Christian Wisdom Meets Modernity

Illuminating Modernity

Illuminating Modernity is dedicated to the renewal of faith in a world that is both Godless and idolatrous. This renewal takes the legacy of faith seriously and explores the tradition in the hope that the means of its contemporary development are to be found within it. This approach takes the historical crisis of faith seriously and makes sincere efforts to receive the strength necessary for a renewal. We call our way the Franciscan option. And yet, one of the greatest resources upon which we hope to build is Thomism, especially those hidden treasures of modern Thomistic thought to be found in Continental and phenomenological philosophy and theology.

The Franciscan option takes the history of faith seriously both in its continuity and in its change. It takes seriously the tragic experiences of the history of faith since the Wars of Religion and especially in late modernity. But it also takes seriously the rich heritage of faith. As Michael Polanyi argued, faith has become the fundamental act of human persons. Faith involves the whole of the person in his or her absolute openness to the Absolute. As Hegel saw, the logic of history is prefigured in the story of the Gospels, and the great and transforming experience of humanity has remained the experience of resurrection in the aftermath of a dramatic death.

The series editors are boundlessly grateful to Anna Turton, whose support for this series made a hope into a reality. We also owe a huge debt of gratitude to Notre Dame's Nanovic Institute for European Studies for giving us financial and moral support at the outset of our project. Many thanks to Anthony Monta and James McAdams for caring about the 'Hidden Treasures'.

Christian Wisdom Meets Modernity

Edited by

Kenneth Oakes

t&tclark
LONDON • NEW YORK • OXFORD • NEW DELHI • SYDNEY

T&T CLARK
Bloomsbury Publishing Plc
50 Bedford Square, London, WC1B 3DP, UK
1385 Broadway, New York, NY 10018, USA

BLOOMSBURY, T&T CLARK and the T&T Clark logo are
trademarks of Bloomsbury Publishing Plc

First published in Great Britain 2016
Paperback edition first published 2018

Copyright © Kenneth Oakes and Contributors, 2009

Kenneth Oakes has asserted his right under the Copyright,
Designs and Patents Act, 1988, to be identified as Editor of this work.

For legal purposes the Acknowledgements on p. ix constitute an
extension of this copyright page.

All rights reserved. No part of this publication may be reproduced or
transmitted in any form or by any means, electronic or mechanical,
including photocopying, recording, or any information storage or
retrieval system, without prior permission in writing from the publishers.

Bloomsbury Publishing Plc does not have any control over, or responsibility for,
any third-party websites referred to or in this book. All internet addresses
given in this book were correct at the time of going to press. The author and
publisher regret any inconvenience caused if addresses have changed or sites
have ceased to exist, but can accept no responsibility for any such changes.

A catalogue record for this book is available from the British Library.

Library of Congress Cataloging-in-Publication Data
Names: Oakes, Kenneth, editor.
Title: Christian wisdom meets modernity / edited by Kenneth Oakes.
Description: New York : Bloomsbury T&T Clark, 2016.
Identifiers: LCCN 2015049935| ISBN 9780567666871 (hbk) | ISBN 9780567666895 (epub)
Subjects: LCSH: Christian philosophy. | Christianity and philosophy. |
Philosophy, Modern.
Classification: LCC BR100 .C54135 2016 | DDC 230.09/04--dc23
LC record available at http://lccn.loc.gov/2015049935

ISBN: HB: 978-0-56766-687-1
PB: 978-0-56768-380-9
ePub: 978-0-56766-689-5
ePDF: 978-0-56766-688-8

Series: Illuminating Modernity

Typeset by Fakenham Prepress Solutions, Fakenham, Norfolk NR21 8NN

To find out more about our authors and books visit
www.bloomsbury.com and sign up for our newsletters.

*For my grandparents
Ross and Sharon Irwin
Elizabeth Oakes
Francis and Marie Oakes*

Contents

Acknowledgements		ix
List of Contributors		xi
Introduction		xiii
1	Why Kierkegaard is the Culmination of the Modern Philosophical Revolution *David Walsh*	1
2	Charles Baudelaire: From within the Veil *David Bentley Hart*	21
3	Martin Heidegger and Christian Wisdom *Cyril O'Regan*	37
4	Romano Guardini: Liturgy, Style, Church *Patrick Gorevan*	59
5	Erich Przywara and the *Analogia Entis*: A Genealogical Diagnosis and Metaphysical Critique of Modernity *John R. Betz*	71
6	Karl Barth and Modernity, with Special Reference to Nietzsche *Kenneth Oakes*	93
7	'Sœur Thérèse, meet Prof. Dr. Husserl': On Hans Urs von Balthasar's Theological Phenomenology *Peter Casarella*	111
8	Karol Wojtyła's Aims and Methodology *Adrian Reimers*	129
9	The Grace of Being: Ferdinand Ulrich and the Task of a Faithful Metaphysics in the Face of Modernity *D. C. Schindler*	149

10 Christology and the *Nihil*: The Wisdom of Cardinal Pierre de
    Bérulle and the Catholic Encounter with Modernity   165
    Aaron Riches

11 Imaginative Conversion   183
    Mátyás Szalay

12 Renewing Christian Philosophy: An Outline   203
    Balázs M. Mezei

Bibliography   233
Index   251

Acknowledgements

The chapters of this volume were originally given as papers at a conference entitled 'Christian Wisdom Meets Modernity', held between 12–14 December 2014 at the University of Notre Dame (UND). The editor would like to thank all of the conference participants and attendees for their time, effort and willingness to brave winter in South Bend, Indiana. Many thanks are also due to Francisco Javier Martínez Fernández, Archbishop of Granada, for his lovely series of opening remarks and his welcome and warm presence throughout the conference. The editor is also grateful to Francesca Murphy, Cyril O'Regan, Laura Betz and the Institute for Church Life (UND) for their time and support during the conference. As the talks were initially intended to be exercises in prosopopoeia, many thanks to David Bentley Hart for summoning the spirit of Charles Baudelaire. Additionally, the editor would like to acknowledge and express his thanks to the Institute for Scholarship in the Liberal Arts (UND) and the Nanovic Institute for European Studies (UND) for their generous financial support both of the conference and of the 'Illuminating Modernity' book series more broadly.

List of Contributors

John R. Betz is Associate Professor of Theology at the University of Notre Dame. He is the author of *After Enlightenment: The Post-Secular Vision of J. G. Hamann* (2009) and co-translator of Erich Przywara's *Analogia Entis: Metaphysics: Original Structure and Universal Rhythm* (2014).

Peter Casarella is Associate Professor of Theology at the University of Notre Dame. His edited and co-edited works include *Jesus Christ: The New Face of Social Politics* (2015), *Cusanus: The Legacy of Learned Ignorance* (2006) and *Christian Spirituality and the Culture of Modernity: The Thought of Louis Dupré* (1998).

Patrick Gorevan teaches at St Patrick's College, Maynooth. He has published several articles in *New Blackfriars*.

David Bentley Hart is currently Danforth Visiting Professor of Theological Studies at Saint Louis University. Some of his books include *The Experience of God: Being, Consciousness, Bliss* (2013), *Atheist Delusions: The Christian Revolution and its Fashionable Enemies* (2009) and *The Beauty of the Infinite: The Aesthetics of Christian Truth* (2003).

Balázs M. Mezei is Professor of Philosophy at the Pázmány Péter Catholic University. He has published widely in philosophy and philosophy of religion in Hungarian and his recent works in English include *Religion and Revelation after Auschwitz* (2013), *Illuminating Faith: An Invitation to Theology* (2015) and the forthcoming *Radical Revelation*.

Cyril O'Regan is the Catherine F. Huisking Professor of Theology at the University of Notre Dame. His books include *The Heterodox Hegel* (1994), *Gnostic Return in Modernity* (2001), *Theology and the Spaces of Apocalyptic* (2009) and a two-volume work entitled *The Anatomy of Misremembering: Von Balthasar's Response to Philosophical Modernity* (2013–).

Kenneth Oakes is a postdoctoral fellow at the University of Notre Dame. He is co-author of *Illuminating Faith: An Invitation to Theology* (2015), and author of *Karl Barth on Theology and Philosophy* (2012) and *Reading Karl Barth: A Companion to the Epistle to the Romans* (2011).

Adrian Reimers teaches in the philosophy department at the University of Notre Dame. His books include *The Truth About the Good: Moral Norms in the Thought of John Paul II* (2011) and *The Soul of the Person: A Contemporary Philosophical Anthropology* (2006).

Aaron Riches teaches theology at the Instituto de Filosofía 'Edith Stein' and the Instituto de Teología 'Lumen Gentium' in Granada. He has published in journals such as *Modern Theology, Communio, The International Journal of Systematic Theology* and *Pro Ecclesia* among others. He is also the author of the forthcoming *Ecce Homo: On the Divine Unity of Christ*.

D. C. Schindler is Associate Professor of Metaphysics and Anthropology at the Pontifical John Paul II Institute on Marriage and Family at the Catholic University of America. His recent books include *The Catholicity of Reason* (2013) and *The Perfection of Freedom: Schiller, Schelling, and Hegel between the Ancients and the Moderns* (2012).

Mátyás Szalay teaches theology and philosophy at the Instituto de Filosofía 'Edith Stein' and the Instituto de Teología 'Lumen Gentium' in Granada. He has published numerous articles in Hungarian and German and is the author of the forthcoming book *Philosophari in Maria*.

David Walsh is Professor of Politics at the Catholic University of America. His many books include *After Ideology: Recovering the Spiritual Foundations of Freedom* (1990), *The Growth of the Liberal Soul* (1997) and *The Modern Philosophical Revolution: The Luminosity of Existence* (2008).

Introduction

Christian Wisdom Meets Modernity

The following chapters are dedicated to the encounter between the presuppositions and claims of modern intellectual culture and the Christian confession that the crucified and resurrected Jesus Christ is the power and wisdom of God and is lord of history and of his Church. These chapters do not assume that Christianity and modernity are two stable and separate essences capable of ready description, nor do they presume that Christian wisdom and modernity meet each other in pure conflict or perfect coincidence. There are, naturally, a variety of positions in between the two poles of conflict and coincidence. There are historical and genealogical studies which contend that modernity is a natural consequence of Christianity, a contingent perversion of it, or an anti-Christian renewal of pagan antiquity. There are also accounts of modernity's relationship to Christianity as one of bemused intellectual disdain or calculated utility in the face of the responsibilities of statecraft, colonization and economic expansion. Finally, there are tales of the relationship between modernity and Christianity told from the perspective of changes and innovations in social practices, educational, ecclesial and political institutions, and technology and the natural sciences.

In comparison to all these tales of Christian wisdom and modernity, the scope of the chapters in this volume is relatively modest. In keeping with the overall focus of the *Illuminating Modernity* series, the figures, texts and issues are primarily Continental and Roman Catholic. The encounter staged in these pages between Christian wisdom and modernity is, then, only one form among many. The ambition of the chapters, nonetheless, is relatively grand. Each presupposes in its own way that the hopes, anxieties and assertions of modern intellectual history deserve to be heard and addressed and that the Christian confession is sufficiently rich, supple and confident to register and reflect upon the cares and worries of our near and distant neighbours.

Overview of Chapters

Chapters 1 and 2 deal with two great figures from the nineteenth century: Søren Kierkegaard and Charles Baudelaire. Beginning with these two seems apropos as David Walsh argues that Søren Kierkegaard is the culmination of modern philosophy and as Baudelaire is the originator of the term '*modernité*'. After an engagement with Martin Heidegger, Emmanuel Levinas and Jacques Derrida, Walsh outlines how Kierkegaard completes the modern philosophical project inasmuch as he moves beyond a metaphysics of presence towards the horizon of the person. Kierkegaard is able to do so inasmuch as he contends that the person, or 'the individual', is to be fundamentally understood as existing in communication with other persons and called forth by God to be this unique person. David Bentley Hart, in a marvelous literary performance, channels the voice and poetry of Baudelaire. Any further description of this piece would seem crude, especially as Baudelaire himself despised didacticism.

Having glanced briefly at two significant philosophical and poetic instantiations of modernity, Chapters 3–9 turn to the engagement between Christian wisdom and modern thought in some of the leading theologians of the twentieth century. Cyril O'Regan chronicles the varied reception and evaluation of Martin Heidegger in three of the premier Catholic intellectuals of the first half of the twentieth century: Edith Stein, Karl Rahner and Erich Przywara. He next turns to Hans Urs von Balthasar's 'comprehensive engagement' with Heidegger, whereby von Balthasar contends with Heidegger both at the level of genealogy and the nature of the sacred. Patrick Gorevan covers the work of Italian-born German priest and theologian Romano Guardini. He traces Guardini's *Gegensatzlehre* ('theory of opposition') through his writings on liturgy and the Church and finishes with Guardini's account of concrete Catholic existence in the modern world. John R. Betz presents the background to Erich Przywara's thought, his unique and ambitious account of the *analogia entis*, and his diagnosis and critique of the intellectual ills of modernity. For Pryzwara, as Betz sees it, the Reformation's insistence upon 'faith alone' and an exclusive transcendence led to the Enlightenment's insistence on 'reason alone' and an exclusive immanence. It is the Catholic vision of the God who is beyond and in creation, which is another way of formulating the *analogia entis*, which overcomes these extremes.

Kenneth Oakes tackles the thorny question of the relationship of Karl Barth to modernity and his understanding of modernity. He then examines Barth's reception and interpretation of Friedrich Nietzsche as a case study for Barth's handling of modern figures. Peter Casarella explores Hans Urs von Balthasar's engagement with modernity through his interactions with phenomenology. These interactions, however, as well as the attempt to develop a theological phenomenology, were anything but simply academic. Casarella shows how von Balthasar's theological phenomenology was undertaken for the sake of reuniting theology and sanctity and the edification of the witness of the saints, and to these ends von Balthasar found the life of St Thérèse of Lisieux and the promise of secular institutes an inspiration for his work. With Adrian Reimers' chapter we turn to Karol Wojtyła (Pope John Paul II) and his theology of the body. After presenting Wojtyła's methodology and relationship to phenomennology and metaphysics, Reimers turns to Wojtyła's understanding of love, chastity, sex and shame and compares Wojtyła's thoughts to those of Max Scheler. Throughout the chapter Reimers helpfully characterizes Wojtyła's work as an exercise in phenomenology but as thoroughly pastoral in orientation and end. D. C. Schindler, in the last of the forays from the twentieth century, presents the metaphysical reflections of the German philosopher Ferdinand Ulrich, especially as they developed in conversation with Hegel and Heidegger. What emerges most clearly from Schindler's presentation is the depths to which metaphysics and ontology are transformed upon the entrance of the categories of grace and especially love. While Hegel and Heidegger offer their own variations of salvation history or the identity and character of God, for Ulrich it is the incarnation which most fully allows being to be seen in its innermost depths as love, as love poured out by the self-giving triune God.

With Chapters 10–12, our attention turns to creative engagement with modernity across three different themes. Aaron Riches uses the work of Cardinal Pierre de Bérulle to tease out the implications of the doctrine of *creatio ex nihilo*. He does so, however, from the perspective of Christology, theological anthropology, spirituality, and with an eye towards the valorization of the *nihil* in some strands of contemporary philosophy. The result is a creative and powerful statement of the continuing significance of Bérulle's thought and practice. Mátyás Szalay offers an historical overview of the imagination with an emphasis upon its relation to the fundamental disposition of the subject. Particular emphasis is given to how the imagination has been understood within modernity and the piece ends with a call for the development of a 'Marian imagination'. Finally, Balázs M. Mezei describes the sweeping and holistic vision of ancient philosophy under the rubric of 'cosmo-theology'. While Plato and Aristotle bequeathed to philosophy a host of concepts, arguments and terms, their relation and meaning within an expansive account of the cosmos was often obscured in the history of philosophy. Christian philosophy has been able both to retain this cosmo-theological vision as well as transform it by the confession of an absolutely transcendent God and by securing the uniqueness of human personhood. It is highly fitting that this volume closes with Mezei's programmatic statement for the renewal of Christian philosophy.

1

Why Kierkegaard is the Culmination of the Modern Philosophical Revolution

David Walsh

When I wrote a book on what I termed 'the modern philosophical revolution' it came as something of a surprise to discover that Kierkegaard was its culmination.[1] I had not planned on assigning him the final chapter since every other thinker was treated in chronological order. To the extent that there is a coherent unfolding of modern philosophy one would expect it to be a succession of ever more penetrating accounts. The arc of thinkers from Kant to Derrida can be seen as converging on an ever more adequate conception of their common project. However we define it there can be little doubt that they are in a conversation driven by mutual critique. The successors correct and enlarge on their predecessors. None can overleap the process by which its inspiration unfolds. Yet that is what occurs in the case of Søren Kierkegaard. He is the exception who arrives largely unnoticed at the end point before the dialectic of philosophy has reached it. Not only is his voice diminished by its publication in Danish but, when it does join the European mainstream through Jaspers and Heidegger, it serves the purpose of the later underwriters. It is no longer the astonishing apprehension of the path that includes them. The successors cannot be eclipsed by the predecessor on whom they build. For that to occur we must be prepared to revise our narrative or at least remain open to its possibility. That is the task of this essay, as we attempt to rescue Kierkegaard from the labels of irrational decisionist as well as unreconstructed religionist. Perhaps in this anniversary year we are finally in a position to consider how one who pondered the modern problematic most deeply could thereby stand most fully within it.

---

[1] David Walsh, *The Modern Philosophical Revolution: The Luminosity of Existence* (Cambridge: Cambridge University Press, 2008).

To suggest that Kierkegaard reached the limit of the modern philosophical revolution requires first that we sketch what that singular development has entailed.[2] This may require some indulgence since it is hardly a universal consensus that modern philosophy follows an overarching narrative. Certainly there are many threads to the unfolding of modernity but part of the challenge has always been to identify the turning points in which their convergence comes into view. Once that is done the structure of the modern philosophical revolution can be grasped. If Kierkegaard is one of those pivots, then he also brings the process as a whole more readily into view. Our second step will be to suggest how he completes the movement of thought that comes after him. In its simplest formulation we may identify his achievement as the breakthrough to the paradox of faith, that 'the single individual is higher than the universal'.[3] The singular individual now becomes the horizon within which reflection occurs. Yet it would not resolve the aporias of identity and meaning so well documented in the ensuing philosophical development if it did not go beyond the isolated individual. Somehow the individual must disclose the inwardness of the person in whom the relationship to others is already contained. Our third section will follow Kierkegaard's discovery of the God-relationship as the one in which the individual is most fully revealed. The individual becomes the person who inwardly contains the whole of being as he or she is held within the inwardness of being that is God. Kierkegaard is thus the one who points the way beyond a metaphysics of presence to the mutuality of persons that had always been its source.

Elements of the Modern Philosophical Revolution

The conventional narrative of modern philosophy and, by extension, modernity itself begins with Descartes who famously declares *cogito ergo sum*. By turning to the self or subject he seeks to ground certainty on what cannot be doubted.

---

[2] It was gratifying to discover that no less a figure than John Paul II had struggled on the eve of his papacy to find the right formulation for the profound philosophical shift that has occurred. He too conceded that it was a 'revolution' in relation to the preceding tradition, and also one that was ultimately a deepening rather than a rejection of the form that philosophy had taken. 'In that sense one may, and even must, speak about *some kind of revolution* which has occurred in the ethics of modern times. The substantive subordination of practicality to normativity had to bring with it, not so much (as in the case of Kant) the rejection of the entire teleological structure which had hitherto been dominant, but its demotion.' Karol Wojtyła, *Man in the Field of Responsibility* (trans. Kenneth W. Kemp and Zuzanna Maślanka Kieroń; South Bend: St Augustine's Press, 2011; Polish original 1991), p. 54 (italics in original).

[3] Søren Kierkegaard, *Fear and Trembling* (trans. Howard and Edna Hong; Princeton: Princeton University Press, 1983), p. 70.

When everything else has become questionable, there is still the indubitability of the questioner. From there the validation of our knowledge of reality as well as our place within it must be erected on the one indefeasible foundation of the self. The autonomous subject becomes the centre from which order extends into social and political reality. Eventually the crisis of the isolated subject becomes apparent when it discovers it can neither find its way toward a sustaining metaphysical horizon nor manage to live without one. The mastery of nature by modern science does nothing to mitigate the unmastery of reason now deprived of any guiding purpose. The forlornness of reason over against the world it dominates is well recognized. Less clearly perceived is the partial character of this observation itself. Omitted is any account of the resistance to groundlessness that has remained a feature of the same philosophical unfolding. The dramatic rupture with theology and metaphysics has obscured the extent to which they endure, and not simply as a remnant increasingly discarded by an ever more virulent rationalism.[4] Awareness of the unsustainability of a truncated reason is present from the very beginning. Not only does Descartes turn toward God as the foundation in the Third Meditation but the impossibility of reason furnishing its own justification only deepens. Kant is surely the high point of its explicit recognition. He is the one who demonstrates that reason would have to presuppose its validity in order to establish it. From that crucial concession philosophy moves toward an ever deeper realization of reason as itself a part of the reality it investigates. Having previously forgotten its own being it now opens toward the horizon of being as such.

That is a formulation reminiscent of the thought of Martin Heidegger whose own trajectory virtually repeats the transition. Beginning with the subjectivity of Dasein, he came to see that existence could never provide the category of its own thinking about itself. The condition of the possibility of existence is that which does not exist because it simply is. Sein is the horizon of Dasein. Of course, how Dasein might know Sein when Dasein is constituted by it is one of the most puzzling questions in Heidegger's reflection. It is the central question around which his thought revolves, as it is for the whole transcendental movement launched by Kant.[5] Just as with Wittgenstein grappling with the question of what language can say about itself, the results may be elusive,

---

[4] This was the narrative of *The Modern Philosophical Revolution*. For a looser confirmation see the anthology of Chris Firestone and Nathan Jacobs, *The Persistence of the Sacred in Modern Thought* (Notre Dame: University of Notre Dame Press, 2012).

[5] Steven Crowell and Jeff Malpas (eds), *Transcendental Heidegger* (Stanford: Stanford University Press, 2007).

even inconclusive, but they cannot be regarded as incoherent. Heidegger may be on a track that is difficult to map, for it is being uncovered in the process of walking it, but that does not in any sense render it a figment. It is real because it is the reality of subjectivity. When thought thinks of itself, it no longer revolves within its own thought world but reaches toward the horizon of being. It was Parmenides, in Heidegger's judgement, who uttered the inceptional proposition of philosophy. To think and to be are the same (Fragment B 3). But what is the being that is the possibility of thought? How can it be thought? Heidegger well knew that the thinking of being is within the horizon of being, not within the horizon of thought alone. It is the stretching of thought beyond itself that is possible because thought moves beyond itself just as being opens itself to the glimpse. It is the event in which meeting takes place. What cannot be met is encountered. This is where all of the paradoxical language of *Vom Ereignis*, the long withheld *Contributions to Philosophy*, is first fully employed.[6] The traces of that shift from talking about being to talking out of being would be enigmatically evident in the many exoteric writings of the succeeding years. But it was only with the eventual publication of *Vom Ereignis* that they could be properly deciphered. Then we would see that philosophy is precisely the accomplishment of the impossible. It says what cannot be said, the word of being that makes its saying possible.

All that is overlooked in the oracular pronouncement of being is the figure who undertakes it. Heidegger himself is missing from the Heideggerian philosophy. This explains the tone of apocalyptic detected by his most acute successors who take note of the inflated self-importance present within it. Vanity, even when not unjustified, perhaps most of all then, remains vanity. It is the fatal misstep that leads a great thinker to presume his superiority to actual historical reality. Not only does this lead to the appalling misjudgements of the practical sphere that taint the name of Heidegger, but it can even contaminate the core of his philosophical project. If the latter is to be rescued then it requires acknowledgement of what Heidegger fails to acknowledge. That is, that despite the world-historic significance of his apprehension of being, as what cannot appear even as it opens the possibility of appearance, that he remains a man within the world. Without a superior claim on reality he remains the servant of being. It is indeed the modesty of his own status that most profoundly guards the transcendence he reveals. In this respect he is no differently situated

---

[6] Martin Heidegger, *Contributions to Philosophy (from Enowning)* (trans. Parvis Emad and Kenneth Maly; Bloomington: Indiana University Press, 1999).

than any other human being. The shepherd of being remains a shepherd. It is precisely when he puts himself first, when he allows his own finitude to intrude on his message, that he most decisively betrays it. If the call of being means anything, it surely means that the one who responds has irrevocably put himself aside. Neither he nor his local cohort can emit any hint of self-aggrandizement. Being that transcends even appearance can be reached only by the readiness to transcend all appearance. Eternity definitively surpasses time. Nothing in time can represent it.

These are not necessarily new problems. Apocalypse has been on the boundary of revelation ever since the rupture of the transcendent intersection with time. What is new is the clarity, an almost unmistakable clarity, Heidegger has brought to bear on it, despite a readiness to deflect his own insight. Yet an inclination to betray an illumination does not in any way detract from its imperative. Rather, it sends us in search of what is missing in Heidegger's thought that would preserve it from the fate of self-distortion. Heidegger's failure to live up to the call of his illumination is emblematic of the failure of the great spiritual aspiration that defines modernity at its best. Impatience at the failure of justice has too often collapsed into an embrace of injustice as the means of securing justice. Mundane success became the measure of a call that is utterly beyond the mundane. In each case the crucial mistake had been to absolve the particular carrier of transformation from the necessity of submission to its imperative. Goodness could be short-circuited without the necessity of becoming good. The individual had ceased to live under the judgement he proclaimed. The absence of an ethics from Heidegger's thought has long been remarked and the response he offered strangely unpersuasive, amounting to a kind of abdication of responsibility for holding one.[7] If one's allegiance is to the ground of ethics within the opening of being then one would seem to bear an even greater responsibility. Respons-ability to being remains responsibility.

The latter was the path pursued by Heidegger's most penetrating successors, Levinas and Derrida. They were his deepest critics because they followed him by going beyond him. Levinas broke new ground by insisting that opening toward being requires a response to the call of the other that comes from beyond being. Heidegger's still contemplative priority is overtaken by the primacy of action that precedes it. Before there is even an I to open toward being, the face of the other is disclosed to me. The other is closer to me than I am to myself.

---

[7] Martin Heidegger, 'Letter on Humanism', *Basic Writings* (ed. David Krell; San Francisco: HarperSanFrancisco, 1977), pp. 213–65.

The leisure of beholding has been taken from me by the urgency of the call that compels my response. Heidegger's prioritization of being to the self that opens has been transformed into the priority of the other whose need breaks in upon me. Being that is more me than myself is identical with the other who is more intimate to me than I am. In each case the I that contemplates has been shattered by the breakthrough from beyond. But where Heidegger's rupture of the primordial still permits a relaxation into the self, Levinas permits no such retreat. The ethics that had eluded Heidegger because it could not establish its priority within being has now gained that indefeasible status. Even the disclosure of being cannot eclipse the other who comes from before it. Being is the face of the other.[8] Ethics is prior to ontology, to use a favoured formulation. The tradition that had always based practical reason on its theoretical foundations could now be secured, if still by no means universally, by the priority of the call of a practical imperative. There is no stepping outside of obligation. What has yet to be explained is how it is possible for me to recognize this. How can I know myself as the holder of an unlimited debt? It must surely have something to do with who I uniquely am for no one can substitute for me in its discharge.

This is the aporia that Derrida zeroes in on in the Levinasian enlargement of being to the other. At first it is merely to point out that Levinas cannot even maintain the priority of the other without a corresponding extension of the understanding of language. The asymmetry of the other to me can hardly even be expressed unless we concede that all of our language is somehow incapable of performing its role. If the other is before I can even pronounce a name then he also overturns the competence of naming. *Sauf le nom* is one of the reflections in which Derrida accomplishes this endless destabilization of the mastery the name seems to provide.[9] The title, playing on 'save the name' and 'except for the name', suggests that the name can be saved only by excepting it from being named. The other exceeds all language that might denote. Of course this is more than a semiotic subversion of the claim of proper names to name what is proper to the person named. Derrida goes on to unfold the existential horizon within which the consequences must be lived out. He develops, for example, an elaborate account of hospitality as the relationship in which the host becomes hostage to the guest. What is owed to the other can never be sufficiently repaid since the only basis on which the relationship can exist is the admission that there is no point at which the claim of the other has been met. Something

---

[8] Emmanuel Levinas, *Otherwise than Being or Beyond Essence* (trans. Alphonso Lingis; The Hague: Nijhof, 1981).
[9] Jacques Derrida, *Sauf le nom* (Paris: Galilée, 1993).

similar applies to the practice of giving which can never give sufficiently, no matter how much is given. Excessiveness is embedded in the relationship to the other before it has even begun. This is why Derrida turns increasingly toward the divine horizon in his later years, including Kierkegaard's meditation on Abraham's sacrifice of Isaac, as the only possible means of containing the impossible dynamic in which his thought unfolded.[10] He sensed, without fully conceding, that Kierkegaard was the one who had taken the fullest measure of the reorientation that the modern prioritization of being and the other thrusts upon us. Not only could the foundation of order no longer begin with the I, but even the possibility of claiming authorship of the works we pen was subverted.

Unlike Levinas who hesitated to embrace the thought of Kierkegaard, possibly out of dislike for the decisionist reputation attached to it, Derrida displayed a far more uncomplicated admiration. He understood the convergence both in the style of literary self-distancing and in the existential purposes it served. Every text opens up the space of *différance* as the possibility from which it arises and is thus incapable of containing. Existence is irrevocably outside the text. Kierkegaard insisted that he was not the author of the works he had written because he was just as much the learner in the process. Writing is itself an opening of existence that occurs in no other way. Derrida's concept of *différance* carries this Kierkegaardian notion of the impossible possibility of writing, as he continually points to the aporias that infect every text. Deconstruction is precisely their reading in this light. Yet despite the increasing seriousness with which Derrida embraces the existential implications of this grammatological beginning, a deepening well attested by the religious turn in his last two decades, the full realization of the consequences eludes him. At best Derrida is serious about remaining unserious. Ironic self-distancing has not, in Kierkegaard's formulation, gone far enough to include itself. Then he would realize that there is no leisure to consider the aporias when one is in aporia. He is the text that must be written, for the deficiency of all written texts has been established. No writing can contain the author whose narrative must arise in living it out. Not even the estimable personal qualities of a Derrida, with his lifelong penchant for inserting himself into various social and political challenges, can reach the limit of complete self-giving. It may be that this has something to do with his inability to arrive at God who alone could receive him completely. Without the God-relationship, the self that can give and receive is hardly real. This is the culmination reached only by Kierkegaard.

---

[10] Jacques Derrida, *The Gift of Death* (trans. David Wills; Chicago: University of Chicago Press, 1995).

Individual Exceeds Universal

The problem for deconstruction is that the semiotic shortfall that infects all communication seems to rebound on the subject who must also fail to become present. Aporetic expression applies equally to the self that utters it. Neither the meaning nor the speaker acquires presence. What is overlooked is that this very analysis derives from a meaning and a self that are knowable despite their defectiveness. The condition of the possibility of deconstruction, as Derrida admitted, is that not everything can be deconstructed. Justice is such an unassailable measure.[11] Everything else can be seen as deviating from it but only because *it* cannot deviate. Scepticism concerning personal identity arises from our inability to denote an indubitable carrier of identity that is not itself simply imputed. Deep down there is nothing deep down, as our house nihilist, Richard Rorty, ruefully intoned. No matter how uneasy we may be about accepting the consequences of the view that we are nothing more than the contingent assembly of our parts, we have real difficulty in constructing an alternative. A metaphysical soul seems too remote a concept to be of any value. Certainly Kierkegaard has no use for it. His reflections head straight for the reality that is emergent in the whole process, for he knew that the soul or self was not a beginning but an end. It is not so much that we are in danger of losing our souls as we are in danger of not having them at all. The ethical life and the soul are correlative. It is by means of right living that we gain our souls, not in the sense of saving them, but of making them real. The ethical life is the attainment of the immortal.

But contrary to the conventional view this has nothing to do with the future. It is a present reality. In fact immortality is the condition of the possibility of acting well, as Kierkegaard made plain in *Either / Or*. The Seducer of 'The Seducer's Diary' can scarcely even be named, for the web of deceptions occludes even his own identity. He etherealizes in concealment, deceiving even himself. Like Giovanni who dissolves in a welter of music, he continually modulates away from who he is. The condition of gaining a substantial presence in himself and in the world is, as Judge William demonstrates, the willingness to make a lifelong commitment. By contrast, the Seducer is incapable of the constancy that friendship requires. The point of Kierkegaard's meditation on the juxtaposition of character types is, however, not to denote them as the result of opposing

---

[11] Jacques Derrida, 'Force of Law: The "Mystical Foundation of Authority"', *Acts of Religion* (ed. Gil Anidjar; New York: Routledge, 2002), pp. 230–98.

choices. Either / Or are not the alternatives with which we are confronted but the possibility of choosing at all. In this sense the choice is not the arbitrary leap Kierkegaard is so notoriously thought to propose but the realization that nothing in time can overcome the inconstancy of time. Only eternity can save time from itself. This is what Judge William explains in his discourse on marriage, a commitment that on its face carries no surety of its accomplishment. Indeed everything seems to indicate its unreliability. What makes it possible for one moment to contain all the moments of a life is that we already stand outside the whole of existence. Kant was right in suggesting that free action begins in eternity but he lacked the linguistic means of expressing it.[12] Kierkegaard found it in the exchange of wedding vows that would otherwise be a reckless leap into uncertainty, if it were not 'signed in heaven, and then it is countersigned in temporality'.[13] The translation of the man and woman into eternity is not an event ahead of them but the condition of binding their lives in mutuality. It is because they are capable of holding the whole of their lives in that moment that they can present it to one another. Marriage transcends the existence it makes possible.

In this way it brings to light the inner reality of every ethical action in which the character or ethos of a person comes into view. But this is not simply a reality to be observed from the outside, as the returning symposiasts of 'In Vino Veritas' (*Stages on Life's Way*) do in taking note of the domesticity of Judge William's house, for they cannot know what is going on within the inwardness of husband and wife. All they can know is that before a marriage has become a public phenomenon it must first have been conceived by its participants who, strictly speaking, are not simply within the lives they are leading. Capable of comprehending the whole of their existence they do not fully exist anywhere within it. Rather than dissolving into the multiplicity of their unfolding they have emerged at the turning point that embraces it all. By taking responsibility they have become the persons who transcend the temporality in which it is undertaken. If they had not instituted such a moment of encompassing commitment they would not cease to be persons, although their hold on personhood would have become correspondingly attenuated. It is only by losing one's life that one saves it. Paradoxical language has traditionally been employed

---

[12] Immanuel Kant, *Critique of Practical Reason* (trans. Mary Gregor; Cambridge: Cambridge University Press, 1997), p. 82.

[13] Søren Kierkegaard, *Stages on Life's Way* (trans. Howard and Edna Hong; Princeton: Princeton University Press, 1988), p. 112. See also Søren Kierkegaard, 'The Esthetic Validity of Marriage', *Either / Or, Part II* (trans. Howard and Edna Hong; Princeton: Princeton University Press, 1987), pp. 3–154.

to convey what cannot so readily be conveyed, even though it is intuited universally. Kierkegaard understood this well for he knew that it was paradox that held the whole movement together and permitted us to talk about it. The self that is gained in self-giving is clearly not the momentary self of our awareness.

It is a far more substantial reality. This is what Judge William knows most clearly, although it is only dimly grasped by Johannes the Seducer. It is the latter who seeks to retain existence from a standpoint within it, to make the moment into a frozen instant of eternity. But the moment cannot be made to last and the attempt to hold onto it results in losing even the fleeting enjoyment that marks the aesthetic life. At least Don Giovanni did not make that mistake as he cast himself headlong into the exhilarating rush so perfectly depicted by Mozart's music. The Seducer is incapable of pleasure, consumed as he is by the need to prevent its passing. Judge William, by contrast, relishes the aesthetic life because he has demonstrated his readiness to go beyond it. Without craving its pleasures he can affirm their reality. Instead of believing that the erotic finds its consummation, and thereby its collapse, in marriage, he is able to assert that it is marriage that provides the possibility of an erotic continuity. It is the institution outside of time that has made the unfolding of time possible. For this reason it cannot be entered into with a partial self. Nothing can be held in reserve as if providing an escape hatch. It is only if one has become the kind of person who can hold the whole of existence in one's hands that one's whole life can be bound. Then, and then alone, have you become the self that, although it exists nowhere within time, makes a lifetime possible. No doubt this is a highly paradoxical conception. It amounts to the claim that we are already at the end before we have set out on the journey. We have no mundane analogue for a transcendence that is prior to itself. But this is, Kierkegaard insists, where a steadfast conviction of the ethical leads us. It is in light of the eternal that our temporal existence is possible. Who we are is disclosed most profoundly in the ideality of our becoming it.

That is all we know, for Kierkegaard refuses to enlist the language of metaphysics that, since Kant, has become an extinct tongue.[14] Yet the problem of a metaphysics that foreswears metaphysics is that it is perpetually in danger of lapsing into solipsism. When nothing can be said we are inclined to concede that nothing can be known. The great challenge is to hold onto permanence when it can no longer be assigned to permanent things. How can there be the

---

[14] 'The metaphysical is abstraction, and there is no human being who exists metaphysically.' Kierkegaard, *Stages on Life's Way*, p. 476.

identity of self or soul when we have conceded their unattainability? It is in rising to meet this challenge that the real greatness of Kierkegaard lies, for he not only recognizes the non-viability of metaphysics but arrives at the horizon that had all along been its source. Existence cannot be comprehended along the lines of an alternative universe outside of the one we inhabit, but must be understood as the unsurpassable boundary of the existence we continually unfold. In answering the question of where the anchor of that which cannot be anchored lies, the centre of a centreless reality, he returns us to the only whole in which the whole can be contained: the person. This is the absence that has been present from the very beginning. All of the discussion of being and beings, of God and the soul and the whole furniture of ontology, has been carried on by persons who remain outside of what they say. Yet they are in no way ethereal or uncertain. Nothing could be more substantive than the person who endures beyond all the changes they undergo. Capable of containing it all, they are themselves uncontained. Indeed they surpass the universal since they are capable of contemplating it. Persons are the ultimate particularities since each is unique and irreplaceable. Contrary to the prevailing notion that ideas of being, substance or identity are necessary to comprehend the reality of persons, we realize that it is the reverse. Our metaphysical conceptions are derived from our self-knowledge as persons who somehow contain their own being and remain the same throughout all of the vicissitudes of their existence. We still do not have knowledge of that which makes our knowledge possible but we do know it as what must be the case. To speak of this as the core of the person is always to suggest an identity that might be extracted, which is just what is impossible. The self that expresses itself is not the self that is expressed.

Kierkegaard may not have elaborated that focus on the inexpressibility of the person but he did bring to light the inner dynamic that underlies it. Nothing can contain the person who contains all. This is the insight that makes him the true originator of the philosophic movement known as 'personalism', although he is often not fully recognized within its genealogy. It is of course true that he does not use the term 'person', preferring usually to talk about the 'individual'. This is among the most decisive concerns for the personalists who understand the individual as what is interchangeable, the instance that can be duplicated elsewhere, while 'person' signifies the unique and irreplaceable one that each of us is.[15] It is a crucial, if still not widely embraced distinction, in part because its

---

[15] Cf. Jacques Maritain, *The Person and the Common Good* (trans. John J. Fitzgerald; Notre Dame: University of Notre Dame Press, 1966), esp. ch. 3, 'Individuality and Personality'.

philosophical significance has not been fully grasped. Even the relevance of the person to the discourse of being that dispenses with metaphysics has yet to be taken on board. But when those acknowledgements are duly made, the singular role of Kierkegaard becomes evident. He is the one who most thoroughly elaborates the interior movement by which, in grasping the universality of the ethical life, the person not only gains a foothold in the eternal, but becomes indeed the substantial reality that is its indispensable concomitant. In making a lifetime commitment one becomes more than one is. The self is the self who not only expresses itself but binds itself. Kant had earlier suggested the same in explaining moral action as the enactment of a universal maxim, for it has simultaneously enacted the self that is beyond the self. By thinking through the issue in individual cases Kierkegaard made the eternity of the self an unmistakable theme.

Yet even that is not the summit of his achievement. There still remains the moment in which the eternity of the self is gained precisely as mine, not to be replaced by any other. The eternal must be contained nowhere but within the 'I' that is invisible to the external world, for I have become the carrier of the whole. This is the disclosure of the horizon of the person within which Kierkegaard's thought unfolds. The obligation that is assumed in light of the eternal demand of duty must be made my own, otherwise the ethical capacity to stand outside of all conceptions of the good to interrogate their goodness could become an evasion of responsibility. The arrow of obligation strikes home only when it has become my inescapable obligation from which I cannot turn aside. Without possibility of avoidance, I have become the uniquely responsible one. The meaning of the ethical life is that it can terminate only in the call that I alone can hear. Beyond the question of whether what is proposed is good, is the question as to whether it is intended for me. Have I been called before the judgement seat? In asking about the good I am simultaneously asked by it. The voice of conscience is ultimately not my voice. It reaches me from the Other who is more within me than I am myself. What makes Kierkegaard the great navigator of inwardness is that he brings out the full weight of this realization. Thought can never dispense with the self within which it arises. But what imparts to that momentary self the realization that it is far more consequential than its present emergence is that it has been called forth by that which is beyond all emergence. The command of God is what secures the eternity of the self. I know who I am within the unsurpassability of the call. It is in this way that the self exists beyond itself as that which shares in the eternity of God. The God-relationship is the horizon of the person.

God-Relationship as the Horizon of the Person

The person is affirmed as a person. There is no greater metaphysical reality nor more deeply disclosed core. It is the God-relationship that constitutes the horizon of the person. This is the realization that made Kierkegaard a religious thinker. He could not speak on behalf of religion, for that would be to claim its authority, an authority of which he himself was just as much in need. The *Upbuilding Discourses*, his most religious works and published under his own name, were written in the knowledge that he too stood just as much in need of upbuilding. His original plan of writing pseudonymously as a way of disguising the religious perspective of his authorship suffered an ironic reversal when he discovered that he could not so easily jettison the arrangement. When Kierkegaard came to write in his own voice, he discovered that it was premature to claim what such authorship implied. It would be tantamount to speaking for God. At best he could aspire toward the divine perspective on things. How indeed can we speak of God when it is the God-relationship that is the horizon of our existence? This was the staggering implication of his displacement of metaphysics with religion, a displacement that the unfolding of metaphysics had made inexorable. Terminologically, 'religion' and 'metaphysics' effect their own overturning since they render external what can only be grasped from within. But the deeper issue is that no one can claim mastery of what is of God. When the substance of our existence turns, not on the achievement of moral heroism, but on the impossibility of measuring up to a relationship that utterly exceeds it, then there is no possibility of reaching a vantage point from which it can be comprehended. The best we can say is that 'in relation to God we are always in the wrong'.[16] When the God-relationship constitutes the core of our existence it cannot be pronounced. This is an insight, not only into religious language, but into the inaccessibility of that by which we are constituted. The innermost can never be said.

It can however be shown. The poetic presentation that Kierkegaard thought would be a stage eventually left behind turned out to say more deeply what could not be said. Nowhere was this more the case than in the meditation that even at the time he knew would make his name immortal, *Fear and Trembling*. Abraham's sacrifice of Isaac was the story that brought the God-relationship into focus because it departed so radically from the ethical universal. What was Abraham to hold onto when he could no longer hold onto the imperative of

---

[16] This is the upbuilding thought that forms the concluding 'Ultimatum' of *Either / Or, Part II*.

duty, the duty above all of preserving his son? The episode not only unhinges our connection with duty but makes it clear that it never was so firmly established. It had always been up to us to maintain it. The duty of following duty remained our responsibility.[17] Nothing could determine that inexplicable free initiative that arises from we know-not-where. Often, accomplishment of duty is as much of a surprise to us as it is to the rest of the world. We do not know what we are capable of, good or bad, before we have undertaken it. Freedom is unfathomable. This is the abyss that all moral philosophy had sought to avoid, preferring to take refuge in talk about nature, sentiment or inclination. Almost anything might occupy the ontic black hole so long as it saved us from contemplating it. Whatever ground is attributed to goodness we can always ask whether it too is good. Indeed ever since Plato first turned our thought to the good as the highest, this has been the ominous threat at the heart of our philosophical reflection. Is the good itself good? Now it can no longer be avoided. This was the crisis that hung over the modern understanding of morality as it became apparent that the questioner stands outside of the good. But unlike Nietzsche, Kierkegaard did not despair of arriving at an answer. Despite his reputation as an existentialist, for whom nothing is higher than the decision of the moment, he had found his way through to what is beyond existence. It was the relationship to God that secures the individual who 'exceeds the universal'.

Beyond universal law are the individuals who enact it. They continually exceed it, not only in the generosity that goes beyond what the law requires, but in the impossibility of anything determining their freedom in advance of its exercise. Kant shows more than a glimpse of this in his marvelling at the impossibility of anything determining the will to action but the will itself. Nothing stands higher in his estimation than a good will. What he did not contemplate is how such a good will might contemplate itself. What could preserve it from the abyss of arbitrariness that its supremacy seemed to open before it? It would have to find a way of putting itself aside so that no hint of superiority could taint its devotion to the good, no whiff of self-approval mar its impeccability. To accomplish this, something more than self-restraint is required for there must be nothing of self left in its actions. That can occur only if the place of the self is entirely occupied by the other. It is relationship to the other that holds it decisively away from itself. Now action springs from the other, from the priority

---

[17] Kant's categorical imperative is addressed to each one personally. '*Act only on that maxim through which you can at the same time will that it should become a universal law.*'

of the other, rather than from the self. That priority becomes all-encompassing only when the other encompasses the whole of the self. This is pre-eminently the case of the God-relationship, the One who calls on us to respond with nothing less than the whole self. Even in the call of others, it is God who calls on us to respond with complete self-giving. It may indeed seem paradoxical to suggest that the solitary individual on whom the entire burden of responsibility rested is now profoundly displaced. Yet that is what has occurred and it is Kierkegaard's genius to have grasped what the modern elevation of freedom requires. Freedom must be prepared to go beyond itself. Only then is it free, when not even a regard for freedom itself stands in the way. By ceasing to be a self it becomes a self most completely. Rather than hold onto its identity, the self must be prepared to transcend it. When we ask where then does it exist, we can only say that it exists solely within itself. Inwardness is the mode in which the self has already gone beyond itself.

To erect freedom on this singular foundation of relationship to the other is of course to anticipate the course of philosophy up to the present. We have scarcely even reached the point at which he seemed to arrive. This is because we lack the conceptual means of explaining to ourselves how the one who has given away the most *is* most all. It seems contrary to the law of being, certainly to the economy of loss and gain. Only in the economy of relationship does it make any sense. But then it remains invisible to the external world since relating is only possible in inwardness. External expression may be a way of marking it, but that remains an external marking. Nothing of the reality that transpires can be accessed from outside. Only those who are prepared to enter into the relationship can know what it is and what it contains. This has always been known within the history of revelation, even if it could not withstand the inclination to think that we could nevertheless find an external measure. To Kierkegaard this was the problem of Christendom, the enduring misconception by which the Church armed for its defence without realizing it had thereby lost what was worth defending. In the logic of relationship, loss is gain and gain is loss. Those who love cannot be deceived, nor can they lose. The self has so completely been displaced that there is not even a self to calculate the cost. Each has exceeded itself and installed the other in its place. They are in one another. Containing one another inwardly they hardly exist in the realm of the external, for only traces of what they have left behind remain. But the whole possibility of self-transcendence is that there is an other to whom the self can give itself. This is why the God-relationship is so foundational. It is the relationship that includes all other relationships. God is the guarantee of mutuality when the mutuality of others has not even been disclosed. Openness is already there because it is the openness of God. He is the one who is present in the relationship to every other, not as a universal principle, but as the one who enfolds them more fully than they do one another. Mutuality is of God.

The inwardness by which we hold all others is a participation in the inwardness of God. It is because we share in the divine inwardness that we can relate to one another inwardly. Within marriage this occurs without the partners realizing they have thereby become selves that can only hold one another in inwardness. It is only when they transcend even their relationship that they realize that they are marked by the God-relation. Each holds the whole of being within him- or herself because there is nothing that may not be asked of them. By going beyond the finite each has become the infinite to whom God can give himself. This is the identity of the self that no longer seeks to preserve its identity. It is in the God-relation that it has most truly become an 'I'. In asking the question of every instance of the good whether it is good, the self has only dimly begun to realize what it is, that is, the self is in every instance the one whose responsibility for the good surpasses every instance of the good. No instantiation of the good will be sufficient to extinguish the demand for even more goodness. The partners in the marriage who enact an unconditional commitment had not quite realized what this entailed. Not only are they capable of containing the whole of their existence in that moment, but they are also incapable of containing the whole of their existence in that instant. Nothing can contain them.

The condition of the possibility of the ethical life is that they bear an unconditional responsibility toward it. They can be bound by the ethical because they stand outside of its bounds. It is their capacity to relate to the infinite, the God-relation, that discloses who they are. Nothing they do sufficiently measures up to what has been required of them. Even marriage is not a finite commitment, one they might eventually discharge as one might amortize a debt. Rather they have entered upon a debt that mounts continually. Even when the partners hold one another through their finite actions, they are themselves held in an infinite relation that remains their true reality. Nowhere visible in the external world, they have begun to disclose their infinity. It is only in their relation to the infinite, the God-relation, that they can perceive who they really are. The unconditionality of their commitment arises from the unconditioned in which they exist. It is the God-relation, the relation to the One who may require more than they are prepared to give, that defines who they are, that is, as persons who must always be prepared to be more than they are.¹⁸ Excessiveness is not only a possibility but the very ground of their possibility. The self that may claim its substance is always eclipsed by the self that is called to surrender it. Responsibility means the impossibility of limiting responsibility in advance. That is the unattainable self, the self of the God-relation, that Kierkegaard so unfailingly targets. It is not only that the individual exceeds the universal but the universal continually points to its own overcoming.

This is why it is silence that marks the knight of faith. Nothing can be said for nothing can convey what must be held inwardly. The case of Abraham fascinated Kierkegaard because he so perfectly exemplified the pure inwardness of the God-relation. Not even the law could become a means of externalizing it. God had commanded him even to go against the law, or at least to demonstrate he was prepared for that extreme. The greatness of Kierkegaard's account is that he respects the impenetrability of inwardness. We do not perceive Abraham's experience. For us the externality of the poetic is the only means of glimpsing what occurs. Even less can we penetrate it from the side of God. We do not know why God issued such a command, a 'teleological suspension of the ethical' that sails dangerously close to overturning it. All we know is that Abraham did not take offense. His heart did not rebel against the divine command or presume to measure it in his own finite judgement. He simply yielded and thereby became the knight of faith. When all was lost he resolved to hold fast to the call that he alone could hear. He could not even cling to the law that had all along been synonymous with the voice of God. Yet it was not the voice of God, who may call on us to act differently. But what did that mean, 'a teleological suspension of the ethical'? The paradoxical formulation – since the ethical is the teleological – is a way of acknowledging the penultimacy of the ethical. Beyond it is the One who is its source. Nothing is higher than the personal relationship to God. Teleology points beyond itself.

Whether God will require the abrogation of the teleological is not for us to know. He could command the impossible and we have no assurance against it, except for the assurance of faith. This is what above all, on Kierkegaard's reading, characterizes Abraham. He is the knight of faith. He trusts that God will not require what God has required of him, to kill his own son in whom the promise of his descendants is contained. Yet nothing provides a ground for that faith, nothing, that is, but God himself. The God whom Abraham knows

---

¹⁸ This is why a man who goes through life on the assumption 'that he is not a criminal but not faultless, either, is of course comic'. Kierkegaard, *Stages on Life's Way*, p. 479.

would not require it of him. He might require that sacrifice of himself, but not of Abraham. Indeed he *would* require it of himself before he would require it of Abraham. Toward Abraham it would only be one more gesture of the love that wishes to draw him near but can scarcely risk its disclosure, lest it overwhelm him. The love that cannot be expressed can only be inwardly embraced. That is the life of faith. Faith is the inwardness that holds fast to the inwardness of God.[19] It is not a holding of beliefs, of propositions, but of the other who is beyond them. This is why no one can substitute for another, for each must enter personally into the relationship. God cannot be known in any other way. Everything else can be known through the mastery that knowledge provides but the person can only be known through the unmastery by which each cedes place to the other. Personal knowledge is the knowledge of personal uniqueness. The whole can only be known as a whole, as it is in itself.

It is through faith that Abraham opens the whole of his existence to God and receives the whole of God in return. Neither side holds anything back. When we ask what it is that God reveals to Abraham we can only say that he reveals his heart, that is, he reveals nothing or at least nothing that we could say. The revelation of God has no content for any content would merely be something more about God. It would not be God himself. That which expresses is inexpressible. Even the divine call, the divine instruction, contains the specific. But how we know it is from God cannot be explained except by knowing God. Only one who knows God can hear the command and follow it out. Faith is that heart-knowledge. It is through faith that Abraham reached it. From the beginning it was faith that led him to trust in God who already revealed himself in the first prompting of faith. By following the path of faith Abraham would arrive at the disclosure of God as the God who can only be known by faith, that is, as the God who can only be known in himself. To say that this is 'mystical' is to use a term that Kierkegaard disliked, for it suggests that it is secret or hidden whereas it is open and available. Abraham may not have been able to say what he knew of God but he did know God. That was enough, for nothing could authenticate the message more truthfully than God himself. God is the message. Faith is its reception. The invitation to open toward it is the path of faith that Abraham followed in order to arrive at the God who had issued the invitation. He became the knight of faith because he showed that faith is the opening

---

[19] '*An objective uncertainty, held fast through appropriation with the most passionate inwardness, is the truth,* the highest truth there is for an *existing* person.' Søren Kierkegaard, *Concluding Unscientific Postscript to* Philosophical Fragments (trans. Howard and Edna Hong; Princeton: Princeton University Press, 1992), vol. 1, p. 203.

through which every individual can gain all by surrendering all. By responding to the call he became the individual who stood outside the whole. He had definitively surpassed the substance of his ethical identity.

To arrive at a theoretical penetration it would be necessary to go beyond Kierkegaard's focus on the individual (*den enkelte*), a term that already arises from the discourse of beings. If the individual bearing of responsibility is to become a paradigm of being beyond beings then it would have to reach for the language of the person. The person is already what is not in being because it is the mask (*prōsopon*) or persona through which it appears. This is how it can grasp what is beyond being. Beyond all that is said or done is the person who is never reducible to what is said and done. It is for this reason that the person bears responsibility. The 'beyond being' is thus not a vague aspiration toward what cannot be said, but the quite concrete reality in which the person is. We know it through the experience of living within it, although there is no 'it' apart from the reality of the person. When we think about such categories as substance, that which endures beyond the changes it undergoes, the suppositum of accidents, it is the durability of the person that is the controlling paradigm. This is not the soul or psyche or 'I' in any empirical or specific sense, for they too can be interrogated as to who the person is. The possibility of asking who a person is derives not only from the inexhaustibility of the person, but much more fundamentally from the unique totality that the person is. We know the person beyond all that the person presents as appearance, for the person cannot simply be in the appearance. The very meaning of the mask is that it is held by that which is not a mask. This is not an abstraction, but the concrete truth that each one of us is. My call to responsibility is the voice of God who, beyond the law, calls me to be uniquely responsible. No one else can take my place for it exists nowhere but within the call. Responsibility is not located in being but rather being within responsibility.

That is what Kierkegaard saw, even if he did not fully elaborate it within the language of the person. He not only called our attention to the personal dimension of all thought but realized that it is the personal that is the horizon of thought. All thinking begins within the movement by which I assume responsibility for it. To say that all that we do or say is a mode of existence suggests that it might be assimilated to some general pattern of reality. But that is to overlook the extent to which the 'I' that attends has stepped outside of what occupies its attention. I can attend precisely because I am not within it. The individual exceeds the universal and yet is not dispersed as if it were universal. By embracing all I affirm that I am even more the unique one. Nothing and no one can take my place. This is the point at which the language of being has been eclipsed, just as it is the place where the incomprehensibility of the unique has erupted. Yet that defeat of generality has not rendered it inaccessible, for it has been transcended by the leap of the personal beyond it. What cannot be said can be grasped. Persons know one another as persons outside the boundaries of the universal to which they are assimilated. We know one another as unique others, without any science to explain it. That is the horizon of all communication between us even though it cannot be included within any horizon. The indispensable cannot be contained. It is the I that can assume responsibility for the whole because it is somehow the whole of reality. That is how God addresses us, as it is also the way that we turn to God. Without intermediaries we encounter one another as utterly unique. There can be no danger of forgetting or losing ourselves in that encounter, since it revolves around the impossibility of avoiding the whole that each of us is. Even without fully embracing the language of the person, Kierkegaard had hit upon its most central feature. Each person is the whole of being. By assuming sole responsibility each one stands outside the whole of being. Those who know this already think within the horizon of the person.

2

Charles Baudelaire: From within the Veil

David Bentley Hart

Merci, Mesdames et Messieurs. Je suis enchanté d'avoir été invité à ce rassemblement, malgré ma condition actuelle. Mort, c'est à dire. Mais tout d'abord, permettez-moi de proposer l'exhortation suivante:

Enivrez-vous!

> Il faut être toujours ivre. Tout est là: c'est l'unique question. Pour ne pas sentir l'horrible fardeau du Temps qui brise vos épaules et vous penche vers la terre, il faut vous enivrer sans trêve.
>
> Mais de quoi? De vin, de poésie ou de vertu, à votre guise. Mais enivrez-vous.
>
> Et si quelquefois, sur les marches d'un palais, sur l'herbe verte d'un fossé, dans la solitude morne de votre chambre, vous vous réveillez, l'ivresse déjà diminuée ou disparue, demandez au vent, à la vague, à l'étoile, à l'oiseau, à l'horloge, à tout ce qui fuit, à tout ce qui gémit, à tout ce qui roule, à tout ce qui chante, à tout ce qui parle, demandez quelle heure il est et le vent, la vague, l'étoile, l'oiseau, l'horloge, vous répondront: "Il est l'heure de s'enivrer! Pour n'être pas les esclaves martyrisés du Temps, enivrez-vous; enivrez-vous sans cesse! De vin, de poésie ou de vertu, à votre guise.

Il est l'heure de s'enivrer! Pour n'être pas les esclaves martyrisés du Temps, enivrez-vous; enivrez-vous sans cesse! De vin, de poésie ou de vertu, à votre guise.[1]

---

[1] *Le Spleen de Paris* XXXIII: 'Make yourself drunk!/ It is necessary always to be drunk. That is the all of it: the sole question. In order not to feel the horrible burden of time, which breaks your shoulders and presses you down to the earth, you must be inebriated without surcease./ But on what? On wine, poetry, virtue, as you please. But make yourself drunk./ And if sometimes, on the steps of a palace, on the green grass of a ditch, in the dismal solitude of your room, you awaken, your drunkenness already diminished or vanished, ask the wind, the wave, the star, the bird, the clock – everything that flees, everything that groans, everything that rolls, everything that sings,

I

The great virtue of the dead is their silence. Having passed beyond the boundaries of the utterable, they are henceforward deprived of the privilege of utterance, and so can no longer bore us with tedious inventories of their regrets or, worse, burden us with the fruits of their wisdom. They keep their quiet vigils in some inner sanctuary, into which we cannot peer and from which not so much as a whisper should escape. So I beg your kind indulgence in thus presuming to address you from beyond the veil that hides that last and most terrible mystery from view. I was summoned hither, by a power I find I cannot resist. How I shall be received back into the society of the deceased, having cavalierly disregarded the cardinal rule of their etiquette, I cannot foresee; but I never was much bound by custom. And I find that, at my present remove from the undulating inconstancies of our personal and collective histories, I can see many things – concerning both myself and the world where once I dwelt – far more clearly than I could from the more limited perspectives afforded the living.

I am not, however, given to systematic formulations, so forgive me if I should wander somewhat from topic to topic.

So, then, what are the chief predicaments of modern man? I would say, first, disbelief in original sin and, consequently, an inability even to imagine what it would mean to strive against it. And by disbelief I do not mean a coarse but perhaps pardonable rejection of the doctrine on the part of a man who, shaking his puny fists at the unavailing heavens, demands possession of his own soul; that is the disbelief of the rebel, whose act of defiance remains, *contre cœur*, an affirmation of the divine, or at least a confession of a *divine* discontent. I mean rather the impotence of an imagination that finds the very notion of sin incomprehensible and a little absurd; I mean the barren conscience of a man who is quite sure that, whatever sin might be, it surely lies lightly upon a soul as decent as his own, and can be brushed off with a single casual stroke of a primly gloved hand; I mean an habitual insensibility to the illuminations and chastisements of beauty, a condition of being wholly at home in a world from which mystery and sin and glory have all been banished, and in which spiritual wretchedness has become material contentment. To that man, the bliss that calls to him in the beautiful would seem only an intolerable accusation, its gracious invitations only a perverse condemnation of his well-earned and lavishly vegetal happiness.

> everything that talks – ask them what time it is, and the wind, the wave, the star, the bird, the clock will answer you: "It is time to make yourself drunk! So as not to be Time's martyred slaves, make yourselves drunk; never cease making yourself drunk! On wine, poetry, virtue, as you please".

So he does not see it, he cannot hear it. And thus the ancient compact between the world above and that below has been forsaken; the glittering scale of natural and supernatural sympathies – of analogies and symbols, of revelations and memories of paradise – has been shattered, its starry fragments scattered in the dust; the way of ascent has been lost.

Forgive me for saying so much in so small a space, but I am a poet, and therefore lazy.

What, though, am I to make of the world into which I was born? How else can I make sense of that complacent love of moral squalor, that luxuriant banality, that is the single spiritual achievement of our age? Here where every bourgeois has been poisoned by the triteness of Voltaire – that philosopher of the concierges – and where every good citizen hears the voice of progress and enlightenment in the inane prattle of journalists, with all their childish laicism? Progress – the doctrine of idlers and Belgians, content to let their neighbours do their work for them – the oafish belief that civilization lies in steam or turning tables rather than in reducing the marks of original sin upon the soul.[2]

I was often rebuked for the insufferable pride I sometimes took in my baptism, as though that constituted some rare and special pedigree; but, in our time – when every bourgeois is a rationalist, when every aristocrat is servile in his eagerness to become as enlightened as the bourgeois, and when even the tradesman or the peasant aspires to be a modern man of reason – to what more ennoblingly antique lineage may one lay claim than that of the baptismal font?

II

How did they ever come to this place, these desolate multitudes, gathered here under Satan's ashen skies? It is no use asking them: they cannot recall. They remember only, as in a dream, departing from frozen harbours bathed in twilight, sailing over dark waters lit by a sickly moon, their groaning barks borne on torpid currents past shores where sheer granite cliffs or walls of iron-grey thorns forbade any landing, and at last drawing up into these oleaginous waters, alongside these dreary quays wanly gleaming with rime. If they could cast their minds further back, they might recall a lost paradise: green and yellow meadows stirred by tender winds, umbrageous woodlands and emerald groves, glass-blue mountain peaks melting into azure skies, glittering bays whose diamond waters

---

[2] See *Mon cœur mis nu*, XXXVII, LXXXI.

break in jade and turquoise surges on sands like powdered alabaster – there the rain falls gently, and is transformed by the setting sun into shimmering curtains of gold – there, beyond the valleys and the limestone caves, lies a palace filled with every delight the senses can endure, enclosing garden courtyards where crystal fountains splash in porphyry basins, intoxicating perfumes hang upon the breezes, and unwithering flowers of every hue shine out amid the greenery's blue shadows […] If only they could recall. But, of course, they do not wish to do so. Occasionally they hear a distant dolorous echo, a faint fading rumour of that forgotten bliss, carried to them over the purple sea, but they only turn away and thrust their hands into their pockets, anxiously feeling for their purses. Their triumph is their diabolical drabness, their pitiless sobriety. (And what is perfect sobriety other than the rejection of love, of communion – the refusal of the God who *is* intimate communion, the love that gives itself with the recklessness of a drunkard?) They wish for no paradise more opulent than the contentment they have already achieved; they will not hear of such a thing.

Herein, I submit, lies the small moral quantum within my own dissipations, which were never so extravagant as I made out in my poems. To play the *flâneur*, the dandy delicately glistening upon the boulevards, can be an act of principled defiance against an age in which dreariness has become the face of sensualism, in which men cosset their appetites precisely by coarsening and deadening them. It is an ambiguous defiance, I admit. The poet, as I once observed, is like an albatross bound down to a ship's deck, all its floating grace reduced to comic awkwardness, confined to an element it cannot master and above which it should forever soar. He is also, I might add, a peacock among the pigeons.

Here, I have written a sonnet, which I call *Genus Pavonis*. (Excuse the roughness of the verse, I entreat you. The dead are masters of every language, having entered into that silence that is in truth the fullness of all sound, enfolding every tongue within itself. But, even so, as a poet my only true idiom is French.)

> The gorgeous opalescence of your tail,
>   Your shrilling voice upon the evening air,
>   Orgulous cock, *mon semblable, mon frère*,
> Your delicate crown – sapphires upon frail
> Stems of silver light – your glimmering mail
>   Of green and jet, your bearing debonair …
>   A mirror that deceives me I am fair –
> The envy of all animals more pale.

And yet I dare not gaze too long, bright jewel
    Of burning beauty, strange unearthly bird:
You strip all rivals of their plumage, cruel
    And jealous; harsher cry was never heard …
Obscure angel, enigma, nature dual:
    A heavenly splendor … vain and absurd.

III

I admit, there is some peril in resisting Satan's world by seeking to outshine one's fellows. Can one ever then become more than a greater Satan among lesser Satans? But, surely, if we are fallen, we should at least strive to be children worthy of an apostate angel. Perhaps our vanquished god prefers we should not – indeed, prefers we have no thought of him at all. For what the modern age has taught us is that the kingdom of hell is essentially a respectable place, where the devil is best served by remaining *incognito*, where sin and remorse and penitence trouble no one with their curbside importunities – "Please, sir, only a *soul*!" – where no one frets about angels or devils, where all good men apply themselves virtuously to becoming machines among machines, without sin because without souls. What world, after all, could be more respectable than one without sin? Where the only transgression anyone truly deplores is to deny that the highest happiness is prosperous mediocrity? Where the only indecency is to suggest that, among the ashes of the modern heart, there might linger a spark of divinity that, blown upon with but a little breath, could be kindled into flame?

In such a world, those who uphold public morals and serve the public weal do so only for Satan's ends. They can rise to no higher god than he. They are guardians of the world of commerce, where everything is valued only as it might be bought or sold, where all giving and receiving are governed by the satanic law that each must try to take more than he gives, where any creed but the worship of Plutus must be brought into ridicule, where everything is plunged into the abysmal shadow of that insatiable Typhon called America – that gas-lit desert of barbarism, with its infantile, gigantic, exuberant vulgarity, its monstrously guileless delight in affluence, its omnivorous vacuity.[3] For these good citizens, the highest good is that machines should wholly Americanize us, that progress should impoverish us of everything spiritual in our natures, until life can no

---

[3] See *Edgar Poe, sa Vie et ses Œuvres*, I.

longer intrude upon us with its fitful energies. Yes, respectable men, men of commerce, men of the most unimpeachable rectitude: under their vigilant gaze the youth will flee his home not when he is 18, but when he is 12, not to seek a hero's adventures or liberate a beautiful captive from a tower or immortalize a garret with sublime thoughts, but to establish a business, enrich himself, surpass his father in avarice and cunning, and perhaps buy a journal for the propagation of enlightened ideals.[4] They shall see to it, that is, that he becomes as virtuous as they.

Against such decency, such respectability, it is necessary to rebel. Only thus can one extirpate the devil from one's heart. And yet, in rebelling, one cannot help but tread the path for a time of the great master of rebellion.

Here – another poem, one called

The Fall of Lucifer

No darkness falls across this golden noon,
And here no cloud or shadow mounts the wind;
Softly falls the dragon, through a ruined sky,
The region of the sullen southern stars.

A meteor, a silver strand of lightning
Upon the hazel dusk, he fell and fell,
Gold his hair and gold his eyes, such bright beauty
In sheer descent upon the languid breeze ...

When, still delighting, sang the angels, sang
The stars...The son of morning, fallen where
None can find him, who in the evening of
That age slipped down along the seam of night ....

Gone now, all glory, all that lovely bright
Magnificence: become the ember's glow,
The aftermath, the deep reproach of those
Cold, bleak, disconsolate, and empty heavens;

And now, amid a race who crave a God's
Miraculous sadness, terrible mirth,
The tawdry splendor of his glory's waste
Must wear another aspect than its own,

And he must walk the dismal floor of earth,

---

[4] See *Fusées*, XXII.

> And range the fallow reaches of the sea,
> And rule the turbulent and lifeless winds,
> And hide in secret chambers in their hearts.

Do not be appalled if I observe that a truly beguiling beauty still sometimes smoulders in his eyes, a virile grandeur still adorns his limbs and shoulders. One cannot arraign modern men for their unconscious diabolism, really, until one reminds them that the devil exists – even if, at times, one must do this by worshiping him. The explicit service of Satan, after all, is more honourable than the brutish servitude to him in which the modern soul labours. By openly adoring the delectable ruins of the fallen angel's beauty, one thereby casts oneself upon the mercy of God. It is a transgression that implores the love of heaven, and is thus a reproach to those whose lifeless consciences know nothing of either the devil or God. Better a forthright Satanist than a complacent bourgeois rationalist, sired by Voltaire in some tidy, comfortably appointed, and aseptic sty. The former can, at least, still revere beauty, even if it be only a corrupted beauty; there remains the possibility of good taste. I, at any rate, was never a complacent rebel. How little the first critics of *Les Fleurs du Mal* understood this, or understood the vacillations of the soul that produced that book, or grasped the meaning of the various impersonations through which that soul told of its wanderings. All my sins I confessed there *as sins*; all my recalcitrance, my every revolt, was directed against God *as God*. It was he from whom I was cut off, he whose absence provoked my misery and loneliness. I never abjured divine love, and certainly enjoyed none of the despicable ease of the contented atheist. When I spoke in the voice of rebellion, I also proclaimed thereby my passionate longing for God's mercy. Voltaire could not be seduced by the devil's shattered glory, true, and could not love what he should not love, but only because he was incapable of rapture before God, and could not love what he should love. That was not moral heroism, but only sterility of imagination.

I beg you to understand that within all of us two allegiances struggle against one another: one to God and one to the devil; one the desire to ascend, the other the desire to descend.[5] And there is no middle way: we yield to one inclination or the other in all that we do and say and think. One cannot therefore reject God but remain otherwise uncommitted. That we might receive mercy, then, and even perhaps absolution, we should acknowledge, without reserve, that when

---

[5] See *Mon cœur mis nu*, XLI.

we transgress we do so as Satanists – and so acknowledge also the God from whose gaze we are far removed.

IV

In the end, however, rebellion must exhaust itself. We grow weary of our paltry carnal transports, our ebulliences of defiance, our abortive expeditions to the frontiers of the respectable world. All this too, in the end, we must give up, or we will have achieved nothing but to bind ourselves more securely to the flesh. This, however, is the greatest trial we can undergo. When defiance dies in our breasts, there follows a fruitless season of the soul; we at first find ourselves deserted, caught in a ghostly twilight between two worlds, a winter of the soul, like a man whose marriage has grown cold or whose garden has grown bare. Nothing we do can prosper at first. We can but wait.

Which brings me, incidentally, to this verse, which I have entitled

Patient Husbandry

The violet of twilight, and the pale brittle gold
Of poplars, the brilliant bleak silver in the fold
Of the dark ailanthus leaf, and the dying fury
Of the last late bloom, limp upon the copper briar,
All like the lovely son of the morning's dimmed glory,
He who once walked like a god in the stones of fire:

Bitter. Beneath the traces of birds' fading songs
The sinuous dragon, still lovely, though he is fallen,
Slips through red thorns, a fugitive shimmer of bronze,
Then disappears – a ghost in the twined fires of autumn.
The thunder echoes distantly, low walls enclose
The tangled waste where you dream of the absent rose.

The bare ruins of your garden still betray the signs
Of vanished beauty, and the spent year yet declines …
But what of that? As the hardened earth sinks in shadow,
Assume the dove's gentleness, the sweet serpent's guile –
You have wedded yourself to a woman of sorrows
And must live every day for her infrequent smile.

One must always endure the briar while the rose sleeps
In the sap's oblivion; gaze then upon her head,

Lowered, lips describing a silent phrase: she weeps
Rarely. Her pain is your sacrifice. With the dead
The seeds of fallen fruit lie dormant for a time.

But the vision thrives in the still earth. In a flood
Of silence, Simon heard a sweet supernal rhyme,
And fled to desert wastes that he might live apart,
And feed its promise with the fever of his blood,
And hold its secret in the fastness of his heart.

I have always felt a certain affection for the Stylite, I should mention, though not on account of his piety. Was he not, I wonder, the truest *flâneur* of all, the subtlest sensualist, the supreme dandy? Was not his asceticism really a kind of wanton revel, the voluptuary's craving for the excitement of absolute abandon, an ecstasy so intense it carried him beyond even the boundaries of pleasure?

Who can say? Mortification is one path to transcendence, I suppose, but not the one I best understood, until perhaps the end. I knew instead the venerable, the sacred paths of wine, women, and song – the blessed delirium of the pure heart's yearning for a forsaken Eden.

And when I speak of wine, I mean just that. Not narcotics, not hashish and opium, both of which I tasted in my time; therein lie only the illusory paradises whereby the wily lord of this world leads astray our natural hunger for the infinite.[6] I mean that ruby or golden nectar by which we resist the tyranny of circadian time and loosen the fetters of daily care. I mean that noble, pure, enlivening draught from the springs of paradise. Children and savages understand what we good citizens have forgotten: by their delight in things that shine and glitter, their love of feathers and bright threads and beads, they declare their contempt for the real and hence their spiritual natures.[7] The disinherited child, under the tutelage of some invisible angel, yet tastes only heaven in all he eats and drinks, and is made drunk by the sun – and by colours, splendours, iridescences – and he sees all things in their newness, and by his play he instinctively remakes paradise.[8] And we, when inebriated, return to the child's estate; drunkenness is the festival of innocence; in the land of the *philosophes*, the drunkard is a prophet. Blessed wine – our moral protest against the arid sobriety of the devil's kingdom of respectability. Wine, which creates communion, which

---

[6] See *Le Paradis Artificiels*, I: *Le Poème du Haschisch*, especially chs 1 and 5; *Du Vin et du Haschisch*, ch. 7.
[7] See *Le Peintre de la Vie Moderne*, ch. XI: *Éloge du Maquillage*.
[8] See ibid.; '*Bénédiction*', in *Les Fleurs du Mal*.

is poured out in us like God's love. Wine, the first holy sign by which Christ revealed himself at Cana – our true Dionysus, the risen lord of indestructible life, of vitality and abundance, great *choregos* in the orgies of innocence.

V

Now, conversely, when I speak of woman, I confess, I am often guilty of a certain dividedness. I was always capable of a more exalted view of woman, if not quite the fawning gynecolatry of some of my contemporaries. Here, a poem:

The Dancing Girl

No soft memory of living flesh can,
Within the crystal lattice of the mind,
Recall her grace, *sa tendresse, sa luxure,*
Or summon up her body's frail complaint,
Its moan of doves and flutes, its mirroring
Of moon's blue light, which seemed to shine in her …
All melts into this dreary anomie
In which all thought is lost; and all the sweet
And ardent turmoils of those distant nights
Are just a fragrance or a voice recalled.

One here must speak in mysteries and say,
The dark reflection of her passing form
In all the gleaming facets of the night,
Between white pillars of the marble earth,
Must indicate what is more real than flesh;
The world is mirror, where the spirit moves
In symbols, glitters, echoes, dreams, and signs,
Fatidic gestures from a nameless world
Beyond time's fragile surfaces, beyond
This labyrinth in which her absence roams.

The glory of her long, unceasing dance
Grows grander in the limpid well of space,
And endlessly her gentle form withdraws
And endlessly draws near, as in all things
That shine and all that, shining, still conceal,
Her motions echo on, and on redound,

Though body is but dream and memory;
And now her dancing fills the frigid world
With figures cast in fire, immersed in night,
More various and strange and true than life.

And yet, one might well ask, why was my principal image of woman so often that of the prostitute? Again, though, when social order is the regime of mechanism, of bodies without souls, of the market, of materialist prudence – when this is decency, is respectability – then transgression becomes a necessary piety. And, in such a world, it is the prostitute – the rejected and reviled, the suffering servant of an age that knows no sin and seeks no expiation – who corrupts the logic of acquisition and consumption with the subversive possibility of a tenderness that exceeds the price remitted; thereby she becomes the emblem of the holy, the sign of love's patient vulnerability. How often I was considered most blasphemous when, in truth, I could scarcely have been more devout.

The Heathen's Apologia

I

Consider Phoebe, how she goes
    Down paths of utter decadence,
    For well this carnal pilgrim knows
That God – all opposites' coincidence –
    Is found upon the left-hand way
    Just as upon the right. And so
    Let honeyed hungers have their sway,
And appetite be infinite yet grow.

II

Consider Phoebe, how she calls
    That virile ephebe to attend her:
    God draws the longing from her soul
That prompts the gentle service she will render.
    The vastness of creation spills
    Into the ocean of her heart,
    The tumult of the cosmos stills –
She finds divinity in every part.

III

Consider Phoebe, how she weeps
    For hearts that have grown hard and cold:

> The knowledge that her sorrow keeps
> Discreetly hid from men will not be told.
> From chaos the great hand of Zeus
> Drew forth the worlds as fruits of love:
> These scorching passions he set loose,
> These pains, return a glory from above.
>
> IV
>
> Consider Phoebe's ecstasy:
> The writhing clutching of her hands
> Is God's eternal majesty
> Weft on the loom of time with shining strands.
> For Phoebe in her agony
> Of joy and canticle of sighs
> Embraces all of earth and sea,
> And clasps infinity between her thighs.

You may disapprove. Perhaps I do as well. But you must see that God himself is the most prostituted of us all, since he is the highest friend of all, the most shared in common, the inexhaustible reservoir of love.[9] Here, where all is sold and nothing given, love can find us only by the supreme condescension of selling itself, of divesting itself of its glory and descending into the brothels of our hearts, where all our loves are purchased loves, thus taking us unawares precisely where our lust reigns supreme. Christ kept company with harlots out of the abundance of his compassion, yes, but also perhaps because he found them holier – more blameless – than the righteous. And was not the dereliction of the cross like the self-abnegation of a lupanar? Was it not there that God gave himself – sold himself cheaply – to those who could not hope to win his love, requiring nothing in return but the paltriest pittance of their faith?

VI

As for song – that, for me, is perhaps the final mystery of divine mercy. I mean the way of beauty, the ambiguous raptures of art. I expect we all hope that divine mercy will come to us in the surprise of an annunciation, the invasion of a splendour that does not wait upon us, but that suddenly seizes us to itself. But,

---

[9] See *Mon cœur mis nu*, LXVIII.

O Lord, could we really bear to meet your gaze in the gaze of your angel? Is any but the purest soul prepared for that encounter?

I was much taken once, at the museum, by one of those childish but oddly touching sacred pictures of the Byzantine Greeks. I half sketched out a poem about it, in fact. Here:

Annunciation

Beneath a canopy of gold – tempera's sky,
Through which smooth gesso's luminosity still breaks –
Her figure, cowled in dark vinaceous purple dye
Marked with three stars, set off against brown hills, bice lakes,
Is turned to meet the lush farrago of his wings:
Soft lavender, cornelian red, and green imbue
His plumage with prismatic splendor, from which springs
An arc of amethyst, a fringe of fiery blue;
And there an edge of silver frosts his pinions' tips.
He stands erect – his brow's the color of the moon,
His incandescent eyes are indigo, his lips
Are coralline – but bent escarpments seem to swoon
Above the scene. Time cannot comprise him: the day
Wears on, indifferent to eternity's press
Of glory; the dark world looks stubbornly away
From his rude revelations of time's changeless depths.

But she in rapture gazes on this presence, bright
With dreadful beauty, at the air about him stained
With iridescence where his wings shed their cool light.
The space between them faintly trembles with its pained
And constant tensions: face to face, the deepest wounds
Of being pass between them. Nacreous and cold,
The gesso's glow still penetrates the trees and stones.
She quickens in life's sleep, and knows that he could hold
Her here forever with his gaze, trapped in his eyes.
Beyond, a fabulous coiled world of ochre lies.

Perfect beauty would be terrifying. We could not bear it; it would convict us of the squalor we have gathered around our souls in our attempts to shield ourselves from remorse. We must labour, therefore, amid imperfect beauty, knowing that therein – inasmuch as beauty is the realm of the spirit – our loyalties to God and to the devil vie with one another. It is the angel within us, after all, that the devil within us seeks to corrupt. Here, amid the darkness of this world, the burning embers of true beauty lie scattered, gleaming jewels of golden fire, sparks of divine glory, and we can only strive to gather them up again. But there also Satan hangs his lures and sets his snares, for he too knows the uses of beauty. Some of these lost splendours were once gems brightly shining in his diadem of stars.

VII

I end where I began. I cannot – we cannot – poor philosopher, above all you cannot – erect again that glorious scale of eminence and analogy that once rose from earth to heaven, but which modern man has pulled down. In my last days on the earth I learned that, in the end, I knew only the way of dereliction, of seeking God's mercy in all the final, frailest gestures of abandonment. In this age, we can find no other path of ascent than that of our last descent into the penury of a strangely disconsolate hope. There is only one who can create for us, in our broken solitude, that star-strewn way of return – and he seems so remote in this age that sometimes it is as if we only dreamed him. One last verse:

John on Patmos

My tongue was as a golden bird
   Tangled in an emerald net,
My eyes were diamonds, my ears heard
   His voice in silver echoes; yet
I knew no way to join the dance
   Until the dancer took my hand,
And led me in a floating trance
   When I could scarcely rise to stand.

Or so, when visions seized my soul,
   It seemed; or when his gentle form
Amid the garden shadows, cold
   And still (as when he calmed the storm
Upon the waters), fixed in prayer,
   Became as pure and strange as light
Departing from the evening air
   Before the melting blue of night.

> I am as gold or emerald,
>   As twilit gems or moonlit silver,
> Beyond all grief, transformed, and held
>   Within a cage of stars, and never
> To leave this island washed by dreams;
>   I can recall as none else can
> The otherness in him: he seemed
>   A shape more beautiful than man.

Thus, in the end, I learned to pray, constantly, out of my deepest despair, my incessant thirst for that boundless love:

O God, you whose name I scarcely dare pronounce, blessed be you for the gift of my suffering: the suffering you impart as a remedy for our impurities, to make the strong fit for holy delights.[10] O, have pity upon me, my God, my God, and upon us all. See what innocent monsters throng the city, O creator both of law and of liberty, you the judge who forgives, who perhaps taught me my taste for horror in order to cure my heart as it were at sword's point. Have pity on all men and women who are mad. Can any be monstrous in your sight, you who created them, who alone know why they exist and how they made themselves and how they might not have done so?[11] Teach me to extend my charity, without so much as a grimace of disdain, to the poor, the abased, the suffering, so to spread a triumphal carpet beneath the feet of Jesus.[12] Teach me also to see how my humiliations have been graces sent by you.[13] Recall, O Lord, how as a child I spoke constantly to you,[14] and forgive me now. I implore your pity, you whom alone I have loved, out of the abyss wherein my heart lies entombed.[15] O, my God, my God, let me not dwell forever far from your gaze.

So I prayed …

In this age of broken covenants, we can offer only these whispered supplications, these uncertain prayers, not always knowing if we are heard. As we have lost the path, we must for now make our way in darkness, groping helplessly, till we learn again how to be led by faith.

Ah, well…The reflections of a forlorn ghost or of a soul in bliss – I cannot tell you which. That secret it is not given me to disclose.

---

[10] See 'Bénédiction', in *Les Fleurs du Mal*.
[11] See *Le Spleen de Paris*, XLV.
[12] See 'Le Rebelle', in *Les Fleurs du Mal, poèmes supplémentaires*.
[13] See *Mon cœur mis nu*, CXV.
[14] See *Mon cœur mis nu*, CIV.
[15] See 'De Profundis Clamavi', in *Les Fleurs du Mal*.

So, then – *alors* –

Agréez-vous, je vous en prie, l'expression de mes sentiments distingués. Merci, Mesdames et Messieurs, merci beaucoup. Maintenant je dois partir – je dois retourner à ce terrible mystère qui attend chaque homme – alors je vais dire: 'Adieu. Adieu.'

3

Martin Heidegger and Christian Wisdom

Cyril O'Regan

Almost from the beginning of his career, Heidegger's philosophy came to be regarded as an opportunity to correct and refresh Catholic philosophy and theology which seemed to have narrowed in scope and succumbed to a fallow rationalism, doing no service to the capaciousness of reason and its complex but neighbourly relation to faith, which was typical of the premodern period. Vatican I (1869), *Aeterni Patris* (1879) and *Pascendi dominici gregis* (1910) were symptoms of a long-standing problem of reaction in Catholic theology as it faced the challenges of (a) the Reformation, in the forms of *sola scriptura* and *sola gratia*, and (b) the Enlightenment, which separated faith from reason, and proposed a fundamentally instrumental view of the latter. Catholic theological thinking increasingly took the form of proof, and if not proof, then appeal to institutional authority. This makes sense of why Catholic thinkers – such as Erich Przywara, Edith Stein and Karl Rahner, and a little later Bernard Welte, Gustav Siewerth and Hans Urs von Balthasar – were genuinely enthusiastic about the contribution (albeit indirect) that Heidegger could make to Catholic thought. In line with Husserl's recommendation to dispense with the objectivizing natural attitude, but in a way much more focused than he, Heidegger was seen to have opened up dimensions of experience and reception of ultimate reality that seemed to leave room for religious exposition and construction. Heidegger, then, had at the very least the prospect of being an agent in the reform of Catholic thought, which would elicit a capacity corresponding to its wideness in much of the premodern tradition, where thought expressed itself as a scientific discourse (*scientia*) only because it was first and last a wisdom or sapiential discourse (*sapientia*). To the degree to which Heidegger's phenomenology moved beyond instrumental rationality, it was a matter of judgement as to whether it should be called a wisdom discourse in the strict Catholic sense, or at least thought to approximate to sapiential expression after the manner of the best models in the classical tradition of Western thought. But for some prominent Catholic thinkers – mainly but not exclusively German – one thing was certain: Heidegger's phenomenological ontology could help to 'wise up' both Catholic philosophical and theological thought.

In most cases of Catholic encounter with and appropriation of Heidegger, *Being and Time* (1927) was the pivotal text wherein Heidegger attempted to articulate an approach to reality equidistant from the standard Aristotle and the standard Kant. Heidegger rejected equally logical and epistemic foundationalism and proceeded to mint a new language for the dynamic between Dasein and Sein.[1] It was obvious to Catholic thinkers that a number of themes and some of the language in Heidegger's articulation of fundamental ontology were religious in suggestion, if not in intent, and they noticed that religious thinkers such as Augustine and Kierkegaard are adduced (even if sparingly) throughout the text.[2] At the very least it gave comfort to Catholic thinkers that they were not engaging a hostile. One can imagine that any awareness of Heidegger's even earlier work (1913–26), especially his Habilitation (1915), which was ostensibly on the *Categories* of Duns Scotus (with a significant portion written by Henry of Ghent),[3] as well as his palpable interest in Augustine, Paul, Luther, Eckhart, Carmelite mysticism, Schleiermacher and Otto, would likely have encouraged Catholic readers of Heidegger to presume actual, and not merely formal, hospitality to Christian thought and practice.[4]

As Catholic thinkers both engaged Heidegger and entertained some measure of assimilation, there were, however, a number of conditions that required satisfaction were appropriation to be justified. In this short essay I would like to draw attention to three: (1) The 'methodological atheism' of *Being and Time* and the famous 'Phenomenology and Theology' essay (1928) was seen to indicate, at the very least, that Heidegger's brand of phenomenology was neutral

---

[1] For a convenient English translation of *Sein und Zeit*, see *Being and Time* (trans. John McQuarrie and Edward Robinson; Oxford: Blackwell, 1967), hereafter *BT*. This edition translates the seventh edition of *Sein und Zeit* (Tübingen: Max Niemeyer, 1953), hereafter *SZ*.

[2] For Heidegger's references to Augustine, see *SZ*, pp. 43–4 (*BT*, p. 69); *SZ*, pp. 171–2 (*BT*, pp. 215–16). For Kierkegaard, see *SZ*, p. 190 n. 4 (*BT*, p. 492) and *SZ*, p. 338 n. 3 (*BT*, p. 497). For a critical evaluation of Heidegger's treatment of Augustine, see Cyril O'Regan, 'Answering Back: Augustine's Critique of Heidegger', in *Human Destinies: Philosophical Essays in Honor of Gerald Hanratty* (ed. Fran O'Rourke; Notre Dame: University of Notre Dame Press, 2013), pp. 134–84.

[3] See Sean J. McGrath, *The Early Heidegger and Medieval Philosophy: Phenomenology for the Godforsaken* (Washington, DC: Catholic University of America Press, 2006), esp. pp. 88–119.

[4] For comprehensive coverage of this material, see Theodore Kisiel, *The Genesis of Heidegger's Being and Time* (Berkeley: University of California Press, 1993). See also John van Buren, *The Young Heidegger: Rumor of the Hidden King* (Bloomington: Indiana University Press, 1994).

regarding religious belief;[5] (2) the reduction of philosophical and theological concepts to their phenomenological and existential bases did not imply their replacement, or, in other words, *Destruktion* was not literal; what was intended was the uncovering of an origin, or basis (*Abbau*), that would redeem the truth, meaning and meaningfulness of philosophical and theological concepts which all too often came unmoored from their originating experiential and existential context; and (3) the metaphysical and theological traditions were not so vitiated that the Catholic wisdom tradition, which was broad as well as deep but which has its twin peaks in Augustine and Aquinas, might not be of contemporary philosophical and theological value.

Stein, Przywara and Rahner responded in different ways and in different tones to the 'gift' of Heidegger,[6] which, given its principled openness to philosophical discourse, was more provocative in Catholic than Protestant thought. Although by and large in Protestantism only Bultmann and his school fully embraced Heidegger's existential analytic of Dasein,[7] it is evident that the theological-epistemological grounds of liberal Protestant theology, which in equal parts supported Luther's *sola scriptura* and Kant's epistemological restrictions on what we can know, meant that only the first of the three issues proved in any way exigent.[8] One could assume that most – if not all – philosophical and theological concepts were the work of the 'whore reason' and/or imposed by an alien authority, and that they signified the pretension to know things about God and the God–world relation that human beings simply cannot know. Evidence

---

[5] For a convenient translation of the oft-cited 'Phänomenologie und Theologie' (1927/28), see 'Phenomenology and Theology', Martin Heidegger, *The Piety of Thinking: Essays by Martin Heidegger* (trans. and ed. J. Hart and J. C. Maraldo; Bloomington: Indiana University Press, 1969), pp. 5–21. This essay has an important evidentiary function in Laurence Paul Hemming, *Heidegger's Atheism: The Refusal of a Theological Voice* (Notre Dame: University of Notre Dame Press, 2002), pp. 64–6, 202.

[6] I am evoking Derrida's sense of pharmakon. For Derrida's exposition of the double signification of the term, see 'Plato's Pharmacy', in Jacques Derrida, *Dissemination* (trans. Barbara Johnson; Chicago: University of Chicago Press, 1981), pp. 65–172.

[7] Bultmann and Heidegger were fellow travellers at Marburg in the 1920s with Bultmann thinking that Heidegger's *existentials* threw light on the kerygma of the Gospel which was distorted in doctrine and by theological conceptualization, and correspondingly, Heidegger allowing a version of Christianity that was purely actualist and without conceptual mediation. In the decade before *Being and Time* Heidegger had pretty much settled on this position. The letters between Bultmann and Heidegger have been collected. See *Rudoph Bultmann/Martin Heidegger Briefwechsel, 1925–1975* (eds A Grossmann and C. Landmesser; Tübingen: Mohr Siebeck, 2009). Arguably, the best book on the topic of the relation between Bultmann's theology and Heidegger's early philosophy is still John MacQuarrie, *An Existentialist Theology: A Comparison of Heidegger and Bultmann* (London: SCM Press, 1955).

[8] After the Second World War, Protestant theologians did try hard to appropriate Heidegger's more language-oriented philosophy in their articulation of the biblical text as a language-event (*Sprache-Ereignis*). Gerhard Ebeling and Ernst Fuchs are two of the more prominent appropriators of Heidegger in New Testament studies.

to the contrary in its own history, the Reformation polemic against reason and tradition continued to be useful in a process of negotiation with modernity. Moreover, this negotiation was made considerably easier if the basic issue could be reduced to the meaning and meaningfulness of the biblical text (although necessarily a meaning and meaningfulness to the side of instrumental rationality which had every right to dominate in the practical sphere). Specifically, the issue narrowed as to whether: (a) there is a kerygmatic core that can be extracted from the historical record and no-longer operative worldview of the biblical text; and (b) the kerygma can in turn be illuminated by a non-metaphysical form of thought that has become available. Thus we see occasion for Bultmann's and Heidegger's association at Marburg, Bultmann's enthusiastic endorsement and adoption of Heidegger's existential categories, and Heidegger's returning of the favour in 1928 and later in his Zürich seminar (1951).[9] In the latter text the Word that gets worded in the biblical text, although perhaps not in it alone, is a primal word. This Word thus escapes the misprisioning of rationalism and metaphysics assigned to almost every other cultural discourse, of which philosophy and theology not only do not enjoy exempt status, but are paradigmatic specimens.

Whatever the felt urgency for reform in Catholic thought with respect to deepening inquiry and enlarging its scope, there were limits. These limits were as much internally as externally imposed. Specifically, while the Catholic philosophical and theological traditions could be submitted to scrutiny, they could be rejected neither automatically nor whole cloth. Greater or lesser levels of comfort might be illustrated by early twentieth-century Catholic thinkers who felt compelled to engage Heidegger in order to move forward in philosophy and theology. These writers attempted to step behind the debacle of a Catholic thinking that not only had become irrelevant but that also effectively left itself without a useable past.

Three Catholic Thinkers: Rahner, Stein and Przywara

The three Catholic thinkers we have mentioned more nearly adapt than adopt Heidegger in their encounter with his thought. Karl Rahner seems to have the least anxiety about the risks a Catholic thinker runs in adopting a discourse

---

[9] The Zürich seminar was given to a group of Bultmannians; see Martin Heidegger, *Gesamtausgabe 15: I. Abt., Veröffentlichte Schriften 1910–1976 Seminare* (ed. Friedrich-Wilhelm von Herrmann; Ingrid Schüßler; Frankfurt: Klostermann, 1986). For a good discussion of the Zürich seminar, see Hemming, *Heidegger's Atheism*, pp. 184–91.

that constructs theological and philosophical discourses as derivative at best, corrupt at worst. As Laurence Hemming rightly points out,[10] Rahner's assimilation of Heidegger is largely opportunistic. He does not feel obliged to obey what might appear to be prohibitions against conceptualist language, nor is he concerned to present a detailed retrieval of some (or any) of the major philosophical or theological figures of the Catholic tradition. In *Geist in Welt* (1939, finished in 1936) Rahner operates as if Heideggerian prohibitions need not count.[11] Quite simply, he is not inclined to cede to Heidegger's fundamental ontology full control over theological discourse. Having studied with Heidegger in the early 1930s, Rahner has more than a casual command of Heidegger's *oeuvre*.[12] Nonetheless, despite this knowledge of *Introduction to Metaphysics* and, more importantly, Heidegger's questioning of the value of the association of philosophy and theology[13] (this time from the point of view of philosophical inquiry), Rahner is relatively insouciant when it comes to drawing on Heidegger to refresh a Thomism already 'transcendentally' refreshed by Maréchal, Rousselot and Blondel. Heidegger helps to correct for rationalism, first as a propositionalist tendency, which favours answer over question and proscribes fundamental orientation, and second, as a functional disconnection between contemplation and action, pushing aside modes of thought that are world-embedding and self-involving. With regard to the last point, in what is essentially an application rather than explication of Heidegger, Rahner operates for the most part as if Heidegger's methodological atheism is precisely that (methodological), and therefore acts as if it does not foreclose on religious belief. Rahner behaves as if reduction to the person dynamically oriented towards her divine ground is not forbidden by Heidegger (even if not necessarily encouraged), and as if a major Catholic figure such as Aquinas (or an Augustinian Aquinas) was under no threat of deletion from the canon of real thinkers, despite his awareness of Heidegger's tendency to maximal and alarming canonical shrinkage. In the

---

[10] On Rahner's opportunistic rather than serious engagement, see Hemming, *Heidegger's Atheism*, pp. 21–9.

[11] For an English translation of *Geist in Welt*, see *Spirit in the World* (trans. William Dych; foreword by Johannes Metz; New York: Continuum, 1969).

[12] The most up-to-date reflection on the relation between Rahner and Heidegger – facilitated by the publication of Rahner's notes on the lectures he took with Heidegger – is by Peter Joseph Fritz. See his very fine *Karl Rahner's Theological Aesthetics* (Washington, DC: Catholic University of America Press, 2014). Other still useful accounts include Thomas Sheehan, *Karl Rahner: The Philosophical Foundations* (Athens, OH: Ohio University Press, 1987); also J. A. Bonsor, *Rahner, Heidegger, and Truth: Karl Rahner's Notion of Christian Truth, the Influence of Heidegger* (Lanham, MD.: University Press of America, 1987).

[13] Heidegger famously disparages the notion of a Christian philosophy as an oxymoron in *Einführung in die Metaphysik* (1935). For a convenient English translation, see *An Introduction to Metaphysics* (trans. Ralph Mannheim; New Haven: Yale University Press, 1959), p. 7.

period of the production of this text as well as *Hörer des Wortes* (1941), the range of Heidegger's texts explicitly engaged is fairly small: mainly but not exclusively *Sein und Zeit* and the *Kantbuch*.[14] Dialogue with these selections in a philosophical investigation into the ontological implications of Aquinas' reflections on knowledge in the Tertia Pars (articles 83–5) enabled Rahner to construct his metaphysics of finitude and reframe the notion of mystery, which had narrowed in Vatican I to an epistemological limit. In its new definition, mystery becomes not only the horizon and goal of all desire, but also what makes it possible.[15]

Rahner, then, without apology, does not seem exercised by a proper reading of Heidegger, such as the kind enjoined by Hemming. Heidegger's thought does not set the conditions for Catholic theology, but rather it supports and augments the Catholic turn to the dynamism of the intellect (synecdoche) that has been afoot for almost 40 years. This pragmatism very much comes to the fore in a short essay that Rahner devoted to the relation between Heidegger and Catholic theology in which,[16] while he declares his principled openness to Heidegger's thought, he cautions against confusing the host and what may be grafted. Still, even with Rahner, there are a few demurrals. He contests Heidegger's proscriptions of God and *summum esse* (and their linkage) and, correlatively, Rahner wonders about an orientation in which there is no term or where in fact nothing is the term. Admittedly, the issue of whether nihilism lies as a hidden implication of Heidegger's thought is already in the air. At one level it is an issue that raises its head in Davos (1929) in Heidegger's famous debate with Cassirer (ostensibly over Kant), in which Heidegger shows himself to be keen: (a) to expose the cultural traditions of the West,[17] as well as metaphysics,

---

[14] Building on hints provided by Thomas F. O'Meara, recently Peter Joseph Fritz makes a compelling case for the influence of Heidegger's Schelling lectures on Rahner. See his 'Karl Rahner, Friedrich Schelling, and Original Unity', in *Theological Studies* 75 (2) (2014): 284–307. The Schelling discussed by Heidegger in the seminar is the Schelling of *Vom Wesen der menschlichen Freiheit* (1809). The lecture course on Schelling is now vol. 42 of the *Gesamtausgabe* of Heidegger's work which is now over 100 volumes.

[15] From *Spirit in the World* on, 'mystery' is an important notion in Rahner's thought. It is correlative to the unthematic awareness by the subject of the ground of existence. Among the many Rahner texts where mystery plays a significant role, see *Hörer des Wortes* (1941). For an English translation, see *Hearer of the Word: Laying the Foundation for a Philosophy of Religion* (trans. Joseph Donceel; ed. and intro. Andrew Tallon; New York: Continuum, 1994), Part 3: The Hiddenness of Being, pp. 55–89. For a somewhat later expression, see 'The Concept of Mystery in Catholic Theology', in Karl Rahner, *Theological Investigations 4: More Recent Writings* (trans. Kevin Smyth; Baltimore: Helicon Press, 1966), pp. 36–73. The original essay appeared as 'Über den Begriff des Geheimnisses in der katholischen Theologie' (1964).

[16] Rahner wrote only one essay on Heidegger (1939). For a convenient translation, see 'The Concept of Existential Philosophy in Heidegger', in *Philosophy Today* 13 (2) (Summer 1969): 126–37.

[17] For an excellent account of the Davos debate, see Richard E. Gordon, *Heidegger, Cassirer, Davos* (Cambridge, MA.: Harvard University Press, 2010).

as bankrupt; and (b) to legislate that thought live in the apocalyptic moment in which it responds to what is needful. What is needful is left unhelpfully specified, and Heidegger's 1933 Rector's Address[18] is, to say the least, not an admirable specification of content. Implied also is that all important thought has an apocalyptic and evental, or 'uncalled for', character – a vision that gets clarified and exacerbated in and beyond the so-called *Kehre*. Przywara, who was at Davos, had already noted this concern in and for Catholic thought in *Analogia Entis*.[19] To conclude this very minimalistic précis, Rahner thinks that Heidegger can play a positive role in the articulation of a fundamental theology at the borders between philosophy and theology by 'wising up' Catholic traditions of philosophical and theological thought that have adopted rationalist and authority protocols. Importantly, Rahner does not suggest, as a number of more recent Catholic religious thinkers have,[20] that Heidegger's thought is the wisdom that gives Western philosophical and theological thought their sanction (not excluding its twin peaks of Augustine and Aquinas).

Edith Stein is as much a philosophical fellow-traveller with Heidegger as a receiver of a secular wisdom that corrects for the abatement of thought in Catholic philosophy. A student of Husserl, Stein is convinced that her mentor is the answer to the subjectivism of modernity rather than the problem (as Heidegger among others come to think). Her early philosophical work develops a view of subjectivity – precisely as intersubjectivity – on lines related to, but dissimilar from, what is enacted in Scheler.[21] Heidegger never comes

---

[18] The publication of Heidegger's Rector's Address at his installation in 1933 in which there is an explicit endorsement of National Socialism started a debate which shows no sign of abating as to whether Heidegger's behaviour invalidated his entire philosophical project. The debate started in France and moved from there to Germany and the United States. On the French side, Victor Farias and Philippe Lacoue-Labarthe are especially important. For the former, see *Heidegger and Nazism* (trans. Paul Burrell, Dominic Di Benardi and Gabriel R. Ricci; ed. Joseph Margolis and Tom Rockmore; Philadelphia: Temple University Press, 1989). For the latter, see *Heidegger, Art, and Politics* (trans. Chris Turner; Oxford: Blackwell, 1990). Those who have been important on the German side include Hugo Ott and Rüdiger Safranskski. On the US side, prominent commentators who have entered the discussion include Tom Rockmore, James F. Ward, Richard Wolin and Michael E. Zimmerman. Richard Wolin helpfully brings together much of the most contentious material. See his *The Heidegger Controversy: A Critical Reader* (Boston: MIT Press, 1991). For a translation of the Rector's Address, 'The Self-Assertion of the German University', see pp. 29–39.

[19] We are fortunate enough now to have a wonderful English translation of *Analogia Entis 1: Metaphysik: Ur-Struktur und All-Rhythmus* (Einseideln: Johannes Verlag, 1962). This volume was compiled by Hans Urs von Balthasar in consultation with Erich Przywara and contains, in addition to the 1932 text of *Analogia Entis*, thirteen later essays, the last dating from 1960. The English translators have added two additional pieces. See *Analogia Entis: Metaphysics: Original Structure and Universal Rhythm* (trans. John R. Betz and David Bentley Hart; Grand Rapids, MI: Eerdmans, 2014). See also Betz's powerful comprehensive introductory essay, pp. 1–115.

[20] Perhaps the commentator on Heidegger, who is as convinced as Hemming of the unequivocal value of Heidegger to unrubbish and rehabilitate theology is Joseph S. O'Leary. See his *Questioning Back: The Overcoming of Metaphysics in the Christian Tradition* (Minneapolis: Winston Press, 1986).

[21] Stein's most important early work overlaps significantly with that of Max Scheler, who explored

to function, as he does in Rahner, as the eclipse of Husserl, even when (or especially when) Stein turns to Aquinas, on the one hand, and to the Carmelite mystical tradition, on the other.[22] For her, Husserl is the wisdom thinker in phenomenology, and when she converts Husserl remains, for her, the one inalienable modern philosophical resource for Catholic thought. Moreover, Stein continues to believe that phenomenology in principle does not have an anti-religious bias, yet she does not move so far as to claim that Heidegger's not-uncongenial modification of phenomenology, given its ontological register, necessarily preserves such neutrality. Here one might think of Stein as an exemplar for Marion,[23] who, in a number of texts in which he attempts to develop phenomenology through thinking a further reduction (of givenness) beyond the eidetic and phenomenological reduction, clearly favours a move of regression behind Heidegger's fundamental ontology. Both Marion and Stein seem to agree that Heidegger's fundamental ontology is in fact biased against revelatory kinds of appearing in a way that Husserl's non-ontological variety of phenomenology is not. Unlike Heidegger's ontological version, Husserl's variant of phenomenology not only proves neutral with regard to religious appearance, but, arguably, is truly welcoming of revelation.

Now Stein worries also – along with (and perhaps because of) Przywara – that *Sein und Zeit* bespeaks nihilism.[24] She also sees how nihilism goes hand in hand with a peculiar Heideggerian proscription that only the finite can be disclosed to a searching intellect, and a view of the self that is erotic all the way through in that its desire neither can nor should be satisfied. Especially in her

---

areas of affect and originally given responsiveness to the other that short-circuited the problem of intersubjectivity posed by Husserl's transcendental turn in *Ideas 1* (1913). See her *On the Problem of Empathy: The Collected Works of Edith Stein (Volume 3)* (trans. Waltraut Stein; rev. 3rd edn; Washington, DC: ICS Publications, 1989).

[22] See *Science of the Cross (The Collected Works of Edith Stein (Volume 6)* (trans. Josephine Koeppel; ed. D. L. Gelber, R. Leuven; Washington, DC: ICS Publications, 2003).

[23] The preference for Husserl over Heidegger in Marion's ongoing project of excavating phenomenology has focally to do with the greater proximity of the former to the third reduction, that is, to givenness, beyond the eidetic and phenomenological reduction. This in turn makes possible the reception of religious phenomena and Revelation. See especially *Reduction and Givenness: Investigations of Husserl, Heidegger, and Phenomenology* (trans. Thomas A. Carlson; Evanston: Northwestern University Press, 1998); also *Being Given: Towards a Phenomenology of Givenness* (trans. Jeffrey L. Kosky; Stanford: Stanford University Press, 2002).

[24] Stein's essay *Martin Heideggers Existentialphilosophie* was essentially an appendix to *Welt und Person* (Louvain: Éditions Nauwelaerts, 1962). If overall the analysis of *Sein und Zeit* is appreciative, nonetheless, Stein worries about the absolutization of death, the prescription of 'nothing' as the horizon of existence and the correlative proscription against God as the horizon and ground of all being. For a good account of this important essay, see Antonio Calcagno, 'Die Fülle oder das Nichts? Edith Stein and Martin Heidegger on the Question of Being', *American Catholic Philosophical Quarterly* 74 (2) (2000): 269–85.

work on Aquinas, *Finite and Infinite Being*,²⁵ Stein diagnoses and problematizes the axiom of finitude, which is constitutive of both *Being and Time* and the *Kantbuch*. In this, she differs from Rahner, who blithely passes over it as he insists that the infinite ground of reality is given to the finite subject, albeit given pre-thematically rather than thematically. From Stein's perspective, Heidegger may have done all thought – Catholic thought not excluded – not only a major service by insisting on the finitude of the knowing and willing subject, but at the same time a disservice in making unavailable the possibility/actuality of an infinite subject that is the ground of searching. Being the good Thomist that she becomes, Stein produces an inversion of Heidegger's priority: higher than possibility is actuality and the reality that gives itself without the constraint of transcendental conditions.²⁶ Arguably, Heidegger does not loom sufficiently large for Stein to be concerned that she is involved in retrieving a figure like Aquinas who belongs to a philosophical tradition judged by Heidegger to be woebegone, even if the language of dismissal has yet to crystallize into the single and singular term of repudiation, that is, 'ontotheology'.²⁷

Erich Przywara's *Analogia Entis* (1932) represents a deeper,²⁸ more concerted Catholic and critical engagement with Heidegger than that exhibited by an opportunistic Rahner and a Stein who, while she consistently supported the phenomenological turn, did not grant Heidegger's ontological inflection/revision any special authority. For Przywara, Heidegger's emphasis on reality as dynamic is of direct benefit to philosophy and thus indirectly to theology, as is also Heidegger's existential manner of approach. In addition, Heidegger's ontological insistence is congenial to Przywara, who thinks that a constitutive

---

[25] The full title is *Finite and Infinite Being: An Attempt at an Ascent to the Meaning of Being* (trans. Kurt. F. Reinhard; Washington, DC: ICS, 2002). It has been noted often how the title of Stein's major philosophical text recalls *Sein und Zeit*. Stein's critical engagement with Heidegger is front-loaded. Early on in the text Stein indicates that the lack in Dasein refers to a fullness in the ground of Being, not emptiness or nothingness (pp. 54–9). For reflection on this important difference, see Rafa Kazimierz, 'On Human Being: A Dispute between Edith Stein and Martin Heidegger', *Logos* 10 (4) (Fall 2007): 104–17.

[26] Stein inverts or reverses Heidegger's prioritization of possibility over actuality in *Sein und Zeit* (p. 38) (*BT*, p. 63), and is convinced that phenomenology vindicates the priority of act rendered in medieval philosophy and especially that of Aquinas. See *Potency and Act* (trans. Walter Redmond; Washington, DC: ICS Publishing, 2009).

[27] See Martin Heidegger, 'The Onto-theo-logical Nature of Metaphysics' ('Die onto-theo-logische Verfassung der Metaphysik' (1956/7)), in idem, *Essays in Metaphysics: Identity and Difference* (trans. Kurt F. Leidecker; New York: Philosophical Library, 1960), 33–67.

[28] The 1932 text is less than a half of the material translated by Betz and Hart; see *Analogia Entis*, pp. 117–315. Betz and Hart also usefully translate a 1959 essay by Przywara reflecting on the relative merits of Husserl and Heidegger. This essay is not found in the 1962 German edition of *Analogia Entis*. See *Analogia Entis*, pp. 613–22. Przywara overall favours Husserl who apparently did not mix philosophy with bad theology as Heidegger did.

problem for philosophy is the turn to the subject.[29] Heidegger is equally agreeable to Przywara in his critique of a pure objectivism, although in this Przywara seems to be aware that here Heidegger continues a line of argument opened by Husserl. And in view of the incorrigibly erotic and zetetic nature of genuine philosophy, it is to be appreciated that in Heidegger one finds a modern philosopher who is a match for the totalizing essentialism of Hegelian thought which represents the *ne plus ultra* of both the leaving behind of the experience that motivates and gives aim to philosophy and the excision of mystery that is a perennial temptation of philosophical thought.[30] For Przywara, Heidegger does not support the view of mystery as an epistemic limit to thought – a no trespass zone familiar in both Kantian and Catholic positivistic circles – but rather a view of mystery as ontological excess requiring maximum human participation. In this respect Heidegger is a figure of anamnesis to be paid close attention by Catholic thinkers and should be granted admission into Catholic discourse.

Both the question of Heidegger's qualifications for a major anamnetic role and the question of his replaceability emerge in Przywara's concerns with what he takes to be Heideggerian reductions. Here I simply give three of the more important. First, as *Analogia Entis* renders it, it is far from clear to Przywara that Heidegger's methodological atheism is merely that. Rather, the textual evidence suggests that Heidegger's commitment to the finite and the temporal is radical and excludes the possibility of the infinite and the eternal. Heidegger's thought represents, therefore, a foreclosure that is possible to sanction neither on philosophical nor on Catholic grounds. There is an anterior obligation to hold out the prospect of an infinite and eternal horizon to the yearning and searching finite self, however one speaks to our access.

Second, the linguistic strain evident in *Analogia Entis* in the torsion given to concepts that are complexified and ramified rather than simplified (*Sosein-in-und-über Dasein*), and the related propensity to neologism, suggests that Przywara is in part persuaded by Heidegger's critique of the metaphysical concept-formation of the West with its penchant for essentialism and shallow forms of clarity. Thus, if not necessarily *Destruktion* in the manner referred to in *Being and Time*, what is required by Catholic thought is at least a critical examination of what is living and dead in Catholic concept-formation and a recovery

---

[29] See *Analogia Entis*, p. 120. Without suggesting that Heidegger's own non-subjective existential position is fully adequate, Przywara shares Heidegger's concern that absolutizing a subjective starting point, whether that of Descartes or German Idealism, represents a philosophical cul-de-sac.

[30] For an attack against Hegel's invidious essentialism and univocalizing of reality, see Przywara, *Analogia Entis*, pp. 144, 15–51, 188–9.

of what is living and covered over by formal consistency, which abides only in a vacuum. A major issue, however, has to do with whether concept-formation is absolutely or relatively compromised in performing a regression from the concept to the originating experience. In using (even if modifying) concepts generated in the philosophical tradition, some of them minted in the Scholastic period, Przywara can be thought to resist unilateral reduction of concepts to existential categories (and presumptively their dismissal, should they not admit of such reduction) and the associated topography in which there is an invariable primary and secondary. To the degree to which Przywara does not license the reduction of concepts without remainder to existential categories, he seems to be insisting on two things: (a) the priority of the existential over the conceptual can only be functional, and (b) even as functional, the priority of the existential is at best relative.

Third, even at this early stage – that is before Heidegger expostulates at length about what is wrong with certain periods of philosophical thinking and what is wrong with any number of its major thinkers (Plato, Aristotle, Descartes, Leibniz, Hegel, even Nietzsche) – there appear to be concerns with Heidegger's genealogical gestures and his apparent foreclosing on the Western tradition of thought. Przywara is no idolater of the classical philosophical tradition, but he is unprepared to throw overboard either Aristotle or Plato, even as he has judicious criticisms of the latter. Even less does he desire to jettison Augustine and Aquinas,[31] who negotiate in complex ways with the classical tradition, learn from it, but also correct and develop it in more radical as well as more measured ways. Heidegger definitely is a philosophical radical that Cassirer is not,[32] but the question is how generative and how reliable can a kind of thinking be that, even with a rehearsal of method, seems to come from nowhere and to link only eccentrically with the philosophical tradition. Moreover, Przywara diagnoses the apocalyptic character of Heidegger's form of thought, what he calls theopanism,[33] as a gratuitous self-presentation of the really real that essentially erases the given of nature – and one might also add the given of culture

---

[31] Augustine and Aquinas are the two magisterial figures in *Analogia Entis*.
[32] Przywara's judgement of the contrast between Heidegger and Cassirer rhymed with the majority. Heidegger was philosophically the more radical and thus gave philosophy a better chance of moving forward, but it was not clear that the radicality did not intimate a kind of recklessness.
[33] For theopanism, see *Analogia Entis*, pp. 19–20, 165–7, 229–30. Of course, throughout his work as a whole, it is the actualism of Barth that provides the classic case. See Betz's useful discussion in *Analogia Entis*, pp. 50–3, where he shows that the event quality of the disclosure of Being, which grants no integrity to the created world, and a more pantheistic view in which the world is everything are dialectically related. With regard to Heidegger this means that a double characteristic of his thought as being figured by the sublime and by the chthonic is not contradictory.

and tradition. The erasure of the given of nature in the commitment to event, whether divine or anti-divine, essentially means that monism is the ultimate issue of too great a stress on equivocity. Therefore, essentially the extremes of pantheism and theopanism meet in the violation of the analogy of being.

Now whatever the outcome of the debate as to whether the so-called *Kehre*, marked by a shift from the analytic of Dasein to Sein, is best designated as a rupture or as a filling out of the tendency to favour ungroundedness over ground, event over stable patterns of the given[34] or a genealogical account of the Western intellectual tradition characterized by decline over the acceptance of tradition, the fact remains that in his readings, especially of Hölderlin (but also of Nietzsche), in which both the recovery and eclipse of the 'holy' assume a central role, Heidegger's thought assumes even closer proximity to Christianity. This proximity requires examination. This is not to say, however, that Heidegger's elucidations of Hölderlin or his thematic of the Holy are immediately taken up in Catholic thought. Although Przywara may have worried about a development that likely would have convinced him of the rightness of his central thesis that Heidegger's thought represents the negation of the analogy of being, for the most part he does not comment on it. We have to wait until the early 1950s for the charge that Heidegger's thought represents a conspicuous remythologization of the matrix of appearance and thus experience in the modern period.[35] And, of course, this argument against the 'later' Heidegger occurs at roughly the same time that Przywara writes his own commentary on Hölderlin,[36] which seems calculated to rescue Hölderlin from invidious interpretations which construct him as a post-Enlightenment utopian or a kind of hyperbolic romantic under the spell of a gorgeous but essentially useless philhellenism.

Here one is safe in thinking that Marion's essay on Hölderlin in *Idol and Distance* is in line with the interpretation provided by Przywara in which the Christian,[37] and specifically Christological features of Hölderlin's great elegies and odes, cannot be excised and, in fact, produces a Christian interpretation that opens up new depths. One might think of Przywara as episodically engaging the 'later' Heidegger, even as Heidegger has ceased to be quite as

---

[34] Perhaps the most influential proponent of the 'Turn' in English-language writing is William Richardson. See his still valuable *Heidegger: Through Phenomenology to Thought* (Dordrecht: Martinus Nijhoff, 1963).

[35] See in particular Przywara's essay, 'Image, Likeness, Symbol, Mythos, Mysterium, Logos', in *Analogia Entis*, pp. 430–62. It seems to be one of the main concerns of the essay to suggest that Heidegger's thought is 'mythic' in significant respects.

[36] Erich Przywara, *Hölderlin* (Nuremberg: Glock & Lutz, 1949).

[37] See Jean-Luc Marion, *Idol and Distance* (trans. and intro. Thomas A. Carlson; New York: Fordham University Press, 2001), pp. 81–136. For recall of Przywara's *Hölderlin*, see p. 105.

urgent for him as he was earlier in his career. Still, even if at a remove, it is not outrageous to suggest that for Przywara Ignatius Loyola and the Carmelites can be added to Augustine and Aquinas as exceptions to Heidegger's genealogy of the Western intellectual tradition as a forgetting of being (*Seinsvergessenheit*). In a sense it was Przywara who lays down two of the basic forms of Catholic exception, that is, both the magisterial theological tradition and the tradition of mysticism in both its contemplative and active registers. Of the major Catholic thinkers, Aquinas was to be rescued from the metaphysical tradition, which is damned or self-damning, on grounds that largely revolve around the Thomistic notions of *esse*, the real distinction between essence and existence, an adequate understanding of *causa* and to a limited extent the relation between natural and revealed theology. Gustav Siewerth and Cornelio Fabro are perhaps the two best examples of this rescue operation,[38] of which Marion's 1995 essay on Aquinas is a belated example.[39] Once again it is possible to see Marion's early, more nearly theologically inflected phenomenology as exploiting Przywara's opening both in terms of the reduction to mystery carried out in *Analogia Entis* and also in his articulation of forms of negative theology as transcending the very kind of conceptualism condemned by Heidegger, which constructs a God as ground (sufficient reason) to whom we cannot pray.[40]

What is noticeable, however, is that by and large Catholic thinkers fairly consistently maintain a defensive posture. There are pleas regarding exemption status, but often the basic terms of Heidegger's genealogical narrative are not questioned. This is the case with Bernhard Welte,[41] and in a different way (virtually more critical) in Przywara and Marion. Questions that have not been asked include whether in his expostulations on the holy Heidegger offers a substantive view of reality, which: (a) forecloses the genuinely phenomenal quality of Christianity by offering an immanentist, more chthonic alternative form of wisdom of true mindfulness (*Andeken*) and patient – even prayerful

---

[38] See Gustav Siewerth, *Das Schicksal der Metaphysik von Thomas von Aquin bis Heidegger* (Einseideln: Johannes Verlag, 1959). Quite non-incidentally, Johannes Verlag is Balthasar's own publication outlet: Cornelio Fabro, *La nozione metafisica di partecipazione secondo San Tommasio d'Aquino (Opere Complete 3)* (Rome: Editrice verbo incarno, 2005). This reproduces a book produced at the beginning of the Second World War which became famous in and through the French rather than Italian edition.

[39] Jean-Luc Marion, 'Saint Thomas d'Aquin et l'onto-théo-logie', *Review Thomiste* 95 (1995): 31–66.

[40] Heidegger disjoins the God of Christian faith from the God of philosophy (and theology) in his essay 'The Onto-theo-logical Nature of Metaphysics', in *Essays in Metaphysics: Identity and Difference*, p. 65. The relevant passage reads: '*Causa sui*', he says, 'is the just and proper name for God in philosophy. Man cannot neither pray to this God, nor may be sacrifice to him. Confronted by *causa sui* man may neither sink onto his knees nor could he sing and dance' (p. 65).

[41] See Bernhard Welte, *Denken in Begegnung mit den Denkern II: Hegel, Nietzsche, Heidegger* (Freiburg: Herder, 2007); also 'God in Heidegger's Thought', *Philosophy Today* 26 (1982): 85–100.

– openness to the deliverances of an amorphous and polymorphous sacral reality; and (b) at the same time suggests that Heideggerian wisdom bears a parasitic relation to Christian wisdom that it would affright and displace in all the modalities, for instance, its basic picture, its practices (prayer and festival) and its mindful forms of life that might be summed up under the term of *Gelassenheit*. These kinds of questions began to emerge in the early 1940s largely through the work of Karl Löwith, and with various levels of commitment became part of Catholic philosophical and theological negotiation with Heidegger.[42] Jean-Yves Lacoste, arguably, offers the most sustained Catholic probing on these questions, even if a somewhat late one. *Experience and the Absolute* represents a self-conscious effort to expose Heidegger's post-*Kehre* thought as a simulacrum.[43] Lacoste concentrates as much on practices, such as liturgy, as the figurations of attunement and openness which are common to Heidegger's *Andenken* and the Christian tradition. If Marion inspired such a mode of investigation, nonetheless, he does not provide the template; it is, rather, Hans Urs von Balthasar. It is to him that we now turn, and it is our consideration of him that concludes the essay.

Balthasar and the Comprehensive Engagement with Heidegger

The theology of Hans Urs von Balthasar represents Catholic theology's most comprehensive engagement with the thought of Heidegger. This is indicated in a number of different ways: (a) Balthasar's engagement is relatively continuous over a period of fifty years from *Apokalypse* to *Epilogue*;[44] (b) Balthasar

---

[42] Karl Löwith, *Martin Heidegger and European Nihilism* (trans. Gary Steiner; ed. Richard Wolin; New York: Columbia University Press, 1995).

[43] Jean-Yves Lacoste, *Experience and the Absolute: Disputed Questions on the Humanity of Man* (trans. Mark Raferty-Skehan; New York: Fordham University Press, 2004).

[44] Hans Urs von Balthasar, *Apokalypse der deutschen Seele: Studien zu einer Lehre von letzten Haltung*, vol. 3, *Zur Vergöttlichung des Todes* (Einseideln, Switzerland: Johannes Verlag, 1993). Originally published by Verlag Anton Pustet, 1939. See also *Epilog* (Trier: Johannes Verlag, 1987). For the English translation, see *Epilogue* (trans. Edward T. Oakes, S.J.; San Francisco: Ignatius Press, 2004). See especially pp. 41–86 which avails of Heidegger to provide evidence for the probity of a Thomistic metaphysics; *Theo-Logic: Theological Logical Theory*, vol. 1, *Truth of the World* (trans. Adrian J. Walker; San Francisco: Ignatius Press, 2000); *The Glory of the Lord: A Theological Aesthetics*, vol. 5, *The Realm of Metaphysics in the Modern Age* (trans. Oliver Davies, Andrew Louth, Brian McNeil C.R.V., John Saward and Rowan Williams; eds Brian McNeil C.R.V., and John Riches; San Francisco: Ignatius Press, 1991), pp. 429–50, 613–56. One can also see significant traces of Heideggerian as well as medieval influence in the foundational volume of theological aesthetics. See *The Glory of the Lord: A Theological Aesthetics*, vol. 1, *Seeing the Form* (trans. Erasmo Leiva-Merikakis; eds Joseph Fessio S.J. and John Riches; San Francisco: Ignatius Press, 1982).

demonstrates knowledge of Heidegger's texts on either side of the *Kehre*;[45] (c) Balthasar's engagement is widespread and while it features *Wahrheit* recycled as *Theo-logic 1*, the conclusion of *The Glory of the Lord 5*, the *Epilogue* and *Apokalypse*, it is not confined to them.[46] One might read *The Glory of the Lord* in its entirety to be an answer to Heidegger's claim to wisdom and to having putting out of action the entire Christian tradition of thought and performance. Balthasar's outline of theological aesthetics presented in *The Glory of the Lord 1* consists of a three-way discussion between the phenomenon of biblical glory, Neoplatonic aesthetic theory with a theological base, and the Heideggerian sublime. *The Glory of the Lord 4* and *5* articulate a counter-genealogy in which Balthasar's tracing of the tradition is essentially the tracing of multiple exceptions – indeed a manifold of exception – to Heidegger's critique of the violent metaphysical tradition. Of course, Aquinas gets exempted twice, the first time quite formally at the end of *The Glory of the Lord 4* and with an exclamation mark at the end of *The Glory of the Lord 5*, which stages something like a vindication of Thomistic *esse* and the real distinction against Heidegger's asseverations[47] but perhaps also indicates something like a defeat of Heideggerian wisdom revealed to be shallow and simplifying when put up against a form of thought of great sophistication that carries real phenomenological purchase. At the formal level, Balthasar hardly goes beyond what is generally laid down in *Analogia Entis*, substantively, however, Balthasar depends on Gustav Siewerth both for his defence of Aquinas and his very respectful and incisive counter-attack.[48]

Of course, *Wahrheit* (1946), later *Theo-Logic 1*, represents Balthasar's most concentrated, critical engagement of Heidegger, as it elaborates its own phenomenological opening of the person to the mysterious ground of being, which

---

[45] By the time of his Habilitation (1915), Heidegger had come to the conclusion that not only the thought of Duns Scotus, but all medieval thought was riddled with rationalism and essentialism. Thereafter he never changed his mind, and never allowed that Aquinas could be the exception to the rule. This meant among other things that the real distinction had no particular force for him. For a good example of Heidegger's painting of Aquinas as a rationalist, see Heidegger's *The Metaphysical Foundations of Logic* (trans. Michael Heim; Bloomington: Indiana University Press, 1984), pp. 44–7. The original text in German (1928), contiguous with *Sein und Zeit*, goes under the slightly different title of *Metaphysische Anfangsgründe der Logik im Ausgang von Leibniz*.

[46] David Schindler does a wonderful job in his *Hans Urs von Balthasar and the Dramatic Structure of Truth: A Philosophical Investigation* (New York: Fordham University Press, 2004) in laying out the evidence for Balthasar's engagement with Heidegger, especially in the opening two chapters. See my appreciative review in *The International Journal for Systematic Theology* 7(4) (Fall 2005): 585–90.

[47] See *The Glory of the Lord*, vol. 5, pp. 611–56. For Balthasar's basic summary of Aquinas in the history of metaphysics, see *The Glory of the Lord. A Theological Aesthetics*, vol. 4, *The Realm of Metaphysics in Antiquity* (trans. Brian McNeil C.R.V., Andrew Louth, John Saward, Rowan Williams and Oliver Davies; ed. John Riches; San Francisco: Ignatius Press, 1989), pp. 393–412.

[48] The best discussion on the dependence of Balthasar on Siewerth is to be found in David C. Schindler, *Hans Urs von Balthasar and the Dramatic Structure of Truth*, pp. 7, 29, 39, 52–4, 56, 279, 282 *inter alia*.

integrates truth, goodness and beauty. If structurally it reminds of Rahner, in that the entrée is a text by Aquinas (that is, *de veritate*, which obviously avails of Heidegger's prayerful thought (*Hingabe*) in its expostulations on truth as the disclosure of being), it more nearly recalls *Analogia Entis* in its celebration of the dynamism of reality, the ecstatic nature of the human subject, a disclosure model of truth and the mystery of Being considered through the ontological difference. Balthasar does not react to Heidegger as if his wisdom was formal and displayed no resistance to Catholic assimilation. Balthasar resists construing the dynamism of reality as a Heraclitean flux, rejects Heidegger's axiom of the finitism of truth, takes issue with the irremediable restlessness of the self which has no term and sets himself against the correlative nihilism of the history of Being (*Seinsgeschichte*).[49] One of the most conspicuous contributions of the text is Balthasar's block on the neutrality of event when speaking of the necessary connection between truth (*a-letheia*) and the good in and through the fidelity (*emeth*) of Being to beings.[50] The shepherd of Being is in the end Being itself, to which the subject responds in the appropriately diffident fashion, characteristic of Ignatian *indifferencia*.[51] It is highly probable that here Balthasar is already dependent on Löwith, one of Heidegger's more renegade children,[52] for the particular way of soldering truth and goodness. In his express treatment of Heidegger in *The Glory of the Lord 5*, Löwith, who has Heidegger's nihilism as his main target, is cited on precisely this point.[53]

Due to his greater exposure to the Heidegger of the 1930s and 1940s, Balthasar moves easily between 'aesthetic' as a cover for a form of embodied seeing to 'aesthetic' in which what is grasped or rather received is beautiful because it is true. Balthasar has plenty of Heideggerian warrant for this connection, 'The Origin of the Work of Art' (1936) being first among equals.[54] This connection plays a key role in Balthasar's sketch of theological aesthetics in *The Glory of the Lord 1*. Nonetheless, the prescribed attunement to reality and solicitude towards it does not involve accepting the pure singularity of appearances and their

---

[49] See von Balthasar, *Theo-Logic 1*, pp. 244–72; also 51, 73, 88, 108.
[50] For *emeth*, see von Balthasar, *Theo-Logic 1*, pp. 38–9.
[51] For Ignatian indifference, see von Balthasar, *Theo-Logic 1*, pp. 49, 76.
[52] On Heidegger's Jewish children who either broke with his thought or modified it in important ways, see Richard Wolin, *Heidegger's Children: Hannah Arendt, Karl Löwith, Hans Jonas, Herbert Marcuse* (Princeton, NJ: Princeton University Press, 2003).
[53] See Hans Urs von Balthasar, *The Glory of the Lord*, vol. 5, *The Realm of Metaphysics in the Modern Age* (trans. Oliver Davies, Andrew Louth, Brian McNeil C.R.V., John Sayward, Rowan Williams; ed. Brian McNeil C.R.V., John Riches; San Francisco: Ignatius Press, 1991), pp. 432–3, 440.
[54] Martin Heidegger, 'Der Ursprung der Kunstwerkes' (1935/36). For a convenient English translation, see 'The Origin of the Work of Art', in *Poetry, Language, Thought* (trans. Albert Hofstadter; New York: Harper & Row, 1971), pp. 15–87.

ineluctable temporality and finitude. Perhaps nowhere else in Balthasar's *oeuvre* can one find quite the level of insistence that appearance in a singular – any singular – is the appearance of a depth of beauty and truth more than, but not other than, the singular.[55] In *Wahrheit*, more through a reading of Heidegger than a reading of Aquinas and Bonaventure, which serves as the substrate of the articulation of theological aesthetics in *The Glory of the Lord 1*, Balthasar creatively retrieves beauty as the transcendental which has been too long on furlough. *Wahrheit* is an exercise in fundamental theology; overall *The Glory of the Lord* is not. And in the end the crucial criterion for a theological aesthetic is the glory of God as revealed in Christ, illustrated in *The Glory of the Lord 6* and *7*.[56] This glory surpasses all adumbration, exceeding and relativizing what, nonetheless, hints at it. This means that as Aquinas and Bonaventure, and their presuppositions, are relativized, so also is any contribution Heidegger might be thought to make to Catholic thought, which is surely less than that provided by these Christian thinkers. Against a background in which it is possible for Catholic theology to envision the figure of Christ in and through categories of analysis provided by Heidegger (e.g. Welte),[57] it is interesting that Heidegger never – or at least almost never – refers to Christ when speaking of Christianity, which apparently is univocally regulated by the ghost of *causa sui*.[58] Perhaps the two places where Balthasar hints at an omission, which is addressed head on later by Marion, are in his treatments of Hölderlin and Meister Eckhart in *The Glory of the Lord 5*.[59]

Bathasar's reading of Hölderlin is less than scintillating and falls well behind that of Przywara, and even more that of Marion, who has the advantage of both

---

[55] von Balthasar, *Theo-Logic 1*, p. 107.
[56] Hans Urs von Balthasar, *The Glory of the Lord: A Theological Aesthetics*, vol. 6, *Theology: The Old Covenant* (trans. Brian McNeil C.R.V. and Erasmo-Leiva-Merikakis; San Francisco: Ignatius Press, 1991); *The Glory of the Lord: A Theological Aesthetics*, vol. 7, *Theology: The New Covenant* (trans. Brian McNeil C.R.V.; ed. John Riches; San Francisco: Ignatius Press, 1989).
[57] Bernhard Welte was a life-long confidant of Heidegger and participated in funeral services. He was convinced that both his philosophy offered insights in fundamental theology and was of use value in systematic theology proper. For an example of the former, see his *Zeit und Geheimnis: Philosphische Abhandlungen zur Sache Gottes in der Zeit der Welt* (Freiburg: Herder, 1975). For an example of the latter, see 'Homouios hemin: Gedanken zum Verhältnis und zur theologischen Problematik der Kategorien von Chalkendon', in *Das Konzil von Chalkedon. Geschichte und Gegenwart*, vol. 3, *Chalkedon heute* (eds Aloys Grillmeier and Heinrich Bacht; Würzburg: Echter-Verlag, 1954), pp. 51–80. For an illuminating account of Welte's theology, see Anthony J. Godzieba, *Bernhard Welte's Fundamental Theological Approach to Christology* (New York: Peter Lang, 1994).
[58] In addition to rebuttals to Heidegger's construction of medieval view of cause by Thomists such as Cornelio Fabro and phenomenologists such as Marion, see D. C. Schindler, *The Catholicity of Reason* (Grand Rapids, MI: Eerdmans, 2013), pp. 119–228, esp. 195–203; also Antonio López, *Gift and the Unity of Being* (Eugene, OR: Cascade Books, 2014), pp. 11–99.
[59] See von Balthasar, *The Glory of the Lord*, vol. 5, pp. 29–47 for Balthasar's treatment of Meister Eckhart, and pp. 298–338 for Balthasar's express treatment of Hölderlin (although there are quite a few other references).

a rich French reception and scholarship.[60] Still, Balthasar succeeds in drawing attention to a tension in Hölderlin's work between reversion to paganism, typical of the philhellenism that beguiled German Romanticism, and a commitment to the figure of Christ. Balthasar draws attention, as Przywara does earlier, to poems such as 'Patmos' and 'The Only One'[61] ignored by Heidegger in his many elucidations. He also interprets 'Bread and Wine' in a Christian manner,[62] even if the figure of Christ blurs with the figure of Dionysos. With considerably more bite, Marion follows this strategy in *The Idol and Distance*.[63] No more than Przywara before him and Marion after him is Balthasar disqualifying Hölderlin from the history of exception, which shadows the history of the non-exception, that is, the history of metaphysics and/or ontotheology or history as metaphysics or ontotheology. He simply wants to suggest that: (a) the poet's Christianity does not prove to be an obstacle; and (b) the poetic moment in which love is figured in Christ is a condition of surpassing anything like the conceptual containment of metaphysics understood as a pejorative. This kind of challenge obviously does not replace the more direct challenges to Heidegger's narrative of mourning, which implicates Plato and Neoplatonism, Aristotle, Augustine, Aquinas, and even Kant to a limited extent.[64] Rather, it supplements it. It intimates that the criteria of exceptionality in Heidegger's genealogical narrative should be fairly applied and broadened. The fast paced genealogy of *The Glory of the Lord* 5 might seem to rule out deep questioning of Heidegger's principle of exceptionality. And it is true that Balthasar is more anxious to suggest different kinds of exceptionality – mystics, saints and fools as well as thinkers – than go deeply into any figure.

The treatment of Meister Eckhart in *The Glory of the Lord* 5 is, however, symptomatic of a deeper questioning. It is not a little interesting that together

---

[60] Marion is especially influenced by the Heidegger commentators J. Beaufret and François Fédier, both of whom are supremely interested in the Hölderlin–Heidegger relation. For Beaufret, see *The Idol and Distance*, pp. 84, 89, 93, 97, 99, 102, 133, 204. For Fédier, see *The Idol and Distance*, pp. 81, 84, 92, 97, 99, 204, 245. Of course, Marion can also call upon French literature which has simultaneously imbibed Hölderlin and Heidegger. The main figure here is the great mid-century French poet, Réne Char. See *The Idol and Distance*, pp. 23, 25, 157. Of course, Heidegger had been in actual communication with Char whose work is influenced greatly by Hölderlin.

[61] von Balthasar, *The Glory of the Lord*, vol. 5, pp. 319, 331, 333, 334.

[62] von Balthasar, *The Glory of the Lord*, vol. 5, pp. 313, 335.

[63] In *The Idol and Distance*, p. 89 n. 12 Marion acknowledges that he has read Balthasar on Hölderlin. For his reading of 'The Only One', see *The Idol and Distance*, pp. 90, 105, 108, 109, 110, 115, 116, 126, 131; for 'Bread and Wine', see *The Idol and Distance*, pp. 90, 92, 95, 105, 106, 125, 126, 131; for references to and treatment of 'Patmos', see *The Idol and Distance*, pp. 90, 94, 103–10, 117–23, 127–31.

[64] Narrative of mourning also includes Descartes and Leibniz whom Balthasar sees as fundamentally separate. For Balthasar's appreciative analysis of Leibniz, see *The Glory of the Lord*, vol. 5, pp. 468–78.

with Heraclitus, Greek Tragedy and Hölderlin, Meister Eckhart and his belated expression in the couplets of Angelus Silesius is judged to belong to the sacred remnant of memory in the constitutive forgetting of Western thought.[65] For Heidegger, Eckhart transcends metaphysics and presumably the causality obsession that constitutes it. As such, he has critical purchase proximally over the medieval philosophical and theological tradition, and ultimately over the entire metaphysical tradition. Eckhart's *Gelassenheit* evinces an ecstatic releasement towards, and solicitude with, disclosure; it represents a posture of waiting, and specifically waiting, on the event of appropriation (*Ereignis*).[66] In Heidegger's own texts the general contrast is emphasized, but Catholic assimilation of Heidegger's Eckhart brings the contrast with Aquinas to the fore. Welte, Schürmann and Caputo are all examples of this,[67] even if in the end both Welte and Caputo lessen the contrast by making Aquinas more Eckhartian rather than going the standard apologetic route of making Eckhart more like Aquinas.

In *The Glory of the Lord* Balthasar offers a positive portrait of Aquinas shortly before he gives his sketch of Eckhart,[68] and he puts an exclamation point on the value of Aquinas in his spirited presentation of Siewerth's Thomistic answer to the regulation of thought by the ontological difference of Being and beings in *The Glory of the Lord*. The rehabilitation of Aquinas, however, goes hand in hand with a critique of Eckhart. Balthasar essentially argues that not only does Eckhart not escape the metaphysical tradition, but that he in fact articulates an *Einheitsmetaphysik*.[69] It does not seem clear to Balthasar how such a construction can escape Heideggerian censure. Certainly, both in its general

---

[65] Heidegger knows well that Silesius is in continuity with Eckhart's emphasis on *Gelassenheit*. Thus inserting Silesius in a critique of the search for grounds of which Leibniz is the main offender is quite deliberate. It gives Meister Eckhart's *Gelassenheit* – and also Heidegger's version – critical traction over Leibniz's imperative of the principle of sufficient reason. See especially *Vom Wesen des Grundes* (1929). See *The Essence of Reasons* (trans. Tom Malick; Evanston: Northwestern University Press, 1969).

[66] The most extensive treatment of *Ereignis* in Heidegger's corpus, the *Beiträge* (1938), was only published posthumously (1989) and was not available to Catholic thinkers until very recently. For a translation, see *Contributions to Philosophy (From Enowing)* (trans. Parvis Emad and Kenneth Maly; Bloomington: Indiana University Press, 1999).

[67] In different ways and in different respects Welte, Schurmann and Caputo valorize Eckhart over Aquinas. For Welte, see *Meister Eckhart: Gedanken zu seinen Gedanken* (Freiburg: Herder, 1978); Reiner Schürmann, *Meister Eckhart: Mystic and Philosopher: Translation with Commentary* (Bloomington: Indiana University Press, 1978); also Schürmann, *Heidegger: On Being and Acting: From Principles to Anarchy* (trans. Christine Marie Gros; Bloomington: Indiana University Press, 1999); John D. Caputo, *The Mystical Element of Heidegger's Thought* (New York: Fordham University Press, 1986).

[68] See *The Glory of the Lord*, vol. 5, pp. 29–47 for Balthasar's treatment of Meister Eckhart; for Hölderlin, see also *The Glory of the Lord*, vol. 5, pp. 298–338.

[69] For Balthasar's critique of Eckhart's thought as an identity metaphysic, see my 'Von Balthasar and Eckhart: Theological Principles and Catholicity', *The Thomist* 60 (2) (April 1996): 1–37.

form as well as in its substance, it should not escape Christian censure. On the substantive theological side, there is much that is problematic by way of the figure of Christ and theological anthropology in general. In terms of general form, Eckhart's thought deconstructs analogy. The ever greater difference of God and world is not honoured, nor, for that matter, is the distinction between Being and beings respected. At the same time the gap between the divine milieu and the plane of immanence is so widened that there is absolutely no *commercium* between the divine and the world and the divine and the self. Here the extremes of absolute univocity and equally absolute equivocity meet. Balthasar seems persuaded, undoubtedly after Siewerth, that analogy and theological difference or differences (God–world; Trinitarian distinction) both protect and surpass the ontological difference. A Heideggerian devotee such as the ex-Catholic Schürmann would disagree. These differences do not support and surpass the ontological difference, but are displaced by it. Negatively speaking, the primacy of the ontological difference is procured by the disintegration of *analogia entis*.

Balthasar rightly sees that the exceptionality of Eckhart functions in a forensic fashion to displace and replace the canonical philosophical tradition. One way whereby Catholic thought does not fall victim to something like a Trojan Horse strategy is to simply expel Eckhart from a viable philosophical tradition because of his destruction of analogy. Another is to rehabilitate him back into the Christian philosophical tradition, first by correcting his correction of Aquinas, and second in acknowledging his moderation within the Rhineland school of mysticism, and especially in relation to Ruysbroeck.[70] It is the second tactic, suppler and more subtle, that is adopted by Balthasar in *The Glory of the Lord 5*.

Genealogy is one side of the Catholic–Heidegger problem, since it functions barbarically to lay waste the intellectual recourses of Catholicism. The other side of the Heidegger problem is that the sacrality prescribed by Heidegger as the fundamental ground, with respect to which the forms of the gods and God are secondary and tertiary respectively, is inhospitable to Jewish and Christian monotheism. Derrida has been eloquent on how the biblical God, who is the source of ethical obligation, is displaced by the polymorphous sacrality that would explain it.[71] Perhaps more inchoately, but nonetheless definitely, Balthasar has a sense of how Heidegger's projection of the Fourfold of earth/sky/human/divine subverts the possibility of the Christian God by proscribing

---

[70] For Balthasar's treatment of Ruysbroeck, see *The Glory of the Lord*, vol. 5, pp. 67–78.
[71] Jacques Derrida, *Of the Spirit: Heidegger and the Question* (trans. Geoffrey Bennington and Rachel Bowlby; Chicago: University of Chicago Press, 1991).

certain forms of transcendence. Transcendence can but be the bulge in the order of immanence. And prayer has to be understood to be an openness to an address that only appears to come from on high. No protest of the ordinary Christian believer who has never heard of *causa sui* will suffice. As mentioned previously, Lacoste deepens and expands on these insights, which were noted by Heidegger's more secular critics, including Adorno.[72] Heidegger's piety and Heidegger's world differ from Catholic Christianity, and the meanings of prayer and festival also change as they are given new coordinates. The relationship between Heideggerian and Catholic wisdom can only be seen to be competitive. This makes Heidegger an ambiguous resource, and Catholic ambivalence necessary. Enlightenment modernity is the ultimate enemy of Christianity as it is all religion, since it has become the air that we breathe, such that the enemy is the enemy as much within as without. And after scrutiny Heidegger, who could and should have been a friend to Catholic thought, is at best an equivocal resource. While, perhaps, we should not reject him totally, we have to be vigilant in our assimilation. Heidegger is a powerful thinker and a thinker of power, and he does not yield easily to piecemeal borrowing, which is the most that can be licensed. He is a thinker of danger, who puts us in danger should we go too far with him. But we can abide with him a while as a critic of modernity and a reminder of our tendency to chatter, forget and worship the convenient and rationale simulacra of the God who is other precisely as not-other (*Non-Aliud*).

---

[72] Theodor W. Adorno, *The Jargon of Authenticity* (trans. Knut Tarnowski and Frederick Will; Evanston, IL.: Northwestern University Press, 1973).

4

Romano Guardini: Liturgy, Style, Church

Patrick Gorevan

Introduction

Romano Guardini, the great German theologian and liturgist, cultural commentator and forerunner of Vatican Council II, was actually born in Verona, Italy in 1885. In the following year, the family moved to Mainz, for business reasons. In their new situation, Italian was always spoken at home, and he retained a lifelong nostalgia for Italy and things Italian. His father introduced him to Dante, and his mother never really left Italy behind, visiting her home place annually, sometimes accompanied by one or another of her four sons. Romano Guardini's last visit there was in 1968, a few weeks before his death. His *Letters from Lake Como* (1923) dwelt on the landscape, life and culture of the area as a living setting in which almost physically to confront contemporary civilization, a constructive if wistful confrontation with what disquieted him. The Italian homeland drew his gaze, as to a place where nature and art were still at one with each another.

Antonio López Quintás has remarked that one could describe Guardini as 'of Italian birth, German formation and European spirit'.[1] The theme of 'Europe', as the solution to the tension he felt between his two homelands, is a keynote of his whole life. He was often drawn by his personal trajectory to reconcile personal and cultural realities of a diverse nature. In 1962, in a memoir, he mused that he had been very much aware of Europe from the very beginning: Europe, a reality which was hardly ever mentioned at the time, but which he was experiencing

---

[1] Antonio López Quintás has written a number of works about Guardini: *Romano Guardini y la dialéctica de lo viviente* (Madrid: Cristiandad, 1966), *Cuatro filósofos en busca de Dio*s (Madrid: Rialp, 1989). The phrase in question is taken from his entry on Guardini in *Gran Enciclopedia Rialp* (Madrid: Rialp, 1972), vol. XI, p. 386.

(with trepidation, for Europe had its weaknesses, as many another great civilizations had) as the only possible basis of his own existence. When he won the Erasmus prize in 1965, three years before his death, the citation praised his extraordinary contribution to the European spirit and hailed him as one of the greatest Europeans of the age.

This sense of being 'on the frontier' of things, being 'between', marked Guardini's life. Bruce Harbert, in 'The Quest for Melchisedech', points to the priest as a man on the frontier: offering sacrifice, sometimes sharing in the exclusion which is the lot of the victim, glimpsing aspects of reality which others ignore.[2] Guardini lived *his* priesthood in his commentary on the issues of the time and of the church, often by straddling boundaries and discovering the common elements shared by body and spirit, inward and outwardness, institution and individual, God and Caesar. William Desmond's claim that the priest and the philosopher are 'intimate others' rather than dualistic opposites is vindicated in Guardini's intellectual life.[3] The '*Gegensatzlehre*', or the theory of oppositions, which is part of Guardini's understanding of concrete living realities, was his method of forging links among polarities in dialogue with one another.[4]

By 'opposition' (*Gegensatz*), Guardini means a living unity among contrasting realities, in which the one does not exclude the other. There is distance between the opposites and they do not collapse into one another, but still enter into dialogue with one another. This is rather different from 'contradiction' (*Widerspruch*), which is a complete mutual exclusion of the contradictory elements. Oppositions can participate mutually and lead to a genuine synthesis, while contradictions have nothing in common with one another. This implies that many phenomena which are regarded as autonomous and complete are actually complementary. He offers the example of the concept, which is usually portrayed as an autonomous phenomenon, but which actually is an opposite pole to the experience of reality.

As Guardini gradually worked out his thought, particularly in the 1920s, he found that the 'opposition theory' was both most congenial to his thought,

---

[2] Bruce Harbert, 'The Quest for Melchisedech', *New Blackfriars* 68 (1987): 529–39.
[3] Cf. William Desmond, 'Consecrated Thought: Between the Priest and the Philosopher', *The Journal of Philosophy and Scripture* 2 (2) (Spring 2002): 1–10 (1): 'The affinity of priest and philosopher holds if there is an ultimate towards which both are oriented. In this affinity the two are intimate others, even if in tension. This tension in affinity is itself double. It can be a source of conflict: either the priest or philosopher might treat its intimate other as a rival, potentially hostile, if not subordinate to its own claim to pre-eminence. It might also be a source of fruitfulness: thought can keep fidelity alert, while fidelity can keep thought poised on a path of discernment.'
[4] Antonio López Quintás, *Cuatro filósofos en busca de Dios*, p. 152.

and arose out of that thought. Guardini states that his early works, *The Spirit of the Liturgy* and *The Church and the Christian*, both have the *Gegensatzlehre* as 'their ruling direction and measure'.[5] Both show how basic ideas like body and soul, individual and corporate body, and freedom and commitment need one another and by entering into dialogue with one another are able to enrich the task.[6]

In this paper I look at the *Gegensatzlehre* at work in these two early writings that express Guardini's lifelong concern, first for *liturgy* and secondly for the being of the *Church*. Thirdly, I look at his prophetic search for the 'conscious unity of Christian existence', a cooperation of faith and 'the concrete actual world' and its echoes in *Gaudium et Spes* and subsequent magisterial and other Catholic writings on Christian engagement with the secular.

Liturgy

One of the earliest and best known examples of Guardini's religious phenomenology is found in his writings on the *liturgy* in which contrasting dimensions – the personal and the communal, the spiritual and the material – work in a creative and beneficial tension: 'In any form of prayer [...] which is intended for the ultimate use of a corporate body, the whole fullness of religious truth must be included. The liturgy condenses into prayer the entire body of religious truth.'[7]

'The liturgy is the lex orandi.'[8] Guardini sought to bring the liturgy into the centre of the Christian's life, and to place it at the heart of the many other, more private, expressions of prayer and reverence. He offers an overview of the rather demanding scope of Christian public prayer:

> Prayer must be simple, wholesome and powerful. It must be closely related to actuality and not afraid to call things by their names. In prayer we must find our entire life over again. On the other hand, it must be rich in ideas and powerful images, and speak a developed but restrained language; its construction must be clear and obvious to the simple man, stimulating and refreshing to the man

[5] Romano Guardini, *Der Gegensatz* (Mainz: Matthias Grünewald, 1925), pp. 210-11, quoted in H. B. Gerl-Falkowitz, *Romano Guardini* (Kevalaer: Topos, 2010), p. 177.
[6] Giuseppe D'Acunto in 'Concretezza e opposizione in Guardini', *Información Filosófica* 8 (2011): 107-20, has shown how Guardini applied 'opposition' to the process of knowledge: intuition of the singular and universal knowledge are not contradictory realities, but inhabit one another.
[7] Romano Guardini, *The Spirit of the Liturgy* (trans. Ada Lane; London: Sheed and Ward, 1937), p. 15.
[8] Guardini, *The Spirit of the Liturgy*, p. 8.

of culture. It must be intimately blended with an erudition which is in nowise obtrusive, but which is rooted in breadth of spiritual outlook and in inward restraint of thought, volition and emotion. And that is precisely the way in which the prayer of the liturgy has been formed.[9]

Guardini was not a liturgical 'specialist' in the contemporary sense of the word, but he wrote widely and influentially about it. He wrote descriptively, influenced by phenomenologists of religion such as Otto and Scheler, and he pointed to patterns of the spiritual life which emerged in the liturgy. Here the great human realities of flesh and spirit, individual and community, freedom and rigour, often opposed to one another, are given a space where they dwell in unison and enrich the interior life.[10] This creative tension which liturgy permits between these apparently opposed realities is shown in Guardini's simple and profound liturgical writings, which display his theory of opposition (*Gegensatzlehre*) to full advantage. In *The Spirit of the Liturgy* (1923), the devotional *Meditations Before Mass* (1939) and *Sacred Signs* (1922), Guardini offers both the main lines of his liturgical thinking, and some practical suggestions for applying them in individual and parish life.[11]

Guardini's writings have influenced Joseph Ratzinger (Pope Benedict XVI) in many areas, but the liturgy should be mentioned in a particular way. He read *The Spirit of the Liturgy* as a theology student, and the little book opened his eyes to the liturgy as the animating centre of the Church, the very centre of the Christian life. In 2000 he prefaced his own *The Spirit of the Liturgy*[12] with the remark that 'its basic intentions coincide with what Guardini wanted to achieve in his own time with *The Spirit of the Liturgy*'. As Guardini had done, he hoped to offer an 'aid to the understanding of the faith and to the right way to give the faith its central form of expression in the liturgy', and, further, he ventured to hope that, in a new way, his own book might also encourage something like a 'liturgical movement', as Guardini's had done, by which people might see the liturgy as the prayer of the Church, a prayer guided by the Holy Spirit, 'in which Christ unceasingly becomes contemporary with us'.[13]

---

[9] Guardini, *The Spirit of the Liturgy*, p. 36.

[10] 'The rediscovery of the liturgy was for him a rediscovery of the unity between spirit and body in the totality of the unique human being, as the liturgical act is always at the same time a corporal and spiritual act.' (Benedict XVI, address to Romano Guardini Foundation, 29 October 2010.)

[11] Romano Guardini, *Meditations before Mass* (trans. Elinor Castendyk Briefs; London: Longmans, 1955), also available as *Preparing Yourself for Mass* (Manchester, NH.: Sophia Institute Press, 1997); *Sacred Signs* (trans. Grace Branham; Dublin: Veritas, 1979).

[12] *The Spirit of the Liturgy* (trans. John Saward; San Francisco: Ignatius Press 2000), p. 8.

[13] Guardini, *The Spirit of the Liturgy*, pp. 6–7.

The Style of the Liturgy

For Guardini, the liturgy has true 'style'. The passing centuries have polished, elaborated and adapted it. An inner world of immeasurable breadth and depth has created for itself so rich and ample an expression, at one and the same time so lucid and so universal in form, that its like has never been seen. This *savoir faire* is shown in an ability to combine opposed elements; here I single out one example: how it can deal with human emotion, channelling and expressing it without exploitation or indulgence: 'The liturgy as a whole is not favourable to exuberance of feeling...The liturgy is emotion, but it is emotion under the strictest control. The liturgy has perfected a masterly instrument which has made it possible for us to express our inner life in all its fullness and depth, without divulging our secrets – *secretum meum mihi*.'[14]

Examples of this 'style', Guardini points out, are to be found in the Collect prayers of Sunday Masses. Each of them is a miracle of compression, in which the depths of the spiritual life are touched upon in a couple of well-balanced phrases, which manage to touch the heart of devotion without ever straying into sentimentality. The Collect prayer for the twenty-seventh week of the year is an example:

> Almighty, ever-living God,
> who in the abundance of your kindness
> surpass the merits and the desires
> of those who entreat you,
> pour out your mercy on us:
> to pardon what conscience dreads, and give what prayer does not dare to ask.

It is hard to imagine anyone not identifying with this prayer, but its detached style allows each of us room to deal with the intense feelings it expresses in our own private way, without 'divulging our secrets'.

This creative tension between the public corporate nature of the liturgy and the individual's private appropriation of its teaching is at the root of his disagreement with the Benedictine liturgical school at Maria Laach, where he had collaborated with Abbot Herwegen and Odo Casel. There came a point where he could not accept Casel's rejection of individual piety and devotion in the name of liturgical correctness. In a seminar in 1922 Guardini claimed that the action of the farmer in his field, stopping his ploughing to say

---

[14] Guardini, *The Spirit of the Liturgy*, p. 22.

the Angelus, was also liturgical, a view echoed, many years later, by Paul VI among many others.[15] Guardini's little work on the Rosary can help us here: his sensitivity to the power of the sacred words, of the repetition and how we 'are here to kneel where prayer has been valid.'[16] This attention to the 'creative opposition' of liturgy and individual piety was not pleasing to the somewhat 'all or nothing' Maria Laach liturgical school, and there was a regretful parting of ways between Guardini and Casel. Guardini felt that liturgy involved the objective, shared meaning to which we have alluded above, but also the reception of this faith in individual spiritual life. He concluded that Casel and his colleagues did not share his interest in promoting liturgical renewal among those who lived beyond the confines of the monastery life.[17]

The Church is Awakening in Souls

The Church is that 'corporate body' referred to by Guardini for which liturgical prayer is intended. The liturgy is at the heart of the Church and coincides with the rule of her faith. Guardini always claimed that he wished simply to be an 'interpreter of the Church'. In her, too, the *Gegensatzlehre* rule of opposition is to be found at work, for she is a living, concrete being, which, for Guardini, was actually awakening in souls.[18]

Guardini's ecclesial spirit comes to the fore in the well-known account he gives us of his conversion. Many famous conversion accounts stress the individual journey through doubt, uncertainty and hesitation, but Guardini points further. He speaks of his conversations with his friend Karl Neundörfer, their struggle to overcome Kantian presuppositions and the moment when he realized that:

---

[15] 'The recitation of the *Angelus* is deeply rooted in the piety of the Christian faithful, and strengthened by the example of the Roman Pontiffs. In some places changed social conditions hinder its recitation, but in many other parts every effort should be made to maintain and promote this pious custom and at least the recitation of three *Aves*. The *Angelus* "over the centuries has conserved its value and freshness with its simple structure, biblical character, [...] quasi liturgical rhythm by which the various times of the day are sanctified, and by its openness to the Paschal Mystery" (cf. PAUL VI, Apostolic Exhortation *Marialis cultus*, 41).' Congregation for Divine Worship and the Discipline of the Sacraments, *Directory on Popular Piety and the Liturgy* (2001), §195.
[16] T. S. Eliot, *Little Gidding*, I. Cf. *The Rosary of Our Lady* in *The Living God – The Rosary of Our Lady* (trans. H. Von Schwecking; London: Longmans Green, 1957).
[17] Cf. Robert Krieg, *Romano Guardini: A Precursor of Vatican II* (Notre Dame: University of Notre Dame Press, 1997), p. 82, and H.-B. Gerl-Falkowitz, *Romano Guardini*, pp. 94–5.
[18] Romano Guardini, 'Das Erwachen der Kirche in der Seele', *Hochland* 19 (1922): 257–67 (259).

'Everything will come down to the statement: "Whoever holds on to his soul will lose it, but whoever gives it away will gain it".' ... If he wants to arrive at the Truth and in the Truth arrive at his true self, then he must let go of himself ... 'To give my soul away – but to whom? ... Not simply "God". For whenever a person wants to deal only with God, then he says "God" but means himself. There must also be an objective authority [*Instanz*], which can draw out my answer from self-assertion's every refuge and hide-out. But there is only one such entity: the Catholic Church in her authority and concreteness [*Präzision*]. The question of holding on or letting go is decided ultimately not before God, but before the Church.' It struck me as if I carried everything – literally 'everything', my whole existence – in my hands, in a scale at perfect balance: 'I can let it fall to the right or to the left. I can give my soul away or hold on to it ...' And then I let the scale sink to the right.[19]

Freedom and dogma; movement and fixity; supernatural faith and natural life; these contrasts among many others show the concrete living reality of the Church in action.

Guardini was convinced that thinking in harmony with the Church leads to freedom. In fact he claimed that 'genuine Catholicity, which is seriously convinced of the supernatural and dogmatic character of Catholicism, is the most open-minded and the most comprehensive attitude, or rather the only open-minded comprehensive attitude, in existence. If by open-mindedness we mean the intellectual outlook which sees and values all objects as they really are, the Church can claim this description, because in [the] face of the superabundant wealth of human experience she occupies the sole perfectly stable, clear and determined position. Both the wealth and the fixity enter into the Catholic mind.'[20]

In his 1922 work *The Church and the Catholic*, Guardini muses on this unity of contrasts: 'this is not a contradiction, but a contrast. One term of a contradiction precludes the other – good and bad, yes and no, for example, exclude each other. Every living thing, however, is a unity of contrasts which are differentiated from each other, yet postulate each other. The firm, yet flexible, simple, yet creative, unity of the living organism can only be grasped intellectually as a web of contrasts. I hope to explain this point thoroughly in another book.'[21]

---

[19] Romano Guardini, *Berichte über mein Leben* (ed. Franz Henrich; Düsseldorf: Patmos, 1984), pp. 70–2. The translation is provided by Aaron Pidel, S.J. at http://whosoeverdesires.wordpress.com/2011/01/29/the-conversion-of-romano-guardini/ (last accessed 21 April 2014).
[20] From Romano Guardini, *The Church and the Catholic* (trans. Ada Lane; New York: Sheed & Ward, 1935), p. 114.
[21] Guardini, *The Church and the Catholic*, p. 36. The book in question, *Der Gegensatz*, was written in 1925 (see fn. 5).

Many of Guardini's followers were influenced by this broader view of the Church which Guardini was able to adumbrate, including but going beyond the institutional concept which had predominated since Vatican I. The Church was presented as something living, which we do not simply join in an external manner, if we wish, but welling up within us by the power of the Holy Spirit conferred at baptism.

Much later on, after the Second Vatican Council, not without his own influence, had broadened and deepened reflection about the identity of the Church, he brought the *Gegensatzlehre* to bear on the various *models* of the Church which were being discussed at the time:

> [t]here is one image which is today seemingly predominant in men's thoughts – the image of the people of God. It is marvelously vivid and full of movement, and expresses immediately something that is particularly important for the thought of our time: the historical element, the church's existing and working in time, her wandering and struggling. But we must not forget the other image which the Lord himself contributed to Christian thought when he spoke of the edifice that he would build upon the rock...There is in her a constant activity and also an abiding sameness.[22]

All of these images are 'veiled by the mystery of the eschatological elements... they can be refuted at every point by the appearances of history...they must be believed, and their fulfillment must be hoped for and awaited.'[23]

In his meditation on the life of the Church also Guardini offers another vital contrast in the life of the Church, that subsisting between the ordinary and the 'extraordinary': '[w]e need men and women to live the extraordinary form of life heroically. But we have just as great need of others to live the ordinary form of life heroically.'[24]

This leads me to a final aspect of Guardini's integrating thought to be touched upon in this paper: his call for the integration of faith and ordinary life.

---

[22] Romano Guardini, *The Church of the Lord* (Chicago: Henry Regnery, 1966), pp. 112–14, quoted in *The Essential Guardini* (ed. Heinz R. Kuehn; Chicago: LTP, 1997), p. 116.
[23] Guardini, *The Church of the Lord*, quoted in *The Essential Guardini*, p. 117.
[24] Guardini, *The Church and the Catholic*, p. 111. Guardini is referring to the evangelical counsels: 'The majority He calls to follow the ordinary, a few the extraordinary road. The ordinary rule of life is that in which the natural and supernatural values and demands are brought into a harmonious balance. The extraordinary rule of life is that in which even in the external conduct of life everything is directed immediately to the supernatural. The former commanded; the latter counselled. The former is open to all men, the latter only to those "who can take it"' (p. 109).

Unity of Christian Life: Faith and the World

In the preface to *Freedom Grace and Destiny*, published in 1948 but given as a lecture in 1943, Guardini worried that 'the conscious unity of existence has been to a large extent lost even by believing Christians. The believer no longer stands with his faith amid the concrete, actual world, and he no longer rediscovers that world in his faith ... To save redemption by the Son, [he] has been forced to abandon creation by the Father.'[25]

The ordinary rule of life, as Guardini points out, that to which most members of the Church are called, is that in which 'natural and supernatural values and demands are brought into an harmonious balance'.[26] Michael Novak offers a telling quotation from Guardini, to the effect that anybody should be able to tell that you are a Catholic even by the way you climb a tree![27]

These ideas are echoed closely by the Second Vatican Council, in particular by *Gaudium et Spes* (43): 'One of the gravest errors of our times is the dichotomy between the faith which many profess and the practice of their daily lives. It is a mistake to think that, because we have here no lasting city...we are entitled to shirk our earthly responsibilities.'

In the years following the Council, a new feature has emerged, a development of its doctrine,[28] echoing Guardini's phrase: 'the unity of Christian existence'. This new feature emerges in *Christifideles Laici* and has been expressed as 'unity of life': 'The unity of life of the lay faithful is of the greatest importance: indeed they must be sanctified in everyday professional and social life. Therefore, to respond to their vocation, the lay faithful must see their daily activities as an occasion to join themselves to God, fulfill his will, serve other people and lead them to communion with God in Christ.'[29] In recent years, since the Synod, it has become common in magisterial and more unofficial spiritual exhortation.[30]

---

[25] Romano Guardini, *Freedom, Grace and Destiny* (trans. John Murray; New York: Pantheon Books, 1961), pp. 9-10, 11.
[26] Guardini, *The Church and the Catholic*, p. 109
[27] Cf. Michael Novak, 'A Letter to Roberto', *Logos: A Journal of Catholic Thought and Culture* 3 (2000): 70-84 (72-3).
[28] The phrase had actually appeared in the Council decree on the life of Priests, *Presbyterorum Ordinis* (14), and it was quoted in some of John Paul II's early addresses to clergy.
[29] John Paul II, Post-Synodal Apostolic Exhortation *Christifideles Laici* (1988), §17.
[30] The phrase 'unity of life' was originally associated with the preaching of St Josemaría, the founder of Opus Dei. He first began to use the term in 1931 (cf. J. L. Illanes, 'The Church in the World', in Pedro Rodríguez, Fernando Ocáriz and José Luis Illanes, *Opus Dei in the Church: An Ecclesiological Study of the Life and Apostolate of Opus Dei* (Dublin: Four Courts Press, 1994, pp. 147-90) and it became a core description of his aim: 'Christians must not resign ourselves to leading a double life: our lives must be a strong and simple unity into which all our actions converge ... We are "citizens of heaven", and at the same time fullyfledged citizens of this earth.' St. Josemaría Escrivá de Balaguer, *Christ is*

Speaking of unity of life brings us to one of the more controverted passages of *Gaudium et Spes*: paragraph 36, which deals with the autonomy of earthly affairs. The passage, famously, seeks to achieve unity between rightful God-given autonomy of creation and its consequent dependence on God:

> Now many of our contemporaries seem to fear that a closer bond between human activity and religion will work against the independence of men, of societies, or of the sciences.
>
> If by the autonomy of earthly affairs we mean that created things and societies themselves enjoy their own laws and values which must be gradually deciphered, put to use, and regulated by men, then it is entirely right to demand that autonomy. Such is not merely required by modern man, but harmonizes also with the will of the Creator...But if the expression, the independence [*autonomia*] of temporal affairs, is taken to mean that created things do not depend on God, and that man can use them without any reference to their Creator, anyone who acknowledges God will see how false such a meaning is. For without the Creator the creature would disappear. For their part, however, all believers of whatever religion always hear his revealing voice in the discourse of creatures. When God is forgotten, however, the creature itself grows unintelligible.[31]

This paragraph echoes Guardini's famous criticism of Kant's drive towards ethical 'autonomy'. Writing in 1939, Guardini had claimed that 'the whole modern view of the autonomy of the world and of man [...] seem to rest ultimately on the notion which made of God the "other" '.[32] He repeatedly attempts to break 'the spell' of Kant's critique of heteronomy, for example, in *Conscience* (1931):

> [Kant] says: 'As soon as I treat the Good like God, as soon as I apprehend the moral law as a demand of God, it is "another" who is commanding me, and I become heteronomous...' But anyone who is really religious is bound to reply in amazement: 'But God after all is not "Another"! How is it possible

---

Passing By: Homilies (Dublin: Veritas 1974), p. 126 (from a homily on Ascension Thursday, 1966). In recent years, *Vita Consecrata*, John Paul II's 1996 Apostolic Exhortation on the renewal of Religious life (§67), encouraged the religious too to exercise themselves in the '*difficili arte vitae unitatis*'. In the *Directory for the Ministry and Life of Priests* (1994), *Priests for the Third Millennium* (1999) and *The Priest, Pastor and Leader of the Parish Community* (2002) the Congregation for Clergy has recommended the practice to priests. Cardinal Martini spoke of 'unity of life in a fragmented world', and many recently formed associations, blogs and initiatives – some consciously taking up the suggestions offered in *Christifideles Laici* – also refer to the ideal.

[31] Second Vatican Council, Pastoral Constitution *Gaudium et Spes*, §36.
[32] Romano Guardini, *The World and the Person* (trans. Stella Lange; Chicago: Henry Regnery, 1965), p. 204, quoted in Tracy Rowland, 'The World in the Theology of Joseph Ratzinger/Benedict XVI', *Journal of Moral Theology* 2 (2) (2013): 109-32 (127). According to Rowland, Guardini actually wrote this consideration in 1965, but this cannot be confirmed. It seems more likely that this is a translation *sans plus* of Guardini's 1939 volume.

to confuse things and concepts in such a way? A man next to me is "another" state authority is "another". But God after all is not "another" in this sense! Of course He is not I. Between Him and me there lies an infinite gulf. But God is the Creator, in whom I have the foundation of my being; in Whom I am more myself, than in myself alone.'[33]

'Without the Creator, the creature would disappear', as *Gaudium et Spes* would later say. Guardini avoids the way the question is still often put; it is not a matter of laboriously making human autonomy 'compatible' with dependence upon God, but of seeing our secular autonomy emerge precisely from an un-grudging and un-jealous Creator, proud rather than suspicious of his children's spontaneity and freedom. It is surely right, as he does, to base the *parrhesia* of faith's engagement with modernity on the bountiful and creative Fatherhood of God.

Conclusion

Guardini was deeply influenced by Max Scheler's approach to doing philosophy, his new Copernican turn beyond Kant; he was struck by his overcoming anthropocentrism with theomorphism, seeing man as the image of God. In 1923 Guardini, beginning a career as a rather youthful and inexperienced Professor of Philosophy of Religion and Catholic *Weltanschauung* at the University of Berlin, sought Scheler's advice and was always grateful for it; it 'showed him his way'. Scheler counselled him as follows: '[Y]ou must do what is meant by the word "*Weltanschauung*": as a responsible, conscious Christian, observe the world, things, people [and their] actions, and then say in a scholarly way what you see.'[34] For Joseph Ratzinger, this was what attracted young people to Guardini: his thought was a way of questioning oneself and seeking truth about God and the world, which is concrete and personal in Christ, by listening and receiving. He recalled that Guardini's favourite word as a lecturer 'was "look",

---

[33] Romano Guardini, *Conscience* (trans. Ada Lane; London: Sheed and Ward, 1932), p. 64. Guardini continues: 'The philosophic thought of our day is engaged in breaking the spell of Kant at all points. It will do so in this respect as well. The moral law is not a law of my ego. To say it is, is an inner defect of vision; even if by "ego" I mean "the subject generally", the structure of human judgment in general, it is part of the indissoluble essence of the moral law that it "meets" me; that for me it is precisely the reverse of "ego". Philosophically, therefore, Kant's axiom is already untrue. But it is so religiously as well. Indeed ultimately it has a strange religious insipidity, which is only to be explained by the fact that Kant was hardly livingly religious at all' (p. 64).

[34] Cf. Gerl-Falkowitz, *Romano Guardini*, pp. 104–5. I have used the translation which appears in Krieg, *Romano Guardini*, p. 91.

because he wanted to lead us to "see", and he himself was in a common interior dialogue with his listeners'. [35]

He has been called a prophet and a martyr for the truth; the ancient term 'confessor' of the faith could well be used about him. He confided to Paul VI, in 1965, that the only thing which will convince modern people is the unrestricted and uninterrupted message of revelation.[36] At any rate, his own desire to see the whole (*das Ganze*), reflected often in its opposed but linked aspects, and his commitment to look on the world from the standpoint of the Church's teaching in its fullness and unity, was what permitted him to draw, from that store-house, things both new and old.

---

[35] Benedict XVI, Address to Guardini Foundation, 29 October 2010.
[36] Cf. Letter to Paul VI, 1965, quoted in Krieg, *Romano Guardini*, p. 69.

5

Erich Przywara and the *Analogia Entis*: A Genealogical Diagnosis and Metaphysical Critique of Modernity

John R. Betz

Occasionally in the history of theology, and more generally in the history of ideas, great thinkers are overlooked and sometimes even forgotten. Sometimes this is a function of the philosophical trends of the time or the theology à la mode; sometimes it is a function of the difficulty of the thinker in question; sometimes it is a function of style or the lack of a sufficiently limpid medium of communication. And sometimes, in the most poignant examples of forgotten genius, it is a function of all these factors, which together conspire to produce a perfect storm of obscurity. Such is the case, I would argue, with the remarkable Jesuit philosopher, theologian, poet and critic Erich Przywara, S.J. (1889–1972), who is almost unknown today, but was one of the great Catholic theologians of the twentieth century.

Of course, this is not to say that Przywara has been forgotten. While the amount of scholarship is not overwhelming, a number of studies of his work have appeared over the years.[1] There have also been some notable indications of his importance. His protégé Hans Urs von Balthasar, for example, spoke of Przywara as 'the greatest spirit' he ever knew, claiming that his 'profundity and breadth is without comparison in our time'.[2] And in his mentor's honour he published not one, but two separate tributes – not to mention using his publishing house to reprint and preserve many of Przywara's works for posterity. Of still greater moment, in an address to German theologians in 1980, Pope

---

[1] For a fairly extensive bibliography, both of Przywara's corpus and of most of the scholarship to date, see http://www.helmut-zenz.de/hzprzywa.html (last accessed 21 December 2014).
[2] Hans Urs von Balthasar, *My Work: In Retrospect* (San Francisco: Ignatius Press, 1993), pp. 50, 89.

John Paul II referred to Przywara as one of the great theologians of the German Catholic tradition, along with Albert the Great, Nicholas of Cusa, Johann Adam Möhler, Matthias Scheeben and Romano Guardini – theologians 'who have enriched and continue to enrich not merely the Church in Germany, but the theology and life of the entire Church'.[3] But can one really say that Przywara continues 'to enrich not merely the Church in Germany, but the theology and life of the entire Church'? The current state of theology in Germany alone would seem to belie it. Indeed, such extraordinary tributes only make it all the more perplexing how anyone of such reputed brilliance and stature could possibly have been forgotten – or at least nearly so – and how such a large and impressive corpus of writings (altogether as many as 40 monographs and 800 articles and reviews) could be mostly untranslated and unread. What indeed is one to make of this discrepancy between Przywara's reputed stature and the actual reception, or lack thereof, that he has received?

There are more reasons for this than can be enumerated here, but, among them, one has to consider the intervening circumstances of the Second World War, which began when Przywara was at the height of his intellectual powers, and left him with a nervous disorder from which he never fully recovered.[4] As a result, the man of seemingly boundless energy, who between 1922 and 1932 authored no less than seventeen books and 230 articles and reviews (and in between gave 237 lectures all over central Europe), gradually withdrew from public and even from Jesuit community life into increasing isolation.[5] And so it is somewhat understandable that, as his own students' stars were on the rise (e.g., von Balthasar, Josef Pieper and Karl Rahner), Przywara himself gradually faded into the background.

---

[3] Papal address to theologians in Altötting, Germany (18 November 1980): 'Sie stehen in einer großen Tradition, wenn ich nur an den hl. Albert den Großen, Nikolaus von Kues, Möhler und Scheeben, Guardini und Przywara denke. Ich nenne diese hervorragenden Theologen stellvertretend für viele andere, die in der Vergangenheit wie in der Gegenwart nicht nur die Kirche des deutschen Sprachraums, sondern die Theologie und das Leben der ganzen Kirche bereichert haben und noch ständig bereichern.'

[4] Whatever underlying condition may have been present, the stress of these years undoubtedly contributed to his illness. As one of the lead editors of the Jesuit journal *Stimmen der Zeit,* which was a major source of Catholic intellectual resistance to the Nazis, he and his fellow Jesuits were under constant threat – a threat that was finally realized when the journal was shut down by the Gestapo in 1941. We also know that on at least one occasion during a lecture on Christian heroism, Przywara was taunted, heckled and egged by Nazi sympathizers; his confrère and fellow editor, Alfred Delp, S.J., with whom he collaborated on the journal between 1939–41, was ultimately executed by the Nazis for 'treason'. See Martin Ederer, 'Propaganda Wars: *Stimmen der Zeit* and the Nazis, 1933–1935', *Catholic Historical Review* 90 (July 2004): 456–72 (457).

[5] See Thomas O'Meara, O.P., *Erich Przywara, S.J.: His Theology and His World* (Notre Dame: University of Notre Dame Press, 2002), p. 9: 'The priest who had appeared to possess energy without limits became anxious, incapable of work, and erratic, a condition only heightened by the opinions of others that it was partly psycho-somatic, exaggerated, or easily remedied.'

But these factors alone do not account for Przywara's present-day obscurity; nor are they the most important. The proximate cause of his obscurity is rather – as even the most cursory examination of his main works reveals – a function of the extraordinary difficulty and nearly unintelligible compression of his thought and style. This is not to deny that Przywara could deliver lectures in a comprehensible idiom; he was, after all, one of the most popular Catholic lecturers in between the two wars. (Indeed, any reader of Przywara would be well advised to begin with his published lectures, such as *Gottgeheimnis der Welt* or *Gott: Fünf Vorträge über das Religionsphilosophische Problem*.[6]) What is at issue here is rather his main philosophical and theological writings, like his *Analogia Entis*, which was first published in 1932.[7] Ironically, this work for which he is best known also has the peculiar distinction of being written – or so it would seem – without any particular audience in mind. As von Balthasar described it in an early review, 'An exposition of this thought-world, which is compressed into 150 pages, would ordinarily require as many as 1000 pages of philosophical epic.'[8] This may not take anything away from its content; it may be that the *Analogia Entis* will be remembered as one of the greatest works of philosophical theology ever written.[9] But as Josef Pieper, no less an admirer, pointed out, it is nevertheless, even for the most learned of philosophical and theological readers, nearly unreadable.[10] It is hardly astonishing, therefore, that the history of theology tends to remember only one giant of the early twentieth century, namely, Karl Barth, and tends to forget the other, whom Barth once called 'the giant Goliath incarnate' – in comparison with whom Barth reckoned all his other (Protestant) opponents as 'dwarfs'.[11] The reason for their dissimilar fate is rather obvious: Karl Barth knew how to write for a large audience; and he knew how to write well, epically, beautifully, and almost always to great rhetorical effect. Przywara, the thinker's thinker, who lacked Barth's stylistic gifts and rhetorical genius, for the most part did not.

---

[6] These early lectures from the 1920s can be found in the second volume of Przywara's *Schriften* (ed. Hans Urs von Balthasar; Einsiedeln: Johannes Verlag, 1962), pp. 123–372.
[7] Erich Przywara, *Analogia Entis: Metaphysics: Original Structure and Universal Rhythm* (trans. John R. Betz and David Bentley Hart; Grand Rapids, MI: Eerdmans, 2014).
[8] Hans Urs von Balthasar, 'Die Metaphysik Erich Przywaras', *Schweizerische Rundschau* 33 (1933): 488–9 (489).
[9] von Balthasar went so far as to call it '*the pharmakon* for the philosophy and theology of our time'. See Hans Urs von Balthasar, 'Erich Przywara', in Hans Jürgen Schultz (ed.), *Tendenzen zur Theologie im 20. Jahrhundert. Eine Geschichte in Porträts* (Stuttgart: Olten, 1966), p. 357.
[10] See Josef Pieper, *Autobiographische Schriften* (ed. Berthold Wald; Hamburg: Felix Meiner Verlag), p. 82.
[11] See Karl Barth, Letter to Pastor Horn, 12 February 1929 (Karl Barth Archive). See also Barth's letters to Eduard Thurneysen in *Karl Barth–Eduard Thurneysen Briefwechsel*, vol. 2, *1921–1930* (Zürich: Theologischer Verlag Zürich, 1974), pp. 638, 651–4, 708f.

By the same token, one cannot be surprised that Przywara is rarely mentioned in popular works on twentieth-century theology,[12] or that the depth of his thought has not been sufficiently probed. (It is a law just as true of the modern academy as it is of the natural world that things with mass sink away, whereas things of low density rise to the top.) And yet, given Przywara's pioneering role in Catholic theology in between the two world wars – not to mention his recent papal commendation by John Paul II – *it is surprising* that he continues to be a *quantité négligeable*, if not altogether unknown, to most Catholic theologians today. To give but one illustration: who today would know that this Jesuit was once hailed as the *doctor universalis*, a title no one has shared since Albert the Great.[13]

By any reckoning this circumstance is unfortunate. Przywara was one of the first great Catholic theologians to break out of the confines of a narrow scholasticism and engage the modern world. At a time when Catholic theology in Germany was marginal (Przywara's own Jesuit training had to be undertaken in the Netherlands due to the anti-Jesuit laws that were still in effect), he helped to make Catholic theology both culturally relevant and intellectually respectable: on the one hand, *vis-à-vis* Protestant theology, which for centuries had enjoyed pride of place in the great German universities; on the other hand, *vis-à-vis* modern rationalism and atheism, which had been on the rise since the Enlightenment. Indeed, Przywara's pioneering engagement on the ecumenical front (his friendly encounters with Karl Barth were the first of their kind) and his profound engagement with modern philosophy and culture (on the basis of a comprehensive knowledge of the history of philosophy from the pre-Socratics to Heidegger) in many respects paved the way for Vatican II, modelling the kind of evangelical renewal that the Council hoped to achieve.[14]

My aim in what follows is thus, in the spirit of *ressourcement*, in some small measure to rectify this situation: to show not only why Przywara is worthy of study, but also why he has enduring implications for the Church's engagement with the modern world. As a matter of necessity, however, given the current state of scholarship, I begin with a double introduction: first to Przywara's role in twentieth-century theology, and then to the central concept of his thought, the *analogia entis*. Upon this basis I hope to show how he creatively deploys the

---

[12] See, for example, Fergus Kerr's survey of *Twentieth-Century Catholic Theologians* (Oxford: Wiley-Blackwell, 2007).

[13] For the reference to Przywara as '*doctor universalis*', see the *Werbetext* for Przywara, *Humanitas: Der Mensch gestern und morgen* (Nürnberg: Glock & Lutz, 1952).

[14] Thus Rahner speaks of Przywara's 'lifelong dialogue with the past and the present, with the entirety of western intellectual history from Heraclitus to Nietzsche', and of 'his openness to all in order to give to all'. See Karl Rahner, 'Laudatio auf Erich Przywara', in idem, *Gnade als Freiheit. Kleine theologische Beiträge* (Freiburg: Herder, 1968), pp. 266–73 (268).

analogia entis as a diagnostic and metaphysical therapy for modernity's dialectical ills.

Przywara's Role in Twentieth-Century Theology

Among the great German theologians of the early twentieth century, the most famous within his lifetime was arguably Karl Adam, whose *Spirit of Catholicism* was translated into multiple languages and is still widely read today. One also thinks of Romano Guardini, who had an undeniable influence on the German liturgical movement and, in recent years, has even appeared on German postage stamps. Compared to Adam and Guardini, Erich Przywara is today the least known. Of the three, however, he was not only (arguably) the most brilliant, but also the most prolific, having authored over 40 monographs and as many as 800 articles and reviews. In fact, by 1962, ten years before his death, Przywara's corpus was already large enough that, in order to preserve a record of them for posterity, von Balthasar published a separate bibliography of Przywara's diverse and scattered writings.

Compared to Adam and Guardini, Przywara also had a comparable, if not greater, range of influence: he was the representative Catholic theologian at the Davos seminar in 1928 and 1929 (where Heidegger and Cassirer famously clashed); he was the first Catholic theologian to engage in ecumenical debate with Karl Barth, who considered him his greatest opponent; he wrote a massive and influential three-volume commentary on the *Spiritual Exercises*; he was a leading editor of the Jesuit journal *Stimmen der Zeit* until the journal was shut down by the Nazis; he was the first major theologian to promote Newman in Germany, editing and introducing the first German edition of the cardinal's works; he was at the forefront of the Catholic reception of phenomenology (specifically engaging the works of Husserl, Heidegger and Scheler); and he was a friend, mentor and spiritual director to Edith Stein, encouraging her first translations of Newman and Thomas, and in all likelihood influencing her decision to enter the Carmelite order.[15]

For us today, however, there is perhaps no greater indication of Przywara's influence than what von Balthasar and Karl Rahner – arguably the two greatest

---

[15] In 1932, the year prior to Stein's profession as a Carmelite, Przywara published *two* works of Carmelite inspiration: one a work of his own religious poetry, entitled *Karmel: Geistliche Lieder*; the other a selection of his own translations of John of the Cross, Teresa of Avila and Thérèse of Lisieux, entitled *Hymnen des Karmel*.

post-war Catholic theologians – had to say about him. As Rahner put it in 1965, 'One must not forget Father Erich Przywara. For the Catholics of Germany in the twenties, thirties and forties he was considered one of the greatest minds. He had a great influence on all of us when we were young.'[16] In 1967 Rahner also honoured Przywara with a *laudatio*, during which he admitted that in the noisy marketplace of ideas Przywara's voice is hardly heard anymore. But, he went on to say, 'Does this mean that the Catholic generation of today has learned what it had to learn from him and, now that it is able to forget the old teacher, can continue nonchalantly along the path of the Church's future without him?'[17] No, he said, 'Without being a prophet I feel compelled to say that we, the generation after him, as well as future generations still have critical things to learn from him. The whole Przywara, especially the late Przywara, is yet to come. He stands at a place in the road that many in the Church have yet to get past.'[18]

Przywara's influence on von Balthasar, who was 'chaperoned' by Przywara from a distance between 1931–3 and later worked with him closely on the staff of *Stimmen der Zeit* between 1937–9, was even profounder.[19] In *My Work: In Retrospect* von Balthasar commemorates him as 'an unforgettable guide and master', adding, 'Never since have I encountered such a combination of depth and fullness of analytic clarity and all-embracing synoptic vision. The publication of three volumes of his works in my [publishing] house is intended as an external sign of thanks; but none of my own books should hide what it owes to him.'[20] And in another of his many tributes, he writes:

> The totality of Przywara's work defies classification; it is not something that one can be finished with, and so most have chosen to ignore it. But whoever has gone through his school, wherever one later ends up, will carry the impression of this encounter in one's thought and life; and every return to the old master will leave one oddly shaken, perhaps because one comes to realize how much younger this old master has remained than all who have come after him.[21]

Clearly, Przywara meant more to Rahner and von Balthasar than he does to most theologians today (about many other things they may have disagreed,

---

[16] See Karl Rahner, *Karl Rahner in Dialogue. Conversations and Interviews 1965–1985* (eds Paul Imhof and Hubert Biallowons; trans. Harvey D. Egan; New York: Crossroad, 1986), p. 14.
[17] Rahner, 'Laudatio auf Erich Przywara', p. 271.
[18] Rahner, 'Laudatio auf Erich Przywara', p. 272.
[19] See Hans Urs von Balthasar, *Our Task: A Report and a Plan* (trans. John Saward; San Francisco: Ignatius Press, 1994), p. 37.
[20] See von Balthasar, *My Work: In Retrospect*, pp. 50, 89.
[21] Erich Przywara, *Sein Schrifttum 1912–1962* (ed. Leo Zimny; intro. Hans Urs von Balthasar; Einsiedeln: Johannes Verlag, 1963), p. 18.

but not about this). And both of them complain in one way or another that we have failed to engage him, indeed, that we have ignored him.[22] They tell us in no uncertain terms that we have been missing something, and that Przywara has something to teach us even today. In what follows, limiting myself to a consideration of Przywara's earlier works, I will attempt to answer, at least in part, the question of what this is.

Przywara and the *Analogia Entis*

Whatever relevance Przywara may still have for contemporary theology is certainly bound up with the *analogia entis*, the 'analogy of being' – a term that he, more than any other, introduced into modern theological discourse. Of course, Przywara did not invent the *analogia entis*; it is a term with a long history, originating in the Thomistic tradition.[23] In fact, Przywara calls Thomas *the* teacher of the *analogia entis*, whether or not Thomas ever used this exact phrase. But for Przywara the *analogia entis* is not just a scholastic technicality. Nor, on his view, does analogy function in theology merely to regulate theological language – guarding, on the one hand, against the presumption of univocity (that is, of thinking that our words mean the same thing when predicated of God and creatures), and guarding, on the other, against the false humility that is indistinguishable from agnosticism and presumes one cannot speak meaningfully of God at all.[24] On the contrary, for Przywara the *analogia entis* has a comprehensive ontological and theological significance.[25] As the standard of a Catholic understanding of reality, it figures in everything, precisely because the way one thinks about the relation between God and the world affects everything else.

---

[22] In 1948 von Balthasar was still hopeful that Przywara would find an audience among those involved in future reforms of the Church: 'Few have a clearer vocation to advise, to clarify, to illuminate and, even if they cannot join in the planning themselves, train those who would do so for their mission, than Erich Przywara.' See his foreword to Erich Przywara, *Vier Predigten über das Abendland* (Einsiedeln: Johannes Verlag, 1948), p. 8. By 1966, however, he lamented that 'our age has chosen the easier path of not engaging him'. von Balthasar, 'Erich Przywara', p. 354.

[23] See Julio Terán-Dutari, '"Die Geschichte des Terminus "Analogia Entis" und das Werk Erich Przywaras', *Philosophisches Jahrbuch der Görres-Gesellschaft* 77 (1970): 164. See Przywara, *Analogia Entis*, p. 306.

[24] Such is the conclusion that has been reached by a number of commentators on Thomas who restrict their considerations largely to *ST* I, q. 13. See, for example, Herbert McCabe's commentary in *Summa Theologiae*, vol. 3, *Knowing and Naming God* (London: Eyre & Spottiswoode, 1964), p. 106: 'Analogy is not a way of getting to know about God, nor is it a theory of the structure of the universe, it is a comment on our use of certain words.' For further discussion and contesting of this view, see the introduction in Przywara, *Analogia Entis*, pp. 40–3.

[25] In the words of Rahner, Przywara transformed the *analogia entis* 'from a scholastic technicality into the fundamental structure of Catholic theology'. Rahner, 'Laudatio auf Erich Przywara', p. 270.

(The incarnation, for example, would be inconceivable apart from it: for if the world is already divine, according to a pantheistic model, the incarnation could not have been the novelty that it was; and, contrariwise, if the world were not in some way related to God as God's creation, then Christ would not have been coming to 'his own', or to that which he had made, according to the prologue of John, but would have been entering into a reality not simply fallen, but fundamentally alien to himself.)

The *analogia entis* thus turns out to be critical to all 'right-thinking' – all orthodox – Catholic theology. Equally, though, for reasons we shall see in more detail, the *analogia entis* turns out to be critical to the apologetics of the Church in the modern world: on the one hand, in its engagement with Protestant (particularly, Reformed) theology, which, in its Barthian forms, tends to reject any created analogy between God and the world (since we are related to God, according to Barth, strictly by faith, by an *analogia fidei*); and, on the other hand, in its engagement with modern secular culture, which is likewise committed (at least *de facto*) to the notion that there is no analogy between God and the world, and that public space and public policy are therefore indifferent to religious concerns. (The secular and the *analogia entis* are, one could say, mutually exclusive concepts.) My immediate task is thus twofold: first, to explain what Przywara means by the *analogia entis* (and, implied in that, how he understands the teaching of Thomas Aquinas); and, secondly, to explain how he creatively deploys the *analogia entis* in his multi-front engagement with modern, non-Catholic (philosophical and theological) forms of thought.

What, then, does Przywara mean by the *analogia entis*? Without going into the prior history of the term, or intra-Thomistic debates about its status in the thought of the Angelic Doctor, for Przywara, the 'analogy of being' basically means two things, which, in Christian terms, would seem rather uncontroversial: on the one hand, that finite being is grounded in and derives its being from infinite being (herein lies the moment of proximity and similarity); on the other hand, that finite being cannot be equated with its ground, with infinite being, but remains both essentially distinct from it and infinitely transcended by it (therein lies the moment of distance and ultimate dissimilarity). The language here is obviously metaphysical. But the *analogia entis* is not an exclusively philosophical principle, for it is equally a principle of revelation that is attested in Scripture.

The *Analogia Entis* in Scripture

In scriptural terms (and I would go so far as to suggest that the *analogia entis* is as biblical a doctrine as that of the Trinity), one might express the principle as follows. *On the one hand*, Scripture speaks of creation as a manifestation or declaration of God's handiwork, as a telling of his glory (Ps. 19.1), and, as such, as a kind of likeness or parable of divine things. In the words of Wisdom, 'From the greatness and beauty of created things comes a corresponding [ἀναλόγως] perception of their Creator' (Wis. 13.5). And, in the echoing words of Paul, 'Ever since the creation of the world his eternal power and divine nature, invisible though they are, have been understood and seen through the things he has made' (Rom. 1.20). Furthermore, Scripture does not merely suggest that creation is a vague analogy, from which the Creator may be inferred, but expressly declares human beings to be the 'image and likeness of God' (Gen. 1.26-7). On the basis of Scripture alone, therefore, it is hard to deny that creation is some kind of analogy, especially when it comes to human beings, whom God is said to have created in his image.[26]

But this is not all. For precisely when one might rest content with an artistic analogy between the Creator and the created, one susceptible of various degrees of distance between them (degrees culminating in the remote, Gnostic deity of Deism), Scripture goes further. For, having established that creation is somehow like God, and thus some kind of analogy (which, of course, presupposes the difference and distance between the things compared), Scripture goes on to affirm God's radical *proximity* and *immanence* to creation. As Paul famously put it to the Athenians, 'In him we live and move and have our being' (Acts 17.28) – granting that the depths of this immanence are unknown to all but the saints, who, having found God in Christ through faith, hope and love, subsequently marvel with Augustine to discover that God in Christ is nearer to them than

---

[26] Of course, the matter is somewhat more complicated than this, because it is precisely here that the confessions will divide. For Catholic theology, creation remains an analogy in spite of the Fall. For even if the image of God is languishing in chains due to sin, it is still an image longing for its redemption. For Reformed theology, on the other hand, as a consequence of the Fall, the analogy of creation is precisely what is in question. The conflict between the confessions could be resolved, however, if one simply distinguishes with Scripture between the image of God (which human beings always and indestructibly are) and the likeness of God (which human beings lost in Adam and can only regain in Christ); or if one understands the *imago* with Augustine and Bonaventure as an *imago ad imaginem*. The relevance of this to the analogy of being is that the latter, rightly understood, comprises all of these moments: that of the image originally made to be a likeness (image = likeness), that of the image no longer a likeness (image ≠ likeness) and that of the image whose likeness is progressively restored in Christ (image => likeness). In other words, though it may not be apparent due to the cataracts of sin, creation remains objectively an analogy, but one that is in our current state obscured, awaiting the revelation of the sons of God (Rom. 8.19), in whom, by the workings of grace, its own diaphanous nature *qua* analogy will again be apparent (cf. 1 Cor. 15).

they are to themselves: that Christ, as Augustine is wont to say, is (ontically) their very life and (noetically) their very light.[27] Indeed, for the author of the letter to the Colossians the radical immanence of God in Christ to the world is nothing less than *the* mystery, which has been 'hidden since the foundation of the world, but has now been revealed to the saints', the mystery of 'Christ in you', which is 'the hope of glory' (Col. 1.27) – the mystery that God is not only immanent to his creation in a general way, but that God indwells his temple, the human being, in a special way (1 Cor. 6.19); and that, as first happened with Christ, whose bodily temple was raised on the third day, God will also raise up the bodily temples of those united to him, as members of his body, on the last day (Rom. 8.11).

On the other hand, however much Scripture testifies to God's proximity to creation – especially to human beings who are created *ad imaginem*, to be God's very likeness, and who are called, moreover, as members of the mystical body of Christ, to be the very temple and throne of His glory – the same Scripture can also say, in the words of the Psalmist, 'Who is like the Lord our God, who is enthroned on high' (Ps. 113.5). Equally, the same apostle who spoke to the Athenians about God's immanence to creation could say that this same God 'dwells in unapproachable light' (1 Tim. 6.16). To be sure, some will dispute Pauline authorship here; but that is beside the point. The point is that Scripture speaks of both realities: of our nearness to God and our distance from God, of our likeness to God and (especially due to the disfigurement caused by sin) of our unlikeness to God. And thus, in view of this similarity *and* dissimilarity, likeness *and* unlikeness, proximity *and* distance, one may speak not only on the basis of philosophical metaphysics, but also on the basis of Scripture of an essentially *analogical* relation between God and creation.

The Analogical Dynamic of Creaturely Existence

Still, though, the nature of the relation between God and the created universe of finite, contingent things stands in need of further specification. For, after all, what do we mean by finite being? And in what sense is it an 'analogy'? Having carefully studied Thomas's *De ente et essentia*, Przywara begins with the Thomistic 'real distinction' (*distinctio realis*) between essence and existence,

---

[27] See Augustine, *In Jo. Tract. XIX*, xii: 'If ... you are illumined by drawing near to him and darkened by withdrawing, your light was not in yourselves but in your God ... If you live by drawing near to him and die by withdrawing, your life was not in yourselves. For that which is your life is the same as that which is your light' (my translation).

which for Thomas runs through all created reality. For as long as one is talking about creatures, including the most exalted of angels, 'what' they are, their essence, is not the same as the sheer 'fact' of their existence. But Przywara does not stop there. Instead, drawing out the full implications of the 'real distinction', he speaks of finite being as a *unity-in-tension* – a *Spannungseinheit* – between essence and existence.[28] Przywara thus renders the Thomistic doctrine not only more precise, but also more dynamic. For, according to Przywara, the creature *qua* creature is defined precisely by this *non-identity* of essence and existence, which in turn accounts for the creature's mutability and movement as a being that is strictly 'in becoming' (*in fieri*).

But, using Przywara's own idiom of the '*in-über*' (which one can translate as 'in-and-above' or 'in-and-beyond', and is more or less a rendering of the Aristotelian 'en-telechy'), the structure and corresponding dynamic of creaturely being can be rendered still more precisely – if also more gnomically – by saying that the essence of the creature is always *in-and-beyond* existence. Here we have Przywara's basic formula for a creaturely metaphysics. For the essence of the creature, as that which, on the one hand, *in*-forms the existing creature, making it *what* it is, on the other hand mysteriously transcends existence at any given moment as a *telos*, which *qua telos* is yet to be attained.[29] Admittedly, on the face of it this might look like an illicit importation of Aristotelian metaphysics into theology, or metaphysics masquerading as theology. But this, too, follows from what Scripture reveals about the human being as the image created to be God's likeness.[30] One could even say that the human being is, ontologically speaking, a stretch – ordered to what lies beyond it. In the words of Benedict XVI, commenting on Genesis 1, 'human persons are beings *en route*, beings characterized by transition. They are not themselves; they must ultimately

---

[28] See, for example, Erich Przywara, *Ringen der Gegenwart, Gesammelte Aufsätze 1922–1927* (Augsburg: Benno Filser-Verlag, 1929), vol. 2, pp. 906–62. See also Erich Przywara, 'Thomas von Aquin als Problematiker', *Stimmen der Zeit* 109 (June 1925): 188–99. For Thomas on the real distinction, see John F. Wippel, *The Metaphysical Thought of Thomas Aquinas: From Finite Being to Uncreated Being* (Washington, DC: Catholic University of America Press, 2000), pp. 146ff.; idem, *Metaphysical Themes in Thomas Aquinas* (Washington, DC: Catholic University of America Press, 1984), p. 136.

[29] Here again, though, we can be more precise. For the essence of a stone is hardly what we would call a transcendent horizon, even if the essence of a stone is not the same as its existence, which is gratuitous. What is at issue is rather the particular being that is the human being, in Heidegger's terms Dasein, for whom the difference between essence and existence, the ideal and the real, is both a question and an experience. This is not to deny that the difference between essence and existence runs through all creation; it is simply to emphasize that nowhere is this difference, as a perceived tension, so great and at times so painfully evident as in the human being.

[30] In the remarkable words of 1 John 3.2: 'Beloved, we are God's children now; what we will be has not yet been revealed. What we do know is this: when he is revealed, we will be like him, for we will see him as he is.'

become themselves.'[31] There is an entire metaphysics implied in this statement. The same can be said of the maxim that derives from Augustine, and which Przywara quotes in the first section of his *Analogia Entis*, 'Become what you are.'[32]

With this creaturely dynamic, however, there also comes the possibility of the tragic, of sin, of 'missing the mark'. For while it is the condition of the possibility for the image to become an actual likeness, it also admits the possibility that the creature could tragically fail to be what it is. But then the question becomes all the more pressing: how is the creature to become itself? Or what would it mean for the creature to become what it is? Following Przywara, we have already established that the human being, as a dynamic unity of essence and existence, is not just fundamentally distended, but fundamentally *ecstatic*. In other words, *contra* the modern myth of autonomy and individualism, it is in the nature of human being that it is precisely *not self-possessed* but finds its being *beyond itself* – and this is all the more so the case the more like God in the scale of creaturely being the creature is: that it can be completed, that it can be one with itself, only beyond itself. Such is the implicit metaphysics of the gospel: 'whoever desires to save his life will lose it, but whoever loses his life for My sake will find it' (Mt. 16.25). Thus, if the rational creature is to become what it is – ultimately, as an image, an analogy, of triune ecstasy – then it too must become ecstatic, which is to say that, following Christ, it must learn to love.

The *Analogia Entis* as a Theo-Cosmic Principle

Thus far we have been discussing the dynamic of creaturely existence *qua* creaturely existence. In short, following Przywara, we have simply been drawing out the implications of the real distinction. Still, though, the question remains

---

[31] Benedict XVI, "In the Beginning," *A Catholic Understanding of the Story of Creation and the Fall* (trans. Boniface Ramsey; Grand Rapids, MI: Eerdmans, 1995), p. 49. One finds this notion, albeit from a quite different perspective, in Nietzsche's Zarathustra, for whom the human being is an Übergang – a 'transition'. See *Also Sprach Zarathustra*, Vorrede 4 in *Kritische Studienausgabe* (eds G. Coli and M. Montinari; Berlin: De Gruyter, 1988), p. 16f.: 'Was groß ist am Menschen, das ist, daß er eine Brücke und kein Zweck ist: was geliebt werden kann am Menschen, das ist, daß er ein *Übergang* und ein *Untergang* ist.'

[32] Przywara, *Analogia Entis*, p. 124. Augustine, *Serm.* 272. To be sure, in its original context Augustine's exhortation has a Christological and ecclesiological inflection: it is an exhortation to the body of Christ to *be* the body of Christ, specifically, to be what we receive in the Eucharist – with the implication that we become *ourselves* (what we essentially are) by partaking of Christ, in whom we find our ourselves (Mt. 10.39). For *what* we are is ultimately who we are in Christ, that is, who God, the Father, from eternity envisioned us to be in his Son (Rom. 8.29). But for Przywara this is nevertheless an exhortation that has its basis in the dynamic of the real distinction, since the grace of participation in Christ presupposes a created nature that is able to receive it.

as to what actually constitutes the analogy here – an analogy that allows one to speak of a certain similarity between creatures and God, but at the same time, and more importantly, requires one to speak of an abiding and even greater difference between them. On the one hand, for Przywara, one may speak of a similarity between God and creatures in that there is an analogy between the unity of essence and existence in creatures and the unity of essence and existence in God. The all-important difference, however, is that whereas creatures are a *gratuitous* unity of essence and existence, in God the unity of essence and existence is from all eternity an absolute *identity*, inasmuch as God's essence is to be. In the words of Thomas, *sua igitur essentia est suum esse*.[33] In other words, God *IS* who he is, whereas human beings are forever *becoming* who they 'are'. In creatures essence and existence are really distinct; in God they are not. Therein, to put it simply, lies the analogy of being.

This then allows Przywara to summarize his doctrine of analogy by saying that God is at once in *and* beyond creation.[34] Thus, the 'in-and-beyond' of essence in-and-beyond existence (which was Przywara's formula for a creaturely metaphysics) turns out (precisely at the point where a creaturely metaphysics opens into a theological metaphysics) to be intersected by another 'in-and-beyond': that of God 'in-and-beyond' the totality of creation. Thus, for Przywara, everything from creation, considered in itself, to God's relation to creation turns out to be structured by this principle of the 'in-and-beyond'. Needless to say, this may also be the point where systematic rigour leads to systematic obscurity. The basic point, however, which may be clearer when translated into a different but equivalent idiom, is that everything from creation (considered in itself), to the relation between God and creation, and even (one could argue) to God as Trinity, is structured – and so provides the room for a dynamic interplay of immanence and transcendence.[35]

---

[33] *ST* I, q. 3, a. 3, corp.; Przywara, *Ringen der Gegenwart*, vol. 2, p. 945.
[34] Przywara first presents this as the Catholic concept of God in an early essay entitled 'God in us and God beyond [literally above] us' [*Gott in uns und Gott über uns*], which was first published in *Stimmen der Zeit* in 1923, and was subsequently reprinted in *Ringen der Gegenwart*, vol. 2, pp. 543–78.
[35] There is some room for speculation about the dynamic of immanence and transcendence within the Trinity in Przywara's writings; but such a vision is arguably nowhere so sublimely expressed as in the writings of Jan van Ruusbroec, for whom the persons of the Trinity at once transcend themselves toward the other persons in love, and precisely thereby remain in themselves in the unity and simplicity of their common essence. As such, they *do* what they *are*; there is, in this sense, no interval whatsoever between them: their pure act is their common being.

The *Analogia Entis* and Catholic Spirituality

By virtue of its inherent dynamic, Przywara's metaphysics of the *analogia entis* thus furnishes, at the same time, the structural 'background' of Catholic spirituality and mysticism. In the words of Augustine, which Przywara takes to be axiomatic for the Catholic concept of God, God is both *interior intimo meo* and *superior summo meo*, 'more inward than my inmost' and 'higher than my highest'.[36] Glossing this text from Augustine, he writes, '*Deus interior* and *Deus exterior*, "God in all and above all," God more inward than we are to ourselves, and yet surmounting and transcending [all things] as infinite and incomprehensible.'[37] For Przywara, this is the metaphysical basis for the unity of Augustine's and Newman's 'opposite virtues' of faith and love. As he puts it, 'Because God reveals himself as simultaneously a God of blessed, mystical intimacy and a God of the coolest distance, the fundamental disposition of the faith-filled soul should be one of "fearing love and loving fear"– a fear that springs from love inasmuch as love fears to lose the beloved; and a love that through fear maintains a holy sobriety and a tender reverence.'[38] Indeed, for Przywara, not only does the *analogia entis* sum up the Catholic concept of God (i.e. as a God who is at once immanent and transcendent), it is also the measure of authentic religious life.

At this point, however, it is crucial to underscore that the *analogia entis* does not imply any static equilibrium or midpoint between the poles of divine immanence and divine transcendence, as though the *analogia entis* could be summed up by a simple 'both-and'. On the contrary, for Przywara, the *analogia entis* is an explicitly *dynamic* structure, tending (from the side of the creature) always in the direction of a greater transcendence. And this is precisely where the Ignatian spirituality at the heart of his metaphysics is apparent: for it is a

---

[36] Augustine, *Confessions* III, 6 (11).
[37] Przywara, *Ringen der Gegenwart*, vol. 2, p. 543. N.B., by divine 'immanence', Przywara hardly means to equate God with things or to endorse anything remotely resembling pantheism. On the contrary, even in God's immanence to creation, being *more interior* to it, he is beyond it. Thus, at no point does the *analogia entis* give the creature a hold on God.
[38] Przywara, *Ringen der Gegenwart*, vol. 2, p. 543. Cf. *Schriften*, vol. 2, p. 22: 'God in creatures, and therefore love; God above and beyond creatures, and therefore fear: "loving fear and fearing love".' See Augustine, in Ps. 118 (22, 6) (trans. Maria Boulding; New York: New City Press, 2003), p. 448: 'You, who are more intimate to me than my inmost self, have set a law within my heart by the action of your Spirit [...] so that I may not dread it like a loveless slave but love it with a chaste fear like a son or daughter and fear it with chaste love'. Cf. John Henry Newman, *Parochial and Plain Sermons*, vol. 1 (London: Longmans, Green, and Co., 1907), p. 322: 'The fear of God is the beginning of wisdom; till you see Him to be a consuming fire, and approach him with reverence and godly fear, as being sinners, you are not even in sight of the strait gate. I do not wish you to be able to point to any particular time when you renounced the world (as it is called), and were converted; this is a deceit. Fear and love must go together; always fear, always love, to your dying day.'

metaphysics of the God who is 'ever greater', *semper maior*. Thus, recalling the theme of divine infinity, which is arguably no less important to Augustine than to Gregory of Nyssa, he rhetorically inquires, 'Even if we were to have the most sublime experience of mystical union, would we then have any right' to say that 'we had arrived at a state of "immediacy" or "maximal knowledge" or "ultimate proximity"?'. He answers with a single paradoxical phrase from Augustine: *Invenitur quaerendus*! ['He is found in order to be sought!'].[39] And at his most lyric Przywara makes the same point as follows:

> All our wandering in Him and to Him is a tension between an ineffable proximity and an ineffable distance. Every living thing [...] is full of His presence. 'He is not far from us; for in Him we live and move and have our being.' But we grow in our sense of His fullness only in the measure that we do not equate Him with any created thing or circumstance, that is, in the measure that we stand at an ultimate distance from every particular shining of His face. He is the infinite light that becomes ever more distant the closer we come to Him. Every finding is the beginning of a new searching. His blessed intimacy [*Inne-Sein*] is the experience of His infinite transcendence [*Über-Sein*]. No morning of mystical marriage is a definitive embrace of His fullness; no mystical night of despair is a detachment from His presence...He compels us into all the riches and changes of world and life in order that we might experience Him anew and more richly as beyond this world and life. And, ultimately, this indissoluble tension of proximity and distance to Him is but the innermost revelation of His own primal mystery, by which He is *in* us and *beyond* us, closer to us than we are to ourselves, such that we love him as proximity *itself*, and, yet again, farther away from us than any other distance, such that we revere Him with trembling as distance *itself*. God in us *and* God beyond us.[40]

As confusing as the terminology of Przywara's *analogia entis* can be, here in a rare example of limpid prose we see its basic point: there is no genuine natural *or* even supernatural experience of God that does not give way to reverent distance and silent adoration.[41] Indeed, even at the height of mystical union, God remains God, and the creature remains a creature. As he puts it at the

---

[39] Cf. Augustine, *In Jo. Tract.* LXIII, i: 'Ut inveniendus quaeratur, occultus est; ut inventus quaeratur, immensus est. Unde alibi dicitur, "Quaerite faciem ejus semper"' (Ps. 105.4). ('He is hidden in order that you might seek him; and in order that you might not cease in your search once you have found him, he is infinite. Thus is it said [...] "Seek his face evermore".')

[40] Przywara, *Schriften*, vol. 2, p. 281; cf. p. 404.

[41] See 'Mystik und Distanz', in *Schriften*, vol. 2, pp. 66–90; 72f.: 'Even the Church is inwardly conscious of Him only insofar as it reveres Him as above her ... Both individual and ecclesial mysticism are essentially bound to the law of distance. Both the individual soul and the community live Christ [*leben Christus*] to the extent that they have a lively consciousness of the ultimate distance between Him and them.'

conclusion of an essay on Thomas Aquinas from 1925, 'Passing through and beyond the madness of all seemingly complete systems, it is the proper task of the creature ever more humbly and resignedly to recognize its true vocation, which is worshipful silence before the mysteries: *Adoro te devote*, **latens** *Deitas*.'[42]

Przywara and the Tradition

At this point, having explained the rudiments of the *analogia entis*, it is important to clarify that Przywara never considered the *analogia entis* to be *his* doctrine, but rather the implicit teaching of the Church through the ages – a teaching that (in keeping with Newman's understanding of doctrinal development) he merely sought to make explicit. Indeed, when criticized, for example, by Karl Barth, he repeatedly claimed that his doctrine of analogy was at the end of the day nothing but an explication of the teaching of the fourth Lateran council: '*Inter creatorem et creaturam non potest tanta similitudo notari, quin inter eos non maior sit dissimilitudo notanda*' ['One cannot note any similarity between creator and creature, however great, without being compelled to observe an ever *greater* dissimilarity between them'.] Such was the Council's decision against Joachim of Fiore, who in the Council's view had threatened precisely to collapse the analogical difference between the unity of the Trinity and the unity of believers, not to mention the threat he otherwise posed of collapsing the immanent Trinity into the three stages of the economy of salvation.

But even though Przywara is in his own estimation little more than a distiller of the Catholic tradition, he is certainly a creative *synthesizer* of it, whose genius consists in seeing the deep unity within the variations of the one tradition – and, by extension, in seeing the synthetic form, the *Gestalt*, of any single great figure within it (as one especially sees in his 'synthetic' works on Augustine and Newman). There are many examples of such synthetic interpretation, each of which illustrates a peculiarly Catholic reading of the tradition, but one of them is most relevant here: the way that Przywara reads Thomas through Augustine. For though the basic structure of Przywara's *analogia entis* comes from Thomas, who lays bare the original *structure* of essence and existence, the rhythmic, beating heart of it comes from Przywara's reading of Augustine. Indeed, only by dint of this creative synthesis does it become clear how the *analogia entis* is the original dynamic of created being. But there is arguably still more of the Church

---

[42] Przywara, *Ringen der Gegenwart*, vol. 2, p. 929 (Przywara's emphasis).

in the *analogia entis*, which is indicated by Przywara's use of the word *Spannung* or tension; for, though he draws more explicitly on Augustine here, his use of this term clearly resonates with the concept of *epektasis* one finds in Gregory of Nyssa. And, in point of fact, for Przywara as for the Cappadocian, given divine infinity this stretching of the creature *in Deum* will last forever.[43]

In any event, as these examples are meant to indicate, Przywara is an ecclesial thinker, a thinker *of the tradition*. As such, it is impossible to call him an original, except by calling him an original *of the tradition*. (And here, in general, Catholic theology distinguishes itself from the cult of originality that attaches willy-nilly to theologians such as Luther, as Johann Adam Möhler pointed out in his *Symbolik*, and philosophers such as Heidegger.) Przywara is not an original in that sense. This is not to deny certain novelties, however, such as his audacious attempt to comprise the entire Catholic metaphysical tradition within a single term, the *analogia entis*, or his creative rendering of the *analogia entis* with a host of explanatory idioms, which are almost as cryptic as what they are supposed to explain. We have already encountered one such phrase, namely, '*Spannungs-Einheit*' or 'unity-in-tension'. Another is the phrase 'in-and-beyond', which is meant to capture various levels of tension between immanence and transcendence. Other such neologisms include '*Spannungs-Schwebe*', '*Gegensatz-spannung*' and '*Beziehung gegenseitigen Anders-Seins*'. (In other words, what we have here is a vocabulary that is every bit as idiosyncratic as Heidegger's, but one that is employed not for the sake of deconstructing the metaphysical tradition – and, in Heidegger's case, distorting it – but rather of disclosing it, so that through Przywara's poetic rendering we can see the *truth* of metaphysics, which is to say that we see in Przywara the anti-Heidegger.)

Przywara's View of Modernity: Genealogy and Critique

Admittedly, few today would put so great a stress upon the *analogia entis*. Even von Balthasar, who never wavered in his conviction regarding its importance, was reluctant to make it *the* formal principle of Catholic theology, especially in the context of his ecumenical debate with Karl Barth who was so vexed

---

[43] The same could be said of the *analogia entis*, since even in its deification, the creature remains a deified *creature*. In other words, the *analogia entis* is never abrogated – not even in eternity. It is a principle that retains its validity even in the most exalted regions of supernatural participation in the divine nature, even at the heights of mystical union; and this is why it can in no way be reduced to a principle of natural theology. See Erich Przywara, *Katholische Krise* (ed. Bernhard Gertz; Düsseldorf: Patmos, 1967), p. 11.

by it.⁴⁴ For that matter, we might wonder along with some venerable scholars of Aquinas, such as Herbert McCabe, whether this doctrine really has any foundation in the teaching of the Angelic Doctor. With them we might ask, 'Isn't analogy just a way of qualifying our use of certain words?'⁴⁵ We might even wonder with Karl Barth whether Przywara's *analogia entis* makes philosophy the foundation of theology in such a way that threatens the purity of theology *qua* theology, not to mention the uniqueness of Christ as the sole mediator between God and human beings. These and similar questions, which are not trivial, demand an answer that only a thorough reading of Przywara's works could properly provide.⁴⁶

As far as Przywara himself is concerned, however, this much is clear: there is no getting around the *analogia entis*. It is a basic category of Catholic thinking about the relation between God and creation, which, as we have seen, is presupposed by the incarnation. Indeed, for Przywara, the hypostatic union is unthinkable apart from the kind of metaphysical relation between divine and human natures that the *analogia entis* describes.⁴⁷ Nor, as we have seen, is it abrogated or superseded by grace – not even at the heights of mystical union. For even in the most exalted regions of the creature's supernatural participation in the divine nature, even in the full and complete integration of the creature into the body of Christ, indeed even when God is 'all in all' within a perfected universe, when the whole of the material universe is a theophany, a burning bush, the distinction between Creator and creature remains. For the creature whom Christ unites to himself (and to the Father) by the gift of their common Spirit remains, even in its union with God, a creature; and God in His Divine Majesty remains the God who, as infinite, is *semper maior* – and so worthy of ever greater love and service. In this sense, for Przywara, the principle of the *analogia entis* is indeed ultimate – both as regards the irreducibility of the

---

⁴⁴ See Hans Urs von Balthasar, *The Theology of Karl Barth: Exposition and Interpretation* (trans. Edward T. Oakes; San Francisco: Ignatius Press, 1992), p. 35. See also Werner Löser, 'Weg und Werk Hans Urs von Balthasars', *Philosophisch-Theologische Hochschule Sankt Georgen. Frankfurt am Main-Virtueller Leseraum*: 'Von Balthasar never wavered in his conviction that the doctrine of the "analogia entis" was of decisive significance for every right-thinking philosophy and theology. It determines, whether implicitly or explicitly, all the expressions of his thought.'

⁴⁵ See again McCabe's commentary in *Summa Theologiae*, vol. 3, p. 106. See also David Burrell, *Analogy and Philosophical Language* (New Haven: Yale University Press, 1973), pp. 119ff.; Ralph McInerny, *The Logic of Analogy* (The Hague: Martinus Nijhoff, 1961); *Studies in Analogy* (The Hague: Martinus Nijhoff, 1968); *Aquinas and Analogy* (Washington, DC: Catholic University of America Press, 1996), pp. 152ff.

⁴⁶ For an attempt to address some of these issues, see the introduction to *Analogia Entis*, pp. 37–43, 83–115. See also John R. Betz, 'After Barth: A New Introduction to Erich Przywara's *Analogia Entis*', in *The Analogy of Being: Invention of the Antichrist or the Wisdom of God* (ed. Thomas Joseph White; Grand Rapids, MI: Eerdmans, 2010), pp. 35–87.

⁴⁷ See Przywara, *Analogia Entis*, p. 98 n. 272.

creature *qua* creature and the *ever greater* glory of God as God. In Przywara's pithy, gnomic idiom, God remains 'in-and-beyond'. And this is why, at the end of the day, whatever one makes of the foreshadowing of the *analogia entis* within the domain of philosophy – that is, whether this is something that one can grasp by the natural light of reason – the *analogia entis* is not reducible to a principle of natural theology.

At issue here, however, is not simply the continued importance of the *analogia entis* as a regulative principle within the Church, but also the question of its relevance for the Church's mission to the modern world. In other words, what does the *analogia entis* have to do with the spirit of Vatican II and the kind of engagement with the modern world proposed in *Gaudium et Spes*? Though Przywara did not have any direct role in the Council's proceedings, it is obvious from his writings that the *analogia entis* has an indispensable role to play: for the simple reason that the problems of modernity are fundamentally *metaphysical* in nature, stemming from a fundamental and (in his view) catastrophic misconception of the relation between God and the world. In other words, in Przywara's view, the modern world is predicated upon a denial of the *analogia entis* – a denial that he traces back not so far as to Scotus (who is perhaps easily misunderstood in this regard), but rather to the Reformation. And ever since, in Przywara's view, the world has been reeling from two destructive dialectics.

The first of these dialectics is between rationalism and voluntarism, which is parodied in the difference between the God of Kant, who is purely immanent to reason, and the God of Luther-Calvin, who totally transcends reason. The second dialectic, which Przywara considers still more basic, is between pantheism and theopanism, i.e. between a reduction of God to the world, which *alone* is regarded as real (in the case of pantheism), and a reduction of the world to God, *who alone* is regarded as real (in the case of theopanism). In other words, for Przywara the entire problem of modernity, which oscillates between an exclusive transcendence and an exclusive immanence, turns on this one word 'alone', as in Luther's ***sola** fide*. For it is precisely the Reformation's cry of faith alone and grace alone, and its concomitant rejection of reason and natural capacities, that led to the Enlightenment's reactionary cry of *reason* alone, and its concomitant rejection of faith and tradition. One extreme thus turns out to be the flipside of the other. As Przywara strikingly puts it:

> As for this identity [*Identität-Eins*] of God and world, which took the place of polarity and its unity-in-tension [*Polaritäts-Spannung-Eins*] of God and world, what does it really matter whether one call it God or world, whether one call

it the world-denying theopanism of Spinoza or the God-denying pantheism of Schopenhauer-Nietzsche? In either case the inevitable consequence was the frightful reeling of modernity between a sensual, pleasure-seeking intoxication with the world and a fanatical, eschatological hatred of the world: is not this the deadly fever that is shaking Europe even now?[48]

To understand how the *analogia entis* relates to these dialectics (as a corrective to them), it is important to recall that the *analogia entis*, as Przywara understands it, functions on two different levels: the first concerns the immanent creaturely tension between essence and existence; the second concerns the transcendent relation and tension between the creature and the Creator. When the *analogia entis* holds sway, these native tensions (each in the form of an 'in-and-beyond') are preserved. In modernity, however, they mutate into dialectics. On the one hand, in place of the tension between essence and existence, we have an either–or: between an abstract, universal rationalism disconnected from history and tradition (characteristic of the Enlightenment) and a radical, individualistic voluntarism (which traces back to Luther and terminates in the historicism, relativism and will to power of Nietzsche). This dialectic then repeats itself in various forms, as in the famous clash between the transcendental essentialism of Cassirer and the hermeneutical existentialism of Heidegger.

In the case of the second dialectic, instead of the tension between God as the first cause who works all things (*Allwirksamkeit*) in and through the secondary and analogous causes of creation, modernity fluctuates between one or another form of reduction, between one or another form of *Alleinwirksamkeit*, in short, between one or another purism: between a theopanism of 'God alone' (in which case God is or does everything and the creature is and does essentially nothing) and a pantheism of the 'world alone' (in which case the world is all there really is and God is essentially nothing). In the case of theopanism the world either lacks ontological density, being a mere manifestation or emanation of the divine (as one sees in various idealisms, Neo-Platonisms and philosophies of the East), or (as with extreme forms of Calvinism such as Barth's) it lacks integrity, being stripped as a consequence of the Fall of any real, dramatic cooperation with grace. In the case of its dialectical flipside, pantheism, which is represented by modern secular atheism, it is not the creature but God who is unreal, who is now thought to be nothing but a concept or projection of the human being: whether God be thought of as a product of self-alienation (Feuerbach–Marx), mythopoesis (Nietzsche) or wish fulfillment (Freud).

---

[48] Przywara, *Ringen der Gegenwart*, pp. 960f.

Still, though, to express the dialectics of modernity in terms of pantheism and theopanism, or even in terms of their noetic corollary, rationalism and fideism, might leave us untouched by the full force of their significance. At some level these terms are abstractions. And this is the danger with Przywara's highly abstract thought, which in many ways trades in abstract typologies. But if we say secular rationalism and religious fanaticism the import of these terms is suddenly – and I would venture to say directly – evident: for the one admits no faith into the public sphere; the other admits no reason into its dogmatism. In other words, from the perspective of Przywara's *analogia entis*, both are at their core *totalizing*, and so both have the capacity – and have variously demonstrated the capacity – to be *totalitarian*. Therein lies the frightfulness of the dialectic of modernity: between the Puritanism of Calvin's Geneva (and radical Islam) and the various purges and rational 'solutions' of modern secular atheism. The one admits no reason; the other admits no faith. Each in its own peculiar way is terrifying. To state the matter thus is admittedly sensational, but is this not the dialectic of our times, the dialectic that continues to rend the world, pitting culture against culture: a dialectic between the secular denial of God (in the West) and the religious denial of man (in the East)? At the very least, it underscores the importance of the *analogia entis*, and how critical it is when dealing with modernity and modern forms of thought that one get one's metaphysics right.

6

Karl Barth and Modernity, with Special Reference to Nietzsche

Kenneth Oakes

The material that follows is divided into three sections. In the first I cover some difficulties regarding Karl Barth's historical and material relationship to modernity and modern theology. In the second section I cover Barth's understanding of modernity, modern theology and the ways in which Christian thought and practice present a problem to modernity. The focus of the third section is Barth's reading of and response to a thinker who readily identified that Christianity presents an insoluble problem to modern intellectual culture and pretentions: Friedrich Nietzsche.

Karl Barth as Modern

Elucidating Karl Barth's relationship to modernity, and in particular to the performance and course of theology in the modern period, has proved difficult for several reasons. First, there was the widespread acceptance of Barth's and the other dialectical theologians' judgements and criticisms of eighteenth- and nineteenth-century theology. Dissatisfied with the state of theology in the late 1910s and early 1920s, Barth and his erstwhile comrade-in-arms traced back the origins of these dissatisfactions to their nineteenth-century predecessors and characterized their own theologies as an antidote. Unearthing Barth's relationship to modernity and modern theology thus requires moving beyond Barth's own self-descriptions and characterization of modernity and modern theology. Secondly, elucidating this relationship depends on broader judgements regarding the intellectual and religious movements and figures of the eighteenth and nineteenth centuries. The legacies of Kant and Hamann, Schleiermacher and Hegel, and Kierkegaard and Ritschl are still contested matters, as are the various Pietisms, Romanticisms, Rationalisms and Orthodoxies of the time period. Barth once told his students that they need only read the first 12 paragraphs of Schleiermacher's *Glaubenslehre* to understand the rest. Yet should Schleiermacher's endeavour be understood from §4 or from §62?[1] Barth also describes Hegel as one for whom problems and oppositions are raised only to be settled and domesticated.[2] Yet should Hegel be interpreted as a philosopher of closure, of 'perfect openness'[3] or some reconciliation of the two? Thirdly, there is the vast array of theological and intellectual influences upon Barth to consider and weigh in relative importance in his thought and the development of his thought: Barth was a seasoned exegete of Scripture and interpreter of Paul; proficient in the classical Protestant confessions; conversant with Lutheran and Reformed divines; familiar with figures such as Kant and Overbeck, the Blumhardts and Herrmann; and he was a Swiss Social Democrat. Even after having identified and accounted for these sources of Barth's theological inheritance, there is then the task of tracking Barth's own creative appropriations of and movements beyond them.

That the issue of Barth on modernity and modern theology is not only difficult but also contentious can be seen in that Barth scholarship itself seems undecided on whether and to what extent Barth's thought may be called 'modern'. Barth scholarship has in fact produced four competing yet compelling portraits of Barth and his theological work as modern, anti-modern, non-modern or postmodern.

Viewing Barth's thought as modern arguably started in Germany in the 1970s and was associated with several theologians at the University of Munich.[4] While ostensibly historical in nature, their research was at times charged with high-stake polemics and the sting of past nationalistic bruises. Barth's apparently anti-democratic statements were thought to contribute to the collapse of the Weimar Republic and Barth was accused of perpetuating one of the worst excesses of modernity – fascism – within his theology. Trutz Rendtorff, for instance, argued that Barth adopts the modern account of the human as a free,

---

[1] Friedrich Schleiermacher, *The Christian Faith* (Berkeley, CA: Apocryphile Press, 2011), §4, pp. 12–18; §62, pp. 259–62.
[2] Karl Barth, *Protestant Theology in the Nineteenth Century: Its Background and History* (trans. Brian Cozens and John Bowden; London: SCM Press, 1972), pp. 396, 414.
[3] See Andrews Shanks, *Hegel and Religious Faith: Divided Brain, Atoning Spirit* (London: T&T Clark, 2011), ch. 2, pp. 35–44.
[4] For an overview, see Stefan Holtmann, *Karl Barth als Theologe der Neuzeit: Studien zur kritischen Deutung seiner Theologie* (Göttingen: Vandenhoeck & Ruprecht, 2007).

self-legislating and sovereign subject and then projects this understanding of human subjectivity onto the divine. Closely related is Barth the anti-modern. Barth's slogan that 'religion is unbelief' stands as a harsh judgement upon the extensive use and promotion of 'religion' in figures such as Schleiermacher, Troeltsch and Rade. Barth's ethics, often taken as a species of divine command theory, also violate the very hallmark of genuinely ethical reflection and action within modernity: that it be autonomous. As for Barth the postmodern, Barth's criticism and abandonment of apologetics and his sense that the various platforms on which modern theologies had attempted to base themselves, whether the subject, reason or historical criteria of authenticity, were not as stable or neutral as they purported to be. There is also Barth's apparent ease in exegeting Scripture's plain sense and focus on Scripture's narratological and literary features rather than hermeneutical theory, extensive recourse to historical reconstructions or issues of oral and textual transmission. Finally, Barth the non-modern is perhaps clearest in many of the sweeping passages on the divine perfections in *Church Dogmatics* II/1, or the doctrine of Christ's offices in *Church Dogmatics* IV, through which one can wind without ever so much as bumping into a modern. In this line of interpretation Barth becomes a type of perennial figure who belongs alongside such doctors of the church as Augustine, Thomas Aquinas and John Calvin, and who offers us a fairly classical doctrinal system which could have come from any age.

The question 'is Barth's theology modern?' has yielded four plausible answers and in doing so raises another question: 'Why such divergent answers?' While the diversity of Barth's influences has already been mentioned, the simplest answer, which is also an academic truism, is that Barth's relationship to modernity often ends up looking suspiciously similar to that of the Barth scholar. A more substantive answer comes from the history of Barth reception. Within Barth's North Atlantic reception, one could show how some of the first Barth texts to appear in English – *Romans* II, the three famous dialectical addresses from the summer of 1922, *Church Dogmatics* I/1 – give the appearance of being anti-modern, and certainly stand among his more combative texts. This portrait of Barth also seems confirmed by the use of his theology, along with those of the other dialectical theologians, to beat back the final remnants of nineteenth-century liberalism within North Atlantic contexts. The continuing appearance in English of the later volumes of the *Church Dogmatics*, especially volume IV, with their growing reliance on and exposition of classical Protestant sources and theologians, and their steady exegesis of Scripture in a seemingly pre-critical fashion, readily give rise to Barth the non-modern. Yet Barth the postmodern seems an inevitable figure after the rise of post-structuralist or post-Marxist thought within US and British universities and the growing appreciation of Barth's nonchalance about modern academic conventions, his suspicions regarding some of the grander claims of modernity and his general distrust of classic metaphysics. Finally, it is only natural that Barth the modern would first appear in Germany given the tendency of German scholarship to historicize its subjects, to view modernity as an unfinished work rather than an untenable project, and the late but steady publication of Barth's earliest, arguably most modern works in the *Karl Barth-Gesamtausgabe*.

Materially speaking, however, one can account for these four divergent yet plausible readings with two observations. The first is that the earliest Barth inherited a host of assumptions from 'the modern theology', that broad stream of theology whose founder was Schleiermacher and whose executor was Ritschl. The second is that through the course of his development Barth kept some of these modern assumptions intact (yielding Barth the modern), and radicalized, criticized and abandoned others (Barth the postmodern, the anti-modern and the non-modern). Such modern assumptions would include a healthy Christocentrism; a concern for ethics and concrete human existence; suspicions regarding both natural and speculative theology; the insistence that theology is a positive endeavour which begins with revelation and should not be based on history, philosophy or psychology; an appreciation for critical historical study of Scripture and church history; worries regarding heteronomy; and the sense that theology can be an ecclesial discipline while still remaining within the academy. Many of these modern sensibilities can be found in one way or another in the likes of Schleiermacher, Ritschl, Herrmann, Rade and Troeltsch, and many of them will stay with Barth for the rest of his life.

Yet in order to see how outcomes can exceed initial conditions, one could select any of these distinctly modern themes and trace them through Barth's development to surprising ends. The earliest Barth, for example, had learned from Herrmann, and thus from Schleiermacher, the importance of theology's *Selbständigkeit*. The concept *Selbständigkeit* is usually translated as 'independence', but one could just as well render it as 'autonomy', 'self-sufficiency' or 'self-reliance'. Theology's *Selbständigkeit* connotes the sense that theology can be a fully-fledged, vigorous and sweeping discipline in its own right. Herrmann had established theology's 'independence' through a peace treaty in which Kant's critical philosophy determined knowing in general while Luther mixed with Schleiermacher determined religious 'knowing'. The earliest Barth accepted this treaty although not without some concerns. What happens in subsequent years, however, is that the desire for theology's independence meant a relativization of the strictures of modern theology and philosophy. If theology is indeed an independent, self-reliant discipline, one which starts and ends with revelation, takes place in the church and concerns itself with the reading and proclamation of Scripture, then what is to stop theology from becoming more aggressive towards or less concerned about the commitments of modern ethics, history, philosophy and biblical criticism? What is to prevent one from engaging with the Protestant Scholastics, reading Scripture according to its plain sense without little critical apparatus and doing theology under the presupposition that the crucified and resurrected Jesus Christ is seated at the right hand of the Father from where he rules and consoles his church? Here one can see how a distinctly modern concern can quickly turn into something strangely non-modern, postmodern or even anti-modern. While the notion of theology's *Selbständigkeit* is a formal matter, one could perform similar experiments with other of his earlier assumptions and will most likely see strange flowers growing from characteristically modern soil.

Barth's Modernity

Barth once remarked he would have been a historian in another life, and his interest in history, or more precisely social history, is readily apparent in the beginning of the 'Background' section of his *Protestant Theology in the Nineteenth Century*.[5] Here Barth discusses eighteenth-century developments in the natural sciences, travel, reading, writing and publishing, political theory and practice, views of nature, architecture, fashion, historiography, educational reforms, voluntary associations, literature and poetry, music and the 'inner life' of 'eighteenth-century man'. In these pages we can readily see that Barth's modernity is vibrant, living and polyphonic.

Similar material can certainly be found in the *Church Dogmatics* or elsewhere in Barth's corpus, but only if one looks hard enough. In contrast to *Protestant Theology in the Nineteenth Century*, in these other places Barth's modernity is leaner in several different ways. First, his modernity tends to be textual and intellectual. At times Barth can deal with modern shifts in social practices, technological developments, the natural sciences, the history and literature of specific regions or cities, but overall his modernity is the intellectual world and

---

[5] See especially the chapter 'Man in the Eighteenth Century', in Barth, *Protestant Theology*, pp. 33–79.

history created by the canonical texts in the fields of theology, philosophy and ethics. Secondly, Barth's modernity is allophone, as the people, texts and issues are mostly Prussian and German. French thinkers such as Descartes, Rousseau or Voltaire may enter the scene occasionally, but the luminaries of the English or Scottish Enlightenments, figures such as Locke, Hume or Lord Shaftesbury, are absent, as are Spanish, Italian or Central European thinkers. Thirdly, Barth's primary interest in modernity is theological and he focuses in particular on how modern intellectual trends affect Christian doctrine and Scriptural exegesis. Developments in philosophy, cosmology, political theory or natural philosophy in and of themselves do not hold Barth's attention for long, and yet he could show interest in them to the extent to which they dealt with theological matters or influenced theological discourse.

In *Protestant Theology in the Nineteenth Century* Barth uses the theme of 'absolutism', or the 'will to form', to characterize the eighteenth century. He defends this procedure of summarizing a century with a specific 'objective spirit' by arguing that the eighteenth century cannot be taken on its own terms, particularly that of 'the Enlightenment', when attempting to offer a 'theological understanding of the whole situation'. To this end, Barth opts for 'absolutism' or 'will to form' instead of 'Enlightenment' for capturing the century's trajectories, events and dreams, and 'absolutism' in particular becomes Barth's 'comprehensive key-word' or the 'form' that he uses to bind together the various facets of eighteenth-century political, social and religious culture.[6]

The course of theology in the eighteenth century 'proves to be just one further instance of this attitude to life in general'.[7] Theology in the eighteenth century is subject to what Barth calls 'humanization'. This term is meant to allude to the revival of sixteenth-century humanism within the eighteenth century, and the humanist ideal of an independent, self-sufficient and self-satisfied humanity aglow with and fascinated by its own splendorous autonomy and capabilities. Within the eighteenth century the humanization of theology meant 'if not the abolition, at least the incorporation of God into the sphere of sovereign human self-awareness, the transformation of the reality that came and was to be perceived from outside into a reality that was experienced and understood inwardly'.[8] If this internalizing movement is what most alarms Barth, and Pietism is singled out for criticism, he nevertheless details four attempts to humanize and tame Christianity. These attempts include the incorporation of

---

[6] Barth, *Protestant Theology*, p. 37.
[7] Barth, *Protestant Theology*, p. 81.
[8] Barth, *Protestant Theology*, p. 84.

Christianity into the state, into bourgeois morality and sensibilities, into science and philosophy, and into the inwardness of the individual.

As for Pietism in particular, Barth details some ways in which Christian thought and practice proved difficult to assimilate.[9] The indigestible elements included, for example, the temporal distance between the historical Jesus Christ and the contemporary believer; the fellow-believer; the authority of Scripture, creed and church; the idea of the divine command; and the concepts of mystery or sacrament. Barth thinks, however, that this general attempt to internalize and domesticate Christianity on behalf of the Pietists and others was not taken in complete earnest, as there remained internal contradictions, the lingering cherishing of Scripture and the material substance of Christian claims. As for this material content, Barth mentions the memory of a God who speaks and a humanity who listens over and against Spinoza's deity; the scandal and offence of a Protestant doctrine of justification by (free) grace through faith; and belief in eternal life, a blessedness which cannot be seen, touched or conquered, but only believed in.

The nineteenth century continues and completes the 'absolutism' of the eighteenth century and its corresponding 'humanization' of Christianity. This humanization, however, proves less than successful. In Barth's narrative, Christianity represents an insoluble problem to the nineteenth-century enlightened 'man' who in supreme self-confidence believes himself to be the measure of all things. Within this framework, the course of nineteenth-century theology becomes a tale of the partial or failed assimilation of Christianity into dominant cultural discourses of ethics, politics, philosophy and history.

When the polemics are muted, Barth offers the standard tale of theology and philosophy within the nineteenth century. The beginning of the century belonged to Herder and the Romantics, quickly went to the great systems of speculative idealism and finally saw the return of positivism in the second half of the nineteenth century. When we overlay the polemics onto this track a variety of different criticisms begin to be heard. Theology in the nineteenth century retreated into the narrow regions of epistemology and ethics that Kant left for it.[10] Modern Protestantism posits and works from the 'sovereignty of the

---

[9] Elsewhere Barth can also note in passing that Christian doctrine had already lost its 'inner content' in the seventeenth and eighteenth centuries through their waves of Pietism and rationalism. Karl Barth, *Church Dogmatics* III/3 (trans. G. W. Bromiley and R. J. Ehrlich; Edinburgh: T&T Clark, 1960), p. 17.

[10] Karl Barth, *Humanity of God* (trans. Thomas Wieser and John Newton Thomas; Richmond, VA: John Knox Press, 1960), p. 16.

universal religious self-consciousness'[11] and substituted the piety of the believer for the majesty and freedom of God. All in all, nineteenth-century theology belongs to Schleiermacher, as the century began with his *Speeches* and ended with his renaissance.

Barth's accounts of specific theologians from the nineteenth century have varying degrees of exposition and sympathy. The tone alternates between calm, curious and incisive, but is seldom dreary or tired. Barth is happy to commend promising elements, which in the case of his narrative means elements which point beyond Schleiermacher and Hegel. For Barth, however, each theologian fails in his own particular way and this failure is gently and swiftly referenced. In accounting for the shortcomings Barth typically alludes to doctrinal material which went forgotten in their theologies. Schleiermacher's theology needs to be reminded of the divinity of the Holy Spirit and the Reformation doctrine of the forgiveness of sin. Menken elides electing grace and the ecclesial setting of Scriptural exegesis.[12] Tholuck renders the opposition of sin and grace a story of the human heart rather than a history of God with his people.[13] Dorner, in whom Barth finds much to commend, seems to prioritize Spirit over Father and Son. Hofmann's presentation of experience and Scripture lacks the necessary interconnection between Word and Spirit.[14] Vilmar needs to be reminded that theology is not only teaching, but both research and teaching.[15] Köhlbrugge's doctrine of Scripture and his exegesis rests on a mechanical doctrine of inspiration, which enacts a kind of violence upon the text. Even Blumhardt's eschatology, especially its chiliasm, seems quaintly at home in the nineteenth century.[16]

As for the philosophers of the late eighteenth and nineteenth centuries, Barth contends that Kant, Fichte, Schelling and Hegel held little interest in the Christianity of the New Testament or of the Reformation. This relative disinterest is apparent in the way that these figures either cautiously criticized or altered Christianity such that it would fit into their own systems. Hegel, who arguably presents the greatest 'misremembering' of Christianity,[17] occupies an

---

[11] Karl Barth, *God Here and Now* (trans. Paul van Buren; New York: Routledge, 2003), p. 68.
[12] Barth, *Protestant Theology*, p. 532.
[13] Barth, *Protestant Theology*, p. 517.
[14] Barth, *Protestant Theology*, p. 614.
[15] Barth, *Protestant Theology*, p. 633.
[16] Barth notes that it was the pastoral nature that meant the academic theology did not take up his insights, even though there was something to be learned from Blumhardt.
[17] For two accounts of Hegel's misremembering, see Cyril O'Regan, *The Heterodox Hegel* (Albany: State University of New York Press, 1994); *The Anatomy of Misremembering: Von Balthasar's Response to Philosophical Modernity*, vol. 1, *Hegel* (New York: Crossroads, 2013).

awkward position in Barth's narrative. As characterizing Barth's placement of Hegel within his narrative would require its own chapter, it can be noted here that Hegel's system offered theologians great promise. In its ambitious attempt to present and follow the sweeping and grandiose work of the triune God *ad extra*, in its understanding that truth is movement, dialectical and historical, that God is infinitely alive, Hegel's works provided the impetus, occasion and challenge for theologians to do the same although they proved unequal to the task.

There also exists for Barth a much smaller and more illustrious group of eighteenth- and nineteenth-century figures who correctly identified an element of Christianity and then consciously rejected it. In *Protestant Theology in the Nineteenth Century* Kant is the figure who recognized what Christianity means for the aspirations of modern thought.[18] In some of his earlier essays it is Franz Overbeck who could point out the distance between modern theology and New Testament Christianity.[19] In the *Church Dogmatics*, however, it is Nietzsche who best understood and then rejected Christianity.

The Crucified and His Host as Problem: Friedrich Nietzsche

A onetime hero in *Romans* II, Nietzsche both continues and concludes one particular stream of eighteenth- and nineteenth-century thought. The figurehead of this stream is none other than Goethe. In order to establish the lineage of Goethe to Nietzsche, Barth points to Goethe's decided penchant for Hellenism, and how the cross becomes included among other irritations: 'tobacco (the smoke), bedbugs and garlic and †'.[20] Yet the telltale indicator of this pedigree is that Nietzsche takes up and completes Goethe's ideal of 'humanity without the fellow-man' (240).

Barth views Nietzsche neither as the culmination of Western metaphysics or nihilism (Heidegger), nor as the father of genealogy or power relations (Foucault), nor as a philosopher of pure positivity and affirmation (Deleuze), nor as a mariner of the divine (Irigaray), nor as the shadowy disseminator of

---

[18] For an analysis of Barth's reading of Kant, see Kenneth Oakes, *Karl Barth on Theology and Philosophy* (Oxford: Oxford University Press, 2012), pp. 140–9.
[19] Karl Barth, 'Unsettled Questions for Theology Today', in idem, *Theology and Church: Shorter Writings 1920–1928* (trans. Louise Pettibone Smith; New York: Harper and Row, 1962), pp. 55–73.
[20] §66 of Goethe's *Venetian Epigrams*; L. R. Lind (ed.), *Johann Wolfgang von Goethe's Roman Elegies and Venetian Epigrams* (trans. L. R. Lind; Lawrence: University Press of Kansas, 1974), pp. 112–15. In *The Will to Power* Nietzsche recommends that 'One must feel about "the cross" as Goethe did.' Friedrich Nietzsche, *The Will to Power* (trans. Walter Kaufmann and R. J. Hollingdale; ed. Walter Kaufmann; New York: Random House, 1968), §175, p. 107.

various textual 'styles' that play with standard notions of truth and presence (Derrida), nor as a mystic (de Lubac). Barth instead sees Nietzsche first and foremost an as ethicist, and more particularly as an ethicist of the 'solitary man'. Nietzsche's thought represents a stimulus for theological reflection and a challenge to theology inasmuch as Nietzsche presents an opportunity for theologians to identify and reject 'this most obvious of all possibilities' (231),[21] the possibility of seeing humanity without the 'fellow-man'.

Barth's takes *Ecce Homo* – not *The Will to Power* fragments, *Nachlaß*, the early *The Birth of Tragedy* or the epic *Thus Spoke Zarathustra* – to be the interpretive centre of gravity (231).[22] Two self-declarations from *Ecce Homo* in particular orient Barth's reading. The first comes from the work's thunderous opening: 'Hear me, for I am he; do not at any price mistake me,'[23] which Barth calls 'a bizarre but genuine form of the first and final proposition of humanity without the fellow-man' (232). The second comes from the work's dramatic conclusion and challenge: 'Am I understood? – *Dionysius against the Crucified...*'[24] These two statements provide Barth with his hermeneutical key for both Nietzsche's life and well as his greatest gift to humanity: the prophet Zarathustra.

The first statement, 'Hear me, for I am he; do not at any price mistake me,' once again has its precursor in Goethe. Barth detects an implicit self-satisfaction in Goethe, but maintains that Goethe's quiet, balanced self-restraint and deep interest in the world prevented the total enfolding upon his own self-consciousness that we see in the self-assertion of Nietzsche's urgent, zealous and absolute 'I am'. Nietzsche 'had to cry out' (232) the 'I am' which Goethe proclaimed with caution and within definite limits and in this way 'Nietzsche was the prophet of that humanity without the fellow man. He did not merely reveal its secret; he blabbed it out' (232). The terrible secret that burdened and animated Nietzsche is this: that 'in a last and deepest isolation he and he alone was the eye and measure and master and even the essence of all things' (232).

In Nietzsche's case, this 'last and deepest isolation' takes the form of

---

[21] Parenthetical references are to Karl Barth, *Church Dogmatics* III/2 (trans. Harold Knight, G. W. Bromiley et al.; Edinburgh: T. & T. Clark, 1960).

[22] An argument has recently been made by Nicholas D. More that *Ecce Homo* is best read as satire: 'Nietzsche's Last Laugh: *Ecce Homo* as Satire', *Philosophy and Literature* 35 (1) (April 2011): 1–15; *Nietzsche's Last Laugh:* Ecce Homo *as Satire* (Cambridge: Cambridge University Press, 2014). Given that Barth finds these lines illuminating and encapsulating of tendencies that appear in Nietzsche's earlier works, More's argument does not substantively affect Barth's reading of Nietzsche.

[23] For an English translation, see Friedrich Nietzsche, *Ecce Homo: How to Become What You Are* (trans. Duncan Large; Oxford: Oxford University Press, 2007), foreword, I, p. 3.

[24] For an English translation, see Nietzsche, *Ecce Homo*, IV, 9, p. 95.

self-obsession, and Barth spends some time detailing how this self-concern is apparent at several points in Nietzsche's biography. Nietzsche's interest in Greek philology, for instance, waned after the emergence of Dionysius as the 'one root of all Greek art' (232), and after Nietzsche's subsequent identification of Dionysius/Zarathustra with himself. Likewise, Nietzsche's brief fanaticism for the causes of evolution and natural science most likely faded after his discovery of the 'will to power' as the essence of all life. Here again an identification or projection takes place, for the will to power remains 'an unmistakable but impressive symbol of his own will' (232). Few would contest that the Schopenhauer in 'Schopenhauer as Educator' is Nietzsche himself, something about which Nietzsche later boasted.[25] Nietzsche's praise of Wagner seemed to last only as long as the composer exemplified Nietzsche's own ideals. Barth interprets Nietzsche's aversion to Christianity and the later Wagner as symptomatic of this repulsion and contempt for that which he could not conform to his own image or become into a projection of himself. This self-concern reappears in Nietzsche's love and fascination for his *alter ego* beside Dionysius, the prophet Zarathustra.[26] As made clear in the Sils-Maria revelation and poem, here again we encounter none other than Nietzsche himself, or at least his ideal self, and indeed another self which can even burden and oppress him. Barth also recounts how Nietzsche can joylessly claim that women 'they all love me',[27] and pointedly responds, 'but he had no use for the fact; he could not love in return' (234).[28] No higher opinion is offered regarding Nietzsche's friendships with males: 'in addition he cannot repay or be faithful to even the best and most sincere of his male friends' (234). Should we be surprised, then, when Nietzsche himself boasts that no other human word could reach him, even from an early age?[29] Or when Zarathustra boasts and laments, 'No one tells me anything new, and so I tell myself to myself'?[30] This isolation is finally and decisively represented in the general subject matter of Nietzsche's writings: Nietzsche himself. As one commentator has recently put it, Nietzsche's writings 'are essentially a species of *talking to oneself*.'[31]

---

[25] Nietzsche, *Ecce Homo*, III, 3, pp. 52–4.
[26] Barth does not mention or explore Heraclitus, Nietzsche's other hero of loneliness and fire. On Nietzsche, Heraclitus and loneliness, see R. J. Hollingdale, *Nietzsche: The Man and His Philosophy* (rev. edn; Cambridge University Press, 1999), pp. 76–7.
[27] Nietzsche, *Ecce Homo*, III, 5, p. 42.
[28] For a brief *apologia* on behalf of Nietzsche on this point, see Hollingdale, *Nietzsche*, p. 175.
[29] See Nietzsche, *Ecce Homo*, II, 10, pp. 33–5.
[30] Friedrich Nietzsche, *Thus Spoke Zarathustra: A Book for All and None* (eds Adrian del Caro and Robert B. Pippin; trans. Adrian del Caro; Cambridge: Cambridge University Press, 2006). p. 157.
[31] Hollingdale, *Nietzsche*, p. 116.

Yet this isolation existed alongside a zealous desire to give and an irritation at his inability to find worthy recipients for his gifts. Barth notes, 'Nietzsche often thought that he lived in indescribable wealth in this isolation, and these were the moments when he could beseechingly and yet also angrily point to the fact that he had infinite gifts to give, that infinite things were to be received from him' (233). The gift Nietzsche offered to the world, even calling it 'the greatest gift it has ever been given',[32] took the form of Zarathustra, his revamped Persian prophet. Nietzsche himself remarks that Goethe and Shakespeare would not be able to breathe at Zarathustra's height; that in comparison to this prophet Dante was a mere follower and not a creator of truth; and that the priests of the Vedas would be unfit to untie Zarathustra's sandals. All this, however, is 'the very least that can be said and it gives no conception of the distance, the *azure blue* solitude in which this work lives'.[33] The towering of this prophet in 'azure blue solitude' above his predecessors coincides with Zarathustra's elevated and solitary position in the epic itself. Barth wonders, 'and what is this position but the "I am" of humanity without the fellow-man, except that this time it is adopted without condition or restraint, in all its weakness? I am – "in azure isolation"' (233).

Zarathustra's struggle between isolation and the will to give of his own burgess reproduces Nietzsche's own. The great prophet sings among the graves, 'I am still the richest and the one to be envied most – I, the loneliest one!'[34] and can both rejoice in the splendorous solitude in his mountain-top cave and yet be impelled to descend so that he may bless others. Nietzsche's Zarathustra can even instruct his disciples on the 'highest' but rarest of virtues: the gift-giving virtue.[35] Yet coupled with this praise of gift-giving is Zarathustra's acceptance of his ultimate fate: 'And whatever may come to me now as destiny and experience – it will involve wandering and mountain climbing: ultimately one experiences only oneself.'[36]

Barth senses the contradictions in play. How could the isolated Zarathustra give wealth, life and joy to others? 'To whom is he, the superman, the absolute "I am" to give himself? And if there is someone, will he thank him for this or any gift?' (234). Zarathustra himself acknowledges this contradiction in his heart's 'double will', torn as it is between the heights and the depths, between

---

[32] Nietzsche, *Ecce Homo*, foreword, 4, p. 4.
[33] Nietzsche, *Ecce Homo*, III, Z, 6, p. 71.
[34] Nietzsche, *Thus Spoke Zarathustra*, p. 85.
[35] Nietzsche, *Thus Spoke Zarathustra*, pp. 55–9.
[36] Nietzsche, *Thus Spoke Zarathustra*, p. 121.

humanity and the overman: 'This, this is *my* precipice and my danger, that my gaze plunges into the heights and that my hand must hold to and support itself – on the depths! My will clings to mankind, I bind myself with chains to mankind because I am drawn upward to the overman; for there my other will wills me.'[37] Even in Zarathustra's flights to the mountaintops, the prophet is still unsettled by his inaccessibility. Sorrow and turmoil burden the overman, Dionysius and Zarathustra, as is especially clear in his laments in 'The Night Song', 'The Stillest Hour' and 'The Wanderer'. The prophet, however, inevitably laughs at his weakness, at his inability to accept and love his loneliness and 'soon rises up again like the eagle, scorning himself for his weakness, and finding joy and exultation and self-glory in the very thing which pains him' (235). Barth wonders, 'which prevails – the complaint or the rejoicing?' (235). Even in his opening remarks in 'Why I am a Destiny', on his being dynamite, the *destroyer par excellence*, Barth queries, 'is this complaining or rejoicing, or both?' (235).

Nietzsche himself feared misanthropy, admitting that '*Disgust* at man, at the "riff-raff", has always been my greatest danger.'[38] Disgust at humanity, no less than humanity itself, must be overcome. The prophet avoids disgust only by 'fleeing to a height "where there are no companions to sit at the well" and drink with him' (234). Zarathustra only overcomes his misanthropy by seeking nests, fountains and homesteads far above the rabble and the unclean. 'Oh I found it, my brothers! Here in the highest regions the wellspring of joy gushes for me! And there is a life from which no rabble drinks!'[39] At this height there is neither food nor homesteads for the unclean. Zarathustra tells his pure companions that 'like strong winds we want to live above them, neighbors to eagles, neighbors to snow, neighbors to the sun: thus live strong winds'.[40] Crowds are tolerable to Zarathustra only inasmuch as they serve as raw material for his hammer. 'Zarathustra has even gained mastery over his *great disgust* at man: man to him is a formless material, an ugly stone in need of a sculptor.'[41] Humanity must either be fled or hammered.

As for the second statement which he uses to orient his discussion, 'Dionysius against the Crucified', Barth sees it as the outcome of the first. Nietzsche could excoriate German nationalism, the philosophy and art of his day, 'scientificality', the moral sensibilities of his contemporaries, anti-Semitism, and yet the Crucified

---

[37] Nietzsche, *Thus Spoke Zarathustra*, p. 113.
[38] Nietzsche, *Ecce Homo*, I, 8, p. 17; see also IV, 6, pp. 92–3.
[39] Nietzsche, *Thus Spoke Zarathustra*, p. 75; Nietzsche, *Ecce Homo*, I, 8, pp. 16–17.
[40] Nietzsche, *Thus Spoke Zarathustra*, p. 76.
[41] Nietzsche, *Ecce Homo*, III, Z, 8, p. 76.

becomes the focal and final antithesis of Nietzsche's project. Nietzsche's polemic against Christianity had a variety of targets. Between *Ecce Homo* and Nietzsche's earlier writings there is 'a certain discrepancy of polemical standpoint' (238). In his *Antichrist*, as well as in the *Will to Power*, Nietzsche charges Paul and the church with the betraying of the true message of Jesus Christ. Nietzsche also complains about the 'No-saying', the blasphemies against the earth in the name of the heavens and the resentment against those strong, free spirits that he sees in Christianity. In a manner worthy of a disciple of the Greeks, Christianity offends the aesthete and even the philologist in him. At other places we encounter professed incredulity at the claims of Christianity. Belief in the God of Christianity has simply been rendered impossible, something which the townspeople themselves have prescience; Zarathustra and the madman only announce what they themselves presume. Nietzsche recounts that he never had time for God, the immortality of the soul, redemption or the beyond, even as a child; 'Atheism is not at all familiar to me as a result, still less as an event: it is self-evident to me from instinct.'[42] Barth detects some hesitation and anxiety at this point. He argues that the 'Dionysius-dithyrambs of 1888 show that he must have had some misgivings on the point. An "unknown God" obtrudes his dangerous being in the speeches of a curious opponent of Zarathustra, and he is not a complete stranger to Nietzsche himself, this hunter, thief, robber bandit, this great enemy, this executioner-God, etc. who tries to penetrate into his heart, his most secret thoughts' (238).[43] Yet the denial of God was not Nietzsche's primary goal. Instead, 'his central attack, into which he flung himself with all his force, was upon what he called Christian morality' (238–9), which is summed up in 'the Crucified'.

That Nietzsche was finally an ethicist, even if only as an 'immoralist', is plain from the last pages of *Ecce Homo* and their refrain upon 'Am I understood'. Each deals with morality/Christianity. The movement begins with 'Am I understood? [...] The self-overcoming of morality out of truthfulness, the self-overcoming of the moralist into his opposite – *me* – this is what the name of Zarathustra means in my mouth.'[44] 'Have I been understood? – I have not said a word just now that I might not have said five years ago through the mouth of Zarathustra. The *discovery* of Christian morality is an event without parallel, a real catastrophe.'[45] It reaches a near feverish pitch in 'Have I been understood? – I have not just

---

[42] Nietzsche, *Ecce Homo*, II, I, p. 19.
[43] Cf. the section on 'The Wizard' or 'The Magician' in Nietzsche, *Thus Spoke Zarathustra*.
[44] Nietzsche, *Ecce Homo*, IV, 3, p. 90.
[45] Nietzsche, *Ecce Homo*, IV, 7, p. 93.

now said a word that I could not have said five years through the mouth of Zarathustra – The *unmasking* of Christian morality is an event without equal, a real catastrophe.'[46] Until it finally reaches its apex in the last line of the book, 'Have I been understood? – *Dionysius against the crucified one*.'[47]

Christian morality is Nietzsche's most dangerous enemy inasmuch as Nietzsche correctly sees that Christianity is a way of life, and one which stands as the reverse image of what Nietzsche is proposing. He meets Christian morality 'as an enemy because it opposes to Zarathustra or Dionysius, the lonely, noble, strong, proud, natural, healthy, wise, outstanding, splendid man, the superman, a type which is the very reverse, and has so managed to do this successfully with its blatant claim that the only true man is the man who is little, poor and sick, the man who is weak and not strong, who does not evoke admiration but sympathy, who is not solitary but gregarious – the mass-man' (239). The doctrines, theology and concepts of Christianity are not even worth repudiating for Nietzsche, but 'this ideal', the valorization of the weak and lowly and base, is. Nietzsche finds in the first chapter of 1 Corinthians the ultimate example of this morality of the sick.[48] It is the morality presumed in this passage, and in the image of the Crucified amongst His host, 'this was what Nietzsche discovered as Christian morality' (240).

Nietzsche grasped that Christian morality confronts the overman with 'suffering man', asks the overman to accept and be with the suffering, to drink from the same wells (241). It is to Nietzsche's credit that he was able to see how 'Christianity places before the superman the Crucified, Jesus, as the Neighbour, and in the person of Jesus a whole host of others who are wholly and utterly ignoble and despised in the eyes of the world (of the world of Zarathustra, the true world of men), the hungry and thirsty and naked and sick and captive, a whole ocean of human meanness and painfulness' (241). Christian morality disturbs the solitary man, and 'aims to pull him down from his height, to put him in the ranks which begin with the Crucified, in the midst of His host' (241). It tells the overman that he too is a man, not a God, and thus belongs to the Crucified and is in fact one of the Crucified's hosts. 'Nor can Dionysius-Zarathustra redeem himself, but the Crucified alone can be his Redeemer. Dionysius-Zarathustra is thus called to live for others and not himself. Here

---

[46] Nietzsche, *Ecce Homo*, IV, 8, p. 94.
[47] Nietzsche, *Ecce Homo*, IV, 9, p. 95.
[48] See, for instance, Nietzsche's comments on 1 Corinthians, among other Scriptural passages, in §45 of *The Antichrist*; Friedrich Nietzsche, *Ecce Homo and the Antichrist* (trans. Thomas Wayne; New York: Algora Publishing, 2004), pp. 147–9.

are his brothers and sisters who belong to him and to whom he belongs' (241). Zarathustra must see himself and his salvation 'in this Crucified, and therefore in fellowship with this mean and painful host of His people, he has thus to see his salvation, and his true humanity in the fact that he belongs to Him and therefore to Him. The Crucified is God Himself, and therefore God Himself is only for those who belong to his host. They are the elect of God. And Dionysius-Zarathustra can be an elect of God only if he belongs to them' (241). The place of the Crucified is always with his host and it would be unimaginable for him to complain: 'Oh when will I return to my homeland where I no longer have to stoop – "no longer have to stoop *before the small ones*!" – And Zarathustra sighed and gazed into the distance.'[49]

Barth commends and credits Nietzsche for identifying an element of Christianity which he thinks was missed throughout the nineteenth century: the Crucified is always with his suffering and broken host. Such is how the Crucified willed and wills to be: for and among humanity, but especially for and among the lowly, despised and broken. Nietzsche perceived the foolishness and offence of the cross, the foolishness of God's decision for the least of these and the foolishness of the forms of life which correspond to this decision. Unlike the majority of the *Aufklärer* or even the modern theologians, Nietzsche understood that Christianity is a problem. It is to his credit that having identified this problem, Nietzsche had the honesty to attack Christianity rather than reinterpret and thereby domesticate it.

Concluding Remarks

For Barth, understanding modernity presents a theological task and problem for the church just as Christianity presents a problem for modernity. In either case, however, Barth's primary interest consists of describing and evaluating what happens to theology in modernity at the hands of both theologians and intellectual elites. Nevertheless, if theology did indeed lose its 'inner content' or become reduced to morality and epistemology, then the blame lies squarely on the shoulders of theologians. Thus Barth's battleground is Christian doctrine, and not necessarily philosophy, metaphysics, cosmologies or philosophies of history. The commitments and conclusions of these disciplines might be subject to collateral attention and then damage but they will do so in the course

---

[49] Nietzsche, *Thus Spoke Zarathustra*, p. 133.

of Barth offering extended and creative accounts of Christian doctrines. In *Church Dogmatics*, Barth can deal with modern figures such as Leibniz, Fichte, Heidegger and Jaspers, but he does so for the sake of developing and clarifying Christian doctrine through attention to a shared area of concern, such as hope, freedom, finitude and nothingness, and transcendence. The goal of these engagements is not primarily apologetics, but the illumination of the subject matter for the sake of theology and its witness. Two aspects of these engagements are striking. First, Barth thinks that theology can offer better accounts of these shared concerns, even from the perspective of the interlocutors themselves. Second, Barth does not think it necessary to switch into some other discourse, such as ethics, natural law or metaphysics, to address the questions and concerns of modernity. Instead he thinks it suffices to offer extended and creative descriptions of traditional doctrinal themes interwoven with exegesis reliant upon the plain sense of Scripture.

7

'Sœur Thérèse, meet Prof. Dr. Husserl': On Hans Urs von Balthasar's Theological Phenomenology

Peter Casarella

Patristic Nuptiality Transposed to the Rhythms of Contemporary Life (1948)

'Theological Phenomenology' is an artifice that von Balthasar uses to show the importance of rethinking the relationship of theology and sanctity. It is a further development of a new approach to a form of theology redirected to the objective faith and living witness of the saints that he had been propounding since at least 1948 when he published his seminal essay on this theme.[1]

What, however, can we learn about von Balthasar's engagement with modernity from these early reflections? The final section of 'Theology and Sanctity' is entitled 'Bride and Bridegroom' and offers insight into the theological core of his still emerging plan to allow Christian wisdom to encounter, correct and purify the excesses of modernity. Viewed in terms of his corpus as a whole, nuptiality as a theological leitmotif opens up the question of the analogy of freedom within von Balthasar's mature Marian anthropology as well as his groundbreaking ideas about the Marian profile of the Church.[2] This programmatic text from 1948, however, yields two decisive points in terms of theological phenomenology. First, of all the sources in the tradition that bring the revealed theology of nuptiality in the Song of Songs to the fore, the Patristic

---

[1] Hans Urs von Balthasar, 'Theology and Sanctity', in idem, *Explorations in Theology*, vol. 1, *The Word made Flesh* (trans. A. V. Littledale with Alexander Dru; San Francisco: Ignatius, 1989), pp. 181–209. This essay first appeared as 'Theologie und Heiligkeit', *Wort und Wahrheit* 3 (1948): 881–97.

[2] Cf. Brendan Leahy, *The Marian Profile in the Ecclesiology of Hans Urs von Balthasar* (Hyde Park, NY: New City Press, 2000).

inheritance and in particular Origen provides the most important impetus to von Balthasar's way of thinking.³ von Balthasar worked on Origen with Henri de Lubac in Fourvière (1933–7). He published 'Le mystérion d'Origène' in 1936–7 and the anthology of excerpts from Origen entitled *Geist und Feuer* in 1938.⁴ Furthermore, Werner Löser in his still valuable book describes Balthasar's Patristic hermeneutics as a 'theological phenomenology'.⁵ This period was fruitful for the recovery of the model of theology based on Origen's witness, for example, Jean Daniélou's *Origène* (1948),⁶ Henri de Lubac's *Histoire et Esprit* (1950)⁷ and von Balthasar's own *Parole et mystère chez Origène* (1957).⁸ Second, no modern theologian had ever attempted a theological reduction of human existence that looked at the possibility that life itself had become fragmented, viz., divided into separate compartments like religion, society, work, family and play, and stood in need of the restorative unification of Origen's deeply Christianized attachment to 'the spell of the Logos'.⁹ von Balthasar wanted to transpose the very idea of a Christocentric *reductio* (literally, 'a leading back' of all things to God) by 'reading' in a unified way the affairs of the everyday that accompany the fragmentation of contemporary life.

'Theology in the Church', writes von Balthasar, 'proceeds always as a continuous dialogue between Bridegroom and Bride (of whom Mary is the prototype)'.¹⁰ von Balthasar agrees here with the school of Rudolf Bultmann that the encounter with revelation is more a personal encounter borne of faith rather than the scientific discovery of objective evidence. But he does not agree with Bultmann about the merely kerygmatic truth of the message of Jesus Christ. What is needed, then, is an account of the nature of the Church that comprises all the evidence given in the marriage of Bride and Bridegroom as a model

---

³ This theme has now been brilliantly exposited in Michelle K. Borras, 'The Paschal Mystery as Nuptial Mystery in the Theology of Origen of Alexandria', PhD dissertation, John Paul II Institute for Studies of Marriage and Family at The Catholic University of America, 2010.
⁴ Hans Urs von Balthasar, 'Le mystérion d'Origène', *Recherches de science religieuse* 26 (1936): 513–62 and 27 (1937): 38–64; and Origen, *Geist und Feuer. Ein Aufbau aus seinen Werken* (Salzburg: Otto Muller, 1938; revised and expanded edn, 1953); English translation: *Origen: Spirit and Fire* (trans. Robert J. Daly; Washington, DC: The Catholic University of America Press, 1984).
⁵ Werner Löser, *Im Geiste des Origenes: Hans Urs von Balthasar als Interpret der Theologie der Kirchenväter* (Freiburg: Josef Knecht, 1976), p. 11.
⁶ Jean Daniélou, *Origène* (Paris: Table ronde, 1948); English translation: *Origen* (trans. Walter Mitchell; New York: Sheed & Ward, 1955).
⁷ Henri de Lubac, *Histoire et esprit: L'intelligence de l'Écriture d'après Origène* (Paris: Aubier-Montaigne, 1950); English translation: *History and Spirit: The Understanding of Scripture According to Origen* (trans. Anne Englund Nash and Juvenal Merriell; San Francisco: Ignatius Press, 2007).
⁸ Hans Urs von Balthasar, *Parole et mystère chez Origène* (Paris: Cerf, 1957).
⁹ Mihai Vlad Nicolescu, *The Spell of the Logos: Origen's Exegetic Pedagogy in the Contemporary Debate regarding Logocentrism* (Piscataway, NJ: Gorgias Press, 2009).
¹⁰ von Balthasar, 'Theology and Sanctity', p. 201.

for the work of the theologian. von Balthasar turns then to a source whose wisdom he considers without parallel: 'No one in recent years has had such a profound understanding of this law of theology, and applied it so thoroughly, as M. J. Scheeben, for whom everything, even what is most formal, is related to the structure of the *Connubium*.'[11] In short, Matthias Scheeben clarifies that theology participates in a special manner in the bridal holiness of the Church through the Holy Spirit. For example, he writes (quoting Scheeben): 'The Holy Spirit anoints with his light the spiritual eye, and so imparts a moral receptivity enabling us to attain a fuller and purer comprehension of the content of faith; and so our knowledge only comes to full strength and life through the realizing of the supernatural life flowing out within us from the Spirit.'[12] The Spirit teaches the theologian who remains open to the gifts of the Spirit and to 'the strictly mystical charismata and experiences of God'.[13] He is turning to the lives of saints not to advocate spiritual elitism or an assimilation of their heroism but 'that we should be enlightened by them on the inner reality of Christ'.[14]

Martin Buber, he notes, says that 'the lives of such men need a theological commentary; their own words are a contribution to this, but a very fragmentary one'.[15] Moreover, he notes that G. W. F. Hegel famously and programmatically saw the Spirit's consciousness of freedom in terms of the 'cunning of reason (*der List der Vernunft*)'. Drawing upon a chapter heading that appears in *Geist und Feuer*, he adds that the contemporary theologian has a different agenda from that of Hegel, one guided by the cunning of love (*der List der Liebe*). Theology today accordingly requires the form of 'a dialectic pushed to the limit in order to rouse and inflame'.[16] *Connubium* is the true source of the unity of a future theology.

In order to return to 'the things themselves' of lived holiness, von Balthasar must part ways with the notion of phenomenology as a neutral science. The methodological bracketing of all that is factual by Husserl leads to a fatal abstraction, says von Balthasar. 'The life of the saints is theology in practice.'[17] The cleavage between theology at prayer (his terms for Patristics) and theology at the desk (what he imputes to the medieval Schoolmen) must be overcome with a new synthesis. The attentiveness and receptivity to the mouth of God,

---

[11] von Balthasar, 'Theology and Sanctity', p. 202.
[12] von Balthasar, 'Theology and Sanctity', p. 202; original text in M. Scheeben, *Die Mysterien des Christentums* (Freiburg i. Br.: Herder, 1958), p. 740.
[13] von Balthasar, 'Theology and Sanctity', p. 203.
[14] von Balthasar, 'Theology and Sanctity', p. 204.
[15] As for the Martin Buber quotation, see 'The Beginnings of Hasidism', in idem, *Mamre: Essays in Religion* (trans. Greta Hort; Westport, CT.: Greenwood Press, 1946), p. 150.
[16] von Balthasar, 'Theology and Sanctity', p. 205.
[17] von Balthasar, 'Theology and Sanctity', p. 204.

that is, the utterance of Revelation as revelation, comes from prayer and must guide all thinking in faith and knowledge that is derived from faith. This entry to the depths of revelation reveals 'the wisdom of God in a mystery, a wisdom which is hidden, which God ordained before the world, unto our glory'.[18]

A First Glance at 'Supernatural Phenomenology' (1950)

Two years after 'Theology and Sanctity', the book *Therese von Lisieux: Geschichte einer Sendung* ('Thérèse of Lisieux: The Story of a Mission') appeared.[19] It was written a full decade before the first volume of the trilogy and at the cusp of the publication of his monumental book on Karl Barth.[20] Balthasar himself reports of two counterweights in the original title. The first admission is quite blunt: 'The Story of a Mission' is a deeper insight into the Little Flower's own title: 'The Story of a Soul'.[21] von Balthasar lays bare in his *Geschichte* the missing dramatic encounter in the psychologistic banalizations of the saint's life. The second counterweight has to do with the intentionality of the 'little way' of St Thérèse. von Balthasar writes that 'it was necessary to set up the counterweight of the "little way" and of the simple fulfilment of a commission against the ever-threatening danger in Carmel and in the Church of a one-sided exaltation of the grandiose subjectivity of the Great Teresa and of the spiritual radicalism of John of the Cross so that these become the absolute canon of mysticism and of holiness'.[22] Here we see another glimpse into von Balthasar's free acknowledgement that Christian spirituality needs to find more quotidian soil if it is to flourish and spread in the world today.

Like the Cuban-American theologian Alejandro García-Rivera, who himself promoted the 'little stories' of Latino popular Catholicism as a starting point for theological methodology, von Balthasar recognizes that the Catholic mosaic is constructed out of many *tesserae*.[23] The brilliance of each one lies in what

---

[18] 1 Cor. 2.7, as cited in von Balthasar, 'Theology and Sanctity', p. 209.
[19] The English translation, *Two Sisters in the Spirit: Thérèse of Lisieux & Elizabeth of the Trinity* (trans. Donald Nichols, Anne Englund Nash, Dennis Martin; San Francisco: Ignatius, 1992), is based upon the 1970 reprint of *Schwestern im Geist*. Essentially, von Balthasar himself bundled two books from the early 1950s into one with a new foreword and a reworking (done by Cornelia Capol) of the citations to *Histoire d'une âme* to correspond to the critical edition.
[20] Han Urs von Balthasar, *Karl Barth: Darstellung und Deutung seiner Theologie* (Cologne/Olten: Hegner, 1951).
[21] Hans Urs von Balthasar, *My Work: In Retrospect* (trans. Brian McNeill, Kenneth Batinovich, John Saward and Kelly Hamilton; San Francisco: Ignatius, 1993), p. 33.
[22] von Balthasar, *My Work*, p. 33.
[23] Alejandro García-Rivera, *St Martin de Porres: The "Little Stories" and the Semiotics of Culture*

it contributes to the whole mosaic. The distinctive contribution of the Little Flower lies in her singular and total grasp of the Christian doctrine of spiritual childhood.[24] von Balthasar clearly misreads Thérèse and the Carmelite tradition to the extent he is claiming that the Little Flower deliberately hid her sense of mission or that the Order of Carmelites put Teresa of Avila and John of the Cross on a pedestal reserved for the real mystics. But these are productive and highly revealing misreadings, ones that yield great insight into the new form of theology that von Balthasar hoped to midwife.[25]

Yet beyond that self-disclosure, he introduces *his* story of *her* mission with the surprising avowal to undertake 'a theological phenomenology'.[26] With this unusual juxtaposition of opposed terms, von Balthasar interjects into his discourse both overtness and a concealment. Does von Balthasar use the term in the sense coined by Edmund Husserl and then refined (sometimes, in fact, in conversation with theology) by Husserl's followers such as Martin Heidegger and Max Scheler? Is that the audience to whom he is appealing in this remarkable plea? If so, what is the new meaning assigned to the task of phenomenology by the adjective?[27]

von Balthasar displayed a keen interest in establishing the building blocks of a phenomenology of the saints from the time that he was writing *Apokalypse der deutschen Seele*. For example, his treatment of the poet Goethe reflected a search for the possible metaphysical dimensions of the poet's morphology and as such shows how he had already begun to cull what he needed for his own theology from a poet whom he held in both reverence and abeyance.[28] His treatment in the *Apokalypse* of Max Scheler's phenomenology of *Ehrfurcht* (reverence, deep respect) also betrays a methodological interest in balancing the active and passive elements of a phenomenological approach into an empathic, loving embrace with the witness of a religious visionary.[29]

(Maryknoll, NY: Orbis, 1995).

[24] Cf. Steven Payne, O.C.D., *St Thérèse of Lisieux: Doctor of the Universal Church* (Staten Island: Alba House, 2002).

[25] I am using 'misreading' here not as an outright falsehood but in the inevitably generative sense of authorship, as in Harold Bloom's recovery of misprision in *The Anxiety of Influence: A Theory of Poetry* (2nd edn; New York: Oxford University Press, 1997).

[26] von Balthasar, *Two Sisters in the Spirit*, p. 39.

[27] Von Balthasar is writing prior to the so-called 'theological turn' in recent phenomenology. There are striking similarities between Balthasar's proposal for a theological phenomenology as a transposition of a metaphysics of analogy and this new development in the French school, but the two positions cannot in the end be assimilated to one another.

[28] See Virginia Raquel Azcuy, *La figura de Thérèse de Lisieux: Ensayo de fenomenología teológica según Hans Urs von Balthasar* (Buenos Aires: Teología, 1997), vol. 2, pp. 334–6 ('¿Fenomenología teológica o "Spiegelinterpretation?"').

[29] See Hans Urs von Balthasar, *Apokalypse der deutschen Seele*, vol. 3, *Die Vergöttlichung des Todes*

Another source for von Balthasar's early path to phenomenology, heavily cited by von Balthasar himself, is the writings on culture of the father of modern sociology, Georg Simmel (1858–1918).[30] In 'Life as Transcendence' (1918), for example, Simmel performs his own blood transfusion into the burgeoning field of sociology of religion (for example, that of Émile Durkheim), one that makes possible the radical idea that openness to the unbounded absolute is the key to grasping the meaning of existence as a whole:

> That man [sic] overcomes himself means that he reaches out beyond the bounds that the moment sets for him. There must be something at hand to be overcome, but it is only there in order to be overcome. Thus even as an ethical agent, man is the limited being that has no limit.[31]

von Balthasar dedicated himself to interpreting Simmel in the *Apokalypse*.[32] Through Simmel von Balthasar was acquainted with a thinker that examined the life of the metropolis and the life of the economy as fields of action for interpersonal encounters undertaken by agents open to life with the Triune God.

The question of whether von Balthasar can be seen as using the term 'phenomenology' in a strict sense still remains open. David Moss takes issue with the assignment of any formal sense of theological phenomenology to Balthasar's treatment of the saints.[33] He argues that von Balthasar displays the witnessing character of holy lives without undertaking a formal analysis (even though he also adumbrates his own phenomenological reduction). He still recognizes the novelty of the approach, for his sense of the formal object of study in the contemplation of the lives of the saints clearly outstrips moralism.[34] von Balthasar himself, for example, says that 'Therese is a warrior even though her battles are fought for love by means of love.'[35] The Little Flower's witness is thus the human archetype of cadaver obedience, the same form of existence that the Son of God displayed passively in his descent into the realm of the dead.[36] In writing her testimony under obedience to her superior while suffering from

---

(Einsiedeln: Johannes Verlag, 1998), pp. 148–52; and Virginia Azcuy, *La figura de Thérèse de Lisieux*, vol. 2, pp. 333–4.

[30] Elizabeth S. Goodstein, 'Style as Substance: Georg Simmel's Phenomenology of Culture', *Cultural Critique* 52 (Fall 2002): 209–34.

[31] Georg Simmel, *The View of Life: Four Metaphysical Essays with Journal Aphorisms* (trans. John A. Y. Andrews and Donald N. Levine; Chicago: University of Chicago Press, 2010), p. 6.

[32] von Balthasar, *Apokalypse*, vol. 3, pp. 231–4.

[33] David Moss, 'Prayer and the Saints', in *The Cambridge Companion to Hans Urs von Balthasar* (eds Edward T. Oakes, S.J. and David Moss; Cambridge: Cambridge University Press, 2004), pp. 84–92.

[34] A similar read on von Balthasar can be found in Danielle Nussberger, 'Theology Made Flesh: Hans Urs von Balthasar and the Saints', PhD dissertation, University of Notre Dame, 2008.

[35] von Balthasar, *Two Sisters in the Spirit*, p. 241.

[36] Moss, 'Prayers and the Saints', p. 89.

tuberculosis, St Thérèse displays to her reader a path to the 'how' of holiness that is practical and imitable without pretending to overcome the necessary *diastasis* that remains between the faithful follower and the divine Beloved. This informal analysis still leaves unanswered the pivotal question about the mode of presentation of holiness in that or in any saint's memoir.

Moss's point still underscores the casual nature of von Balthasar's coinage of a term. von Balthasar posits the idea of a theological phenomenology but, for example, fails to identify a reduction. In von Balthasar's own words, the task seems eminently practical: 'few things are likely to vitalize and rejuvenate theology, and therefore the whole of the Christian life, as a blood transfusion from hagiography'.[37] Rather than announcing a new method, von Balthasar is pointing to the need to move the study of the saints into the heart of the task of theology. Without a blood transfusion the patient is likely to remain sickly. This practical undertaking still requires a form of thinking that looks at the display of holiness in the manner of what philosopher Thomas Prufer called 'datives of manifestation', that is, not just *what* the saints manifest (what Prufer calls genitives of manifestation) but their manner of 'manifesting to'.[38] As genitives of manifestation, the saints show timeless virtues. These moral teachings on holiness are quite necessary, but the so-called 'blood transfusion' – to carry out the entirety of its intended effect – needs to attend also to the form of presentation of holiness.

There are several excellent studies that render the main lines of Balthasarian theology into a phenomenological key. Robert Sokolowski's *Eucharistic Presence* and Virginia Raquel Azcuy's *La figura de Teresa de Lisieux* are illustrative.[39] Both works merit careful scrutiny even though they diverge sharply on the question that is the focus of our attention. What separates these studies is decisive for grasping the possibilities and limits of the marker 'theological phenomenology'. Sokolowski assimilates the Balthasarian method into a Neo-Aristotelian reading of Husserlian phenomenology under the rubric of 'a theology of disclosure'.[40] The method of disclosure for Sokolowski is in spite of its rigour and clarity an antidote to modern theology's obsession with method. A theology of disclosure

---

[37] von Balthasar, *Two Sisters in the Spirit*, p. 39.
[38] Thomas Prufer, 'Husserl, Heidegger, Early and Late, and Aquinas', in idem, *Recapitulations: Essays in Philosophy* (Washington, DC: The Catholic University of America Press, 1993), pp. 72–90.
[39] Robert Sokolowski, *Eucharistic Presence: A Theology of Disclosure* (Washington, DC: The Catholic University of America Press, 1994), and Virginia Raquel Azcuy, *La figura de Thérèse de Lisieux*.
[40] See Peter Casarella, 'Questioning the Primacy of Method: On Sokolowski's Eucharistic Presence', *Communio: International Catholic Review* 22 (Winter 1995): 668–701; and Oscar Cantú, 'Identity through presence and absence: Robert Sokolowski's theology of disclosure and his contribution to eucharistic theology', PhD dissertation, Pontificia Università Gregoriana, 2011.

holds in check the modern tendency to keep the transcendentals of beauty and truth in abeyance through a claim for methodological neutrality by attending to their appearance in sacramental form and action. Azcuy's approach highlights the early Balthasar's fascination with an existentialism stemming from Goethe and Scheler and thus introduces a counterpoint to the possible essentialism that may arise in seeking out datives of manifestation in the lives of saints.[41]

The real distinction between essence and existence, especially as articulated by von Balthasar's master Przywara, precludes any ranking of one over the other. A life in its unity reveals a pattern of existences whose meaning transcends the fleetingness of existence. In that act we can discern the form of goodness that constitutes the highest act of existence. von Balthasar considered the good the highest act of existence and differentiated his 'theo-logic' from that of Jean-Luc Marion on this basis.[42] The phenomenological path opened up by von Balthasar can thus be negatively demarcated as not essentialist, not existentialist and not centred on the Dionysian dynamics of a good beyond being. Within this field of alternatives, Przywara's notion of the 'rhythm' of the *analogia entis* as one that hovers between positive and negative theologies characterizes the positive content of the new coinage: 'theological phenomenology'.[43] Accordingly, there is no unmediated access to the essential forms of human acting in their metaphysical constitution apart from the displays of freedom made evident in lived existence. By the same token, the rhythm of existence maintains its unity by virtue of the vertical relationship to the absolute. Without this openness to transcendence to a being whose very essence is existence (in a coincidence of opposites that transcends finite understanding), lived existence degenerates into the chaos of Heraclitean flux.

---

[41] See Azcuy, *La figura de Thérèse de Lisieux*, vol. 1, pp. 106–7.

[42] Ilkamarina Kuhr approaches the question through a thoughtful comparison with the work of Jean-Luc Marion in *Gabe und Gestalt: Theologische Phänomenologie bei Hans Urs von Balthasar* (Regensburg: Puistet, 2012). According to his *Theologik*, vol. 2, *Wahrheit Gottes* (Einsiedeln: Johannes Veralg, 1985), Balthasar's understanding of the good was closer to that of Claude Bruaire than to that found in Marion's still introductory theological work, *Dieu sans l'être. Hors-texte* (Paris: Presses Universitaires de France, 1982). On Bruaire in this regard, see, above all, Antonio López, *Spirit's Gift: The Metaphysical Insight of Claude Bruaire* (Washington, DC: The Catholic University of America Press, 2006).

[43] John R. Betz, 'Translator's Introduction', in Erich Pryzwara, *Analogia Entis: Metaphysics: Original Structure and Universal Rhythm* (trans. John R. Betz and David Bentley Hart; Grand Rapids, MI: Eerdmans, 2014), p. 79.

Ecclesial Renewal in Lieu of Solitary Authorship (1954–84)

What evidence remains for von Balthasar's commitment to theological phenomenology after 1950? In his testament from the 'apex' of life (his term), Balthasar says that the integrated testimony of the new ecclesial communities is his favourite part of the aesthetics: 'In a concert one instrument must no longer sound like *one* instrument – the ensemble is involved, the whole orchestra…In their integrity [these twelve theologians] let the sound of what I have wanted to make heard ring out.'[44] von Balthasar published through Johannes Verlag fellow travellers to fulfil his mission as the concert master of true catholicity. In order to shed light on these dynamics, we can look at a trajectory of texts that were published in the decades that followed the book on Thérèse: *Gelebte Kirche. Bernanos*; *Im Gottes Einsatz Leben*; and *Unser Auftrag*. These texts lay the groundwork for the trilogy. The book on Bernanos was completed four years after the completion of both the book on Barth and the study of Thérése.[45] Even though his writings are not primarily poetic, the book is an analysis of an important figure in the history of what von Balthasar calls *katholische Dichtung*.[46] von Balthasar explicitly disavows presenting Bernanos as a saint or even as a lay theologian.[47] He is even qualified about assigning to him the designation of 'practicing Catholic'.[48] The approach to Bernanos constitutes in the end a phenomenology of 'a lived witness of a great Christian'.[49] In a manner highly reminiscent of the recently completed treatment of Thérèse, Bernanos's literary production is transposed to the key of a Christian mission to become engaged in the world.[50]

Engagement with God is the concise introduction to what is offered in a more ample way in the *Theo-Drama*.[51] It offers more than a preview. The key is the claim made upon the believer of God's involvement, *Gottes Einsatz*. von Balthasar is not talking about an intrinsically unfathomable reality that we

---

[44] von Balthasar, *My Work*, p. 108.
[45] Hans Urs von Balthasar, *Gelebte Kirche. Bernanos* (Cologne/Olten: Hegner, 1954); English translation: *Bernanos: An Ecclesial Existence* (trans. Erasmo Leiva-Merikakis; San Francisco: Ignatius, 1996).
[46] Maurice de Gandillac wisely states: 'Le mot *Dichtung* est difficile à traduire. Suivant les contextes, nous rendons *Dichter* par <<créateur,>> <<poète,>> <<écrivain,>> ou <<romancier>>'. Hans Urs von Balthasar, *Le chrétien Bernanos* (trans. M. de Gandillac; Paris: Éditions du Seuil, 1956), p. 9 n. 1.
[47] von Balthasar, *Bernanos*, p. 17.
[48] von Balthasar, *Bernanos*, p. 19.
[49] von Balthasar, *Bernanos*, p. 101.
[50] von Balthasar, *Bernanos*, pp. 202–3.
[51] Cf. Margaret Turek, 'Foreword', in Hans Urs von Balthasar, *Engagement with God: The Drama of Christian Discipleship* (trans. R. J. Halliburton; San Francisco: Ignatius, 2008), p. x.

know only partially, that is, *quoad nos*. The Scriptures reveal a distinct form of involvement on God's part. *Einsatz* is a form of involvement that penetrates into the depth of another reality: one thing is placed in the midst of the other. The engagement is revealed to be a double bind and a paradox. God acts through the mission of the Son of God sent by the Father to offer a new form of freedom to humanity. The Son of God descends into the depth of human suffering (in fact, to a realm called 'hell')[52] so that the adopted children may be placed by God into the divine communion. *Gottes Einsatz* thus defines a double engagement, from the divine persons to suffering humanity and from the uniting of the cry of each suffering individual to the prior engagement by God. Too many attempts have been made in modern Christianity, von Balthasar opines, to erect humanitarian and social programmes that lose sight of the centrality of this double engagement and its essentially paradoxical nature.

For von Balthasar only a Christianity that chooses to disavow its core message sees the fundamental challenge of our age as an ethical encounter between Christian values and the forms of progress championed by the world. The fundamental challenge is to grasp the dramatic encounter between chooser and chosen in both the history of Israel and in the revelation of the person of Jesus Christ, the latter being disclosed as 'God's engagement'. The section of the *Theo-Drama* on finite and infinite freedom is sketched in outline here.[53] The whole of revelation leading up to the loving obedience of Jesus casts a negative judgement on the attempt to rely one-sidedly on a structural change in human existence.[54] Without extracting the individual from the created gift of interpersonal communion, the interior transformation made possible by God's engagement on our behalf must by necessity precede structural transformation. von Balthasar is greatly concerned about eschatology and the centrality of the irreducible claim for a victory over death. This is decisive not just for an otherworldly articulation of last things but for seeing the ineluctable place of mortality and injustice even now within a philosophy of history: 'The subject of secular history, however, is not an abstract humanity that exists throughout the centuries, but rather the concrete number of human beings, thousands of whom die at every moment.'[55] Instead of advocating a social utopia, the leitmotif of this work is rooted in the sacramental realism of the gospel of John. He talks about

---

[52] Cf. von Balthasar, *Engagement with God*, p. 36.
[53] Hans Urs von Balthasar, *Theo-Drama*, vol. 2, *Dramatis Personae: Man in God* (trans. Graham Harrison; San Francisco: Ignatius, 1990), pp. 189–429.
[54] von Balthasar, *Engagement with God*, p. 79.
[55] von Balthasar, *Engagement with God*, p. 57.

'staying' and 'abiding in the source'.⁵⁶ Following Origen, von Balthasar attempts to translate the doctrine of ceaseless prayer into an integrated form of existence, action and receptivity to the grace of God revealed in the person of Jesus Christ. That way of being in the world, however unanticipated that may be, is what it means to abide in the source.

There is another key to reading this text, especially if considered together with his testimony from life's 'apex'. von Balthasar writes on the title page of this book: 'These pages belong to Luigi Giussani and his movement Communion and Liberation.'⁵⁷ Strangely, the dedication is not to be found anywhere in the English translation of 2008. Peter Henrici reports that the friendship with Giussani and his movement (along with a growing group of doctoral students and the collaborators from the journal *Communio*) were the three real sources of inspiration that sustained von Balthasar in his last years.⁵⁸ The friendship with Giussani indeed went very deep. Balthasar published Giussani's books and gave talks and retreats for the movement. The friendship included the warning by von Balthasar that the movement should never become enclosed in itself, content with itself and its successes.⁵⁹

Why did von Balthasar believe that his support for such communities was more important than publishing his own works? First and foremost, von Balthasar is adamantly opposed to the idea of a remnant Church.⁶⁰ At the same time he acknowledges that the task of engagement is left to a small flock. At face value, there is an outright contradiction between disavowing triumphalism and encouraging his readers to think that the future of the Church lies in a new aristocracy of genuine saints.⁶¹ The starting point of von Balthasar's commitment to ecclesial existence for the sake of the world has to do with the

---

⁵⁶ von Balthasar, *Engagement with God*, pp. 48–51. One source for the latter idea is Romano Guardini, as we can see from the very title of von Balthasar's biography, *Romano Guardini: Reform from the Source* (trans. Albert Wimmer and D. C. Schindler; San Francisco: Ignatius, 2010).
⁵⁷ Hans Urs von Balthasar, *In Gottes Einsatz leben* (Einsiedeln: Johannes, 1971), p. 5. The first edition of *Reinhold Schneider: Sein Weg und Sein Werk* (Cologne/Olten: Hegner, 1953) was 'written for and dedicated to the Secular Institutes'. The new dedication of 1971 is but a further specification of the same theme.
⁵⁸ Peter Henrici, 'Erster Blick auf Hans Urs von Balthasar', in *Hans Urs von Balthasar: Gestalt und Werk* (eds Karl Lehmann and Walter Kasper; Cologne: Communio, 1989), p. 58.
⁵⁹ Hans Urs von Balthasar, 'Introduzione', in Luigi Giussani, *Alla ricerca del volto umano* (Milan: Jaca, 1984), p. 6.
⁶⁰ von Balthasar, *Engagement with God*, pp. 96–7.
⁶¹ This phrase does not occur in *Engagement with God* but is developed at some length in his book on Reinhold Schneider; Hans Urs von Balthasar, *Tragedy under Grace: Reinhold Schneider on the Experience of the West* (trans. Brian McNeil; San Francisco: Ignatius, 1997). For an astute commentary, see Juan M. Sara, 'Secular Institutes according to Hans Urs von Balthasar', *Communio: International Catholic Review* 29 (Summer 2002): 309-36 (328); and Peter Henrici, 'Erster Blick auf Hans Urs von Balthasar', p. 58. von Balthasar, 'Introduzione', p. 6.

choice of a state of life in the light of the evangelical counsels of poverty, chastity and obedience. von Balthasar maintained that the witness of Christ through the counsels was *not* reserved to priests and the religious and sought to re-evaluate the idea of a secular institute on this very basis. Daniela Mohr has mounted a remarkably thorough but ultimately unconvincing argument that von Balthasar overdetermines the theology of the evangelical counsels by applying the norms of the religious life to the whole of the Christian life.[62] Her criticism nevertheless brings to light the central issue in considering the counsels as an expression of theological phenomenology. Theological phenomenology ultimately reveals that life lived in obedience to the evangelical counsels is a life lived at the heart of reality. Given this radical claim, von Balthasar must now explain how this unique and particular vision of Christian discipleship can serve as an ordering principle for life itself.

von Balthasar carefully delineates the unity and difference of marriage and the consecrated life. This is the fulfilment of the promissory note delivered in 'Theology and Sanctity'. This unity bespeaks an ordering that transcends the social or religious exchange that takes place between married couples and those who pray in monasteries and convents. The unity, as D. C. Schindler illustrates, can be seen in the scope of rational reflection seen within two concentric circles.[63] The inner circle starts from faith, gives rise to theology and issues forth in the vows to consecrated life. The outer circle starts from reason, gives rise to philosophy and issues forth in the vows to sacramental marriage. The circles are ordered to one another in a manner that also allows for their mutual penetration. This ordering of affairs between the Church and the world shows how the witness of the Church lies not above or apart from the mission to serve the world but within its very heart. In choosing a state of life, one is not elevating oneself to a higher or lower plane than other followers of Christ. At the same time, the choice of a state of life does not take place within a metaphysical vacuum; it stands within an ordered grasp of reality as a whole: '[F]or Balthasar, the importance of the secular institutes lies in their proposal of a new unity between "the worldly state and the state of God [*Weltstand und Gottestand*]," between the original impulse of the Gospel and the needs of today's post-Christian world.' [64] The integration of the two circles of existence is the mode of knowing, being and acting whereby these two dimensions of reality

---

[62] Daniela Mohr, *Existenz im Herzen der Kirche. Zur Theologie der Säkularinstitute im Leben und Werk Hans Urs von Balthasars* (Würzburg: Echter, 2000).
[63] D. C. Schindler, *The Catholicity of Reason* (Grand Rapids, MI: Eerdmans, 2013), pp. 324–33.
[64] Sara, 'Secular Institutes according to Hans Urs von Balthasar', p. 310.

remain distinct yet intertwined. Integration without any loss of distinction thus also names von Balthasar's interior grasp of the social mission of the Catholic communion.

The View from Life's Apex (1975)

One true virtue of Balthasar's theological explorations lies in the author's persistent search for a common theme to his own activity as a writer. The essays written at ten-year intervals and collected in English translation as *My Work: In Retrospect* offer testimony to the earnestness as well as the inherently problematic nature of that search.[65] The one penned at the age of 70 is a case in point. He avows at that juncture to have reached what the Bible takes to be 'life's apex' even though he freely admits that he put on the very same airs of immodesty in a retrospective written just ten years earlier. He makes two introductory points about his mature perception of his writing activity, muses rather briefly on the achievement of the trilogy and then reveals what he takes to be the lasting import of his legacy.

Cornelia Capol, a recently deceased member of the Community of St John who accompanied von Balthasar with great devotion from an early stage, describes the essay from the apex as different in kind from the earlier retrospectives: 'Finally, in a kind of pause, as one already looking toward the close of his life, he gave once again an account of what had been achieved, in a clear shift of emphasis away from his "authorship" in favor of pastoral work in the communities he founded.'[66] The two introductory remarks by von Balthasar clarify the kind of 'pause' that the heretofore determined 'author' may have intended. First, von Balthasar opines borrowing from Hector Berlioz that 'one is so taken with a fixed idea [...] that it is present even in works that are not so-called masterpieces.'[67] The style and the truth of the fixed idea necessarily converge so that the idea has its own form of expression in the author's work. The idea becomes 'actual' when the reader sees the idea in its originality, that is, not as a refraction of the fads of the day. Another form of actuality arises when the author's readership responds to the irreversible publicness of authorship by confirming the actuality of a theme that the author may not originally have seen as decisive. Balthasar says he has no right *or possibility* of taking an actuality of

---

[65] von Balthasar, *My Work*.
[66] Cornelia Capol, 'Foreword', in von Balthasar, *My Work*, p. 7.
[67] von Balthasar, *My Work*, p. 94.

this sort away from his readers. Any author must admit that works have a life of their own, and he or she can explain only their origins. The author cannot retrospectively maintain control over how the meaning of a work evolves in changing circumstances. At face value, this stance is the opposite of virtuosity but conceals other, even more revealing vulnerabilities. von Balthasar's avowed sense of his own authorship is, in spite of himself, close to Promethean; his sense of a need for self-dispossession is self-consciously Marian.

The second prefatory remark is less cryptic but even more telling: 'The activity of being a writer remains and will always remain, in the working-out of my life, a secondary function, something *faute de mieux*.' What, then, is the primary goal of his life if not writing? von Balthasar testifies that *all* of his activity as a writer is subordinated to one task – 'renewing the Church through the formation of new communities that unite the radical Christian life of conformity to the evangelical counsels of Jesus with existence in the midst of the world, whether by practicing secular professions or through the ministerial priesthood to give new life to living communities'.[68] In short, von Balthasar would rather serve the cause of Jesus in aiding in the founding of new Christian communities than write books. But he is obviously not pretending to encroach upon the specific domain of pastoral planning for which he possessed only limited skills. For von Balthasar the concrete cause of Jesus is followed in the Church, and the concrete proposal to which he alludes here is his proposal of what he called the secular institutes. In short, he is suggesting that the founding of the Community of St John is by far his greatest achievement and not one that can be separated from his activity as a writer.

What then is the ecclesial *raison d'être* of von Balthasar's massive *opus*? If one is going to write books in the service of the Church, von Balthasar continues, then the activity of the writer has to be judged in two ways, that is, first in terms of the writer's fundamental disposition and then in terms of the writer's ability to disseminate that disposition 'in the multiplicity of responses to the demands of the present'.[69] In order to articulate the fundamental disposition, the brief essay 'from the apex' offers a succinct summary of the trilogy. In 1975 he had just completed *Theodramatik* II, 1 (in English, *Theo-Drama* vol. 2). The volumes of the trilogy dedicated to aesthetics were complete, but the volumes on drama and logic remained incomplete. What can be learned from this about von Balthasar's confrontation with modernity? von Balthasar implies that even

---

[68] von Balthasar, *My Work*, p. 95.
[69] von Balthasar, *My Work*, p. 95.

to say that his own contribution lies in the recovery of beauty misses the mark. He betrays a consistent concern since his first encounter with the rigorous mode of discernment in St Ignatius of Loyola of the dangers of aestheticism. His main advice to his readers is to try to appreciate the thoroughly unmodern and deeply Biblical character of his path to aesthetics: beauty is surpassed 'in "glory" in the sense of the splendour of the divinity of God himself as manifested in the life, death and Resurrection of Jesus and reflected, according to St Paul in 2 Cor. 3.18, in Christians who look upon their Lord and in doing so are transformed by his glory'.[70] His remarks about the reading of the *Theo-Drama* are equally illuminating. The many reductionist tendencies of modern theology all aim away from the 'epic' genre of scholastic thought and towards drama, but none of these individual tendencies are capable of attaining the proper synthesis because they lack an integrating 'dramatic instrumentation' of the literary and lived theatre, and thus life itself.[71] The convergence of the *disiecta membra* of modern theology in a properly theo-dramatic centre is the chief focus of Balthasar's retrospective. From that vantage point one can grasp his prioritizing of divine polyphony over modern ideas of pluralism and his elision of hasty 'de-Mediterreanization' with 'de-biblicization' by virtue of the modernizer's neglect of Palestine and its connection to the east.[72] He summarizes with this testimony:

> Only when God appears on the world stage (and at the same time remains behind the scenes) can one work what the persons of the drama stand for, what "laws" this dramatic action follows, a dramatic action ultimately without parallel, because it constitutes the ultimate drama. *All this is what every Christian knows in a spontaneous and unselfconscious way and what he strives to live out.* What I am trying to do is to express this in a form in which all the dimensions and tensions of life remain present instead of being sublimated in the abstractions of a "systematic" theology.[73]

von Balthasar's self-distancing from the main lines of modern theology goes much deeper than the rejection of the academic label of 'systematics' (a move already present in Barth's *Church Dogmatics*).[74] von Balthasar also abjures

---

[70] von Balthasar, *My Work*, pp. 96–7.
[71] von Balthasar, *My Work*, p. 98.
[72] von Balthasar, *My Work*, pp. 103, 99.
[73] von Balthasar, *My Work*, p. 98; italics added.
[74] On Barth's resistance to 'systematic theology', see Eberhard Busch, *Karl Barth: His Life from Letters and Autobiographical Texts* (trans. John Bowden; Philadelphia: Fortress, 1976), pp. 211-12, as cited in D. Stephen Long, *Saving Karl Barth: Hans Urs von Balthasar's Preoccupation* (Minneapolis: Fortress Press, 2014), p. 10. For von Balthasar one can still try to render key concepts like revelation and faith into the function of guiding principles for a systematic theology, but the project of

fundamental theology as a discipline that ignores the self-authentication of the Word of God and its profoundly personal and direct impact on the human heart.[75] The value of Balthasar's synthesis is that the diverse vectors of thought and intellectual protagonists moving in multiple directions (including Eastern religiosity and Marxism) will now be led into one central arena so that each of the valuable non-Christian insights can be held up for view in the proper light of God's action on behalf of humanity.

The central second volume of the *Theo-Drama* bears the title *Dramatis Personae*, that is, a cast of characters.[76] In other words, the key to navigating the shoals of modern theology is to begin with the assignment of roles, an assignment that like God's will is allotted on earth as it is in heaven. 'Testing everything and retaining what is good'[77] required a deliberate boldness that was counterbalanced by a more temperate approach. This dual approach is first addressed by announcing the leitmotif of nuptiality in the essay 'Theology and Sanctity' and comes in new ways to dominate his mature theological reflection. With the latter development the nuptial rhythm in theology now erupts in theo-dramatic terms. Theo-drama thus becomes the fundamental disposition at the very centre of the trilogy.

How had von Balthasar disseminated the fundamental disposition of the trilogy in his more occasional works written between 1965 and 1975? The author's discussion 'from life's apex' provides a rare glimpse into von Balthasar's self-image among academic theologians. Some might be surprised that he defers to Karl Rahner as the true master of occasional writings even as he continues to battle the fundamentals of his theological orientation.[78] He also highlights the role of thinkers whose wisdom, he says, sustains him daily – the theology of Origen (especially in the anthology that he himself assembled under the title of 'Spirit and Fire') and the poetry of Paul Claudel, whose work he had also translated and assimilated.[79] Not surprisingly, the essay concludes with a *passionate* plea to his readers to recognize the influence of Adrienne von Speyr and of similar ecclesial projects of renewal on his thinking. The Communion and Liberation movement, though only given that title in 1969 by Luigi Giussani,

---

systematizing always remains subject to the countervalent proviso of pneumatology. Cf. Sergio Silva, 'La teología fundamental de Balthasar', *Teología y Vida* 50 (2009): 225–41 (231–5).

[75] Ibid., 100–1.
[76] In the original German: 'Die Personen des Spiels'.
[77] Cf. 1 Thess. 5.21.
[78] von Balthasar, *My Work*, p. 100.
[79] von Balthasar, *My Work*, pp. 108–9.

is mentioned by name in the essay. In both these respects, the passion of this closing reflects the 'pause' about which Capol wisely spoke.

Conclusion

What, then, is 'supernatural' or 'theological phenomenology'? Moss avers that 'Balthasar's approach here does not so much aspire to the pretension of a sheerly scientific and objective phenomenology, as it tries to respond to the givenness, or inner order (*taxis, ordo*) of God's love.'[80] Edith Stein's work would be an example of theological phenomenology in this sense.[81] Expanding upon Moss's initial insight, we could then say that the 'reductions' or 'bracketings' in Balthasar's transpositions approximate the 'creaturely metaphysics' of Erich Pryzwara's *Analogia Entis* (1932) inasmuch as von Balthasar seeks the Christian rhythm 'whereby the lives of the saints become real parables of the inner-divine life of God, based as these lives are upon that foundation of that coincidence of mission and person that characterizes the chief protagonist in the drama of salvation: Jesus Christ.'[82] As Moss himself suggests, there is an earlier tradition of 'reduction' that inspires von Balthasar, namely, the one that guides St Bonaventure's *De reductione artium ad theologiam*.[83] The medieval cousin of theological phenomenology is what St Bonaventure in his First *Collation on the Six Days* calls *metaphysica reducens*.[84] Christ is at the centre of all reasoning. In Heideggerian terms, Christ is the proper focus of what we need to elicit from our engagement in the world beyond *ta physika*, beyond beings understood as beings.[85] The task of sanctity embodied in the lives of the saints leads us back to that 'logical' and meta-anthropological centre of our thinking about God and God's manifestation in the world of human activity.

---

[80] Moss, 'Prayer and the Saints', p. 85.
[81] Cf. Alasdair MacIntyre, *Edith Stein: A Philosophical Prologue 1913-1922* (Lanham, MD: Rowman & Littlefield, 2006).
[82] Moss, 'Prayer and the Saints', pp. 85-6.
[83] Cf. Emma T. Healy, 'The Theory of the *Reductio*', in St Bonaventure, *De Reductione Artium ad Theologiam* (St Bonaventure, NY: The Franciscan Institute, 1955), pp. 119-21; and José Daniel López, 'Aportes sístematicos y metodológicos de una fenomenología de la encarnación para una antropología trinitaria', in Sonia Vargas Andrade (ed.), *Antropología trinitaria para nuestros pueblos* (Bogotá: Publicaciones CELAM, 2014), pp. 75-87 (82).
[84] *Collationes in Hexaemeron* I, 17 in St Bonaventure, *Opera Omnia* (Ad Aquas Claras: Quaracchi, 1882-1902), vol. 5, p. 332. Cf. Emmanuel Falque, 'The Phenomenological Act of *Perscrutatio* in the *Proemium* of St Bonaventure's Commentary on the Sentences', *Medieval Philosophy and Theology* 10 (2001): 1-22.
[85] Martin Heidegger, *Introduction to Metaphysics* (trans. Ralph Manheim; New Haven, CT: Yale University Press, 1959), p. 17.

8

Karol Wojtyła's Aims and Methodology

Adrian Reimers

Interpreting Wojtyła: A Proposal

The theology of the body lies at the heart of Karol Wojtyła's thought. The nature of human love is the conceptual focus of his thought and writing up to the October 1978 Conclave, as well as a kind of link between his scholarship and his papacy, for the first major catechesis of his papacy was precisely the theology of the body. In other words, if we regard *Person and Act* as his philosophical masterwork and culmination of his philosophical reasoning, then we are led into thinking that Karol Wojtyła's principal concerns were philosophical, and his election to the papacy the abrupt end of an interesting philosophical career. If *Person and Act* is his central work, then our task is threefold: to interpret this difficult book as a contribution to an ongoing conversation among certain continental philosophers; to tease out the ontology implicit in this personalist phenomenology; and to determine whether he has broken with the Thomistic tradition, for which he frequently expresses admiration. I suggest, however, that for a more accurate reading of the Wojtyłan corpus, his thought should be interpreted in terms of the later work *Man and Woman He Created Them*, originally written in Polish and eventually presented as the theology of the body audiences.[1] Precisely *this* is his fundamental work in relation to which all his other writings make sense.

---

[1] Cezary Ritter, 'Posłowie: Uwagi historyczno-edytorskie w związku z Jana Pawła II katechezami "Mężczyzną i niewiastą stworzył ich"', in Karol Wojtyła, *Mężczyzną i niewiastą stworzył ich* (Lublin: Wydawnictwo KUL, 2008). See also M. Waldstein, 'Introduction', in John Paul II, *Man and Woman He Created Them: A Theology of the Body* (trans. Michael Waldstein; Boston: Pauline Books & Media, 2006), pp. 6–11.

This thesis also helps to resolve a controversy among Catholic philosophers about the nature of his thinking. *Person and Act*, his presumed *Hauptwerk*, is manifestly phenomenological. In it Wojtyła openly acknowledges his debt to Max Scheler, and the English translation and edition of the work appeared as volume X in the series *Analecta Husserliana*. There Wojtyła uses language familiar to phenomenologists, speaking of consciousness and intentionality, juxtaposing his presentation of the human act with that of more traditional philosophy. In this same work, however, Wojtyła offers clear signals that he is not simply and completely a phenomenologist, as he rejects certain positions that seem central to classical phenomenology, for instance, that cognition or knowledge is an activity of consciousness, as he instead insists that knowledge must be prior to and foundational for consciousness.[2]

Furthermore, his philosophical thinking began with Thomism. Although the evidence for this can be discerned throughout his writings, we may simply take his word for it. Narrating the story of his journey to the priesthood to French journalist André Frossard, Pope John Paul II told about his first encounter with Thomistic metaphysics as an underground seminarian in Kraków. His tutor, Fr Kazimierz Kłósak, gave him a copy of Kazimierz Wais's *Metaphysics*[3] with the instructions to study it and prepare to be examined on it. Young Wojtyła read the book and was profoundly affected by it, despite its difficulty and reputed dryness: 'When I passed the examination, I told my examiner that in my view the new vision of the world which I had acquired in my struggle with that metaphysics manual was more valuable than the mark which I had obtained... This discovery, which has remained the basis of my intellectual structure, is also at the root of my essentially pastoral vocation.'[4] He subsequently completed his doctoral dissertation on St John of the Cross at the Angelicum in Rome under Fr Garrigou Lagrange, O.P. Like the Spanish mystic's thought, Karol Wojtyła's analysis is undergirded with a deep understanding of Thomas Aquinas. Nevertheless, Karol Wojtyła certainly does not read like a Thomist, addressing characteristically Thomist questions using identifiably Thomist arguments. What then do we make of Wojtyła's thought?

This question comes most sharply into focus when we ask about Wojtyła's

---

[2] Karol Wojtyła, *Osoba i czyn: oraz inne studia antropologiczne* (Lublin: Towarzystwo Naukowe KUL, 2000), pp. 80–1; Italian translation Giuseppe Girgenti and Patrycja Mikulska as *Persona e atto* ['Person and Act'] in Karol Wojtyła, *Metafisica della persona: Tutti le opere filosofiche e saggi integrativi* (Milano: Bompiani, 2003), pp. 870–1.

[3] Kazimierz Wais, *Ontologja czyli metafizyka ogolna* (Lwów: Towarzystwo 'Biblioteka Religijn', 1926).

[4] André Frossard, *"Be Not Afraid": Pope John Paul II Speaks Out on his Life, his Beliefs, and his Inspiring Vision for Humanity* (trans. J. R. Foster; New York: St Martin's Press, 1984), p. 17.

metaphysics. On the one hand, he insists on the importance of complementing the 'philosophy of consciousness' with the 'philosophy of being'.[5] In *Love and Responsibility* he argues that a metaphysical understanding is necessary for properly understanding the sexual drive,[6] and in *Osoba i czyn* ('Person and Act') he almost offhandedly remarks that the work he has accomplished in that book can be completed by a metaphysical account of the soul.[7] Others, such as John Crosby and Juan Manuel Burgos, do attempt a metaphysics of the person, but Karol Wojtyła does not. Furthermore, while he defends the dignity and freedom of the person, insisting on his or her spiritual character, he does not develop the concept of the soul at any length.

The Key to the Man's Identity

To understand Karol Wojtyła's thought aright we must know what he was trying to do. I suggest that Karol Wojtyła/Pope John Paul II is very much like St Augustine, who used philosophical, theological and rhetorical skills to present and defend the Christian faith in an age of social and political chaos and ecclesiastical turmoil. Likewise, St John Paul II also saw himself *primarily as a pastor*. Everything that he spoke and wrote was ordered directly or indirectly to a pastoral end. Indeed, he himself directly affirms as much: 'In these two aspects of my life and activity, the pastoral vocation prevailed over that of teacher and scholar; it gradually turned out to be deeper and stronger; but if the two locations are a long way from each other, there was never any rupture between them.'[8] John Paul describes this pastoral role in biblical terms, recalling Jesus' questions to Peter at the end of John's Gospel (Jn 21.15-17). If this is so, then all his works – not only his homilies and the spiritual articles written for the Catholic press in Poland, but also his scholarly work from the 'Lublin Lectures'[9] to essays appearing in *Roczniki Filosoficzne*,[10] *Analecta Husserliana*[11] and *Person*

---

[5] See Karol Wojtyła, 'In Search of the Basis of Perfectionism in Ethics', in Karol Wojtyła, *Person and Community: Selected Essays* (trans. Theresa Sandok; New York: Peter Lang, 1993), pp. 45–56; Karol Wojtyła, 'The Transcendence of the Person in Action and Man's Self-Teleology', *Analecta Husserliana* 9 (1979): 203–12; and especially John Paul II [Karol Wojtyła], *Fides et Ratio*.

[6] Karol Wojtyła, *Love and Responsibility* (trans. Grzegorz Ignatik; Boston: Pauline, 2013), pp. 34–7.

[7] Wojtyła, *Osoba i czyn*, p. 300.

[8] Frossard, '*Be Not Afraid*', p. 18.

[9] Karol Wojtyła, *Wykłady Lubelskie* (Lublin: Towarzystwo Naukowe KUL, 2006); German translation: *Lubliner Vorlesungen* (eds Anneliese Danka Spranger and Edda Wiener; Stuttgart-Degerloch: Seewald Verlag, 1981).

[10] Several of these can be found in Wojtyła's *Person and Community*.

[11] See, for example, Karol Wojtyła, 'The Intentional Act and the Human Act, that is, Act and

and Act – were created ultimately, albeit indirectly, to serve the pastoral end of bringing men and women to Christ. Reflecting on his struggles to defend the faculty of theology at the Jagiellonian University, he wrote: 'Sustaining me throughout this struggle was the conviction that scholarship, in its many different manifestations, is a priceless treasure for a nation. Obviously in my exchanges with the communist authorities, it was the study of theology that I was arguing for, since its survival was under threat.'[12]

Karol Wojtyła self-understanding as a pastor enables us to understand the directions of his writings as well as the apparent lacunae in his thought. As others such as Rocco Buttiglione have pointed out, Karol Wojtyła made remarkably creative use of phenomenological tools of analysis within the context of a solidly Thomistic philosophical and theological framework. However, he does not (like some others, such as Edith Stein[13]) attempt a formal reconciliation of the two as such. Although he speaks often about freedom, he does not deeply address the 'nuts and bolts' of the contemporary discussion of the alleged conflict between human freedom and scientific laws. He admires, uses[14] and subjects to critical scrutiny the thought of Max Scheler,[15] but he never analyses Scheler's thought for its own sake. More generally, Karol Wojtyła does not seem to be especially eager to contribute to the philosophical literature or involve himself in the arcane disputes and analyses that characterize the contemporary culture of journals and conferences. And so we find ourselves confronting a paradoxical figure. On the one hand, he manifestly cares deeply about serious philosophical and theological issues, to the point of writing the very dense but thoroughly coherent and creative *Person and Act*. On the other hand, he does not identify himself and strive to locate his work within the philosophical or theological community. He talks with academics on their own terms, but always as a kind of outsider. Karol Wojtyła/John Paul II is always the pastor, even when he does serious academic philosophy or theology. This explains the somewhat odd tone

---

Experience', *Analecta Husserliana* 5 (1976): 269–80; 'Subjectivity and the Irreducible in the Human Being', *Analecta Husserliana* 7 (1978): 107–14; and 'The Degrees of Being from the Point of View of the Phenomenology of Action', *Analecta Husserliana*, 11 (1981): 125–30.

[12] John Paul II, *Rise, Let Us Be on our Way* (trans. Walter Zięmba; New York: Time Warner, 2004), pp. 87–8.

[13] See Edith Stein [Sr Teresa Benedicta of the Cross, O.C.D.], 'Husserl and Aquinas: A Comparison', in idem, *Knowledge and Faith* (Washington, DC: ICS Publications, 2000), pp. 1–63.

[14] See Wojtyła, *Osoba i czyn*, p. 70; *Persona e atto*, p. 856; also Wojtyła, *Love and Responsibility*, pp. 125, 158.

[15] See Karol Wojtyła, 'On the Metaphysical and Phenomenological Basis of the Moral Norm in the Philosophy of Thomas Aquinas and Max Scheler', in *Person and Community*, pp. 73–94; and especially his *Habilitationschrift: Valutazione sulla possibilità di construire l'etica cristiana sulle base del sistema di Max Scheler*, in Wojtyła, *Metafisica della persona*, pp. 263–449.

of his remarks in *Fides et Ratio*, where he encourages philosophers to be bold and courageous in their work.[16] He 'stands back' while urging scholars forward.

Wojtyła's Metaphysical Silence

One of the most puzzling aspects of Karol Wojtyła's thought, especially for the philosopher reading Wojtyła philosophically, is his metaphysical silence. Although Karol Wojtyła does sometimes speak about metaphysics, he does not develop his own metaphysical thought. In *Love and Responsibility* we read that the human sexual drives are related not only to the biological order but also to the order of existence;[17] subsequently he titles one major section 'Metaphysical Analysis of Love' and another 'Metaphysics of Shame'. [18] In *Person and Act* he describes metaphysics as the 'realm of thought in which are founded the roots of all the sciences', and takes the occasion to discuss the importance of the *potentia–actus* relationship.[19] In John Paul II's audiences on the creed, he cites the metaphysical arguments for the existence and attributes of God.[20] Most famously, perhaps, he calls for 'a philosophy of *genuinely metaphysical* range, capable, that is, of transcending empirical data in order to attain something absolute, ultimate and foundational in its search for truth'.[21] He never, however, connects or develops these themes into a metaphysical treatise of his own.

The most evident and puzzling instance of Wojtyła's apparently casual treatment of metaphysics is his reticence concerning the soul, whose reality and immortality he does affirm.[22] Where he does treat the soul, he refrains from the traditional Aristotelian-Thomistic categories of matter and form. In *Love and Responsibility* Wojtyła offers a purely philosophical account of the human person in order to ground his *personalistic norm*, arguing that the person, as a spiritual being, cannot be used as a means to an end.[23] However, he refrains from the expected arguments that would locate this spiritual nature in the rational soul. Finally, at the very end of Part Three of *Person and Act*, whose project is to provide a deep analysis of the essence of the human person, we

---

[16] John Paul II, *Fides et Ratio*, §§80, 85, 97.
[17] Wojtyła, *Love and Responsibility*, p. 37.
[18] Wojtyła, *Love and Responsibility*, pp. 57–83 and 158–77.
[19] Wojtyła, *Osoba i czyn*, p. 113; *Persona e atto*, p. 915.
[20] John Paul II, General Audiences of 29 January and 5 March 1986; available at http://www.vatican.va/holy_father/john_paul_ii/audiences/alpha/index_it.html (last accessed 3 September 2003).
[21] John Paul II, *Fides et Ratio*, §83.
[22] Karol Wojtyła, 'Thomistic Personalism', in Wojtyła, *Person and Community*, pp. 167–75 (67–9).
[23] Wojtyła, *Love and Responsibility*, pp. 24–8.

read: 'And perhaps in this consists the verification, albeit only indirect, of the affirmation that the soul's reality, as well as its relationship with the body, can be adequately expressed only in metaphysical categories.'[24] The student of Karol Wojtyła is confronted, therefore, with an author who affirms the importance of metaphysics, of the 'philosophy of being', but whose development of this in his own writings is almost casual.

Karol Wojtyła does indeed have a metaphysics, one whose theoretical basis is taken from the thought of St Thomas Aquinas. Practically, however, it is taken from the faith, and we see this in his theology of the body. Furthermore, it is there that we see how he relates this with phenomenology. And so we turn to Karol Wojtyła's treatment of metaphysics and phenomenology in his writings on human love in *Man and Woman He Created Them*.

Metaphysics and Phenomenology in Scripture

John Paul II's audiences on the theology of the body begin with an analysis of the Genesis accounts of the creation of human beings. In his conversation with the Pharisees concerning the legitimacy of divorce (Mt. 19.3-8), Jesus directs his interlocutors to the beginning, to the Creator's original intention for human beings: 'So God created man in his own image, in the image of God he created him; male and female he created them.' After briefly treating the first creation account in Genesis 1, he turns his attention to Chapters 2-3. The distinction is important and instructive for our investigation.

Scripture scholars find important differences between the respective creation accounts in Genesis 1 and 2, and so, in one way, it is not surprising that John Paul II relies on these. What *is* intriguing is the shape of his analysis. Rather than looking to the theological differences between the Priestly and Yahwist authors, he looks at these texts *philosophically*. In John Paul II's analysis of the creation accounts in *Man and Woman He Created Them*, his Aristotelian Thomism and phenomenology are both at work and in complementary ways. To put the matter briefly, John Paul II reads Genesis 1 metaphysically and Genesis 2 phenomenologically.

---

[24] Wojtyła, *Osoba i czyn*, p. 300; *Persona e atto*, p. 1163.

Genesis 1

John Paul II could not be clearer about the metaphysical import that he finds in the first creation account.

> The first account of the creation of man ... contains hidden within itself a powerful metaphysical content. One should not forget that precisely this text of Genesis has become the source of the deepest inspirations for the thinkers who have sought to understand 'being' and 'existing.' ... [Man] is defined in a more metaphysical than physical way.[25]

John Paul goes on to observe that the account affirms the entity of good, because having concluded his work of creation, God sees all he has made 'and behold, it was very good' (Gen. 1.31). He argues that the 'first chapter of Genesis has formed an incontrovertible point of reference and solid basis of a metaphysics and also for an anthropology and an ethics according to which *"ens et bonum convertuntur"*'.[26]

The most important aspect of the first creation account, of course, is the creation of human beings in the image and likeness of God, which has a 'cosmological character: man is created on earth together with the visible world'. And yet man is not like other things in the world. John Paul II notes: 'man…is not created according to a natural succession, but the Creator seems to halt before calling him into existence, as if he entered back into himself to make a decision, "Let us make man in our image, in our likeness" (Gen. 1.27)'.[27] Because he is created in the image and likeness of God, man cannot be reduced to 'the world', cannot 'be understood or explained in his full depth with the categories taken from the "world", that is, from the visible totality of bodies'.[28] This concept of the human being as 'image and likeness of God' is, for John Paul II, 'the immutable *basis of all Christian anthropology*',[29] and in *Love and Responsibility* Karol Wojtyła links this directly with the notion of *person*. Indeed, we can say that *person* expresses the philosophical content of the biblical phrase 'image of God'.

However, John Paul II does not spend much time on Genesis 1. This is the objective account, without any trace of subjectivity. John Paul II does not himself develop his own theoretical reflections on metaphysics, but simply rests

---

[25] John Paul II, *Man and Woman He Created Them*, 2.5, p. 136.
[26] John Paul II, *Man and Woman He Created Them*, 2.5, p. 137.
[27] John Paul II, *Man and Woman He Created Them*, 2.3, p. 135.
[28] John Paul II, *Man and Woman He Created Them*, 2.4, p. 135.
[29] John Paul II, *Mulieris dignitatem*, §6 (emphasis in original).

with the observation that these metaphysical considerations are rooted in the first creation account in Genesis.

Genesis 2

In his theology of the body audiences, John Paul II devotes one audience to Chapter 1 of Genesis and seventeen to Chapter 2, which he characterizes as 'subjective in nature' and 'psychological'. Where Chapter 1 lists a sequence of decisions and actions by the Creator, Chapter 2 tells a story with descriptions of states of mind, of human subjectivity. Although some Scripture scholars have privately criticized John Paul II's treatment of this chapter as 'playing fast and loose' with the Scriptural text, his analysis differs significantly from what one usually finds in Scripture commentaries. John Paul II's treatment of Genesis 2 is a *phenomenological* analysis.[30]

'Naked, but without shame'

To see what he is doing, consider this verse: 'Both the man and his wife were naked, and they were not ashamed' (Gen. 2.25). Why does Scripture mention this fact? The most obvious answer is that the Scriptural author is preparing for the first couple's reaction of shame after their sin: 'I was afraid, because I was naked' (Gen. 3.10). However, this begs the question why Scripture even mentions nakedness and shame in the first place. Biblical scholarship answers like this: 'Man and woman were as yet without sin and the consequences of sin: they had, therefore, none of what a later theology would call the concupiscence of the flesh.'[31] Although John Paul II agrees with this and, indeed, follows this line of analysis, he devotes most of his attention to exploring this verse *subjectively*. Granted that the first couple's lack of shame derives from their innocence, what does this *mean* experientially? In particular, what is the meaning of shame?

The phenomenological method is much more than a kind of introspective description of personal experiences. Even when concerned with emotions and states of feeling, the point of phenomenology is to get precisely to the essence of the reality at hand. The phenomenology of *shame* is a case in point. In his analysis of chastity in *Love and Responsibility*,[32] Wojtyła devotes significant

---

[30] John Paul II, *Man and Woman He Created Them*, 3.1 to 19.6, pp. 137–204.
[31] Bruce Vawter, 'Genesis', in Reginald C. Fuller (ed.), *A New Catholic Commentary on Holy Scripture* (Nashville: Thomas Nelson, 1975), pp. 166–205 (178).
[32] See the section 'The Metaphysics of Shame', in Wojtyła, *Love and Responsibility*, pp. 158–77;

attention to 'The Metaphysics of Shame'.³³ Since he begins by citing Max Scheler's analysis of shame, we do well first to look briefly at Scheler's approach in his *Über Scham und Schamgefühl*.³⁴

Shame is important to Scheler both in itself as a manifestation of something intrinsic to the human person, as well as in regards to other things. He writes, '*The unique position and situation of the human being in the great hierarchy of the universe*, his situation between the divine and the animal, in no feeling is made so clear, so sharp and so immediately expressive as the feeling of *shame*.'³⁵ Let us pause to note how different this is from the traditional position. Classically, what differentiates the human from the brute animal is intelligence, the power of reason, and he is distinguished from the divine, from God and angels, by his corporality. Scheler, however, looks for this difference in a form of subjective experience. What is this experience? Scheler compares shame with other subjective phenomena, such as reverence and disgust, and finds its essence in the peculiar self-awareness of the human person in an experience of conflict.

First of all, because the human being is a kind of bridge between the divine and the animals, he experiences a certain dualism within himself. He thinks himself to be the dominant species, ruling over the animal world, but at the same time he is aware of his generative organs, those that determine his sex, as most clearly and fully shared in common with the world beneath him. As a result he feels shame, and he clothes those parts of his body.³⁶ Scheler distinguishes between two levels of shame: the bodily and the soul-ish ('*seelisch*'). He has a reproductive system similar to those of the animals and hence experiences powerful desires to copulate. He also has a higher consciousness with its desire to love another with devotion. These two are often in tension or even conflict, and this is a source of shame. A being that is incapable of one or the other of these inclinations feels no shame, but as both animal and spiritual, the human person does.

A second factor is the act that Scheler calls '*Rückwendung auf ein Selbst*', 'turning back on a self'. By this he means a redirection of one's attention away from the external situation to one's own self as a self. For example, a mother may run naked from the house to save her baby. When her concern for the

---

'Metafizyka wstydu', in *Miłość i odpowiedzialność*, pp. 156–72.
³³ Wojtyła, *Love and Responsibility*, pp. 157–77.
³⁴ Max Scheler, *Über Scham und Schamgefühl* [On Shame and the Feeling of Shame], in M. Scheler, *Schriften aus dem Nachlass*, vol. 1, *Zur Ethik und Erkenntnislehre* (Bern: A. Franke, 1957), pp. 65–154.
³⁵ Scheler, *Über Scham und Schamgefühl*, p. 67. One is reminded of Mark Twain's quip, 'Man is the only animal that blushes. Or needs to.'
³⁶ Cf. Scheler, *Über Scham und Schamgefühl*, p. 75.

endangered child absorbs all her awareness, she has no concern for herself. Only when the emergency is over and she realizes that her body is exposed to public view does she feel shame. Similarly, the artist's nude model feels no shame so long as she remains mentally in the role of *a model*. However, should she fall out of that role, by becoming aware that the artist might have a sexual interest in her or that she may be interested in him, she experiences shame. In this 'turning back on a self' the person moves out of the realm of the general or universal and becomes conscious of him or herself as an individual. As such, shame is constituted as a 'protection feeling' of the individual over against the universal.[37] Scheler concludes:

> So, it can be seen that the essence of the feeling of shame is on the one hand the turning back of the individual upon himself, and the feeling of the necessity of individual protection of self before all spheres of the universal, and on the other hand, a feeling in which the undecidedness of the value-choosing higher functions of consciousness with respect to objects concerning which the lower instinctive drives express a strong attraction manifests itself as a *tension* between both levels of consciousness.[38]

This complex of feeling and behaviour need not manifest itself in any one specific mode of action. Indeed, Scheler is happy to contrast the strikingly different manifestations of shame among English ladies and gentlemen in comparison with some almost naked peoples in Africa. The way and extent to which the body is covered out of shame may vary from culture to culture, but shame itself is universal.

What Scheler does is not the kind of analysis that we find in the Aristotelian or modern analytic tradition. Either of these may well question why a particular kind of feeling or emotion deserves philosophical study. For the phenomenologist shame, for example, is more than a feeling or emotion; it is rather a factor that shapes human life. Shame powerfully influences how people dress and comport themselves before others, how young men and women court and even the extent to which a person may become unwelcome within his or her society. Shame is present as a *unit of meaning* which works to form human life. By this I mean that the particular phenomenon, in this case shame, *represents* a reality in the person's and the community's life. In his or her effort to discover the *essence* of the phenomenon, the phenomenologist seeks the meaningful key to it. In this instance, with an eye to discerning what is essential to shame, Scheler compares

---

[37] For this entire analysis see Scheler, *Über Scham und Schamgefühl*, pp. 78–9.
[38] Scheler, *Über Scham und Schamgefühl*, p. 90.

the nexus in which we find shame to those in which we experience disgust and reverence. The process is somewhat analogous to that of the linguist who tries to discern the full meaning of a word by examining its role in the language and comparing it with other, apparently related, words. The process is not one of subjective introspection, as though one could understand shame and the feeling of shame merely by examining his or her own memories and current feelings.

As Karol Wojtyła understands it, phenomenology offers a disciplined method of analysing important human realities from the point of view of human consciousness. He outlines this method succinctly in the 'Introduction' to *Person and Act*, where he explains the complementary processes of *induction* and *reduction*,[39] by which the investigator attains an intellectual grasp or understanding of the object under consideration. This method itself does not differ sharply from Aristotle's, as described in Book II of *Posterior Analytics*,[40] but it is applied from a different direction. Such interior data of consciousness are not ordinarily studied by the more objective philosophy of being because they do not directly appear under the objective approach. Classical philosophy can study in depth the sense appetites and relate these to the higher powers of reason and will, addressing, among other things, the tension between the sense appetites and the rational appetite. Such an analysis does not look at the phenomenon from the interior perspective, from the side of personal consciousness of the reality that is at stake. So, although all true philosophy must, whether proximately or remotely, be founded on experience, phenomenology has the advantage of reflecting upon experience as experienced.

Such an approach serves both the intellectual requirements and the pastoral orientation of Wojtyła's thought. The concept of shame is particularly important for Karol Wojtyła's project of analysing chastity and sexual love for two reasons. The first derives from Aquinas's discussion of temperance (of which chastity is a part), where he argues that temperance has two parts: shame (*verecundia*) and continence.[41] It is precisely around these two parts that Wojtyła structures his presentation of the virtue of chastity in *Love and Responsibility*.[42] The second reason, one which becomes thematic in the early parts of his presentation of the theology of the body, is Genesis 2.25: 'the man and his wife were both naked, and were not ashamed'. Consequently, shame is an important theme in Karol Wojtyła's thought about the relationship between sex and love.

---

[39] Wojtyła, *Osoba i czyn*, pp. 62–6; *Persona e atto*, pp. 845–50.
[40] See Aristotle, *Posterior Analytics*, II, 19, 100a, 1–15.
[41] St Thomas Aquinas, *Summa Theologiae*, II, II, 143, 1.
[42] Wojtyła, *Love and Responsibility*, pp. 158–92.

Although not identical to it, Wojtyła's analysis of shame reflects Scheler's. In *Love and Responsibility*, he writes that 'the phenomenon of shame occurs when that which by reason of its essence or its purpose should be interior leaves the sphere of the interiority of the person and becomes in some way exterior.'[43] Shame is a distinctly human, and hence personal, phenomenon because the existence of the person is an interior one. That is to say, the person does not live simply from his or her sensory responses to and physical interactions with the environment, but primarily from his or her interior life. 'This interior life is the spiritual life. It focuses on truth and the good.'[44] Shame responds not to a physical threat, but to the other's possible knowledge or awareness of oneself, and it is particularly an issue where the body and its sexual characteristics are concerned. Wojtyła observes: 'In a particular way the object of shame is the parts and organs of the body that determine its sexual distinctness. Among people an almost general tendency exists to conceal them from the sight of others, especially from the sight of persons of the other sex.'[45] Here the 'threat' arises precisely from the interiority of both the subject and the other person. The sudden exposure of one's naked body to the cat is not an occasion for shame, but to a water meter reader it would be.

The root of this embarrassment, according to Wojtyła, lies in concupiscence. Addressing himself to the question of dress and the exposure of one's body, Wojtyła writes: 'Unfortunately, man is not such a perfect being so that the sight of the body of a person, especially a person of the other sex, awakens in him only a disinterested fondness that is followed by a simple love for that person.'[46] His argument in *Love and Responsibility* is that concupiscence gives rise to shame because the essence of concupiscence is to regard the other as an object for use or enjoyment. 'Hence we have that lived-experience of inviolability (X [she]: "You must not touch me even with the interior desire itself" – Y [he] "I must not touch her even with the interior will to use; she may not be an object of use").'[47] Because it arises from the interiority of the human person, shame is metaphysical; we experience shame because we know that it is not right to be treated only as an object for another's satisfaction. Let us note that it is not the demonstrated or evident fact of concupiscence in a particular case that gives rise to the feeling of shame, as though one tends to feel shame only when another

---

[43] Wojtyła, *Love and Responsibility*, p. 158.
[44] Wojtyła, *Love and Responsibility*, p. 159.
[45] Wojtyła, *Love and Responsibility*, p. 159.
[46] Wojtyła, *Love and Responsibility*, p. 174.
[47] Wojtyła, *Love and Responsibility*, p. 164.

manifests his lust. Shame is present even when one's nakedness is exposed to another who immediately turns away. It arises because the person desires to be seen as a *person* by a person. Wojtyła calls this 'metaphysical' because shame so conceived is rooted deeper than the physical or even sensitive plane, but arises from the person's spiritual (and hence trans-phenomenal and trans-material) character itself.

When we turn to *Man and Woman He Created Them*, the notion of shame is put to work theologically. If the man and woman were naked but without shame, then we may ask how this could be. Their lack of shame is thoroughly contrary to our own experience. Although the original couple were thoroughly aware of the meaning of their bodies in their sexual differentiation, and specifically they knew that they could unite so as to become 'one flesh', they nevertheless felt no shame. Psychologically, they seemed not to be like us and in ways that are significant. Shame, this *unit of meaning*, was not a factor in their experience and behaviour. This touches some of the most perplexing questions about human nature and original sin. Briefly, what was it like to be human before the Fall? And what was the precise impact of the original sin?

One approach that John Paul II rejected was the appeal to a *status naturae purae*, a 'pure' human nature hypothetically abstracted from reference to the supernatural.[48] There is no question of attempting to deduce a 'pure' human nature from philosophical premises having no reference to God or his creative activity. We see this effort not only in the thought of earlier theologians, but also in contemporary philosophy of religion, which has a remarkably difficult time making sense of the concept. Instead of looking for a pure human nature, John Paul II appeals to the *status naturae integrae*, the *original condition* according to the Creator's intentions, which in *Man and Woman He Created Them* he calls the 'beginning'.[49] His theological starting point is the revealed text of Genesis. If the Scripture mentions 'nakedness' in relation to shame both before and immediately after the Fall, then it is significant. Specifically, from the authoritative text we have an insight into the subjectivity of the first man and woman: although naked, they felt no shame.

Is this legitimate? Can we psychoanalyse Adam and Eve on the basis of a pair of brief texts? Or does this truly constitute 'playing fast and loose' with

---

[48] See 'Natura i doskałność' [Nature and perfection], in Karol Wojtyła, *Aby Chrystus się nami posługiwał* (Kraków: Wydawnictwo Znak, 2009), p. 154. A Spanish translation is available as 'Naturaleza y perfección', in Karol Wojtyła, *Mi visión del hombre: Hacia una nueva ética* (trans. Pilar Ferrer; eds Juan Manuel and Alejandro Burgos; Madrid: Biblioteca Palabra, 2010), pp. 44–8.

[49] Wojtyła, *Man and Woman He Created Them*, 1.3, p. 132.

the Scriptures? The answer is simple. John Paul II, like Christian thinkers from the earliest centuries of the faith, applies philosophical analysis to the data of revelation. The Fathers used Platonic categories, the medieval scholastics Aristotelian methods. *What Pope Wojtyła does in the early sections of his theology of the body is apply phenomenological analysis to the Scriptural text.* If phenomenology can help us to penetrate into the essence of shame, then it may be useful for investigating these texts.

When, like Scheler, we examine ordinary human experience, we find that human beings of both sexes naturally flee from exposure of their nakedness to others, and from a phenomenological analysis we learn something about the essence of human sexual experience. Into this analysis, there is now inserted a novelty: In the original condition, according to the biblical text, a young man and woman who are attractive ('This at last is bone of my bones and flesh of my flesh') feel no shame over their nakedness. The Christian thinker acknowledges in faith that this revelation is true. What, then, is she or he to do with it? John Paul II proposes, in effect, that this verse from Genesis, along with Genesis 3.7, 10, presents us with a new datum to be examined phenomenologically. The only difference between this proposed analysis and that which the philosopher normally does is that John Paul II works from an account based on an experience that is closed to us who live after that first sin. Implicit in this is the assumption of a fundamental continuity between our present 'historical' situation and that of 'original man', that by considering the testimony of the Scriptural text we can retrieve at least a glimpse of the original condition of human beings. John Paul II writes:

> It is impossible to understand the state of 'historical' sinfulness without referring or appealing to the state of original ... and fundamental innocence (and in fact Christ appeals to it) ... *Thus, historical man is rooted, so to speak, in his revealed theological prehistory;* and for this reason, every point of his historical sinfulness must be explained ... with reference to original innocence.[50]

We find an important methodological clue to John Paul II's approach at the very beginning of his analysis of 'original nakedness':

> When we speak of original human experiences, we have in mind not so much their distance in time, as rather their foundational significance ... These experiences are always at the root of every human experience ... Indeed they are so

---

[50] Wojtyła, *Man and Woman He Created Them*, 4.2, p. 143.

interwoven with the ordinary things or life that we generally do not realize their extraordinary character.[51]

In other words, our project is not so much to 'go back in time' to events whose narration is mythical, but rather to examine the roots of our own experience with the help of a revealed datum about the ultimate basis of this experience.

Original innocence

John Paul II calls the state of human nature according to the Creator's plan 'original innocence'. Without sin, man and woman can be naked without shame, a condition that we cannot replicate. The constitutive difference between this state and our own is the presence of concupiscence, which resulted from the original sin. It follows, therefore, that the original couple could have lived humanly without the impact of concupiscence upon their relationship. But if this is the case, what sense can we make of sexual desires? From an 'objective' standpoint, one can (as St Augustine in fact does in *City of God*) maintain that in the Garden, the human appetites were entirely under the control of intellect and will. Augustine's discussion is amusing, indeed humorous, as the saint describes those who can wriggle their ears, pass gas and so on at will, arguing that if men can do such things then surely the innocent Adam and Eve could also have controlled their genital organs at will, commanding them to respond according to the demands of reason.[52] But we may find this oddly troubling. Is there not something *right* about passionate sexual desire within marriage? Is the original innocence really nothing more than the dispassionate decision making of Kantian wills, choosing to act sexually in fulfilment of some divinely ordained end?

John Paul II is, in fact, well aware of the problem. But how does one solve it? The Scriptures are clear that the original creation was 'very good', that the Garden was a place of human happiness and that the original couple found delight in each other. The man must certainly have experienced the woman's attractiveness and she his. But this would necessarily, by hypothesis, have been without concupiscence. Therefore, in conducting our phenomenological analysis of shame and desire, we must be able to separate *desire* from *lust*. The first man and woman must, if they were to have united so to become 'one flesh', have been able to experience desire, not only in their minds but in their bodies, such that their bodies would be able to join in the marital act. An important

---

[51] Wojtyła, *Man and Woman He Created Them*, 11.1, pp. 169–70.
[52] Augustine, *De civitate Dei*, XIV, 24.

theme, therefore, that runs through the first two sections of *Man and Woman He Created Them* is that of the distinction between desire and concupiscence. This distinction is premised, however, on the notion that, our own contrary experience notwithstanding, the desire of the man for union with the woman is not the same as his sexual craving, the insistent urge to have and enjoy. If concupiscence consists in the reductive desire to possess and enjoy the other as the bearer of sensually satisfying characteristics, then it remains to give an account of the drawing together of the two that does not depend on such a reductionist desire.

We see our author's first effort to address this problem in *Love and Responsibility*, where he distinguishes sensual attraction from fondness and love for the person as a whole.[53] The first is characterized by a utilitarian attitude of use and enjoyment. The second, however, is characterized by the attitude of gratitude and self-gift, and precisely here is the vital insight that he will develop in his theology of the body. The relationship between the man and the woman in the state of original innocence – that primordial state according to the intentions of the Creator – is not one characterized by the logic of sensual desire but by the 'hermeneutics of the gift'.[54] This fundamental intentionality, based not on acquisition but on the human person's capacity to make a gift of him or herself, is an essential constituent of that *original innocence*, which John Paul II discovers in the Scriptural text and analyses phenomenologically. If the principle cited above is true, that 'original human experiences ... are always at the root of every human experience',[55] then in the interior depths of each person today lies the capacity and in fact the orientation toward the gift of self. Deeper than the powerful sense craving for sexual satisfaction is the need to give oneself completely to another and gratefully to receive another's offer of that gift. The ethical task, then, becomes one of recapturing as closely as possible the love which came naturally in that state of original innocence by fostering an ethos of virtue, especially the virtue of chastity. The insight that John Paul II develops here is that the virtuous life so understood approximates and approaches the ethos of original innocence, a state which cannot be attained again here on earth and whose restoration must wait until the resurrection of the body.

John Paul II takes this theological analysis a further step, one which reflects and deepens Scheler's insight into the roots of shame. He writes:

---

[53] Wojtyła, *Love and Responsibility*, pp. 58–66. See also *Osoba i czyn*, pp. 133–8, 169–77; *Persona e atto*, pp. 942–48, 989–96.
[54] Wojtyła, *Man and Woman He Created Them*, 13.2ff., pp. 178ff.
[55] Wojtyła, *Man and Woman He Created Them*, 11.1, pp. 169–70.

Adam's words in Genesis 3:10, 'I was afraid, because I am naked, and I hid myself,' *seem to express the awareness of being defenseless*, and in the sense of insecurity about his somatic structure *in the face of the processes of nature that operate with inevitable determinism*. In this disturbing statement one can perhaps find the implication of a certain 'cosmic shame' in which the being that is created in the 'image of God' and called to subdue the earth and rule over it ... is in such an explicit way subjected to the earth, particularly in the 'part' of its transcendent constitution represented precisely by the body.[56]

Shame before a determinate universe

Shame thus also expresses a metaphysical reality, the uncanny relationship of human beings in their confrontation with the material universe, to whose inexorable laws they are subject, but to which they are also superior. 'Cosmic shame', which is more than an emotion but a 'unit of meaning', touches two issues at the heart of Wojtyła's philosophical and theological personalism. In the text just quoted he writes of '*the awareness of being defenseless*, and ... the sense of insecurity about his somatic structure *in the face of the processes of nature that operate with inevitable determinism*'. However, the thought that 'ultimately I am powerless' is a formula for despair, leading to existential paralysis. For real people, it is truly a matter of shame, the shame of discovering that one's value in his or her own eyes might be completely without foundation.

By their will persons determine what they will do and in so doing determine the kind of being they are. Because they can act freely, determining themselves, persons are responsible for what they do and what they make of themselves by their acts. It is precisely here that John Paul II's 'cosmic shame' appears as a factor underlying human consciousness. If I, who can know the world and understand so many of its workings so that I can decide what is best to do, cannot control myself, if I cannot control the thoughts of my mind and the organic responses of my sexual faculties, then I am ashamed. I am subject to that which my spiritual nature should make me superior.

John Paul II does not speculate on the interrelationship between the physical order and human sin, nor does he address how a Garden of Eden, in which there was nothing harmful and where nature responded to human work, is even conceivable. What he does address in these theological reflections is that sense of disquieting embarrassment that St Paul wrote of in Romans 7.21-4 between the desires of his mind and the resistance of the flesh.

---

[56] Wojtyła, *Man and Woman He Created Them*, 27.4, p. 242.

Philosophy serving theology

This account of John Paul II's treatment of shame and original innocence is but a sketch of part of the project of developing an adequate anthropology, a project that is ultimately theological. Just as the early Christian theologians adopted Platonic thought and the medieval scholastics that of Aristotle, Karol Wojtyła adopts modern phenomenology. As he realized early on, phenomenology alone cannot adequately found Christian moral theology.[57] This conclusion notwithstanding, he finds in Scheler's thought a fount of valuable insight.[58] Even a cursory reading of *Love and Responsibility* reveals that phenomenology can provide a rigorous philosophical method to analyse human experience. Karol Wojtyła's 'discovery' was how this philosophical tool can serve theology. Confident in the power of his philosophical tools, John Paul II frequently insists on the rigour and conclusiveness of his arguments in *Man and Woman He Created Them*.[59]

Conclusion

From the early days of his career, Wojtyła was convinced that the central problem of our time is that of human persons and their capacity for love. It is the problem of the adequate anthropology. If its ultimate development must be theological, there nevertheless remains a vital role for the philosopher in its development. What Wojtyła worked on through his career and what John Paul II proposed in his theology of the body audiences is a coherent phenomenological account of the human person, an adequate anthropology.[60] Such an anthropology must be adequate not only to scientific data and established theories, but also to the real structure of human experience. As we have seen, although a zoologist may understand fear responses among animals, and a psychologist or anthropologist relates these findings to the human psyche, these in themselves do not yet account for the important human experience of shame. From the standpoint of an adequate anthropology, however, one can more convincingly account for what belongs to the human person and grasp the essentials of interpersonal relationships. This account may not of itself fully

---

[57] Wojtyła, *Valutazione*, pp. 40-1.
[58] Wojtyła, *Valutazione*, p. 446.
[59] See, for instance, Wojtyła, *Man and Woman He Created Them*, 31.1-31.6, pp. 253-6.
[60] Wojtyła, *Man and Woman He Created Them*, 13.2, pp. 178-9.

resolve the metaphysical conundrums that bedevil the conversation concerning the relationship of mind and matter, of soul and body. That is not its point. Such an account, rather, will enable us to move forward into disputed areas on the basis of a philosophy that takes into account the totality of human experience.

In sum, Karol Wojtyła/John Paul II sought throughout his life to teach what love is, why love is exclusive to persons and how we can attain love. And precisely this is the role of the pastor.

9

The Grace of Being: Ferdinand Ulrich and the Task of a Faithful Metaphysics in the Face of Modernity

D. C. Schindler

Ferdinand Ulrich closes the Foreword to what is generally regarded as his *Meisterwerk*, *Homo Abyssus*,[1] with a sentence from St Paul expressing what Ulrich takes to be the task, not only for his book, but for Christian wisdom in general in its engagement with the modern world: 'We take all thought captive in obedience to Christ' (2 Cor. 10.5). It would not be so remarkable, perhaps, to cite such a text as a programmatic envoi for a theological work, but the presence of this passage in Ulrich's Foreword is quite paradoxical for a number of reasons, of which two are particularly relevant in the present context. First of all, Ulrich is insistent that his work is not theology but philosophy; his aim in *Homo Abyssus* is the strictly metaphysical one of unfolding the meaning of being *qua* being, and unfolding man for whom that meaning represents an essential task. As we will see, for Ulrich, obedience to Christ is what allows reason to be genuinely and faithfully philosophical. Second, Ulrich's fundamental critique of modern philosophy is that it has falsely appropriated Christian revelation, and that this false appropriation has distorted its conception of the nature of being. In this case, it is precisely the light of faith, recognized as faith, that allows us to restore the integrity of reason in its natural operation. So we might put the paradox, somewhat provocatively, thus: according to Ulrich, taking modern thought captive to Christ is necessary to liberate it from theology.[2] In

---

[1] Ferdinand Ulrich, *Homo Abyssus: Das Wagnis der Seinsfrage* (eds Martin Bieler and Florian Pitschl; Freiburg: Johannes Verlag, 2nd edn, 1998); hereafter *HA*.
[2] Less provocatively, but more accurately, we would have to say that taking thought captive to Christ liberates it from *pseudo*-theology – i.e. the presumption of theological data outside of the proper spirit of faith.

the following paper, we hope to present at least enough of a glimpse of Ulrich's thought, which remains largely unknown today, to see the sense of this claim.

If we were to characterize Ulrich's philosophy, as he presents it in *Homo Abyssus*, in a single sentence, we might say that it is a Thomistic metaphysics which attempts to think through Aquinas's understanding of being specifically within the context of the present age – this means, above all, on the one hand, in constant dialogue with Hegel, whom Ulrich considers the culmination of modern thought, and, on the other hand, in response to Heidegger, whom Ulrich takes to represent one of the most profound efforts to overcome the problems of modern thought. His is precisely a philosophy of being as love. Whereas Hegel might be said to judge all things from the perspective of the concept as absolute spirit, and Heidegger from the perspective of the truth of being – for there is no higher place to stand, as it were, for these two thinkers – Ulrich is best read as judging all things from the perspective of love, interpreted in the most complete way possible, and this means in all of its ontological, anthropological and theological depth. There is nothing greater than love. It is absolute. It is the one thing necessary. Love is not meant, here, as a mere emotion or sentiment; nor is it meant merely as an act of the will. Rather, because love lies ultimately at the source of all things, the world is an expression of love, it has love as its form and purpose, or in short: love is the meaning of being.[3]

Ulrich regularly uses the phrase, 'the necessary meaning, or sense, of being' (*der notwendige Seinssinn*). The word 'sense' here (*Sinn*) presents three things at once: meaning, that is, intelligible structure; mode or manner (i.e. to do something in one sense or another); and, as it were, 'directionality' (i.e. to go in this or that sense). The sense of being is, we might say, neither a static fact, nor a formless process, but a 'dramatic structure', a complex simplicity that unfolds its abiding unity according to a particular order. As love, moreover, it is *necessary* not only in the sense that Ulrich brings out in the playful etymology of the German word *Not-wendig* – that which relieves (*wendigen*) every distress or need (*der Not*) – but also in the straightforward sense of being inescapable (*ne-cessarium*).[4] There is nothing higher than love that could determine it from above, but rather love is that which determines all other things. Its *sense* is inevitable, and being cannot but obey this sense. According to Ulrich, this means that wherever the necessary sense of being is betrayed, that sense nevertheless always remains, and indeed every part of it remains. It is just that in this case

---

[3] See Ulrich, *HA*, pp. 20–6; cf. Ulrich's reference to the *ratio boni* as another expression of 'necessary sense of being' (p. 461).
[4] See Ulrich, *HA*, pp. 61–2.

these parts present themselves, no longer as an integrated whole (a complex simplicity) but instead in an endless variety of perverted forms, all of which have profound implications for how we think, live and experience reality – that is, every aspect of our relation to God, the world, ourselves and others.

The ultimacy and inescapability of the sense of being is why it offers a particularly illuminating vantage from which to enter into, to interpret and understand, and to judge the thought of a particular thinker or period. Ulrich describes his philosophical engagement with others as a 'metaphysics in repetition', by which he means the task of re-enacting a thinker's thought precisely as an obedient listening with it to being, making the necessary sense explicit in such a way that the thought is judged and made fruitful in the truth.[5] It is as a metaphysics in repetition that we ought to understand his critique of modernity. What distinguishes Ulrich's particular approach to this theme is that his is not a mere moral critique of modernity – i.e. a claim that modern thinkers turned away from the good through various acts of the will. Nor is it a mere intellectual critique – i.e. a claim that modern thinkers failed to make a particular distinction or other, or failed to grasp some decisive concept. Instead, it is a failure of love, in the most comprehensive sense of the term, which means among other things that it is both intellectual and moral at once, and inseparably. For Ulrich, in the 'metaphysics in repetition', every fundamental distinction in the logical structure of being is at the same time an act of human freedom (*menschlicher Freiheitsvollzug*), and so can be described both conceptually and in terms of a disposition or way of relating.[6]

Moreover, because the necessary sense of being comes to expression concretely in accordance with the way in which it is received, the historical circumstances of its received expression have significance for the meaning of being. We who philosophize at the present time do so in a world into which God has entered through his self-revelation in Christ, in and through the Holy Spirit. The love that is the necessary sense of being is ultimately the love of the Trinitarian God of Christ, who was incarnate of Mary by the Holy Spirit and

---

[5] Compare to Heidegger, from whom the phrase comes: *Kant and the Problem of Metaphysics* (trans. J. S. Churchill; Bloomington: Indiana University Press, 1962), p. 211. See Ulrich, *HA*, pp. 194–7, and esp. 349–59. Cf. 'Das Problem einer "Metaphysik in der Wiederholung"', *Salzburger Jahrbuch für Philosophie* 5 (6) (1961/62): 263–98. While Heidegger explains that a '*Wiederholung*' of a problem is a 'disclosure of the primordial possibilities concealed in it', Ulrich explains that the '"metaphysics in repetition" is firstly and ultimately nothing other than the obedience of thought with respect to superessential being, which obedience gives proof of itself in its following of being's transnihilation in the positing and procession of the essence, and so forth'; Ulrich, 'Metaphysik in der Wiederholung', p. 290.

[6] See, for example, Ulrich, *HA*, p. 469. Cf. Ulrich 'Metaphysik in der Wiederholung', p. 284.

whose incarnation has extended into space and time in the Church. Ulrich draws a remarkable inference from this: to philosophize at all is unavoidably to make some judgement about the nature of being simply, and at the same time to make a judgement about the nature of humanity, from whom the meaning of being is ultimately inseparable. But even more than this, in the given circumstances of history, whether or not one is a believer, one cannot avoid making some basic judgement, not only regarding the nature of God, but more specifically regarding the nature of God as revealed by Christ in the Church. The significance of this implication increases the more profound and essential one's thinking is. To reject this implication and thus to close the meaning of being from the meaning of God is therefore not in fact to exclude that meaning. To the contrary, one would thereby inevitably build what Ulrich refers to as 'theologoumena' into one's thinking, but precisely without recognizing them as such. The only way to avoid thus making one's philosophy a 'pseudo-theology' is therefore to recognize the theologoumena for what they in fact are, namely, aspects and implications of God's free self-revelation. The paradoxical conclusion is that it is only a person with faith that is in principle capable of philosophizing in a manner that avoids falsely anticipating and appropriating the truths of the faith, and so betraying its proper nature. To put it simply, only a 'faith-ful' metaphysics can be a faithful metaphysics. It is therefore precisely for the sake of remaining faithful to metaphysics that Ulrich says that, in *Homo Abyssus*, he has 'transcended ontology into anthropology, and transcended anthropology into Christology'.[7] Our aim in the rest of this paper is to elaborate what he means by this especially in relation to modern philosophy.

At the heart of the various paradoxes that emerge at every turn in Ulrich's thought lies a central one that is entailed in the meaning of being as love, and that is the paradoxical character of a *gift*. In a true gift, the giver gives himself in what is given but in an essentially hidden way, or to put the point more adequately, there is a real *separation* (*Trennung*) of the giver and the gift, though it is a separation that does not thereby eliminate the giver's presence in it. The gift instead represents a mediation of that presence without thereby surrendering the goodness of the gift in itself. What this means becomes most evident when we consider two ways in which a gift can fail: on the one hand, a person can give a gift thoughtlessly, simply to fulfil some social convention, perhaps, but, as we say, without 'really meaning it'. In this case, the person does not give *himself* in giving the gift, he is not present in it; instead, the gift is simply

---

[7] Ulrich, *HA*, p. 1.

an object, separate from him. This sort of exchange tends to take the form of a transaction. On the other hand, a person can give a gift without any such separation: he holds onto it in handing it over, he does not succeed in letting it go in a decisive and definitive manner, into the possession of the recipient. In this case, the gift is *not* a gift, but instead an extension of the giver, which thus fails to be communicated in a genuine and true way to the recipient. One might want to say that the problem, here, is that the giver is in this case *too* present in the gift, but if we consider it more profoundly we would have to say that the giver in this case is not *in* the gift at all, but rather hovers over it, demanding some sort of recognition or recompense. He is outside of the gift, but the gift, as a mere extension of the giver, is not 'outside' of him. It is therefore not truly communicated to the recipient. The paradoxical character of a gift becomes evident precisely here: it is only in giving *gratuitously*, in a generous *letting go*, of the gift that the giver becomes, so to speak, part of the gift, that he can be said truly to give himself in giving the gift, and indeed to give himself thus *away*. We note in this context that it is the particular mark of a *person* to be capable of the sort of self-transcendence that the giving of a gift, thus interpreted, represents, which is why the notion of gift is inseparable from that of personal love.

Ulrich's interpretation of the nature of a gift is significantly different from the better known view of Jean-Luc Marion,[8] and this difference is in part what accounts for their divergent judgements regarding the role of metaphysics. For Marion, there is what we might describe as a certain divide between ontology and semiology, between what a thing is in itself (substance) and its reference beyond itself to what is other (relation). To put the matter in somewhat simplistic terms, for Marion, to focus on one's reception of a gift on *what* is given, on the gift as a thing in itself, is precisely to forget the giver. In this case, the more one takes possession of a thing, the less one receives it as a gift.[9] Ulrich's view is more supple, fluid and paradoxical: one does not genuinely receive a gift *unless* one takes it fully into oneself; to refuse to take hold of the gift, to have it simply pour through oneself as if one were a bucket with a hole, is in fact to frustrate

---

[8] See, for example, Marion's presentation of gift in *Being Given: Toward a Phenomenology of Givenness* (trans. Jeffrey L. Kosky; Stanford: Stanford University Press, 2002), pp. 71–118. As John Milbank has pointed out, even in his critique of Derrida, Marion shares many of Derrida's assumptions concerning gift: see Milbank, 'Can a Gift Be Given? Prolegomena to a Future Trinitarian Metaphysic', *Modern Theology* 11 (1) (1995): 119–61.

[9] Marion's interpretation of the parable of the prodigal son illustrates this point well: see *God without Being: Hors-Texte* (trans. Thomas A. Carlson; Chicago: University of Chicago Press, 1991), pp. 95–101. It would be interesting to compare this to Ulrich's interpretation of the same parable: *Gabe und Vergebung* (Freiburg, i.Br.: Johannes Verlag Einsiedeln, 2006). Ulrich takes up many of the same insights as Marion, but does so within a decidedly metaphysical context.

the giving, to refuse to allow the giver to make a gift. A generous giver wants the recipient truly to delight in *what* he gives, and not simply in the giver himself; in his giving of the gift, he takes a special joy precisely in his being forgotten for a moment: his joy would be lessened if the recipient of a gift immediately cast it aside so as not to interrupt his gazing at the giver. There is no opposition *in principle* between the in-itself reality of a gift, and its relatedness, its transparency to the giver. But because there is no opposition, explicit gratitude does not, on the other hand, interrupt the delight in the thing itself, so that one has to *turn away* from the giver in order to enjoy the gift. Instead, the giver is always present *in* the gift, and gratuitously so, which is what allows the gift given and received to effect a profound intimacy, a true personal communion. The substantial reality of the thing in itself is no obstacle to but precisely a creative mediator of the personal intimacy.[10]

This has implications, of course, for the way we interpret God's relation to the world. Marion and Ulrich both think of this relation in terms of *gift*, but while Ulrich connects gift and being, Marion refuses this connection. According to Ulrich, God gives himself in giving what is other than himself, he gives being to the things that are, and this is an essential aspect of what it means to say that God is love. Now, this does not mean of course that being is some *thing* that is given. While Ulrich affirms, in contrast to Marion, that being is in fact a 'medium' of sorts between God and the world, he nevertheless wholly accepts Aquinas's statement that there *is* no medium between God and the world: *non potest aliquid esse medium inter creatum et increatum*.[11] Ulrich can affirm both because of his particular interpretation of being as love: being is no reality that would stand in itself between God and the world. Instead, being is 'pure mediation',[12] it '*is*' 'nothing', not in the negative Hegelian sense of an empty concept that is most universal because it is least determinate, nor in the Heideggerian sense of a 'clearing' that gives itself by withdrawing, but

---

[10] Ulrich illustrates this point from another angle when he presents a child who is playing with blocks. The child builds a tower, and proudly shows the creation to his mother. She looks, not at him, but at the tower, and imaginatively enters into his vision of the thing, describing the various features with admiration. This presence of the tower between the mother and the child in fact enables a more profound and even immediate intimacy than if she were to look past it and address him directly.

[11] Aquinas, *De veritate* 8.17; cf. Ulrich, *HA*, p. 15. In this respect, Ulrich does not construct some philosophical concept as a mediator between God and the world that would substitute for the Person of Christ. He therefore satisfies Barth's concern regarding the Catholic *analogia entis*: on this, see Martin Bieler, 'Analogia Entis as an Expression of Love according to Ferdinand Ulrich', in *The Analogy of Being: Invention of the Antichrist or the Wisdom of God?* (ed. Thomas Joseph White; Grand Rapids, MI: Eerdmans, 2010), pp. 314–40.

[12] Ulrich, *HA*, pp. 25–6. This phrase comes originally from Gustav Siewerth, *Der Thomismus als Identitätsystem* (Frankfurt: Verlag Schulte-Bulmke, 1939), p. 171; see Martin Bieler's introduction to Ulrich, *HA*, p. xvii.

rather in the Thomistic sense of a likeness of the divine goodness,[13] which does not cling to itself in opposition to the other, but is itself always already in relation to its other: 'The pure mediation of being, which is "nothing", unveils the infinite loving presence of God.'[14]

As Martin Bieler has observed,[15] the decisive statement about being, which lies at the heart of Ulrich's thought and thus animates the whole of it, occurs in *De potentia* 1.1: according to Aquinas, created being, *esse*, is '*completum et simplex sed non subsistens*'. What might otherwise appear to be a contradiction for the classical mind – namely, the non-identification of perfection and subsistence – becomes for Ulrich a profound expression of the paradox of love, which has everything precisely in, as it were, not keeping anything to itself. Being is perfection, as Aquinas repeatedly says, but it has its own perfection only in its other: there 'is' no 'to be', except in the endless abundance of the many things that are; or to put it another way, being 'is' only as having always already given itself away and having always already been received by the various *entia*. The many things that *are*, on the other hand, are called beings only by virtue of their derivation from *esse*, which means that they are themselves limited expressions of the complete and simple act of being. The essence constricts and limits *esse* through its participation in, its par-taking of, the 'to be'. This limitation, however, is not a mere negative imposition on what would otherwise be perfect in itself; instead, it is itself a positive expression of what we might call the radical humility of the non-subsistence of *esse*. In this respect, the very smallness and particularity of a created *ens*, interpreted in light of love, proves to be the proper locus of being in its fullness, the place wherein the mystery of being comes magnificently to expression. Here, again, we find an echo of generosity as a hidden presence.

There would be a number of ways to develop and enrich what is stated here in a rather schematic form: Ulrich's *HA* is an excruciatingly sophisticated reflection on this mystery, and a relentless pursuit of the implications of both the necessary sense of being and its distortions. In the present context, I will only unfold two aspects, which bear directly on the relationship between philosophy and revelation, and ultimately on Ulrich's particular characterization of the essence of modernity. The first aspect is a remarkable analogy that opens up between the 'onto-logical'[16] difference between 'to be' and 'that which

---

[13] Aquinas, *De veritate*, 22.2.2. Cf. Ulrich, *HA*, p. 20.
[14] Ulrich, *HA*, p. 20.
[15] Bieler, '*Analogia Entis*', p. 322.
[16] Ulrich tends to hyphenate this word, apparently in order to emphasize that the ontological

is' (*Sein* and *Seiende*, or *esse* and *ens*) and the grace–nature relationship. To speak of the grace–nature relationship is not primarily an attempt to figure out how to relate one thing to another conceptually, but rather above all to understand the way a concrete or created being encounters God's call, his invitation, in history. In the middle ages, the word 'supernatural' came to be used in theology as a way of expressing the *gratuity* of grace, its *transcendence* of nature, the fact that God's personal invitation to share in his triune life is not, so to speak, 'built into' human beings as a constitutive part of their essential definition.[17] Instead, grace perfects nature only by elevating it beyond itself. At the same time, however, according to the scholastic axiom, grace pre-supposes nature, which means it concedes, we might say, a certain *primacy* to nature in its healing elevation and perfection. To put it in 'Ulrichian' terms, the perfection that grace gives, it gives in a certain sense as *belonging* 'natively' to nature *qua* nature.[18] This is part of the radical gratuity, the infinite generosity, that constitutes the very nature of grace.

Now, it is just at this point that the connection with the ontological difference becomes visible. Ulrich speaks about the 'superessentiality of being', a phrase, I suggest, that ought to be understood by analogy to the 'supernaturality of grace' just described. Ulrich means by this phrase, most directly, that *esse* is really distinct from essence in all created being, so that it can be said to transcend all things that are without itself being either an existing thing in its own right, or a mere logical concept. As we saw, this is only non-dialectically possible insofar as being is understood as pure mediation or radical generosity. As such, however, *esse* does not simply 'precede' the things that are: *esse* rather 'pre-supposes' the very essences it makes be.[19] For this reason, the 'to be' can be said to *belong* properly to things; it is so radically given away to things and subsequently so deeply received by them, it can be said in fact to be the *result* of a being's constitutive principles.[20] But if the gift of being is so deeply inscribed in things as to be in some sense the things themselves (an *ens* is an

---

difference is not just a fact, as it were, but an event co-enacted between being (*on*) and man (i.e. reason, *logos*).

[17] On the pre-history of the term, and the evolution of its usage and significance, see Henri de Lubac, *Surnaturel: études historiques* (Paris: Desclée de Brouwer, 1991), pp. 325–428.

[18] As Stefan Oster explains in his exposition of some of the basic features of Ulrich's metaphysics, Ulrich appropriated and transposed into a metaphysical key Kierkegaard's insight into the super-generosity of love: 'According to Kierkegaard, love, insofar as it "builds up," always acts in such a way as to presuppose – and, in so doing, to let itself be given – what it itself creatively achieves.' Stefan Oster, 'Thinking Love at the Heart of Things. The Metaphysics of Being as Love in the Work of Ferdinand Ulrich', *Communio: International Catholic Review* 37 (Winter 2010): 660–700 (677).

[19] Of course, this is not meant to be read as if some agency was being attributed to *esse*.

[20] See Aquinas, *Super Boethium de Trinitate*, 5.3.

esse habens), it means that the essences of things cannot be thought of as self-enclosed quantities ('essence-blocks', as Ulrich puts it), but are themselves forms of generosity in their own order. Substances concretely subsist as poured out, so to speak, into their accidents, living beings subsist in their proper operations by which they enter the world and the world enters them, and human beings have the actuality of their essence in the ecstatic and 'redditive' acts of intellect and will in which they affirm the meaning of being and bring that meaning to fruition.[21] In all of this, we see analogous expressions of self-transcendence, of self-possession in self-gift, which is a reflection of the created being that is itself *similitudo bonitatis divinae*.

When we say that there is an analogy between the superessentiality of being and the supernaturality of grace, we do not simply mean that the two things 'look alike', or have some features in common. Instead, we mean to say that there is a *real unity* between these, though of course it is coincident with an ever-greater difference.[22] To put the point more concretely, to see the superessentiality of being, as Ulrich unfolds it, is to understand being as inherently generous, to see that all things have their own proper existence always already in relation to things different from themselves in a dynamic of giving and receiving.[23] It is to see nature as *inwardly* self-transcending, but to see this self-transcendence at the same time as subsistence, as the possession of perfection, so being complete, rather than as processual dissolution. Only such a nature is capable of encountering grace *ontologically*, that is, of receiving grace into the roots of its being so that the whole of it is transformed without becoming something else. Only such a nature can be viewed as having an intrinsic openness to grace.

Ulrich sees modern thought as forgetting the ontological difference, and therefore embracing a conception of nature that is opaque in relation to grace. What is decisive in the modern notion is a kind of 'essentializing of being', i.e. a rejection of the superessentiality of the 'to be', which can take an almost endless variety of forms. The crucial dimension is the systematic tendency to reduce *esse* to the multiplicity of *entia*, that is, to absorb *esse* in its 'nothingness' into the

---

[21] At the same time, of course, it is necessary to affirm an abiding distinction between 'first actuality' and 'second actuality'. The point here is that this distinction should not be interpreted in a chronological fashion, or even in a unilateral way metaphysically. The first act does not simply come 'before' the second if being is interpreted concretely.

[22] Ulrich suggests that grace has helped to liberate being in its superessentiality, but does not for all that form an essential *part* of that superessentiality. To make it such a part would in fact be to 'hypostasize' being, and at the same time to incorporate a theological a priori into one's philosophizing. On this, see Ulrich, 'Metaphysik der Wiederholung', p. 295.

[23] The paradigm of this giving and receiving is man in his community of love, which is where the meaning of being becomes explicit. This is why Ulrich says that the creative act 'aims at' man as its destination.

essence of the things that are. Concomitant with this is the reduction of being to a concept: if reality is comprised of *entia* alone, then *esse* becomes exactly 'unreal', and so has existence only as a thought in the mind (*ens rationis*). The full weight of this reduction can be felt only if we recall that what is thereby eliminated is precisely what Aquinas had called the likeness of divine goodness. Behind this, as we shall see in a moment, is a radical reconception of God that amounts to a betrayal of the Trinitarian unity of the Divine Persons. But for the moment, we note simply that this reduction cancels out the generosity inscribed in being, so that things become nothing more than themselves in their sheer facticity or in the abstraction of logical identity (A=A). In this case, the encounter with grace can appear only as a violent intrusion or a cosmetic alteration (hear: merely forensic justification), and ultimately both at once.

But there is an even deeper dimension to Ulrich's interpretation of the ontological difference in relation to the question of nature and grace. Here we come to the second aspect, which is no doubt one of Ulrich's most novel contributions to philosophy. In addition to the analogy between the superessentiality of being and the supernaturality of grace, there is a further analogy between the salvation-historical situatedness of nature's encounter with grace and what Ulrich calls ontological spatio-temporality.[24] We will deal here only with the temporal aspect of his idea. Inspired in part by Heidegger – though, as we shall see, departing dramatically from Heidegger's own view of the matter – Ulrich sees the ontological difference as unfolding the fundamental form of time, which 'proceeds from being', according to the ontological difference. Time can therefore take a perverted form when being is not properly received – i.e. not received as a gift, as love. To put the matter somewhat oversimply, Ulrich associates the 'having-been' (*das Ge-wesene*), i.e. the past, with the reality of the essence (*das Wesen*), and associates the 'yet-to-be', the future (*die Zu-kunft*), with the ideal fullness of being, the 'to be'. The living present, then, is being in its concrete subsistence ('*Da-Sein*'), which is as it were the intersection of past and future in which each opens toward the other, or the non-reductive unity of the two dimensions of being. In this case, the future is understood as growing organically out of the past, and the past as opening up to its fulfilment in the future. The present, then, as the ever-fruitful unity of the two, is an 'already-not yet', an actually determinate reality, which one nevertheless receives anew at every moment, and therefore beholds with ever new eyes.

A failure to receive being as love, and indeed to receive it *in* love, thus entails

---

[24] See Ulrich, *HA*, pp. 169–85.

as one of its consequences the fragmentation of time. It is not a surprise that the most decisive casualty of this fragmentation is the living present, which tends to be reduced to a simple, positivistic facticity. But as thus closed up in itself, things 'already' are what they are: the present is received as always already a 'thing of the past'. This is a way of talking about the 'essentializing' of being: in this essentializing, we experience things as nothing more than what we already know; the world in this case never has anything generally *new* to reveal to us; we take everything, not as a gift, but simply as given, which is to say we take things for granted. It would not be difficult to recognize this experience in the rationalism and empiricism of the early modern thinkers, but Ulrich points to Hegel as the culmination of this essentializing of being, insofar as he interprets the movement of history as the unfolding of the concept, which must subsequently be gathered back up into the concept as spirit made fully actual. Philosophy, for Hegel, is therefore not a constantly renewed reception of the revelation of being in the morning of the living present, but instead the owl of Minerva that takes flight only at dusk, after the day is spent, to take hold of what has already been into the logic of the concept.[25]

In making this judgement, Ulrich evidently has much in common with Heidegger, who likewise interprets Hegel as having brought to a certain completion the modern thinking that has always-already forgotten and so closed the ontological difference. But it is instructive to see how different is their response; according to Ulrich, Heidegger betrays a tendency to absolutize the future in his overcoming of the essentialization of being. There is a sort of relentless prioritizing of possibility over actuality, of an openness to receive that must continue past any particular reception, or a listening to being that cannot get caught up in any particular word that is heard: a listening, not to hear, but simply to listen. Ulrich explains that Heidegger's resolute fixing of the ontological difference leads to a kind of mythologizing of being (*das Seinsmythos*), which is the transformation of the revelation of being into a *myth* that, as such, occurs indeed (*sich ereignet*), but in a time that lies precisely

---

[25] To be sure, Hegel describes philosophy as 'a continuous awakening. Such work is not only deposited in the temple of memory as forms of times gone by but is just as present and living now as at the time of its production ... The history of philosophy has to do not with what is gone, but with the living present'. G. W. F. Hegel, *On Art, Religion, and the History of Philosophy: Introductory Lectures* (ed. J. Glenn Gray; Indianapolis, Hackett, 1997), pp. 245–6. But he then goes on to explain just a few pages later that 'Every philosophy is the philosophy of its own day, a link in the whole chain of spiritual development, and thus it can only find satisfaction for the interests belonging to its own particular time' (p. 251).

outside of history, a primordial age that never finds any concrete realization in history, but is always yet to come.[26]

Now, Ulrich's critique of Hegel and Heidegger becomes especially clear – and essentially concrete – when he transposes it into the terms of salvation history. According to Ulrich, Heidegger's thought is tempted to cancel out the incarnation in favour of the 'godly god' who is always yet to come. The ontological correlate of this theological position is a hypostasizing of the superessential being over against its always already having been mediated through the essence to concrete subsistence. Effectively, Ulrich says, Heidegger attempts to return thought to 'an Old Testament attitude of expectant waiting or into the "not-yet" of Greek metaphysics'.[27] But in a world into which God has entered, this apparently 'pre-Christian' position is inescapably an *anti-Christian one*,[28] a rejection of the incarnation, which then has vast and profound philosophical implications for one's ability to remain faithful to the ontological difference. Hegel's thought clearly falls into the opposite temptation: in Ulrich's words, he 'logicizes the Spirit', which means he absolutizes the *Logos*, absorbing the Holy Spirit, who is in fact the fruitful unfolding of the truth of the Logos, the 'ex-egesis' of the Word, in the free movement of history, back into the 'pastness' of the incarnation. The hyper-rationalism of Hegel's spirit as a fully actualized concept, in other words, is a philosophical expression of the failure to interpret the Son as co-spirating the Spirit in fruitful union with the Father.[29] Instead of a *logos of love*, we have a rational substitute *for* love.

But the metaphysics of modernity plays itself out theologically at an even deeper level than that of salvation history: what is at stake in the 'risk of the question of being' is an interpretation of the nature of God himself, or even more directly, of person and nature in the inner life of the divine communion. At a decisive moment in *HA*, Ulrich makes the pregnant and provocative claim

---

[26] Although Heidegger is known for elevating the thinking of the 'early Greeks' as a uniquely profound experience of the difference of being from beings, he eventually came to the judgement that what he meant by the thinking of being '*als solches*' did not occur even there, and was an event yet to occur. See Martin Heidegger, *Contributions to Philosophy (of the Event)* (trans. Richard Rojcewicz and Daniela Vallega-Neu; Indianapolis: Indiana University Press, 2012), and *On Time and Being* (trans. Joan Stambaugh; New York: Harper and Row, 1972).

[27] Ulrich, *HA*, p. 3. He does not name Heidegger explicitly here, but is describing the 'type' that Heidegger represents.

[28] This is the fundamental problem that inevitably arises if one attempts to take Heidegger's 'non-theistic' philosophizing as a purifying propaedeutic to Christian faith. For an example of this approach, see Laurence Paul Hemming, *Heidegger's Atheism: The Refusal of a Theological Voice* (Notre Dame, IN: University of Notre Dame Press, 2002).

[29] It should be noted that this is only one way of expressing the issue. Ulrich presents many others: for example, he interprets Hegel as attempting to provide a philosophical *substitution* for the *Virgo-Mater*, who represents in her flesh, in *person*, the mediation of the infinite by the finite.

that the 'fate of modern metaphysics is made possible by [the] "impotence of God's Fatherhood"'.[30] Ulrich's own explication of this claim is extraordinarily complex, and it is not possible to follow it out here in any detail. We will instead focus on a single point. A basic theme at the centre of Ulrich's metaphysics, as we have seen, is the superessentiality of being interpreted positively as love and therefore as a perfection. We claimed that there is an analogy between this superessentiality and grace. Inside of this, there is the ultimate principle of the analogy, which is the 'supernaturality', or one might say the 'hyper-ousial' character of the Trinitarian Persons with respect to the divine nature or *ousia*. Ulrich claims that the 'ultimate condition of possibility' of a proper reception of being in the ontological difference is the 'unfathomable unity and differentiation of Person and Nature in God that is experienced in faith'.[31] We understand a cause in its effects; the interpretation of being, as God's 'first effect',[32] is by implication an interpretation of the nature of God.[33] According to Ulrich, the hypostasizing of being over against concrete subsistence, and the corresponding absorption of *esse* into the essence of real beings, is at its roots a 'depotentiating' of the Father, whereby he is interpreted as impotent to generate, incapable of giving his substance in a fully complete way – which would imply simultaneous separation and unity, discontinuity with perfect simplicity – to the Son. Because of this impotence, there is so to speak something withheld, a 'remainder', which is not generously given and which the Son therefore has to 'take' for himself. This taking presents itself as a supplemental act necessitated by the failure of the gift, by which the Son completes what the Father was impotent to achieve himself, and at the same time and in that very act turns against the Father in his self-initiated assumption of this negativity in the work of the incarnation. The Holy Spirit, then, is logically required to effect a resolution of this contradiction in God.

This very brief sketch of the fragmentation of triune life in the failure to receive being in and as love alone already reveals how the path of Ulrich's thinking of being leads into the abyssal – *ab-gründig* – depths of the inner mystery of God, a path that cannot properly be followed except within sacramental thanksgiving and thoughtful, contemplative prayer. The primary point in the present context is to see that, when one takes a position in the drama of

---

[30] Ulrich, *HA*, p. 57.
[31] Ulrich, *HA*, p. 118.
[32] Cf. Aquinas, *De potentia*, 3.4.
[33] An indirect but, in the concrete order in our particular historical circumstances, a *necessary* implication.

salvation history, between the historical incarnation and the *parousia* of Christ in the Holy Spirit, one is not outside of God, but *inside* of the drama of the Trinitarian life. Similarly, when one interprets the meaning of being, and thus enacts a particular reception of the meaning of time, one is not *outside*, but rather already *inside* of the drama of redemption. This is why we can speak of 'layers', or perhaps better of 'facets', of analogy in these non-reducibly different orders. As we said above, the term 'analogy' that we have been using here designates not only a similarity of features, but a real relation. To put this another way, there is a kind of *causality* at work here: the absolute and unsurpassable gift in the Trinity is what makes possible both God's self-gift in creation and the more direct self-gift in the incarnation. Moreover, it is this entrance into history, in the fullness of time, that has made possible a proper experience of time in the inter-relation of past, present and future, and, inseparably from this a proper reception of being. More specifically, Ulrich insists that it is the grace of the incarnation that, on the one hand, liberates the density of the living present, and on the other hand liberates the meaning of being as love. As he puts it, it is in fact grace that in a certain sense 'safeguards [*ausspart*] the space of the super-essentiality of being'[34] and it does so, we might say, precisely by transcending being in the mode of generous gift. To identify being and grace by hypostasizing being over-against concrete substance, or to collapse being into essences and thus seize from below what is offered as a gift, is to transform the gratuity of a theological event into what Ulrich calls a 'metaphysical a priori', that is, it is to make grace for all intents and purposes 'a constitutive element of being'. It is in light of this insight that Ulrich affirms Przywara's judgement that 'the absolute philosophies of modernity are … de-theologized theologies'.[35]

We are now more or less in a position to understand the claim made at the outset, namely, that thinking in obedience to Christ is what can set modern philosophy free from (pseudo-)theology. The deepest depths of the original meaning of being as gift have been definitively revealed in the coming of Christ. Thought can either take over what is revealed as its own, and so render the incarnation simply a 'thing of the past', or it can defer the gift as something always yet to come. While this latter option may seem to keep philosophy pure by affirming the gift only as an ever open possibility, in fact it amounts to the

---

[34] Ulrich, *HA*, pp. 112–13.
[35] Ulrich, *HA*, p. 56, citing Erich Przywara's *Analogia entis: Metaphysik*, vol. 1 (Munich: Kösel and Pustet, 1932), p. 41; *Analogia entis: Metaphysik: Ur-Struktur und All-Rhythmus* (Freiburg: Johannes Verlag Einsiedeln, 3rd printing, 1996), p. 70; *Analogia Entis: Metaphysics: Original Structure and Universal Rhythm* (trans. John R. Betz and David Bentley Hart; Grand Rapids, MI: Eerdmans, 2014), p. 164.

hypostasizing of being as self-withdrawing over-against the God who is *already* revealed in the incarnation and therefore constructing an *alternative* interpretation of gift, which cannot avoid becoming something that is always still yet to be given. The only possibility that genuinely liberates philosophy in its thinking of the superessentiality of being as such is *actually to receive the gift* of divine revelation specifically *as* a gift, and therefore as irreducibly and forever distinct from being as nature. This actual reception is inseparable from the gift of self which is an entry into the living present, the 'place' wherein nature is what it is only as ever newly received here and now. It is in this way that nature is free from any false anticipations and pre-emptions in one direction or another, and so held in perfect readiness for grace. A startling implication of this interpretation is that the readiness for grace is thus revealed to be not a provisional state that has to be determined somehow in abstraction from grace and that will be superseded by the reception of grace, after which, presumably, nature will no longer need to be held in readiness; instead, nature's openness to grace shows itself as a state of perfection, which we can understand, again, only when we think most fundamentally in terms of gift.

What Ulrich's philosophy reveals is that the problem of modern thought ought to be understood, and responded to, most fundamentally as a problem that is at its roots ultimately both theological and philosophical, and this becomes properly evident when we engage with modernity on the basis of the one thing necessary – on the basis of love, as the meaning of reality as a whole.

10

Christology and the *Nihil*: The Wisdom of Cardinal Pierre de Bérulle and the Catholic Encounter with Modernity

Aaron Riches

In his book, *Nihil Unbound: Enlightenment and Extinction*, the Scottish 'speculative realist' philosopher Ray Brassier makes a radical argument for the nihilist entailment of the Enlightenment rightly received.[1] According to Brassier, fidelity to the 'vector of intellectual discovery' that was 'initiated by Galileo in the physical realm, continued by Darwin in the biological sphere, and currently being extended by cognitive science to the domain of mind',[2] is obliged to pursue the disenchantment of matter to the fact of literal extinction.[3] A genuine philosophical 'realism' in accord with this modern 'vector of intellectual discovery', Brassier insists, must be fundamentally based in one objective fact of the reality of our world and being that we know with certainty beyond every subjective experience of meaning: 'the earth will be incinerated by the sun 4 billion years hence' and eventually 'all matter in the cosmos will disintegrate into unbound elementary particles'.[4] The pathos of modern and postmodern philosophy, according to Brassier, lies in its unanimous resolve to avoid the revolutionary entailment of this 'Enlightenment logic of disenchantment'. Rather than confirming this truth of reality that we know, and speculating from the basis of this reality, philosophy from Kant to Derrida is distinguished by its

---

[1] I am grateful to Josef Seifert and Chris Hackett, who both read and commented on this text in an earlier draft; I am also grateful to Msgr. Javier Martínez, Cyril O'Regan and D. C. Schindler, for the helpful criticisms and questions they raised when the paper was originally presented.
[2] Ray Brassier, *Nihil Unbound: Enlightenment and Extinction* (London: Palgrave Macmillan, 2007), p. 40.
[3] Brassier, *Nihil Unbound*, p. xi.
[4] Brassier, *Nihil Unbound*, pp. 49–50.

resolve to 'stave off the "threat" of nihilism by safeguarding the experience of meaning – characterized as the defining feature of human existence'.[5] Against this loss of philosophical nerve, Brassier seeks to assert the 'speculative opportunity' of the material fact of *homo sapiens*: the human has no possibility apart from the disintegration of matter, and as such his destiny is the *nihil* unbound.

The nihilist 'vector of intellectual discovery' diagnosed and embraced by Brassier was anticipated and confronted Christologically in the sixteenth century by Cardinal Pierre de Bérulle. While we could fruitfully detain ourselves to nuance the different senses of meaning of *nihil* taken by Brassier and Bérulle respectively, for both the *nihil* is a fundamental fact of human being and the experience of being human. While for Brassier this means that human being is essentially orientated *ad nihilum* – this is his *telos* and destiny – for Bérulle it tends to signify that human being is originally constituted *ex nihilo*, such that this is the first metaphysical and spiritual fact of his existence and experience such that he cannot be self-sufficient in anything because all he properly possesses of himself is 'nothing'.

Made a Cardinal and named 'the Apostle of the Incarnate Word' by Pope Urban VIII in 1627, Bérulle is best known as the founder of the so-called 'French School of Spirituality', which came to dominate modern French piety from the mid-seventeenth century through to the twentieth century.[6] Bérulle's life was above all dedicated to the direction of souls and to the renewal of the priesthood, for which he founded the French Oratory. At the heart of his vocation as a director of souls was his role as perpetual visitor of the Reformed Carmelite nuns in France, whom he was instrumental in bringing from Spain (he personally accompanied a small group of Teresa of Avila's sisters to France in 1604). In addition, he played a significant role in the courts of two French kings, Henry IV and Louis XIII, in the context of which he argued tirelessly for a pan-Catholic political solidarity on the continent, an argument he humiliatingly

---

[5] Brassier, *Nihil Unbound*, from the back cover synopsis.
[6] For the works of Bérulle, see Michel Dupuy (ed.), *Pierre de Bérulle: Oeuvres complètes* (Paris: Éditions du Cerf, 1995–); all citations of Bérulle are from these texts. The literature in English on Bérulle is limited. In what follows I have relied greatly on the excellent book of Erik Varden, *Redeeming Freedom: The Principle of Servitude in Bérulle* (Rome: Studia Anselmiana, 2011). Also see William M. Thompson (ed.), *Bérulle and the French School: Selected Writings* (Mawah, NJ: Paulist Press, 1989); and Henri Bremond, *A Literary History of Religious Thought in France*, vol. 3, *The Triumph of Mysticism* (London: SPCK, 1936). The French literature on Bérulle, by contrast, is exhaustive. Some of the key French texts I have used include: Michel Dupuy, *Bérulle: Une spiritualité de l'adoration* (Paris: Desclée de Brouwer, 1964) and *Le Christ de Bérulle* (Paris: Desclée de Brouwer, 2001); Stéphane-Marie Morgan, *Pierre de Bérulle et les carmélites de France: La querelle du gouvernement, 1583–1629* (Paris: Cerf, 1995); Richard Cadoux, *Bérulle et la question de l'homme* (Paris: Cerf, 2005); and Rémi Lescot, *Pierre de Bérulle: Apôtre du Verb incarné* (Paris: Cerf, 2013).

lost when France marched on Spain at Casale in January 1629. Bérulle's various missions and voluminous writings find their unity in his concern for the practical reality of the Christian life lived, and in the conviction that the human being can entertain no greater delusion than that of his own self-sufficiency, which is not only a metaphysical absurdity but the root of the fallen condition of enslavement to sin.

From *Néant* to *Néant*

Created *ex nihilo*, the human being is for Bérulle, in his essential constitution, a creature who literally possesses 'nothing' of himself. This of course is neither meant to deny that human beings really do exist and live (which would imply that divine creation makes no difference), nor is it to claim that human being has no substantial being in himself, nor freedom to realize acts through his own initiative. It is rather to say that the basic fact of human being and action must involve always, first of all, its being 'anteriorly receptive' (to use a term of David Schindler Sr) to the gift of God apart from which the human being is simply a non-existent.[7] This metaphysical insight lies behind Bérulle's devotion of servitude, which has often been misrepresented as a reactionary baroque '"victim" spirituality',[8] but is in fact based in the reality of contingent being: the human is a fragile existent hovering between being and nothingness. And so while 'light and force of nature does not contain a greater miracle than man',[9] nevertheless this miracle exists only as dependent on an Other. The question of humanism in this light has nothing to do with a clash between humanist optimism and Augustinian pessimism, but concerns rather a question of ontological fact: the human is a creature made from nothing, who of himself is nothing. In this regard the relation of Bérulle to Pico della Mirandola is illustrative.

In *De hominis dignitate*, which exercised a permanent influence on Bérulle,[10] Pico's concern is to articulate an idea of the human as a *Proteus*: 'his specificity is paradoxically to combine in himself, the centre of the cosmos, the material, animate and spiritual, along with the ruling, knowing and loving functions of

---

[7] Cf. David L. Schindler, 'Norris Clarke on Person, Being and St Thomas', *Communio* 20 (1993): 580–92.
[8] Ephraim Radner, *The End of the Church: A Pneumatology of Christian Division in the West* (Grand Rapids, MI: Eerdmans, 1998), p. 341.
[9] Bérulle, *Discours de l'état et des Grandeurs de Jésus* (*Oeuvres complètes*, vol. 7), p. 423.
[10] See Varden, *Redeeming Freedom*, pp. 32–3.

the three angelic orders of the Thrones, Cherubim and Seraphim'.[11] Between these attributes, according to Pico, the human is free to choose who he will be. All of this, on one level, Bérulle upholds, and indeed he writes of the human as made with 'existence as the elements, with life as the plants, with sentience as the animals, and with intelligence as the angels'.[12] But whereas for Pico the emphasis lies on how the human being is the centre containing all the attributes of being, from which springs his vocation as *universi contemplator*,[13] for Bérulle the orientation is different. Man is at the centre of the cosmos, not so much as containing all things, or as surveyor of all things, but rather as a being radically implicated and so pulled between all things.[14] The human being is between heaven and hell, between God and the devil, between the angels and the animals, between spirit and matter, and ultimately between the pure *esse* of God and the *ex nihilo* from which he is made. And so whereas for Pico the greatness of the human being lies in his privileged access to every corner of reality, for Bérulle the human being is rather more stretched by the anterior tensions of between-ness. And so, whereas the freedom of the human for Pico rests in his protean capacity to choose who he will be, the freedom of Bérulle's human being is burdened by competing servitudes he cannot escape from following. In this way Bérulle could be read as clarifying Pico in a way that recovers the central Catholic insight that it is precisely human salvation or damnation that is worked out in the drama of the everyday.

The original servitude that, for Bérulle, marks the fundamental human experience is the simple fact that apart from God the human does not exist.[15] Human being only 'is' in relation and receptivity to God. Crucially this original servitude is not primarily moral, but rather is more strictly a metaphysical fact. Before the touch of Luciferian pride, then, the servitude of being is not experienced as something demeaning, rather it converts to this kind of experience only through the lie of the grasp at self-sufficiency (which is the root of original sin), and the concrete experience that follows from the consequence of original sin. In the distortive refusal to admit the limitation of the human being, to wish to exist for oneself and not by the gift of an Other, the original servitude of being gives way to an enslavement to sin, which is the second servitude.[16] Although extraneous to his fundamental being, the enslavement to sin, to the *néant*

---

[11] John Milbank, 'Dignity Rather than Right', *Open Insight* 5 (7) (January 2014): 77–124.
[12] Bérulle, *Discours de l'état*, p. 424.
[13] Varden, *Redeeming Freedom*, p. 33.
[14] Bérulle, *Court traités* (*Oeuvres complètes*, vol. 6), p. 77.
[15] On the three servitudes of Bérulle, see Varden, *Redeeming Freedom*, pp. 37–44.
[16] Bérulle, *Oeuvres de piété* (*Oeuvres complètes*, vols 3 and 4), no. 35.

du péché, is organically related to the *nihil* from which the human being was created insofar as it is a reversion of his being to that which is perfectly not-God. By proudly asserting to live for himself, the human being can reach and grasp for himself only the *néant* of his origin, which alone is his proper 'possession' apart from God.

The third type of servitude is the servitude to Jesus Christ, the Saviour who redeems the human being from the slavery of sin. This third servitude differs from the first two in that it requires a deliberate practice of abandonment and dispossession, what Bérulle calls *anéantissement*. Herein the true interiority of the human being is realized, not in being most in himself, in the sense of being self-contained, but in realizing his insufficiency, his nothingness before God, whereby he experiences a passage from the original *néant* to *néant* of human being created out of nothing to the *autre néant* of being a pure *capax Dei*.[17] It is precisely in this way that Bérulle recommends the Delphic exhortation, *nosce teipsum*, beloved of Renaissance humanism. For Bérulle, the Delphic exhortation properly lived does not lead to ego-centrism or anthropocentrism, but leads rather to God in whom the 'self' is truly known. 'It is good ... to know oneself', Bérulle writes, 'because in knowing oneself we come to know God'.[18]

But to know God is to love God. The capacity to love God is the essence, for Bérulle, of the human vocation. And this vocation to love is exactly what was crippled by the grasping attempt at self-sufficiency that lies at the heart of Adam's Fall. And so it is concretely the vocation to love that the Saviour came to redeem and in which we participate in our vow of servitude to him. It is for this reason that Bérulle commends the spiritual practice of *anéantissement*, which is not so much a self-annihilation as it is a realization of the self as infinitely belonging to God in Jesus Christ to such an extent that, to deny Christ is to deny one's very self. '[I]t is no longer I who live, but Christ who lives in me' (Gal. 2.20). This realization of the 'I' as constitutively belonging to Christ is not a masochistic self-negation, but rather a response of love giving back to love encountered. And love consists in this: that is, 'not that we loved God but that he loved us' (1 Jn. 4.10), and thus love of God is first of all to receive that which is returned through servitude. Servitude and the practice of *anéantissement*, thus, are nothing other than a radical response to the recognition of the always

---

[17] The point here seems to me to be that which Augustine makes when he describes the spiritual journey as double movement from the exterior to the interior, from the inferior to the superior (*ad exterioribus ad interiora, ab inferioribus ad superior*). The more interior the 'I' becomes the more it moves inward while simultaneously opening to what is beyond and radically other.

[18] Bérulle, *Oeuvres de piété*, no. 184.

prior gift of God's love of us, through alone the human task and capacity to love is truly possible. Either the human being annihilates himself in the loveless delusion that he can create himself or he annihilates himself in ravishing love of being *capax Dei* thanks to the saving gift of our Saviour. 'Jesus alone is our accomplishment.'[19] The true 'royalty of man' thus lies in the Saviour himself, in whom we see that 'human nature was not created to remain within the terms of nature, but was made for grace and the destiny of a state elevated far beyond every [natural] power'.[20]

The Vow of Servitude and Christology

Given the foregoing, how would Bérulle respond to the nihilism of Brassier's 'vector of intellectual discovery'? Of course it is impossible to say, but a broadly Bérullian response would begin by affirming that the *nihil* is indeed a constituent aspect of what we call 'human' and that at one level human being is indeed destined in some sense for a *nihil* unbound. It would be prudent to qualify that this 'unbinding', in a Bérullian sense, is convertible with that of Brassier, for whom the *nihil* is the univocal destiny of all things. For a Bérullian the unbinding of human being into nothing can only be either into the nothingness out of which creation was originally spoken or into the unbounded love of God in Christ in whom it is 'no longer I who live, but Christ who lives in me'. But the deeper question, from a Bérullian point of view, concerns the very concrete question of what practice of life corresponds to unbounded love, to the movement from the *néant* of *creatio ex nihilo* to the *autre néant* of becoming a pure *capax Dei* in Christ. The Bérullian answer is Mary: she is Queen of Heaven precisely because she is *ancilla Domini*, because she claims nothing for herself before the Lord. This central Marian dimension was given practical expression by Bérulle in the famous vows of perpetual servitude to Mary and to Jesus, which he imposed or recommended on all those who either sought or were canonically placed under his spiritual care.

Bérulle's theology of the vow aims to achieve in the human soul a maximal receptivity to God patterned on the *fiat* of the Blessed Virgin: 'let it be done unto me according to thy word' (Lk. 1.38).[21] Internalizing the vow thus meant learning, like Mary, to desire 'to have no self in our self' in order to let 'the spirit

---

[19] Bérulle, *Oeuvres de piété*, no. 135.
[20] Bérulle, *Oeuvres de piété*, no. 85.
[21] On Bérulle's theology of servitude, see Cadoux, *Bérulle et la question de l'homme*.

of Christ be the spirit of our "self"'.²² In the vow, then, as in the Marian *fiat*, the human self is actualized in a negation of self-sufficiency to receptivity.

Patterned on the *fiat* of Mary, the vow of servitude is not only a vow of servitude to God following the example of Mary but also a vow to the Mother in imitation of the filial submission of her Child. In this way the logic of both the vow to Mary and the vow to Jesus is profoundly Christocentric: 'The servitude by which we submit to the Son of God in the order of nature is internal to the servitude by which we submit freely and voluntarily to be servants of Blessed Mary.'²³ Accordingly the highest form of Christian piety is Marian in shape and content since it must, to be Christian, involve a real pattern of following into the incarnate ground of his ultimate filial obedience to the Father, which leads directly to the Cross. We consecrate ourselves to Mary, then, because the Logos dispossessed himself to be utterly dependent on her, taking the flesh of her womb and learning the gestures of human love at her breast in order to complete his mission on Calvary. In this way the pattern of the Son's kenosis, from the frailty of his human infancy to the brutal wounding of his Passion, is the most concrete icon of filial obedience and it reveals, in the most tangible way, *who* Jesus is.²⁴ And in this form of being, of dispossession and being submissive to the initiative of an Other, Christ, according to Bérulle, gives us to ourselves (*nous-mêmes à nous-mêmes*).²⁵ The patient dependence and ready receptivity of the Logos becoming flesh is internal, thus, to the ultimate revelation of what it means to be truly human. This fact of Christ, as the true centre and revelation of human being, animates the metaphysical heart of the vow, which is rooted in a traditional insight native to the dogma of the hypostatic union: the humanity

---

[22] Bérulle, *Discours de l'état*, p. 119. It would not be illegitimate here to wonder if Bérulle's sense of the nothingness of the human before God does not lack something on the *personal* level. It is of course true that, as a contingent being, the human adds nothing to God, but as a created spirit, as one who is a divinely will as a *person*, the human being is an unrepeatable singular with a vocation to love in a singular way in the context of a dialogical relation to God in Christ. Nothing in Bérulle excludes this personal aspect, but it is, from a contemporary point of view, an aspect of his thought that perhaps deserves creative completion and expansion.

[23] Bérulle, *Collationes* (*Oeuvres complètes*, vol. 1), p. 234.

[24] An important point of Bérulle's Christology, in this regard, is clarified by John Milbank, who writes that, for Bérulle, the 'Son's reception [to the Father, which we can equally call his filial obedience or his servitude] is spontaneously active to such a maximum degree that we can say that he is "independent" of the Father, precisely *because* of his substantive relation to him'. John Milbank, *Beyond Secular Order: The Representation of Being and the Representation of the People* (London: Wily Blackwell, 2014), p. 239. Milbank's insightful comment, precisely on Bérulle, signals why freedom and obedience in Christology can never be juxtaposed; or better, how, in the filiation of Jesus, they are united without confusion or separation.

[25] Cf. Bérulle, *Oeuvres de piété*, nos. 34 and 245.

of Jesus does not subsist as 'human' but only 'is' insofar as it subsists in the hypostasis of the Logos.[26]

Drawing explicitly on Thomas Aquinas's subsistence doctrine of the hypostatic union, wherein the subjective unity of Christ is grounded in the divine hypostasis such that there is only one and divine *esse* in Jesus Christ, Bérulle takes this fact of the human nature of the Word as itself the ultimate exemplar of our true being, and the servitude we owe to the Saviour and source of our being. Just as the human nature of Jesus only exists as subsisting in the divine Logos, so through the vow the human being practically enacts the nothingness of his being apart from the Incarnation.[27] The hypostatic union, thus, is key to the truth of what it means to be human: contemplation of the nothingness (*néant*) of Jesus' human nature apart from the Word unlocks the metaphysical truth of human being and the ultimate vocation of the human to loving union with God through Christ. As Bérulle puts it:

> [B]y an ordinance of God this humanity [of Christ] is deprived of its subsistence and proper personality and is thus totally given over to the eternal Word; such that this humanity ... cedes ... its 'self', its proper action, and all that takes origin whatever from it to the eternal Word. From the first moment of coming into being, this nature lacks its own subsistence.[28]

The metaphysics of the hypostatic union here becomes internal to the pattern of kenosis and to the revelation of what it means to be truly human.

In light of the foregoing we can see that the paradigm of our practical *anéantissement*, for Bérulle, is concretely Christocentric in four basic ways: (1) it recalls the original Marian *fiat* through which the Incarnation becomes a fact; (2) it is patterned on the servitude of the Son to the Mother who gave him his flesh and nurtured his fragile being; (3) it follows his filial obedience to the Father's will, which leads to the Cross; and (4) it is rooted in the ontological

---

[26] Cf. Thomas Aquinas, *Summa theologiae* III, q. 2, aa. 2-3; and q. 17, aa. 1-2; Pope Pius XII, *Sempiternus Rex*, 30-1 (DS 3905); and Karl Barth, *Church Dogmatics* I/2 (trans. G. T. Thompson and Harold Knight; eds G. W. Bromiley and T. F. Torrance; Edinburgh: T. & T. Clark, 1956), pp. 163-5. For the best contemporary writings on this aspect of traditional Christological doctrine, see Ivor J. Davidson, 'Theologizing the Human Jesus: An Ancient (and Modern) Approach to Christology Reassessed', *International Journal of Systematic Theology* 3 (2) (2001): 129-53; and 'Reappropriating Patristic Christology: One Doctrine, Two Styles', *Irish Theological Quarterly* 67 (3) (2002): 225-39.

[27] On Bérulle's Christology, see Philip McCosker, 'The Christology of Pierre de Bérulle', *Downside Review* 124 (435) (2006): 111-34; Edward Howells, 'Relationality and Difference in the Mysticism of Pierre de Bérulle', *Harvard Theological Review* 102 (2) (2009): 225-43; and Miklos Vetö, 'La Christologique de Bérulle', introduction to Pierre de Bérulle, *Opuscules de piété (1644)* (Grenoble: Jérôme Millon, 1997), pp. 7-136. Cf. Varden, *Redeeming Freedom*, pp. 53-74. On Bérulle's debt to Aquinas in this regard, see McCosker, 'The Christology of Pierre de Bérulle' p. 129, no. 2.

[28] Bérulle, *Discours de l'état*, p. 118.

dispossession of Christ's humanity in the hypostatic union, which is 'deprived of subsistence and personality ... both of which it receives from the eternal Word'.[29]

Heliocentric Revolution

The Christocentric impulse the vow of servitude sought to provoke is reinforced by Bérulle's heliocentric 'science of salvation', summed up in the revolution he announces in *Discours de l'état et des Grandeurs de Jésus*. Bérulle writes:

> An excellent mind of the present age wanted to maintain that the sun is the true centre of the universe, and not the earth ... This position runs contrary to all appearance, which obliges us to conform our senses to believe that the sun is in continual movement around the earth. This new opinion…is useful and should be followed in the science of salvation: for Jesus is the immovable Sun who in his grandeur moves all things ... Jesus is the true centre ... [around which] The earth of our hearts ought to be in continual movement towards him.[30]

The heliocentric revolution set off by Copernicus in 1543 did not begin as a battle between the Church and the 'scientific revolution'. Copernicus himself had dedicated *De revolutionibus* to Pope Paul III, who embraced it not least for how he took it as confirming the Platonic sun symbolism of which he was fond in philosophical and theological matters. While not all churchmen welcomed the Copernican proposal the way Pope Paul did, others such as John of the Cross took it up as a basis of spirituality.[31] As John of the Cross writes in his commentary on *Llama amor viva*:

> This happens in the same manner as when at the movement of the earth all material things in it move as though they were nothing. So it is when the Prince moves, who Himself carries His court, instead of His court carrying Him.[32]

Himself formed in the spirituality of Carmel, Bérulle was undoubtedly acquainted with this text, and it may in fact form the basis of his own revolution in the 'science of salvation'.

---

[29] Bérulle, *Discours de l'état*, p. 117.
[30] Bérulle, *Discours de l'état*, p. 85.
[31] See José Luis Sánchez, *San Juan de la Cruz en la revolución copernicana* (Madrid: Editorial de Espiritualidad, 1992).
[32] Juan de la Cruz, *Llama de amor viva*, canzión 4,4, in Eulogio Pacho (ed.), *San Juan de la Cruz: Obras Completas* (Madrid: Monte Carmelo, 2010).

Bérulle's receptivity to the Copernican revolution was reinforced by his adherence to the doctrine of divine illumination, which he inherited above all from Denys the Pseudo-Areopagite. As Denys writes: 'the sun ... by the very fact of its existence, gives light to all those things which have any inherent power of sharing its illumination, even so the [divine] Good ... sends forth upon all things according to their receptive powers, the rays of Its undivided Goodness'.[33] As for Pope Paul, so for Bérulle, the Copernican revolution was taken as an analogical confirmation of the doctrine of divine illumination: how, as Bérulle puts it, 'in the order of grace, God ... renders man capable of knowledge of the eternal truths and of the jouissance and firm possession [thereby] of the divine and uncreated good'.[34]

If the doctrine of illumination was understood as reinforced by the new heliocentrism of Copernicus, the break with the old Ptolemaic view was at the same time a radical therapy against an anthropocentric view of reality. In this regard, the first spiritual achievement of the Copernican revolution was to make plain that the human could not in himself be the centre or centring principle of any valid cosmology or science, much less an authentic spirituality or humanism. And so, at the beginning of *le grand siècle*, Bérulle proposed the quintessentially modern revolution unleashed by Copernican science in order to reinforce the doctrine of illumination while at the same time decentring the human from certain anthropocentric tendencies native to Renaissance humanism. In this regard, the Copernican revolution of Bérulle is instructively contrasted with the transcendental 'Copernican revolution' inaugurated by Kant a century and a half later.

Under the banner of the revolution wrought by Copernicus, Kant offered his own revolution in thought.[35] Just as the heretofore presumed 'centre' of the universe was declared the periphery to a new centre, the sun, so Kant offered his transcendental method: reality is not the centre of cognition but rather cognition is the centre of reality. Consciousness was thus, according to the 'Copernican revolution' of Kant, made to supply the necessary conditions under which the world could be thought of as intelligible. But according to French philosopher Quentin Meillassoux, associated with the same school of 'speculative realism' as Brassier, what Kant in fact achieved was to turn the Copernican revolution precisely on its head. Whereas the Copernican programme was

---

[33] Denys, *De divinis nominibus*, 4.1 (PG 3.693b).
[34] Bérulle, *Oeuvres de piété*, no. 137.
[35] Immanuel Kant, *Critique of Pure Reason* (ed. and trans. Paul Guyer and Allen W. Wood; Cambridge: Cambridge University Press, 1998), p. 110 (B xvi).

a revolutionary decentring of the human being and the 'royalty of man', the Kantian move, by contrast, achieved a *counter*-revolution that re-centred the meaning of reality now wholly on the finitude of the human subject. And so, according to Meillassoux, 'when philosophers refer to the revolution in thought instituted by Kant as "the Copernican revolution", they refer to a revolution *whose meaning is the exact opposite*'.[36] Whereas the Copernican revolution asserts that 'the observer whom we thought was motionless is in fact orbiting around the observed sun', Kant's 'Ptolemaic counter-revolution', as Meillassoux calls it, refigures the subject as central to the process of knowledge.[37] Against this backdrop we see that the Copernican revolution of Bérulle is at once more 'revolutionary' and more 'modern' than that proposal of Kant, that is, if by modern and revolutionary we mean authentically Copernican and fearless of the 'vector of intellectual discovery' it unleashed. And this leads us to the issue of the famous meeting of Bérulle and René Descartes.

It has been sometimes suggested that Bérulle 'gave Descartes his mission to find a new basis for certainty'.[38] Among nineteenth-century scholars it was indeed widely held that Bérulle had exercised an abiding intellectual and spiritual influence over the philosopher. All of this has been thoroughly called into question by Jean-Luc Marion.[39] In *Sur la théologie blanche de Descartes*, Marion shows that while Bérulle and Descartes did meet in the autumn of 1628,[40] and while Bérulle did encourage the young philosopher to pursue his new philosophy, there was in fact nothing like an abiding influence: in fact, much the opposite. What Marion takes as the foundational doctrine of Descartes' thought – his doctrine of the created 'eternal truths' – breaks absolutely and at the very root with Bérulle.

The doctrine is elaborated in a series of letters Descartes wrote in 1630 to the Minim friar, le Père Mersenne. In these letters Descartes argues that the 'eternal truths' which had heretofore been thought of as native to the mind of God are in fact as created as creatures. In this way Descartes was able to place an absolute

---

[36] Quentin Meillassoux, *After Finitude: An Essay on the Necessity of Contingency* (trans. Ray Brassier; London: Continuum, 2008), pp. 117–18.
[37] Meillassoux, *After Finitude*, pp. 117–18.
[38] Richard Popkin, 'The Religious Background of Seventeenth-Century Philosophy', in Daniel Garber and Michael Ayers (eds), *The Cambridge History of Seventeenth-Century Philosophy* (Cambridge: Cambridge University Press, 2003), pp. 393–422 (402).
[39] Jean-Luc Marion, *Sur la théologie blanche de Descartes: Analogie, création des vérités éternelles et fondement* (Paris: Presses universitaires de France, 1981), pp. 140–59.
[40] See Stephen Menn, *Descartes and Augustine* (Cambridge: Cambridge University Press, 1998), pp. 46–8. The dating is based on Adrien Baillet, *La vie de Monsieur Descartes*, 2 vols (New York: Garland, 1987 [1691]), but which, as Menn notes, may in fact have occurred in 1627 (*Descartes and Augustine*, p. 49 n. 30).

gulf between the truths of created being and the uncreated truth of God himself, which Marion argues is constitutive and presumed in his subsequent writings. The principal target of Descartes was Francisco Suárez and his doctrine of analogy;[41] nevertheless the idea of the created 'eternal truths' set Descartes on a path that would lead him already in 1630 (only one year after Bérulle's death and two years after their meeting) to a position he himself understood as diametrically opposed to Bérulle.

The key letter as regards Bérulle is dated 27 May 1630. Therein Descartes offers three theses on the causal relation of God to the 'eternal truths'.[42] (1) God created the eternal truths in the same way as he created all things – *ut efficiens et totalis causa* – such that excludes every exemplarity between the eternal truths and God himself; (2) insofar as the eternal truths proceed from God as Creator, they do not emanate from him; and (3) insofar as emanation is a false mode of understanding the eternal truths, so likewise the solar model of illumination must be categorically rejected – the eternal truths are not rays of light that shine from the Light that is God as the rays of the sun illumine the earth. While Descartes did not name Bérulle in this letter, Marion suggests that he is nevertheless the target. What is demonstrable is that Bérulle openly and prominently, in several of his *Opuscules de piété* and in his *Grandeurs de Jésus* proposed the doctrine of illumination in Dionysian fashion, centred on the solar motif. Indeed for Bérulle, the eternal truths are uncreated and therefore it is only by a grace of God that the human mind is rendered capable of contemplating them.[43] As Marion notes, this doctrine of illumination formed, for Bérulle, the basis of the dignity of the sciences and that knowledge of created things which 'aspires to the uncreated life', which indeed aspires to the Logos himself. And here, the doctrine of illumination is linked directly to the Copernican decentring of human sufficiency in matters of being and knowing. The ultimate truth to which the human heart aspires is indeed a truth radically outside of the human mind and outside the power of the mind to dominate: it 'runs contrary to all appearance' and is only ultimately known through the dispossessive receptivity of being open, in Marian fashion, to the grace of the light of God himself.

---

[41] Marion, *Sur la theologie blanche de Descartes*, pp. 110–39.
[42] Marion, *Sur la théologie blanche de Descartes*, p. 142.
[43] Bérulle, *Oeuvres de piété*, no. 137.

The Bérullian Programme and the Magisterium of John Paul II

The Bérullian programme as I have outlined it consists in two basic proposals: Copernican Christocentrism, and servitude to Mary and Jesus. The former clarifies what is in fact the true centre; the latter clarifies the form of dispossession required to take the authentic path of human freedom that unites the human being with his true centre. These two aspects of the Bérullian programme find a clear echo in the Christological humanism proposed through the pontificate of John Paul II.

Bérulle did not textually influence John Paul in any form. To my knowledge, Karol Wojtyła, neither in his pre-papal writings, nor in his writings as pope, did ever make reference to the French Cardinal. And yet Bérulle did exercise a powerful if indirect influence over the pontificate. The most concrete evidence of this consists in two words: *totus tuus*.

John Paul's apostolic motto was taken from Louis de Montfort's famous consecration to Mary: 'I am all yours and all I have is yours, O dear Jesus, through Mary, your holy Mother.'[44] Educated at St-Sulpice in Paris, de Montfort was formed at the heart of the so-called French School of Spirituality founded by Bérulle. According to Henri Brémond, de Montfort is 'the last of the great Bérullians'.[45] Whatever else may be Bérullian in de Montfort, his prayer of consecration to Mary is a perfect example of a Bérullian vow of servitude, and here the link with Bérulle is concrete. De Montfort learned the devotion of the vow at St-Sulpice under the tutelage of Louis Tronson, who was himself introduced to the vow of servitude by Jean-Jaques Olier, who had been formed by two of Bérulle's most important disciples, Vincent de Paul and Charles de Condren, the latter having succeeded Bérulle as superior general of the Oratory in Paris.

The Montfordian consecration, from which John Paul took his motto, consists precisely in a vow 'in honour and in union with the submission to which eternal Wisdom willingly submitted himself' in taking the Virgin as his Mother. While the consecration has been sometimes taken as a quaint baroque pietism, it was for de Montfort a vow of concrete discipleship rooted in a radical reaffirmation of the baptism promise. For John Paul, moreover, *totus tuus* was not merely a personal vow of servitude but, following the gesture of Cardinal Wyszyński's

---

[44] *Totus tuus ego sum, et omnia mea tua sunt. Accipio te in mea omnia. Praebe mihi cor tuum, Maria.*
[45] Bremond, *A Literary History of Religious Thought in France*, vol. 3, p. 393.

dedication of Warsaw to Our Lady of Częstochowa and the 'Great Novena' by which Poland was meant to consecrate herself to Mary, it was a vow of Christian servitude in defiance of the servitude demanded by the modern state and the atheist ideology of 'socialist man'.[46] This is perhaps the best light in which to understand John Paul's recommendation of de Montfort in *Redemptoris Mater*, where the Pope offered the servitude of consecration as the key to his Marian Year and his promotion of the authentic Marian doctrine of the Second Vatican Council, that is, of 'the Blessed Virgin Mary … in the mystery of Christ and of the Church'.[47] For John Paul, *totus tuus* signified the disposition of spirit by which the Church herself must live as rooted in the metaphysical truth that Christ is the unique centre of reality. And this leads to the trace of Bérulle's Copernican Christocentrism at the heart of the Wojtyłan pontificate.

The opening words of *Redemptor hominis*, 'The Redeemer of man, Jesus Christ, is the centre of the cosmos and of history', signals already a Christocentrism profoundly harmonious with that of Bérulle.[48] Where the encyclical may bear its concrete genealogical root in Bérulle is in the programmatic invocation of *Gaudium et spes* 22: 'Christ … in the very revelation of the mystery of the Father and of his love, *fully reveals man to himself*.'[49] John Paul famously quotes the text in his Magisterium more than any other single text of the Council.[50] It was, moreover, crucially proposed by him at the Extraordinary Synod of 1985 as the hermeneutical key of *Gaudium et spes* and perhaps of the Council as a whole.[51]

It has been noted many times that the root of this text is likely based in a sentence of Henri de Lubac's *Catholicisme*.[52] It has also been recounted, no less than by John Paul himself, how de Lubac and he worked together at Vatican II on 'Schema 13', which eventually became *Gaudium et spes*,[53] and how they

---

[46] See Varden, *Redeeming Freedom*, pp. 210–11.
[47] John Paul II, *Redemptoris Mater*, §48.
[48] John Paul II, *Redemptor hominis*, §1.
[49] *Gaudium et spes*, §22; as quoted in John Paul II, *Redemptor hominis*, §8.
[50] David L. Schindler, 'Introduction to Henri de Lubac', *The Mystery of the Supernatural* (trans. Rosemary Sheed; New York: Crossroad, 1998), p. xxvii.
[51] See Tracey Rowland, *Ratzinger's Faith: The Theology of Pope Benedict XVI* (Oxford: Oxford University Press, 2008), p. 32. Cf. Karol Wojtyła, *Sources of Renewal: The Implementation of the Second Vatican Council* (trans. P. S. Falla; New York: William Collins & Co.: Glasgow, 1980), p. 75: 'We seem here to have reached a key point in the Council's thought. The revelation of the mystery of the Father and his love in Jesus Christ reveals man to man, and gives the ultimate answer to the question, "What is man?"'
[52] Henri de Lubac, *Catholicisme: Les aspects sociaux du dogme* (Paris: Les Éditions du Cerf, 1938), p. 264–5. Cf. Paul McPartlan; see his 'Henri de Lubac – Evangelizer', *Priest and People* (August–September 1992), pp. 343–6; and David L. Schindler, *The Heart of the World, Center of the Church: Communio Ecclesiology, Liberalism, and the Liberation* (Grand Rapids, MI: Eerdmans, 1996), pp. 51–3.
[53] John Paul II, *Rise, Let Us Be On Our Way* (trans. Walter Ziemba; New York: Warner Books, 2004), p. 165.

solidified their friendship at the Council around the common conviction that the urgent task of the Church was to resource and propose a robust Christian humanism to counter the human crisis of the modern world. In all events, it is not to overdraw the facts to suggest that, in his programmatic recourse to *Gaudium et spes* 22, there is a Lubacian debt at the heart of John Paul II's magisterium. And insofar as here there is a Lubacian debt, there are perhaps grounds for a direct genealogical link to Bérulle.

If he was not a 'Bérullian', de Lubac found himself nevertheless accompanied throughout his career by the writings of the great French Cardinal. As early as *Surnaturel*, published in 1946, de Lubac held Bérulle up as an example of a baroque method of theological anthropology that refused the dualistic relation of nature and the supernatural.[54] And as late as his penultimate work, the book on Pico published in 1974, he dedicated a significant chapter to the Founder of the Oratory in which he depicted him as a model of authentic Christian humanism.[55] Of all de Lubac's invocations of Bérulle, the fundamental Bérullian motif on which de Lubac seized, and which most basically sums up de Lubac's own theological programme, is that of God in Christ 'giving man to himself (*nous-mêmes à nous-mêmes*)'.[56] As de Lubac wrote in 1949, in 'Le mystère du surnaturel':

> There are certain depths of his [the human being's] nature that can only be opened up by the surprise of revelation. In revealing himself to us, Bérulle used to say, God 'has revealed us to ourselves'.[57]

De Lubac invokes this theme, with direct reference to Bérulle, of the revelation of man to himself on at least four occasions.[58] While he does not quote Bérulle in *Catholicisme*, it is not hard to hear a distinct echo of the French Cardinal in

---

[54] Henri de Lubac, *Surnaturel*, pp. 162–3; cf. p. 163 n. 1: 'Bérulle distingue parfaitement, en maints passages, l'ordre de la nature et celui de la grâce; par exemple, *Opuscule* 160, 1: "Le monde de la nature et le monde de la grâce sont deux états, deux ordres et deux mondes bien différents et bien séparés, encore que l'un sait et se retrouve dans l'autre." Mais il sait aussi le paradoxe de la nature humaine: "Une de nos différences d'avec les autres créatures, c'est qu'elle on été créées parfaites en leur condition et sans attente d'aucun autre nouveau degré qui leur manquât; mais la nature de l'homme n'a pas été créée pour demeurer dans les termes de la nature; elle a été faite pour la grâce, et destinée à un état élevé par dessus sa puissance." Cette attente, pense-t-il, est essentielle à l'esprit, car "Nos esprits sont émanés de Dieu avec rapport à Dieu, comme portant son image et semblance, et ils sont créés pour entrer en communication de sa propre essence: *divinae consortes naturae*".
[55] Henri de Lubac, *Pic de la Mirandole: Études et discussions* (Paris: Aubier-Montaigne, 1974).
[56] Bérulle, *Oeuvres de piété*, no. 34.
[57] Henri de Lubac, 'Le mystère du surnaturel', *Recherches de science religieuse* 36 (1949): 80–121 (118).
[58] In addition to 'Le mystère du surnaturel', cf. Henri de Lubac, *Le mystère du surnaturel* (Paris: Aubier, 1965), p. 265; 'La foi chrétienne: Petite introduction au symbole des apôtres (1991)', in *La foi chrétienne* (Paris: Cerf, 2008), pp. 517–33 (503–4); and *Pic de La Mirandole*, pp. 130–42.

that text of *Catholicisme* paraphrased in *Gaudium et spes* 22 and taken up as one of the basic keys of the magisterium of Pope John Paul II: '*le Christ achève de révéler l'homme à lui-même*'.[59]

The title Pope Urban gave Bérulle, 'Apostle of the Incarnate Word', appropriately signifies the truth of theology for Bérulle: there is no doctrine of God or of the human being that can have any Christian validity outside of the fact of the Incarnation. In our own context the papal title can also be taken as a programme for the encounter of Christian wisdom with modernity and the modern world. For in the Incarnation Jesus truly assumes the whole history of servitude of our fragile being, the servitude we suffer on account of sin and the servitude of redemption we are obliged to live in relation to the Virgin Mother, through whom we are related to her Son. In a word, he assumes the *néant* of our being, and he does this nowhere more concretely than in the fragility of being a child born of a Mother who, like all children, must die. In his birth and death he empties himself to catch up the radical contingency of our being into the perfection of his divine filiation. There is no corner of worldly reality, then, and no corner of truth or of history, that is not internal to who Christ is in the Incarnation: even the *néant* of the modern world belongs more to him than it does to us.

This puts Christian wisdom in a position of genuine freedom before the world, whether the modern world or the postmodern world. As long as Christian wisdom holds firm to the true centre, she holds firm to all that is essential. The Bérullian programme in this regard is at once radically open and decisively prophetic. And in this, the Bérullian programme anticipates the openness of the Second Vatican Council, which sought to encounter the modern world without need of the language of condemnation, while at the same time anticipating what George Bernanos identified as the prophetic truth of the Syllabus of Errors of Pope Pius IX. Bernanos writes:

> [It was for the sake of the human spirit that] the Catholic Church condemned the modern world in a time when it was difficult to understand the reasons for this condemnation, but which are now justified more every day. The famous *Syllabus* ... appears today as truly prophetic. The tyranny [of the modern

---

[59] In this light it is highly significant that in 'La foi chrétienne: Petite introduction au symbole des apôtre (1991)', while discussing the doctrine of revelation in *Dei verbum*, de Lubac invokes precisely *Gaudium et spes* §22 only to declare that while the idea that 'en se révélant à l'homme, Dieu révèle l'homme à lui-même' can be found in many of the Fathers, it is in a 'special and magnificent way expressed by Cardinal de Bérulle' and in his 'Oratorian tradition', where we find a discipline of 'meditation on this theme of the revelation of man in the revelation of God' (pp. 503–4).

world] is not behind us, it is before us, and we have to face it now or we never will.⁶⁰

The metaphysical tyranny of Brassier's 'vector of intellectual discovery' helps us to focus precisely on this fact and on the decision it compels: either the unbound *nihil* of human extinction or the *néant* of the human being in Christ. This means that the Church ought indeed to be truly open, and without fear, to the modern world. But the truth and integrity of this openness will in all cases be measured by the freedom with which the Church makes her prophetic proclamation. Jesus Christ is the true centre, the one Sun around which the soil of the human heart still moves.

---

[60] George Bernanos, *Essais et écrits de combat* (Paris: Éditions Gallimard, 1995), vol. 2, p. 1321.

11

Imaginative Conversion

Mátyás Szalay

At the Crossroad where Conversion becomes Relevant

'Conversion', a crucial phenomenon for Christian faith and wisdom, has been seriously questioned and undergone a radical transformation in modern times.[1] When pondering 'conversion' one considers the very act that brings out the ultimate consequences of any rational philosophical reflection. Any intellectual effort and philosophical labour, however impressive it might appear, falls short if it is not motivated or prompted by an existential embrace: the truth it illuminates. The true insights that are elaborated in a theological or philosophical reflection are the opposite of isolated and neutral facts; they are given to consciousness as 'invocations', as appeals upon which to act both internally and externally. Such calls are only responded to properly if their true intuitions become manifested and incorporated. If theory or contemplation is not only distinct but separated from action in the sense of charity, it turns out to be nothing but a merely fascinating '*Glasperlenspiel*'.[2]

If conversion is an appropriate topic to reflect upon at the end of any philosophical and theological conference, it is especially relevant at a conference on 'Christian Wisdom meets Modernity'. For an encounter with modernity to become fruitful it must do more than enumerate the shortcomings of modern thought; it becomes fruitful as it is able to elucidate how modern criticism of

---

[1] For an impressive summary of this point, see Paul Ricoeur, 'L'imagination dans le discours et dans l'action', in idem, *Du texte à l'action: Essais d'herméneutique, II* (Paris: Seuil, 1986), pp. 213-36 (215-16).

[2] The allusion here is to Herman Hesse's novel *The Glass Bead Game*. Hesse's term refers to a new synthesis of different arts. It is a ludicrous and yet mechanical activity based on associations through which different themes, such as philosophical thoughts and musical melodies, form a new unity. The game, which seems to lack any meaning beyond the diversion and self-aggrandizement of the players, becomes more and more sophisticated thanks to the variation of several themes.

the Christian faith enriched Christian wisdom, albeit often willy-nilly. The modernist contribution is arguably rightly interpreted when understood as paving the way for an even more radical conversion than that promoted by the previous epoch's culture, a point to which I will return in my conclusion.

The intellectual preparation for conversion that modernity provides is twofold. On the one hand, it destroys the conceptual impediments to fully embracing the divinity. One might suspect, for example, that the sophisticated vocabulary and conceptual architecture of the late scholastic concealed rather than revealed the very centre of the discussion: the divine *logos*. On the other hand, it elaborates a more poetic and at the same time more systematic language capable of receptive collaboration with the ongoing divine self-revelation. This should not be taken as a kind of 'progress', however, for what is being revealed in time is nothing other than what the four Gospels already contain in a more perfect form and in inexhaustible richness. Thus what is argued here concerning the general contribution of modernity has to be understood as aspects that are true of any historical time after Christ. Indeed, 'conversion' can hardly be called 'progress' in the colloquial sense, for one always (re)turns to the same divine subject. In this sense modernity, despite all justified criticism, is a time and place where and when community with God was just as possible as in any other period because of divine grace.

The specifically modern heritage that allows for a more radical conversion today can be considered in three aspects: (a) the subject of conversion – who does it; (b) the act of conversion – how it happens; (c) the received divine self-revelation – the one to whom we turn. These three aspects are deeply interrelated, such that whatever features are highlighted as relevant for the modern understanding of conversion imply the others and the unity of all three. In what follows, then, I will briefly consider some of the interconnections of the act of conversion with how modernity understands the divine as well as the human capacity of being converted.

In what follows I shall discuss only one feature of conversion's modern interpretation: the role of the imagination. I consider this feature of the modern interpretation essential for understanding the theologically and philosophically positive and negative impact of modernity on Christian wisdom, as well as for grasping the future possibilities that arise when modernity's account on conversion is looked at critically. The imagination is essential for several reasons. Of all the soul's faculties it is the imagination that is most relevant for the Christian understanding of conversion, rather than, for example, emotional or intellectual capacity or memory. The imagination is primordial in its capacity for both ascent (*anabasis*) and descent (*katabasis*). As regards the anagogical ascent, the imagination provides the intellect with the concrete images that serve in any analogical understanding of divinity. This is the more active anagogical ascent by identifying traces of Divinity in creation. There is also a second, more receptive role of imagination. In connection with the movement of *katabasis* the imagination intends to translate experiences beyond imagination into concrete realities that are still to be assumed and appropriated by the self.[3] While in the first usage the activity aims at responding to the divine call and consists in discovering the analogy within created reality and thus prepares the self for contemplation, in the second phase imagination is more connected to the divine mission that unfolds in contemplation and prayer. The response to the mission is expressed in the form of sub-creative activity,[4] that is, collaboration with the divine precisely by 'realizing', by embodying its call, by giving it a certain shape and form.[5] Here the imagination plays two distinguished roles which are deeply connected to conversion: (a) in the sense of turning to God from creation; and (b) in the sense of turning to creation when moved by the encounter with the divinity.

Equally, the modern theory and praxis of the imagination can rightly be considered one of the most relevant issues for grasping the transformation of the concept of 'conversion'. For while all human faculties undergo a radical revision during this epoch, the cultural understanding of the imagination turned to the opposite of its original ancient and Scriptural meaning: what was considered sin or sacrilege by the Old Testament and Plato came to be celebrated as the key to humanity's progress. This change played an enormous role in conversion being increasingly interpreted not in terms of 'response to God' but, in a reductive way, as a mere self-fulfilment of human nature. In order to understand better its

---

[3] This double aspect of the *anabasis* and *katabasis* of the imagination is visible in the great 'phenomenological' analyses of contemplation by Richard of St Victor, *De gratia contemplationis seu Benjamin major*, Patrologia Latina 196, col. 63-202; bk. I, ch. VI (70-2).

[4] Here I am referring to the key term of Tolkien's aesthetics. See J. R. R. Tolkien, *The Monsters and the Critics and Other Essays* (London: Harper Collins, 2006), esp. 'On Fairy-Stories', pp. 109-61; 'Fantasy remains a human right: we make in our measure and in our derivative mode, because we are made: and not only made, but made in the likeness of a Maker' (p. 145). Also see Tolkien's poem 'Mythopoeia' in which he refutes C. S. Lewis's opinion that myths are nothing but 'lies breathed through silver', and Wayne G. Hammond-Christina Scull (ed.), *The J. R. R. Tolkien Companion and Guide* (Houghton Mifflin, 2006), pp. 620-2. The expression 'sub-creation' has a long history, and some thoughts from Hugh of St Victor will have to suffice. Hugh distinguishes the work of God (*opus Dei*) from the work of nature (*opus artificis*), and argues that the labour of the craftsman and artist imitates nature (*opus artificis imitator naturam*) and borrows its forms from nature (*a natura formam mutuatur*). See *Euriditio didascalia* (*Didascalicon*), Patrologia Latina 176, bk. I, chs X and XII, cols 747-8 and 760.

[5] As for this kind of imagination, see Thomas Aquinas, *ST* I, 1, q. 13, a. 9.

modern transfiguration, then, a brief look at some premodern accounts of the imagination is in order.

Imagination in Premodern Times

In the following I am going to elaborate only four essential aspects of imagination that I consider important for elucidating the link between conversion and imagination.

(1) Moral and spiritual ambiguity. Both Biblical and ancient cultural sources, however different they are, confirm that all human faculties can be used in a spiritually and morally positive or negative way and thus the function of the imaginative faculty is considered spiritually and morally ambiguous. It is enough to think about how the intellect, the memory, the emotive or the volitional faculties are liable to turn against God and thereby become self-destructive. Yet what is so obvious in the case of, for example, the volitional faculty, namely that there is good and bad will, becomes rather oblique concerning imagination.

This particular short-sightedness that is so characteristic for post-Christian culture is a modern heritage, as will be demonstrated in the following point. It is enough to note here that perhaps the most striking fact about ancient and early Christian accounts of imagination is their high sensibility for the possible moral and spiritual destruction produced by the evil usage of imagination. Some authors such as St Augustine[6] or St Thomas[7] look almost with suspicion at imagination, especially if actively and not passively engaged in knowing divine reality. Based on the Adamic myth of the first book of the Bible, and its tale of the fall of imagination and on their experience of religious life, of the imagination is often depicted as the first faculty to be tempted and perverted.

At the same time it is affirmed that the imagination is the faculty which most

---

[6] St Augustine is the first Latin author who used the term 'imagination' in a consistent way, combining the biblical distrust of images with the negative Greek or Neoplatonic account of *phantasia* as a hindrance to spiritual contemplation (*noesis*) (as in Plotinus, *Enneads* 5.5). See further Richard Kearney, *The Wake of Imagination* (London: Routledge, 1998), p. 117.

[7] Thomas Aquinas attributes to the imaginative faculty two capacities. One he regards as less than the intellect, for imagination apprehends only the images of the bodies while the intellect alone apprehends the essences of the things. God, then, cannot be seen by the imagination but can be 'seen' by the intellect. The other Aquinas describes as a passive use of the imagination that receives the divine infusion of images. The certainty and clearness of this type of imagination is beyond any intellectual grasp. Without faith however, imagination would not be able to exercise this highest function. Faith as a kind of knowledge is determined by the image of Christ. It is in this sense that Thomas allows for the possibility of a radical amendment of the intellect by a certain type of imagination. Cf. Aquinas, *ST*, I, 1, q. 12, a. 13.

clearly manifests our divine image or nature for witnessing the supernatural presence and grace amidst fallen creation. The imagination is thus the faculty that is designed to explore ever new ways of glorifying God by offering testimony of the divine presence. It is the imagination that when well applied reflects the glory of God precisely by letting emerge and elaborating and expressing a new understanding, in all spheres of life, of the analogy between Creator and creation. This analogy even goes beyond the *analogia entis*, for it is most eloquently present in the dialogue between divine and human love. Meeting this difficult task involves the imagination performing a real '*Gratwanderung*', a tightrope walk, for it simultaneously looks feverishly after similarities between God while acknowledging the *semper maior dissimilitudo in tanta similitudine*[8] present in any analogy (*analogia entis, analogia libertatis, analogia salutis, analogia fidei, absolute catalogical analogy*).[9] The way the imagination deepens and widens analogy appears like a never-ending trail of grasping which exceeds all intellectual knowledge and philosophical or poetic undertakings: the self-giving love of God as manifested in the scandal of the Cross.

(2) The fundamental attitude in imagination. The second feature concerns the essential role played by the 'fundamental attitude' in any act of imagination. However different the Christian understanding of the human might be from an ancient view, there is a basic agreement that the spiritual and moral evaluation of a particular faculty depends on one's fundamental attitude. No faculty can be rightly regarded as separated from the soul and its fulfilment is not so much due to functioning well or poorly but to how the soul as a whole relates itself to reality and to what is most real, to God.

The fundamental attitude is the basic disposition of the person towards the divine, understood both as the Divinity beyond being (*epekeina tés ousias*[10]) and as the supernatural that pervades all spheres of the natural, that is, the life-world and the human self. The soul's disposition determines the function of all its faculties and their fulfilment depends on how they let themselves be engaged and inspired by the divine reality rather than any skills or talents. Even the lightest touch of divinity received through acts of imagination, volition,

---

[8] '*Quia inter creatorem et creaturam non potest tanta similitudo notari quin inter eos maior sit dissimilitudo notanda.*' Denzinger-Schönmetzer, *Enchiridion Symbolorum*, §806.
[9] For a helpful account of 'catalogical analogy', see Wolfgang Treitler, 'True Foundations of Authentic Theology', in *Hans Urs von Balthasar: His Life and Work* (ed. David L. Schindler; San Francisco: Ignatius Press, 1991), pp. 169–82 (esp. 174).
[10] Plato, *Republic*, 509b.

memory or emotions contains more truth and reality than even the fullest and most perfect worldly being.

(3) Incarnation as the fundament of imagination. The full perfection of the fundamental attitude is reached in the unconditional *fiat* of the Virgin Mary and it sets the insuperable measure and principle for all times. Thanks to her fundamental attitude, the Virgin Mary is doubtless the most perfect imaginative human person and thus she is the archetype for any imaginative act in the right sense. Her contemplation of 'the Word made flesh' or 'the crucified Son of glory' contains *in nucleo* everything that any human person should know or imitate regarding the imagination.

A long process of clarification of the essential aspects of the 'fundamental attitude' regarding the imagination was inaugurated when the imagination of 'the wise man' (the model of antiquity) was replaced by the Virgin Mary's contemplation of her incarnated Son. Thanks to this radical switch, in contrast to the imagination (*eikaseia*) which was subdued to reason (*nous*) in classical thought, the modern soul, at least according to the programme laid out by Romantic thinkers like Schiller and other theorists of creative imagination, thinks that it has to free itself from the intellect's tutelage. (This move is considered necessary by modern thinkers who claim that the intellect is regulated and even captivated by authorities such as tradition, the state and foremost by the Church.) Modern theorists who are quick to observe this new freedom of imagination in relation to reason are reluctant to acknowledge that it stems from the fact that the event of incarnation, which, while being rational as the manifestation of the *logos*, is beyond human rational comprehension. It is not the irrationality of being but the excess of rationality in the divine act of love that allows for this new freedom of the imagination. The manifestation of the *logos* as the origin of everything gives everything a new and rational access, for it provides a novel entry into the inner principle of being: God's personal love for the creation. What is hard to swallow for modern apostles of the imagination, such as Voltaire, is that rational insight into this most general principle of everything, when becoming manifested in the flesh, is only open through personally participating in the divine *passio*, that is, the self-expression of God as love.

The event of the incarnation, as well as any event in the *vita Christi*, especially the scandal of the Cross, is also certainly beyond any type of human imagination. And yet the manifestation of divine love provokes and arouses imagination like nothing else. Who is the one capable of such perfect sacrifice, of such measureless self-giving? What are the signs, the living traces of such love in the life-world? How can we respond to such a gift? These and other questions arise and can be answered only when the gift is received 'imaginatively', with reason being directed to discover and appropriate this mysterious gift in all its extensions and dimensions as it is carefully guided by the active reception of the 'groping imagination'.[11]

The mysterious divine lover who is revealed in and through Christ is radically more distant as being endlessly more glorious than the One in Plato. Yet at the same time Christ is the vivid centre and the principle of being and thus the closest to each and every human heart. This tension between incomparable presence and absence, between utmost distance and closeness, not only provokes thought but gives to human reflection two seemingly opposite dangers. Despite their differences, these dangers stem from the same origin. Any hasty explanation that favours the systematic aspects over respect for the phenomenological data of this 'paradoxical' divine reality – the utmost transcendence in the greatest immanence and vice versa – runs the risk of eliminating the tension by dissolving one of these true manifestations into another. These two temptations which pervade the history of Western thought (identified by von Balthasar as cosmological and anthropological reduction[12]) have determined the development of the imagination in two opposite directions: claiming the imaginative construction of (a) the last principle of the cosmos in which humanity finds its proper place, and (b) the innermost self to which the whole of reality is reducible. Both of these fatal reductions rest on a negative fundamental attitude: a withholding of the affirmation (*fiat*) of the divine reality shortchanges the imaginative faculties. The imagination whose wings are clipped cannot overcome the limits of human rationality and so has to force reality into the narrow borders established by the modern narcissistic ego that can only see itself.[13]

(4) The 'Marian imagination' of the divine love. It is important to see, however, that the cosmological and anthropological models of imagination are reunited

---

[11] I am referring here to something like that which is described by Merleau-Ponty: 'Peut-être Bergson a-t-il compris d'abord la philosophie comme simple retour à des données, mais il a vu ensuite que cette naïveté, seconde, laborieuse, retrouvée, ne nous fond pas avec une réalité préalable, ne nous identifie pas avec la chose même, sans point de vue, sans symbole, sans perspective. « Coup de sonde », « auscultation », « palpation », ces formules, qui sont meilleures, laissent assez entendre que l'intuition a besoin d'être comprise, qu'il me faut m'approprier un sens qui, en elle, est encore captif.' Merleau-Ponty, *Éloge de la philosophie* (Paris: Gallimard, 1953), p. 25.

[12] See Hans Urs von Balthasar, *Glaubhaft ist nur Liebe* (Einsiedeln: Johannes Verlag, 2000), pp. 8-32.

[13] See especially Friedrich Nietzsche, *Thus Spoke Zarathustra*, XXXVI, 'The Land of Culture'.

and radically surpassed in the imagination that is motivated by divine love and directed towards its divine source. One can see this incomparable excellence in the dignity and the conscious representation of the subject matter (its fullness); the ego's stance before the object (humility); its self-realization (total vocation); and the quality and intensity of the attitude (total self-giving).[14]

While the imagination which exemplifies the fundamental attitude still remains mysterious, several significant aspects can be outlined. (1) Its primordial subject matter is God, regardless of its concrete intentional object. This means two things: (a) it is fully positive inasmuch as it is based on the affirmation of the created reality even if there is a sword that penetrates the heart; and (b) it is motivated by consideration of a certain object as divine gift and thus intends to uncover what this gift of the superabundant love of God means concretely for one's own self, one's own community and for humanity. (2) The ego's stance of the fundamental attitude is characterized by the utmost 'ontological humility', the stance which the creature as such has to occupy when faced with the source of his or her whole existence. The Marian imagination is nothing other than a tracing of the superabundant meaning of a given phenomenon back to its ultimate source. Instead of forcefully looking for some amendments to some default reality, it begins with wonder (*thaumázein*) at the fullness and perfection of what there is. (3) While this grateful recognition of the gift-character of all that exists is truly objective, it is far from being impersonal, for there is no impersonal gift. Any 'gift' as such is personal not just because it can be received only by persons but above all because it can only be given by a person and the giving of the gift reveals the nature of the giver. One can thus talk of a Marian imagination when following this 'logic of the gift' that is thus performed within the complex structure of personal vocation. Receiving the gift is tantamount to 'active- participative listening' to the supernatural call as well as to the imaginative elucidation and disentangling of the proper vocation in response to the call. (4) The 'Marian imagination' that is based on the total self-giving of both God and the human person strictly follows the logic of descending, whose emblematic starting point is the incarnation: the *logos* becoming manifested, incarnated, concretely realized. The imaginative act is realized by the concrete and lived encounter between the divine and the human, and it is this 'inspiring' (Holy Spirit) event, beyond any expectation or conceptualization and yet based on sense perception, that triggers and elevates the imagination into the concrete

---

[14] The aspects analysed in relation to the 'fundamental attitude' I owe to Alexander Pfänder, *Zur Psychologie der Gesinnungen* (Halle: Max Niemeyer Verlag, 1913); *Die Seele des Menschen. Versuch einer verstehenden Psychologie* (Halle: Max Niemeyer Verlag, 1933).

phenomenon. The imagination is far from abstraction; on the contrary it is this active reception, this always innovative chasing for the meaning of the invisible *actus essendi* that nonetheless is more real and present than anything tangible. This ontologically fundamental aspect of being (the wonder of existence) epistemologically manifests itself as superabundant meaning; it is precisely what (in a second phase) the imagination seeks to express in an always inappropriate, but at least more proportionate form. The radical insufficiency of any sensual, logical or even metaphorical expression gives rise to renewed attempts to formulate and manifest that content which clearly lies beyond any language and therefore is always poetic at its root.

The Modern Account of the Imagination

The fruitful tension between the unconditional love of God and the radical insufficiency of human response has been interpreted by modernity as paradoxical confusion. The scandal of the God-man in whom the supernatural coexists with the natural, which is the starting point of any 'Marian imagination', was taken over by the ideal of the Promethean and Titanic divinization of humanity in its gradual ascension.[15] Instead of *theosis* initiated by the radical movement of conversion, the new programme for humanity prescribes the invention of the new Adam. The substantial transformation of human nature in Christ suffers an inversion and becomes humanity's desperate seeking of the impossible: becoming its own creator. While this process is well aware of the necessity of 'redemption', most modern thinkers prefer and elaborate apparently 'more reliable (philosophical, scientific and social) trajectories' for reaching happiness than an apparently powerless redeemer hanging on a cross.

When God's self-giving love in Christ is put into parentheses by philosophical reflection, the relationship between supernatural and natural is judged to be paradoxical and problematic and new and inventive modes are needed to resolve it. Instead of accepting the tension through the *sequela Christi*, that is, discovering and acknowledging the supernatural within the natural sphere, modernity offers not just clear distinctions but an increasing separation of the

---

[15] In her analysis of Russian Messianism, Prof. Marta Kwaśnicka distinguishes between the Promethean and the Titanic. While Promethean rebellion is performed in the name of the nation or/and humankind, including self-sacrifice for others, the Titanic rebels against God and social rules. The best example is Dostojewski's Underground Man. Different types of imagination lie a different type of imagination is at work.

two spheres. Since this results in insufferable dualism, the following conceptual step can only be the reduction of one of the conflicting aspects into another: hence the cosmological or/and anthropological reductions mentioned above. In the case of the cosmological reduction, the tension between divinity and humanity is replaced by the conceptually more transparent and simplified dichotomy of the cosmos and human person, with the latter being dissolved into an elevated concept of nature. The anthropological reduction goes the other way around, for it reduces both nature and the supernatural to the other centre of this tension: the artificially 'elevated' concept of autonomous and divinized human self. Both of these modern projects rely on and consider *fantasy* to be the basic power for transforming the 'mind'; it is primordially by this faculty that the modern self hopes to overcome the deficient human condition and restore the perfection of fallen nature. The specifically modern approach claims that both programmes are feasible on their own, by the inventive and genial application of human resources.[16]

The concept of the 'imagination' as understood in the Judeo-Christian and Greek heritage undergoes a radical mutation in these modern Promethean accounts. For antique and early Christianity the noblest accepted form of the imagination, and not just spiritually but also morally, is the divine inscription of images. Even though images were imposed on the soul, human reception of them required active collaboration inasmuch as it depended on the free will that obediently followed the orders disclosed through and by the spiritual experience. It is the genius of the artist that is the modern substitute for this inspiring and uplifting collaboration, the proper realm of which is prayer. Imagination's functioning following modern standards cannot be subsumed anymore under the term 'sub-creation' and thus characterized by active receptivity. Instead, the modern autonomous and spiritually emancipated self discovers the hidden potentialities of what is called 'creative imagination'. The latter is based on the rejection of the deficient nature of the given phenomenon which should then be improved by human inventions.

While the Marian imagination interpenetrates the dialogical sphere (*Zwischenreich*) of natural and the supernatural and dwells essentially between being and what is beyond being, in modern fantasy *descent* (*katabasis*) is less

---

[16] 'The modern movements of Renaissance, Romantic and Existentialist Humanism replaced the theocentric paradigm of the mimetic craftsman with the anthropocentric paradigm of the original inventor. Whether drawing from the scientific idiom of experimenter, the colonial idiom of explorer or the technological idiom of industrial engineer, the modern aesthetic promotes the idea of the artist as one who not only emulates but actually replaces God.' Kearney, *The Wake of Imagination*, p. 12.

primordial and is reduced to the intellectual *ascent* (*anabasis*) of the autonomous mind. Thus the imagination necessarily works on the lower plane. Even if modern fantasy preserves some ascending and transcendental tendencies of going beyond subjectivity, it typically remains on the level of a construct. This 'fantastic' (imaginative in a derivative and deficient way) self-projection considers 'pure nature' to be raw material not yet suitable for human purposes and which should be overcome through a 'creative' combination of its elements.

Feuerbach's philosophy of religion is relevant here, for he draws the ultimate consequences from the Kantian thought according to which there is a spontaneous constitutive activity performed by the imaginative faculty prior to discovering the capacity of the thing in itself (*ding an sich*) as it is given to consciousness. The intellect can only know the products of this 'creative imagination'. If this explanation of Kant about the creative capacity of the autonomous self is true in the natural sphere, then it has to be coercive as well in the supernatural realm and the object of faith. This renders religions mere exercises in fantasy. For Feuerbach, Christianity's unique status among the religions is safeguarded by being the most fantastic religion in which fantasy completely coincides with the desires of the 'heart' (*Gesinnung*). Religion is the highest expression of fantasy which is directed completely by the natural desires of the heart towards the 'transcendence' which is now a projection of the immanent. Feuerbach characterizes the specific Christian fantasy in this way:

> Christianity is distinguished from other religions by this, that in other religions the heart and fantasy are divided, in Christianity they coincide. Here the fantasy does not wander, left for itself; it follows the leadings of the heart; it describes a circle, whose centre is feeling. Fantasy is here limited by the wants of the heart, it only realizes the wishes of feeling, it has reference only to the one thing needful; in brief, it has, at least generally, a practical, concentric tendency, not a vagrant, merely poetic one. The Miracles of Christianity – no product of free, spontaneous activity, but conceived in the bosom of yearning, necessitous feeling-place us immediately on the ground of common, real life; they act on the emotional man with irresistible force, because they have the necessity of feeling on their side. The power of fantasy is here at the same time the power of the heart, – fantasy is only the victorious, triumphant heart. With the Orientals, with the Greeks, fantasy, untroubled by the wants of the heart, reveled in the enjoyment of earthly splendor and glory; in Christianity, it descended from the palace of the gods into the abode of poverty, where only want rules, – it humbled itself under the sway of the heart. But the more it limited itself in extent, the more intense became its strength. The wantonness of the Olympian

gods could not maintain itself before the rigorous necessity of the heart; but fantasy is omnipotent when it has a bond of union with the heart. And this bond between the freedom of the fantasy and the necessity of the heart is Christ. All things are subject to Christ; he is the Lord of the world, who does with it what he will; but this unlimited power over Nature is itself again subject to the power of the heart; – Christ commands raging Nature to be still, but only that he may hear the sighs of the needy.[17]

In Feuerbach's modern approach, the imagination becomes redirected towards the other person's necessity in contrast to its being directed in Christianity towards the divine nature revealed in Christ. Christ, the divine *logos*, is subdued to a fantasy which springs not from the self-revelation of the superabundant divine gift, but by a very lack of being, by the 'sighs of the needy'. In this way the divine nature is made functional and its essence only serves to fulfil the needs of the human.

Fantasy and the Transformation of the Self

As argued in the first point, the most striking feature of the imaginative faculty is that it can be used in service of conversion to God as well as *aversio a Deo et conversio ad creaturas*. Modern thought depicts the latter as necessary for the emancipation of the human soul and humankind's autonomy for self-realization. In contrast to the use of the imagination described under the second point, this latter deficient performance of the same imaginative faculty has been called '*fantasy*'. This type of imagination is not preoccupied with reality but with illusory and parallel universes. While such an imaginative act is possible within any historical epoch, it is only celebrated as the standard measure of the imagination in late modernity.

As previously argued, the most decisive feature is the *fundamental attitude* (the basic disposition towards the divine persons) in which the imaginative act is rooted. In the following I would like to offer a comparative phenomenological analysis of the imaginative or fantastical, or at least those features relevant for the transformation of the self that replaces the classic idea of religious 'conversion'.

First, while imagination is triggered by the surplus of meaning that is

---

[17] Ludwig Feuerbach, *The Essence of Christianity* (trans. Marian Evans; London: Trübner 1881), ch. XV, pp. 148–9. I have substituted the word 'fantasy' for 'imagination', as in the original German Feuerbach does not once mention '*Einbildungskraft*' or '*Vorstellungskraft*', but rather uses '*Phantasie*'.

perceived with gratitude and invites us to penetrate into the being of the given phenomenon, the act of fantasy *is initiated by the consciousness of necessities* (as seen in Feuerbach). Fantasy is employed to overcome the shortcomings of the given reality as they appear to the observer whose view is based on self-centred expectations. Imagination is the proper response to the invitation to discover the hidden face of the divine Giver in all things. It is the recognition of the gift character of anything that is given as related to the act of divine donation. Fantasy, on the contrary, comes to existence when the gift (the *datum*) is reduced to 'data', something simply there, not just embedded in the context of life-world but also fully due to the meaning-giving intentional acts that constitute it. The starting point of fantasy is clearly a world that ceases to appear as a *signum*, or better yet a *symbolum*, a sign that refers to and makes visible its own sources and is only meaningful and truly itself in the soul by becoming reunited with these sources, as in the *symbolum Apostolorum*.

The second feature concerns the ultimate intentional object or the focal point of the act. The imaginative faculty cannot design its own purpose and finality, but relies on the intellect and the final end which is envisaged by the soul. If the 'God-man' ceases to occupy the centre of imagination, it is necessarily replaced by the 'man-god', for, as with any part of the soul, it is natural for the imagination to be oriented to the supernatural.

The third is a matter of the principle by which the act is performed. By this tragic switch in the 'logic of incarnation', upon which the real imagination is based, the imagination turns to its opposite. Any imaginative function not founded on the descent of God prior to any ascent of the human intellect follows the logic of 'de-incarnation'. Fantasy is, despite all appearances, not more but rather less material than imagination. The materialistic tendency in fantasy is due to the fact that the autonomous reality and material consistency of the phenomenon is the first thing fantasy gets rid of. It then has to come up with a kind of pseudo-materiality that is now fully under conscious control, to serve the complete satisfaction of the human self, its creator.

The fourth feature concerns the relationship to the intellect. We have already touched on this under the second point but can clarify further the relationship between the act of the intellect and the different usage of the imaginative faculty. While the imagination gives rise to contemplating the whole phenomenon in its 'wonderful' existence as such and in relation to its origin, fantasy paves the way for problem-centred reasoning that is often expressed as technical thinking. Technical progress in the modern area is due to this 'fantastic attitude' in service of improving human conditions by inventing different types of 'prostheses' in order to fully master nature. In order to fabricate such 'prostheses', fantasy prompts reason to single out the data in question which need to be improved. Both the function of the intellect and the imagination thus remain *analytical*. By rejecting the 'given' as unsatisfactory, fantasy has nothing else to offer but a new combination of already existing elements. The analytical nature of fantasy not only characterizes its mode of procedure, but it also structures the more general principle that results from a fragmented worldview (based on the lack of an unconditional 'yes' to creation), which again reflects and reproduces itself in the acts of fantasy. This is radically opposed to the synthesis offered by any imaginative act that focuses on the gift-character of the given, and which can thus discover and highlight something truly general while being able to see the whole in the fragment.

The fifth feature is its link to the concrete life-world, as a matter of poesis versus praxis. It follows from the points above concerning contemplation and reasoning that in modernity the primordially poetic character of imagination is replaced by its practical application. Fantasy lacks and contradicts both the poetic and the epic attitude of the imagination. The imagination which looks for the link between eternity and temporality has to be simultaneously *poetic* in order to grasp the super-temporal logos of all events and being, and *epic* for any revelation of truth is embedded in a story. *Any truly imaginative act creates a feast in which the sacred's dynamic presence amidst the profane is celebrated.* Fantasy, on the contrary, is always developed on the basis of secular time, for it is nothing else but the constant projection into the future of the deficient past through a presence that is lacking real content. Since paradoxically for fantasy the future is the only 'perfect' tense, the present cannot be but a fleeting moment.

Based on these five characteristics of fantasy, five conclusions can be drawn regarding how 'conversion' is conceived when performed in the context of fantasy. Fantasy is a deficient function of the imaginative faculty and thus it cannot induce the perfection of the soul that starts out with conversion, understood as completely re-turning to God. Instead of this complete and radical *metanoia* (μετανοῖεν) that is engendered by God's loving sacrifice, the 'transformation of the self' brought about by the help of fantasy becomes the gradual victory of the ego's domination over the objectified self and others.

First, the transmutation provided by fantasy stems from considering the self as a freely modifiable *datum*. Modernity formulates two programmes which are, despite their differences, based on the same attitude. One, like Rousseau and Nietzsche, tries to recover some Golden Age and return a culturally corrupted self to a state of childlike innocent nature. The other project, conversely, attempts to leave behind the childish self and accelerate its emancipation into maturity. The common ground of both is their rejection of the divine gift and the gratitude it elicits. Nothing in human nature, they would argue, is given, and so we have full autonomy to become what we want. Fantasy, either through self-mastering or innocent joyful playing, aims to establish the bearable lightness by being oblivious of its origin.

Secondly, at the end of this transformation the 'new Adam' will be born, whether as *homo sovieticus*, *homo germanicus* or *homo liberalis*. Thirdly, the 'new Adam' promised by modern fantasy does not depend on the divine gift and its first momentum, which is the flesh. This basic link, embodied by Christ, between divinity and humanity is always too risky, for it escapes the complete control that the vain human self intends to have over himself. In modern reflection the de-incarnated self, once being dissociated from the divine body, is easily reducible to the abstract 'cogito', and later shrinks to the pure abstraction of a 'transcendental ego'. Despising the flesh goes along with abolishing the organic link between the created world and the self, in the process creating a basic estrangement from the world. In order to overcome this artificial bewilderment the world has to be first demystified and purified of all divine traces in order to be re-created in the image and likeness of humanity. When this new playground of fantasy still seems dull and empty, it is then replaced with a creature of the mind.

Fourthly, the technical progress promoted by fantasy does not only serve the exploitation of nature in general, it also implies and begins with the systematic transformation of the human self. The antique and Christian idea of a radical revision of the fundamental attitude is obfuscated by the continuous social education of 'manners' as an ideal of perfect self-mastery (embodied, for example, in the modern ideal of the English gentleman). This complete control over oneself is essential for self-realization on the individual as well as on the social level. Since this change does not happen from the inside, the process of self-mastery first and foremost requires the objectification of all faculties: not only a more and more meticulous self-analysis but also the 'outsourcing' of the soul's faculties. The intellect, the emotions, the memory and even the senses are not only enforced by technical inventions, but also replaced by them. There is one exception, however, that should not be alienated from the modern self: the will, for within fantasy it becomes the master of all other faculties.

Fifthly, the type of 'conversion' motivated by fantasy is a future projection of the past self. In another words, there is no real new beginning. Any discontinuity between past and future remains wishful thinking, for all future projections are rooted in a deficient past. Only 'reforms' are possible. The burdens of the past, such as never-ending conflicts or wounds that never heal, cast a long shadow on any future identity both on an individual and communitarian level. 'Progress' here means nothing other than a desperate fleeing from one's own past that continuously threatens to invade the future. If there is no arch-image that one can turn to by the imagination, it is inevitable that there is an endless reproduction of one's own image which increasingly resembles that horrifying portrait of Dorian Gray.

Yet there is another consequence of understanding conversion on the basis of 'fantastic self-projection': the denial of the responsive character of any human project. Instead of positive freedom as an obedient *sequela Christi* that responds with self-denial and gift of the self to the divine love, modernity proposes a negative freedom from the absolute origin. Freedom loses its nature as a gift which introduces the dynamic of a loving exchange and becomes interpreted in terms of power. An act is deemed 'free' if it is not embedded in the divine–human dialogue but is instead completely initiated and performed by the will of an abstract self detached from any corporal, cultural or traditional influences. Such a concept of a 'pure act' constrains any consideration of conversion within the context of *vocation*, understood as a beginning in which one responds to the divine call. The moment of self-awakening that leads to conversion is no longer a moment of discovering oneself within the divine–human relationship, but is transformed into the puzzle of an abstract ego confronted with non-ego (as in Fichte).

Imaginative Conversion

Imaginative conversion is opposed to the modern tendency of self-realization based on fantasy. This diametrical relationship becomes visible in regard to different essential aspects. First of all, imaginative conversion means a radical change that is introduced by turning to the divine Person whose presence is discovered imaginatively and then acknowledged wholeheartedly. This process is an active spiritual and bodily reception rather than a constitution exercised by the abstract ego. Thus it is not the ego that is actively re-constructing the self but rather the self that is given a new life through the encounter with the divine. The responsive character of the transformation is essential.

The whole movement is determined by the reception and interpretation of the divine to which one turns. This centre can only be the very basis and finitude of all creation: Christ himself. Not Christ as concept or even as figure of the redeemer, not merely Christ of theological discourse or a philosophical system, but above all Christ as person, as his form (*Gestalt*) appears through and from the gospels. Christ as the vivid reality of personal encounter transmits the Father through the Holy Spirit and thereby reveals humanity to humanity: the new Adam to the old self. Conversion as a radical change of one's perception of reality and the response to it, and primordially to what is most beautiful, true, and real, is enabled by the attitude of Marian obedience. The 'Marian imagination' is focused on Christ, on the divine *logos*, and just as in the gospel it can be elevated to the unimaginable love of the Father. Elevation, however, is only possible inasmuch as the imagination embraces renouncement and discipline. The act of Marian imagination is based on the recognition that there is no other source but Christ, the incarnate divine *logos*, who is capable of revealing God. By obeying the Holy Spirit the imagination serves one basic purpose: intuiting the Father by penetrating into the sensible reality in order to stretch analogy to the extremes. Going beyond being is the precise moment of the specific sacrifice performed by the imaginative faculty: the imagination has to be silenced and needs to die. This sacrifice of the imagination consists in a reverent restraining of oneself from hastily putting forward an image. This vigil is perhaps that the most fruitful deed of all imaginative actions, for the proper and correct image, will come as a gift.

Rediscovering Imaginative Conversion in Postmodern Times

If one considers premodern imagination as mimetic (symbolized by the mirror), then its modern paradigm is productive (symbolized by the lamp) and in the postmodern period it is parodic (symbolized by the labyrinth of the looking glass).[18] For postmodern culture characteristically undermines the modernist belief in the image as an authentic image. It is difficult to make predictions concerning what will be the next stage of this continuous transformation of our understanding of the imagination. As with any epoch, the postmodern imagination finds itself at a crossroad: either preserving and bringing to culmination the modern fantasy, or giving into the contemporary demise of the

---

[18] Kearney, *The Wake of Imagination*, p. 12.

imagination.[19] Yet there is a third option, for which I have tried to argue in this essay: reviving the more original heritage of the Church Fathers and retrieving a 'Marian imagination'.

This is all the more necessary since a survey of the cultural panorama today conveys that the postmodern usage of imaginative faculty aggravates its modern forms: apparently nothing can resist the postmodern fantasy so eager to reshape the world in order to squeeze out the last drop of judicious enjoyment and diversion. The infantile and yet omnipotent ego that is at the same time anxious and disturbed is replaced the obedient imagination of the grateful child that receives any gift with the consciousness of being fully given to him – as pointed out by Ferdinand Ulrich.[20]

It is undeniable that if postmodern imagination gives in to the modern temptation it will repeat the tragic failures of the autonomous modern fantasy that is behind the technical-industrial transformation of the Western world and the destruction of the bloodiest century, as Hans Jonas has shown. As repeatedly noted,[21] modern fantasy resembles the Golem that, by aiming to aggrandize the human in the end cannot but deprive humanity of any trace of imago-nature – on the spiritual and cultural levels.

Any right interpretation of the dubious and deeply obscure signs of our epoch, like Auschwitz, in order not to be misguided by any form of pessimism or optimism, should be carried out within the horizon of eschatological hope. When considered in this broadest context of all, the modern heritage consists not only in the recognition of the witchcraft of unleashed autonomous human fantasy, but also in witnessing the immense capacities of an imaginative faculty willing to collaborate with God. The more secularization advanced, the harder the Christian imagination worked, not only on defending Christian truth, but also on the endeavour of putting forth the kerygma of the Christian faith. When understood and realized through and by Marian obedience, a newly acquired modern freedom from State and Church as institutions and social forces, and from some empty forms of 'tradition', allowed for a more devoted faith in God.

---

[19] As noted by Kearney, one of the most important characteristics of postmodern imagination is that it displays its own artificiality. Instead of producing, the postmodern imagination is satisfied with endless reproduction of the images without any origin. See Kearney, *The Wake of Imagination*, pp. 4–6.

[20] Ferdinand Ulrich, *Der Mensch als Anfang. Zur philosophischen Anthropologie der Kindheit* (Einsiedeln: Johannes Verlag, 1970).

[21] Gerschom Scholem, *Die Vorstellung vom Golem in ihren tellurischen und magischen Beziehungen* (Zürich: Rhein-Verlag, 1954), pp. 235–89. Also see Eric Voegelin, *Modernity without Restraint: The Political Religions, The New Science of Politics, and Science, Politics, and Gnosticism* (Collected Works vol. 5) (ed. Manfred Henningsen; Columbia: University of Missouri Press, 1999), pp. 280–3.

It is enough to think of such rebellious figures of imagination full of Christian spirit like Péguy, Bernanos, Gertrud von le Fort, Dostoyevsky, etc. This freer and more personal response to God which ignited the imagination belongs to that part of the legacy of modernity which postmodern thinking has to appropriate and develop.

The cultural change introduced by modernity both closes a door and opens a window for Christian conversion: the postmodern imagination, more mature than ever (given the double disillusion of the failure of anthropological and cosmological reduction), can only proceed on the secure and yet adventurous path which stems from the Church's tradition of the 'Marian imagination'.

Renewing Christian Philosophy: An Outline

Balázs M. Mezei

Introduction

In this paper I investigate the tradition of 'philosophy' and 'philosopher' with respect to their importance in Christianity.[1] I argue that the meaning of the traditional notion of philosophy as an abstract science has changed significantly. The reason for this is that the 'cosmo-theological' character of traditional philosophy proved to be untenable. If this pattern is not valid in our time, then the question arises if the role of philosophy, as conceived during the Christian centuries, can be continued in and beyond our age. My answer has two aspects: on the one hand, the cosmo-theological character of philosophy needs to be explored; on the other hand, Christian thought still has the potential to open itself to future renewal. Thinking philosophically is a fundamental human feature, and I suggest that 'trying to become wise', the striving for the discovery and realization of the meaningfulness of reality, is still the main concern of human beings reflecting on their historical existence today. In this sense, the encyclical letter of *Fides et ratio* by John Paul II offers guidance, inasmuch as its author calls for 'courage' in thinking. Following this call, the present paper contends that the three mains tasks of a Christian philosophy today are as follows: (a) a sufficient understanding of the tradition determined by cosmo-theology; (b) a sufficient understanding of the importance of the trauma of totalitarianism of the twentieth century as the dividing line between tradition and contemporary reflections; and (c) a sufficient understanding of human beings striving to grasp the meaning of personhood in an open universe on the basis of the meaningfulness of reality.

---

[1] An earlier version of this text appeared in *Logos i ethos* 2 (35) (2013): 109–46.

What is Philosophy?

If one asks what philosophy is, one faces first of all a linguistic problem. The word 'philosophy' comes from the Greek and its meaning is not very clear initially. There is a grammatical and semantic difference between 'philosophy' and 'philosopher', because the latter refers to the lover of the 'wise one' (*sophos*), while the former is about the lover of 'wisdom' (*sophia*).² This difference between philosophy and philosopher is important, because it shows that the activity of the philosopher, that is 'the love for the wise one', may not be reduced to the abstract term of 'philosophy'. The activity of the philosopher, according to its original setting, is closer to a personal relationship, as the basis of community, than to the abstract intellectual procedures of philosophy as we tend to understand this term today.

In the most important first documents of Greek philosophy, the writings of Plato and Aristotle, 'wisdom' cannot be detached from 'being wise' or 'the wise one', because the overall direction of these archaic forms of thought is in a sense theistic or, as we would put it with a later Greek expression, 'metaphysical'. Their theism or metaphysical character is relatively indistinct, and this is more so in Plato than in Aristotle. However, these authors appear to agree on the point that the philosopher investigates nature and culture *not* for the sake of a self-contained abstract science, and not for the sake of technological expertise, but rather with a metaphysical aim. This aim, as both Plato and Aristotle seem to agree, is divinization, the exact content of which cannot be precisely determined on the basis of their writings.³

On the other hand, these writings contain an encyclopaedia of then cutting-edge knowledge about fields as different as politics and cosmology, morals and civic law, mathematics and logic, biology and geography.⁴ These writers and their

---

² Pythagoras called himself φιλόσοφος, not σοφός, and here the 'philosopher' clearly means 'the lover of the wise one'. See the parallel expressions: φιλόβιβλος, 'lover of book'; φιλόξεινος, 'lover of guest'; φιλόδημος, 'lover of people'; etc.
³ As Socrates says, 'That is why a man should make all haste to escape from earth to heaven; and escape means becoming as like God as possible; and a man becomes like God when he becomes just and pious, with understanding.' *Theaetetus* 176 b, as in *Plato: Complete Works* (ed. J. M. Cooper; Indianapolis: Hackett, 1997), p. 195. And Aristotle: 'Therefore if, as they say, men become gods by excess of virtue, of this kind must evidently be the state opposed to the brutish state; for as a brute has no vice or virtue, so neither has a god.' Aristotle, *Nicomachean Ethics* (trans. David Ross, Oxford: Oxford University Press, 2009), 1145 a, p. 118. 'The escape from the earth to the dwelling of the gods' is a mythological figure of speech in the framework of cosmo-theology.
⁴ In the *Republic*, Plato offers a list of the sciences: arithmetic, geometry, physical or optical astronomy, mental astronomy, physical harmonics, mental harmonics and finally dialectics (525–32). We can speak of Plato's ethics and politics (in many parts of the *Republic*), law (in the *Laws*), literature and music (in the *Republic*, the *Laws* and in many other dialogues), anatomy (*Timaeus* 61ff.) and

followers conceived philosophy not only metaphysically but encyclopaedically as well. Philosophy, in other words, used to be the name of the all-encompassing knowledge which tried to synthesize various scientific branches with metaphysics. At the same time, as Pierre Hadot among others explain it, the centre of philosophy after the post-Platonic and post-Aristotelian periods was a certain way of life, an ascetic *Lebensführung* which renounced culture and civilization and entrusted itself to the universal spirit of divine providence.[5]

Plato and Aristotle did not appear to be strongly distinct thinkers in antiquity. In Neo-Platonism, Plato represented the omniscient master and Aristotle the ingenious disciple: Plato offered the general framework; Aristotle was to be thanked for filling in the details.[6] Their difference, however, became more evident especially in Arabian thought and, following the influence of Muslim scholarship in the West, in European Christianity as well.[7] Appropriate investigations uncovered their different approaches to reality, and their methodologies were subsequently distinguished along the lines of the difference between a significantly theoretical and a rather practical kind of reasoning. While this difference is detectable in their writings, it was only in the Italian Renaissance that certain thinkers recognized this difference as emblematic. Raphael's famous fresco *The School of Athens* (1511) expressed this understanding.[8] On the

geography (*Phaedo* 109ff.; *Timaeus* 22–6; *Critias* 3). Systematically, the passage in the *Republic* offers a synthetic view in which astronomy, and especially mental astronomy, occupies the second highest place, and dialectics, that is to say the investigation of the hierarchy of the sciences on the basis of 'conversation', is on the top of all sciences. Aristotle's theory of the sciences is put forward in his various works under the appropriate title, such as ethics, physics, cosmology, meteorology, rhetoric, metaphysics, etc. In the *Metaphysics*, Aristotle offers a hierarchy of the sciences in which the theoretical sciences (mathematics, physics and theology) are placed higher than their relatives in the practical realm (geometry, astronomy) and they are all opposed to the accidental sciences about categories and the distinctions between possibilities and actualities. Theoretical sciences fundamentally differ from the practical and productive sciences (or arts); and 'there is no science of the accidental is obvious; for all science is either of that which is always or of that which is for the most part'. Aristotle, *Metaphysics* 1025 a–1027, as in *The Complete Works of Aristotle* (ed. Jonathan Barnes; Princeton, NJ: Princeton University Press, 1991), p. 87.

[5] Pierre Hadot, *Qu'est-ce que la philosophie antique?* (Paris: Gallimard, 1996). We find clear traces of this ascetic way of life in what we know about Socrates from Plato. For instance, in the *Symposium* we read: 'One day, at dawn, he started thinking about some problem or other; he just stood outside, trying to figure it out. He couldn't resolve it, but he wouldn't give up. He simply stood there, glued to the same spot. By midday, many soldiers had seen him, and, quite mystified, they told everyone that Socrates had been standing there all day, thinking about something. He was still there when evening came, and after dinner some Ionians moved their bedding outside, where it was cooler and more comfortable (all this took place in the summer), but mainly in order to watch if Socrates was going to stay out there all night. And so he did; he stood on the very same spot until dawn! He only left next morning, when the sun came out, and he made his prayers to the new day.' *Symposium*, 220 c–d, as in *Plato: Complete Works*, p. 502.

[6] We find this approach for instance in Plotinus's works.

[7] Franz Rosenthal (ed. and trans.), *The Classical Heritage in Islam* (Berkeley: University of California Press, 1975). Miklós Maróth, *Die Araber und die antike Wissenschaftstheorie* (Leiden; New York: Brill, 1994).

[8] Raphael's typology nevertheless follows Aristotle's classification of the sciences into theoretical and

fresco in the Vatican Museums, Plato and Aristotle are facing the observer and Plato points upwards to the sky with his right forefinger while Aristotle makes a gesture of a downward grasp equally with his right hand. Plato holds the *Timaeus*, the central book of ancient cosmology, and Aristotle carries his *Ethics* as a reference to practical wisdom. Raphael's message is obvious: Plato represents the knowledge of the cosmos, the 'skies', the 'things on high', while Aristotle stands for the pragmatic knowledge of moral action. One kind of knowledge is theoretical, the other is practical; one is speculative, the other is constructive. This typology is apt to be represented artistically and it also discloses a philosophical insight. Raphael created a symbol of the most fundamental typology in the history of philosophy, a typology influencing deeply the subsequent centuries.[9]

From the philosophical point of view, Raphael's distinction seems to be generalizing. We do find that the outline of a systematic metaphysics in Aristotle and Plato reveals an intimate knowledge of the empirical sciences, such as astronomy, geography or biology. Nevertheless, the history of philosophy after Plato and Aristotle can be comfortably seen as belonging to one type or the other. This interpretation permeates Western philosophy at least up to the nineteenth century when the difference between German transcendentalism and Anglo-American pragmatism expressed a strong antagonism reminiscent of the divergence depicted in *The School of Athens*. In our days, we still find the Raphaelite-looking distinction between Continental philosophies on the one hand and Anglo-American kinds of thought on the other hand.

Philosophy, in our sense today, appears to be a Janus-faced tradition, the significance of which is now challenged from two important sides. On the one hand, authors like Martin Heidegger claimed that philosophy in the classical sense had reached its end, because it dissolved in the various branches of the natural, mathematical or social sciences.[10] On the other hand, scientists, such as Stephen Hawking, have recently claimed that philosophy lost its relevance for our contemporary culture, because it did not have an answer to the challenges of scientific development.[11] Moreover, certain theological schools, especially

---

practical in the *Metaphysics*, 1025 a ff.
[9] According to A. N. Whitehead, 'It was Plato who formulated most of philosophy's basic questions – and doubts. It was Aristotle who laid the foundation for most of the answers. Thereafter, the record of their duel is the record of man's long struggle to deny and surrender or to uphold and assert the validity of his particular mode of consciousness.' A. N. Whitehead, 'Review of J. H. Randall's *Aristotle*', *The Objectivist Newsletter*, May 1963, p. 18.
[10] Martin Heidegger, 'The End of Philosophy and the Task of Thinking', in idem, *Basic Writings* (ed. David Farrell Krell; San Francisco: Harper, 1993).
[11] Stephen Hawking with Leonard Mlodinov, *The Grand Design* (New York: Bantam Books, 2010).

that of Karl Barth, revisited the earlier thesis of Protestant theology about the uselessness of philosophy as opposed to faith and gave it a new momentum.[12]

The Cosmo-Theological View

The works of classical philosophers, and many of their followers, are indeed a goldmine for anyone interested in antique forms of human thought. However, there are some fundamental features entailed in these philosophies and which determine the entire tradition of philosophy that may appear as strange or plainly unacceptable today. I do not only mean such points as Plato's description of the inner organs of the human body, because besides its symbolic purpose the description is childish for today's readers.[13] Nor do I merely mean Aristotle's apparent logical conclusion to the water-like nature of the human eye, as opposed to its supposed light-emissive nature, which he verified by observing the decomposing of eyeballs.[14] Similar descriptions and *prima facie* verifications belong to the collection of ancient grotesqueries.

Nevertheless, there is an incomparably more important feature of the works of ancient philosophers, namely the overall pre-Copernican character of their worldview. Plato's meditations on the role of the blood in human bodies betray the author's ignorance of circulation, but this failure did not influence other parts of his philosophy.[15] Yet the pre-Copernican view of the universe offered an understanding of the cosmos as an organic unity in which human beings possess a central place so that they can view the circulation of the stellar bodies and accommodate their entire life to these movements. This universal understanding permeates the whole attitude, general features and particular views of these authors so that no important part of these philosophies can be

---

[12] Cf. Kenneth Oakes, *Karl Barth on Philosophy and Theology* (Oxford: Oxford University Press, 2012).
[13] One example: 'Moreover, the neighboring organ situated on its left turns out to have a structure which is meant to serve the liver in keeping it bright and clean continuously, like a dust cloth provided for wiping a mirror, placed next to it and always available. Hence, whenever impurities of one sort or another, the effects of bodily illnesses, turn up all around the liver, the spleen, a loosely-woven organ with hollow spaces that contain no blood, cleans them all away and absorbs them. In consequence it becomes engorged with the impurities it has cleaned off, swells to great size and festers. Later, when the body's cleansing is complete, the swelling subsides, and the spleen once again shrinks back to its normal size.' *Timaeus* 72 c, as in *Plato: Complete Works*, p. 1273.
[14] 'True, then, the visual organ proper is composed of water, yet vision appertains to it not because it is so composed, but because it is translucent – a property common alike to water and to air. But water is more easily confined and more easily condensed than air; wherefore it is that the pupil, i.e. the eye proper, consists of water.' Aristotle, *De sensu* (trans. J. I. Beare), available at: http://ebooks.adelaide.edu.au/a/aristotle/sense/ (last accessed 28 March 2013).
[15] *Timaeus* 79 e. Plato conjectured that the blood is in motion in the body, but he did not recognize the role of the heart.

understood without taking into account the pre-Copernican view. This view is not merely 'astronomical' in our sense today, but rather an overarching mystical perspective in which the origin and end of human beings, the meaning of the universe itself, the role of history, societies and the sciences are conceived as forming a meaningful whole, which is described precisely by what they called 'philosophy'. One of the most succinct summaries of this view can be found in Cicero's famous *Scipio's Dream*.[16]

I term this perspective 'cosmo-theology'. I am aware of various uses of this expression,[17] yet the phrase is still serviceable for present purposes: it points out

---

[16] In Cicero's *Republic* we read '"Men are created under these terms, that they are to look after that globe which you see in the middle of this precinct, which is called earth; and they are given a soul from those eternal fires which you call constellations and stars, which are spherical globes endowed with divine minds and accomplish their rotations and revolutions with amazing speed. And so, Publius, both you and all pious people must keep your soul in the guardianship of the body, and you must not depart from human life without the order of him who gave you your soul: you must not seem to run away from the human duty assigned by the god. [...] That way of life is the way to the heavens and to this gathering of those who have ceased to live and after having been released from the body now inhabit the place you see" (it was a bright circle shining among the stars with a most radiant whiteness), "which you have learned from the Greeks to name the Milky Way." And from that point, as I studied everything, it all seemed to me glorious and marvelous. There were stars which we never see from this place, and their size was such as we have never suspected; the smallest one was the one furthest from the heavens and closest to earth and shone with borrowed light.' Cicero, *On the Commonwealth. On the Laws* (ed. James E. G. Zetzel; Cambridge: Cambridge University Press, 1999), p. 97. See also Plato's *Republic* where we find a description which highlights the relationship between naked eye observation of the starry heavens and the mental image of perfect heavenly circulations and order. 'We should consider the decorations in the sky to be the most beautiful and most exact of visible things, seeing that they're embroidered on a visible surface. But we should consider their motions to fall far short of the true ones – motions that are really fast or slow as measured in true numbers, that trace out true geometrical figures, that are all in relation to one another, and that are the true motions of the things carried along in them. And these, of course, must be grasped by reason and thought, not by sight. [...] Therefore, we should use the embroidery in the sky as a model in the study of these other things.' *Republic* 529 c–d, as in *Plato: Complete Works*, pp. 1145–6. See also the famous passage in the *Timaeus*: 'We must next speak of that supremely beneficial function for which the god gave them to us. As my account has it, our sight has indeed proved to be a source of supreme benefit to us, in that none of our present statements about the universe could ever have been made if we had never seen any stars, sun or heaven. As it is, however, our ability to see the periods of day-and-night, of months and of years, of equinoxes and solstices, has led to the invention of number, and has given us the idea of time and opened the path to inquiry into the nature of the universe. These pursuits have given us philosophy, a gift from the gods to the mortal race whose value neither has been nor ever will be surpassed. I'm quite prepared to declare this to be the supreme good our eyesight offers us. [...] Let us rather declare that the cause and purpose of this supreme good is this: the god invented sight and gave it to us so that we might observe the orbits of intelligence in the universe and apply them to the revolutions of our own understanding. For there is a kinship between them, even though our revolutions are disturbed, whereas the universal orbits are undisturbed. So once we have come to know them and to share in the ability to make correct calculations according to nature, we should stabilize the straying revolutions within ourselves by imitating the completely unstraying revolutions of the god.' *Timaeus* 47 b–c, as in *Plato: Complete Works*, pp. 1249–50.

[17] My expression of cosmo-theology originates in the term 'cosmo-theism' coined by Lamoignon de Malesherbes and applied in our time by H. von Glasenapp and Jan Assmann. An alternative origin of the term can be traced back to Kant's distinction between 'cosmotheology' and 'ontotheology' in the *Critique of Pure Reason* (B 659/A 631). Assmann uses the term 'cosmotheism' in his various writings, such as in *Moses the Egyptian* (Cambridge, MA: Harvard University Press, 1997), p. 142. According to my understanding of *cosmo-theology*, the term refers to this: The basic structures

that the ancient authors considered the universe to be the expression of a divine entity and human beings to be expressions of important, perhaps even decisive, moments of this universe. Cosmo-theologians were thinking in universal terms, because they aimed at the whole of a pre-Copernican cosmos and sought, in some way, to influence it. They were theologians in that they considered the cosmos divine and saw human beings as moments of the divine functioning of the universe. That is, this view considered the cosmos and human beings as forming a living whole produced and directed by a divine being immanent to, or in some sense transcendent to, the universe. Physical nature, especially astronomical objects, was seen as the central expression of the cosmo-theological character of reality which shaped nature, culture and history. The human mind, as Plato already suggested, should be adapted to the movements of the 'intelligences in the heaven', that is, to the planetary and stellar movements in order that human beings may be harmonized with the universe and thus, through the correction of the error of physical nature, with the godhead.[18]

Inasmuch as this approach to reality was shared by the most influential philosophers not only of the Hellenic era but even for many centuries after it, including the Christian centuries, we can safely say that their worldview was cosmo-theological. While it is often claimed that philosophy introduced the rule of '*logos*' after the epoch of '*myth*', the fact is that this '*logos*' of the philosophers was often closer to mythology than to our rationality today. The difference between a mythological and a cosmo-theological approach to reality consists in their levels of precision: the mythological view is closer to the world

---

of reality become accessible especially in the phenomena of the sky (sun, moon, planets, stars, constellations, etc.), that is, in their movements and relationships. The cosmo-theological pattern determines theistic and monotheistic schemes of earlier and later religious forms, to some extent those of Christianity as well, and thus imbues human consciousness in a fashion which remains effective in various ways even in the age of science. As to the history of the content of this notion, one must refer to Charles-François Dupuis (1742–1809) whose monumental *Origin de tous les cultes, ou la religion universelle* (Paris, 1795) demonstrated – however also distorted – the importance of cosmic experience in the emergence of religious beliefs. Dupuis was a genius who tended to misinterpret his own important discoveries. Franz Cumont describes the content of cosmo-theology (in his words 'cosmic emotion') as follows: 'The resplendent stars, which eternally pursue their silent course above us, are divinities endowed with personality and animated feelings. On the other hand, the soul is a particle detached from the cosmic fires. The warmth which animates the human microcosm is part of the same substance which vivifies the universe, the reason which guides us, partakes of the nature of those luminaries which enlighten it. Itself a fiery essence, it is a kin to the gods which glitter in the firmament. Thus contemplation of the heaven becomes a communion.' Franz Cumont, *Astrology and Religion among the Greeks and Romans* (New York: Dover Publications, 1960), pp. 79–80.

[18] As to the harmony between the stars and the mind, see again *Timaeus* 47 b–c. The problem of transcendence is raised by the passages in Aristotle's *Metaphysics* (1072–3) where it seems that the unmoved mover of the universe has to have a substance in order to produce physical movement. On the other hand, the expression 'κινεῖ δὴ ὡς ἐρώμενον' (1072 b) seems to suggest that the *way* this ultimate principle moves the universe is emotional.

of tales, while always disclosing some moral, sometimes even cosmo-theological insights. The cosmo-theological view, however, presupposed a more accurate knowledge of nature, mathematics and astronomy, so that its premises and conclusions could be understood as scientific and used for formulating fairly precise inferences. It is important to add, however, that the cosmo-theological view substantially changed in Christian thought: while in Cicero we find an animated and divine universe, with the earth and human beings at its centre, the centre of reality for Christianity is God himself; and the universe comes to the fore only as an expression of God's free creative act. Nevertheless, as we can see in many authors from St Augustine to St Thomas or Dante, the cosmo-theological view possessed a deep influence on Christian philosophy, theology and art.[19]

Even though some trends in traditional philosophy became specialized in the problems of physics, logic, rhetoric, morals or even biology, the overall cosmo-theological pattern determined its fundamental concepts and procedures. The hierarchical view of the cosmos served as the pattern of a moral and political hierarchy; logical relations were seen as expressed to some extent by the observable relations among stellar objects, all considered as embodying a rational living being. Theology was shaped in accordance with 'the teachings of the heavens', so that even the notion of an unmoved mover could be conceived of on the basis of the only apparently motionless point in the northern sky, the Polaris.[20] Certainly, it would be a mistake to say that the cosmo-theological view of the universe was a simple copy of optical experience. Cosmo-theologians were sophisticated thinkers, as Plato shows for instance, and they never dared to identify the ultimate truth with optical or any kind of sensual perception. As Plato writes, we 'need to suffer of the things in the heavens' if we want 'to have a part in the true science of astronomy'.[21] That is, we need optical experience,

---

[19] See Thomas Aquinas, *Summa theologiae*, I, 70, 3: 'One being may be nobler than another absolutely, but not in a particular respect. While, then, it is not conceded that the souls of heavenly bodies are nobler than the souls of animals absolutely, it must be conceded that they are superior to them with regard to their respective forms, since their form perfects their matter entirely, which is not in potentiality to other forms; whereas a soul does not do this. Also as regards movement the power that moves the heavenly bodies is of a nobler kind' (trans. Fathers of the English Dominican Providence). Widespread doubts about the soul-filled character of stars (even in the sense of Thomas) were confirmed with the discovery of the telescope and Galileo's investigations presented in *The Starry Messenger* of 1610. However, way beyond this time the conviction that the stars are living beings in a certain sense could be found even among leading scientists.

[20] See Aristotle: 'The first principle or primary being is not movable either in itself or accidentally, but produces the primary eternal and single movement.' *Metaphysics* 1073 a, as in: *The Complete Works of Aristotle*, p. 177. As it appears from the text, the first mover must be of a sort of substance which is able to move other substances, such as the spheres, the stars and the planets.

[21] The expression 'to suffer of the things in the heavens' (τὰ δ' ἐν τῷ οὐρανῷ ἐάσομεν) is mistranslated in several works. Sometimes we even find the translation that we should 'leave the things in

but without mental work or a kind of mystical experience we cannot have an insight into truth. On the other hand, it would be an exaggeration to say that logic, mathematics, morality and politics were nothing more than replicas of 'the teachings of the heavens'. In all these fields, genuine and specific discoveries were made and used for further arguments and conjectures. However, the overall pattern of cosmo-theology determined the framework and the main structures of a conceptual world in which philosophy lived, moved and existed; and the sight of the heavenly bodies, the stars and the planets, the seasons and vegetation offered a schema without which 'philosophy' would have been meaningless.

The most important features of the cosmo-theological view are as follows: (1) the notion of lower nature as fundamentally moldable by higher or divine nature; (2) the notion of nature as containing structures reproducible in particular products of human action; (3) the notions of objectivity and subjectivity; (4) imitation as the essence of human action; (5) human beings conceived along the lines of the 'intelligences of the heavens'; (6) the lack of the notion of genuine difference and genuine newness; (7) history as a cyclical process.

'Nature' in the sense characteristic of the 'earth' is by its essence open to formation by cosmic influences, the rules of the 'heavens'. Based on this notion of nature, 'phusis' or 'natura' became understood as the target of modification, influence and exploitation. Higher nature is eternal and cannot be changed; lower nature is receptive to higher nature and follows the latter as much as possible. Human beings are free to follow or unfollow higher nature, and they are able to reach the ultimate source of reality and participate in the overall configuration of the universe.[22] Moreover, humans can imitate the heavens in that they produce things which are new to nature yet use natural processes as their principles, such as simple or more complicated machines. It seems that the main intention of machine-building in antiquity may have been the production of a replica of the world, such as Plato's μίμημα (*Timaeus* 40 d) and similar planetariums. Engineers such as Heron of Alexandria produced more particular machines as well. For instance, as Claudian describes, cleverly arranged magnets were used to set in motion sacred sculptures in the temple of Mars and Venus to create the scene of a sexual union of the two deities during liturgy.[23] These

---

the heavens alone', which is incorrect given the meaning of ἐάω: concede, let. See *Republic* 530 b–c. Such a mistranslation fits in with a misinterpretation of Plato as the philosopher of abstractions.

[22] See especially Aristotle's description of the ultimate principles of the heavens in *Metaphysics* 1072 ff. Plato speaks of ταὐτόν and θάτερον (the Same and the Other: the sphere of the fixed stars, and the sphere of the planets) in *Timaeus* 35, 37, 44.

[23] Claudianus, Claudius: *Works* (London: W. Heinemann, 1922), vol. 2, pp. 234ff.

efforts were dependent on the view of nature as governed by higher influences; and of human beings as mediators of such influences. Humans, nevertheless, conceived themselves as replicas of higher entities, such as planets and stars, and thus their shadow-like being did not allow the emergence of the notion of genuine subjectivity.[24]

The ancient notion of objectivity, as embodying the eternal and valid structures of reality, was modeled above all on the 'skies' and their apparent regular movements. It is beyond question that the everyday objectivity of sense-perception helps the emergence of a massive feel of objectivity; but precisely the latter is most importantly represented by the impression of the 'eternal movements' of the stars.[25] In the framework of cosmo-theology, the notion of objectivity was reinforced by the experience of the movements of the 'heavens'. I should stress that the main faculty related to the cosmo-theological experience is vision. It belongs to the nature of human sight that, even though its contents are determined by the optical mechanisms of the eye, its production appears preeminently 'objective'. The cosmo-theological view of reality was based on naked eye observation and thus the overwhelming nature of the cosmo-theological experience received an additional support from the objectivity characteristic of human vision. Subjectivity was defined in accordance with this objectivity: In this framework, the subject was conceived as the complementary pole, *the negative* of objectivity. Thus subjectivity became an *optical subjectivity* which is capable of the sight of the universe and defined accordingly as an integral part of it. Subjectivity was defined objectively.[26]

As a consequence of the objective view of the universe, the main activity of human individuals, their societies and even history had to be conceived as imitations or replicas of the objective order of the heavens. From times immemorial, the main feasts of developed societies have been determined in accordance with

---

[24] Plato famously claimed (*Timaeus* 41) that there are exactly as many stars in the heavens as souls, some of them living on the Earth. This parallelism shows that human beings are actually stellar objects in an earthly modification.

[25] Kant famously referred to the 'starry sky' as the most important external source of wonder: 'Two things fill the mind with ever-increasing wonder and awe, the more often and the more intensely the mind of thought is drawn to them: the starry heavens above me and the moral law within me.' Kant: *Critique of Practical Reason*, Part II, Conclusion; available at http://www.gutenberg.org/cache/epub/5683/pg5683.html (last accessed 28 March 2013).

[26] Here we can mention one of the central views of Robert Lanza, the main representative of biocentrism. As he repeatedly writes, the 'external world' is derived mainly from optical experience, but quantum theory does not confirm the well-grounded nature of our optical experience. To which I would add, in cosmo-theology, the extreme objectification intrinsic in visual perception serves as the basis of an entire system, the remnants of which still determine our worldviews, especially physics.

the movements and constellations of heavenly bodies, most importantly the sun and the moon. Even Christianity continued this tradition so that, among other feasts, Christmas and Easter are still settled on by characteristic stellar times – the shortest day of the year (in accordance with the premodern calendar) for Christmas, and the first full moon after the spring equinox for Easter.[27] Human individuals were called to imitate the heavenly movements, stellar and planetary relations, and even the notion of an *imitatio Christi* continued this tradition of a cosmic simulation put into an allegorical context. That is, imitation of the skies, the will of the gods or God, the imitation of great prophets, kings, and heroes, all belonged to the essence of the cosmo-theological view. Thereby human beings became replicas or reflections of paramount personalities, even mythical ones with stellar connotations, such as Hercules or Perseus. The notion of human personhood, in the sense we know of it today, could not have its rightful place in the mind of the ancients. Imitation as the central feature of human activity – a feature which did not exclude but merely determined the notion of free will – hampered the insight into the value of genuine newness in the realms of human action or history. More importantly, the universal hierarchy of analogies blocked the perception of the value of genuine difference, the power of 'the wholly other', as we meet this expression today in philosophy as well as in theology.[28]

Similarly, history could not be seen otherwise than a reflection of the 'eternal circulations' of the heavenly bodies. Historical epochs, the fall and rise of political powers, were also considered to be reflections of events in the sky, even if it must have been very difficult to establish the precise correspondences in concrete cases.[29] Nevertheless, a 'cyclical' view of history did not possess a perfect pattern

---

[27] Dupuis, *Origine de tous les Cultes*, vol. V. Dupuis realized that the fundamental texts of Christianity reflect the cosmo-theological view. He misinterpreted, however, his own discovery inasmuch as he concluded that the figure of Christ was a literary fiction based on the experience of the Sun. This is a non-sequitur. While these texts are clearly determined by the cosmo-theological pattern, their authors saw this pattern as materialized in real occurrences on Earth. The essence of the cosmo-theological pattern is precisely this: that real occurrences reveal it; and the task of a biographer, such as an evangelist, was to show this pattern as realized in real goings-on in everyday circumstances. In other words, Dupuis was seriously mistaken to believe that the figure of Christ was not real; he was right nevertheless in showing that the figure of Christ was seen as revealing a higher order of things as conceived in the natural experience of the sky.

[28] The modern use of the expression '*totaliter aliter*' originates in Rudolf Otto's 1917 *The Holy* and was subsequently applied by Karl Barth in a characteristic sense to point out the absolute difference between the human world and divine reality.

[29] Virgil, nevertheless, connected the rule of Augustus to a new planetary situation in the Fourth Eclogue:

> Now the last age by Cumae's Sibyl sung
> has come and gone, and the majestic roll
> of circling centuries begins anew:

on the sky: as was evident for the ancient astronomers, celestial orbits did not represent a perfect circle. A 'cyclical' notion of history could not be conceived, accordingly, as the realization of an eternal cyclical pattern in which the same things recur forever. The cosmo-theological view contained the recognition that the human eye could not see perfect circulations, only imperfect ones. That was the reason why Plato advised his readers to concentrate on *mental* astronomy, based on the imperfect optical astronomy, since the latter only approximated abstract arithmetical structures. Nevertheless, the supposition that a perfect formula can be spelled out, or at least that the mystically perfect circle can be realized, was a sufficient ground for the cosmo-theologians to ponder about the cause of the difference between the observable imperfect cosmos and the perfect formula. The explanation we have is ingenious: as Plato expounds in the myth of the 'chariot allegory', the once perfect circulation of the heavens was broken by a destructive principle, embodied in the black horse of the chariot.[30] We can interpret this allegory as an explanation of a catastrophe of a cosmic dimension, which had to have three kinds of consequences. First, this catastrophe leads to the unraveling of the various heavenly spheres, each corresponding to a certain level of perfection or imperfection. Second, the catastrophe launches the cosmic wandering of souls which leads from the star-form to human and subhuman existences, and then back to the stellar form again. Thirdly, the catastrophe is the beginning of a historical process of decline and renewal. As can be seen, the cyclical nature of history could well fit in with a notion of history of fall and redemption and did not necessitate a uniform return of selfsame structures.[31]

Departing from Cosmo-Theology

What I attempted to delineate briefly above leads us to realize two things: First, the Western tradition of philosophy was fundamentally determined by the cosmo-theological understanding of the universe. Second, this understanding

---

      justice returns, returns old Saturn's reign,
      with a new breed of men sent down from heaven.
      Only do thou, at the boy's birth in whom
      the iron shall cease, the golden race arise,
      befriend him, chaste Lucina; 'tis thine own
      Apollo reigns. (Trans J. B. Greenough)

[30] *Phaedrus* 246 a–254 e.
[31] Plato remains silent about the *meaning* of the process of fall and redemption. Sometimes he hints at an aim, namely the self-contained life of the universe. Fall and redemption are necessary for the purification not only of the souls but also of the godhead, since the universe as a perfect and eternal whole has 'his own waste providing his own food' (*Timaeus* 33 c).

was not merely peripheral or negligible, but defined the whole conceptual schema of philosophy, its fundamental notions, relations, objectives and, most importantly, philosophy's understanding of human beings. It is an understandable endeavour to flesh out the meaning of many of our philosophical concepts by going back to the very sources, especially to Greek and Latin philosophy. However, it is a serious mistake to believe that such a return could replace the more important task of clarifying the fundamental structures of the cosmo-theological worldview and its relation to our traditional philosophical notions. A 're-Hellenization' of philosophy, as well as a return to Aristotle in order to find a sound notion of reason or moral virtue, are important philosophical proposals, yet they remain insufficient: we need to see not only the original meaning of certain conceptions, but their overall situation as well, in the cosmo-theological view.[32] And we need to see the development by which these notions became abstracted from their original matrix and acquired a meaning in which the cosmo-theological layer was still present. The notion of a virtue is certainly one of these important concepts in which the original cosmo-theological nucleus of 'ἕξις' – the capacity of producing action in a fashion analogous to the intelligible and 'habitual' movements of stars – became blurred, individualized and structured in a moral system in which forgetfulness gradually suppressed the cosmo-theological pattern.[33]

Modern philosophy could not fundamentally detach from this tradition of cosmo-theology, because the possibility was not yet given to face the tradition in its entirety and to explore its essential structures.[34] However, the slow demythologization of philosophy had a strong beginning already in the texts of Plato and Aristotle. While in these authors the cosmo-theological background is often obvious, in many passages of their writings the pattern remains hidden. The reader may have the impression that this latency is the result of tactful editorial work. For instance, Plato would have been able to spell out the philosophical relevance of the Myth of Er at the end of the *Republic* in clear astronomical terms, yet he chose an obscure mythical form. Similarly, Aristotle's concise style

---

[32] Balázs Mezei, *Reason and Revelation after Auschwitz* (New York: Bloomsbury, 2013), pp. 269–84.
[33] Aristotle's discussions point to the astronomical dimension at crucial points. For instance, in the *Nicomachian Ethics*, one discussion on *sophia* leads to the conclusion that *sophia* cannot be identical with politics or government, because human beings are not the most perfect beings in reality, 'since there exist other things far more divine in their nature than man, for instance, to mention the most visible, the things of which the celestial system is composed'. (1141 a–b). This is a reference to stellar entities which Aristotle considers 'gods' (*Metaphysics* 1026 a; 1074 b).
[34] I need to mention Dupuis again, for he produced an overall analysis of the cosmo-theological pattern. However, his superficial naturalism and logical non-sequiturs hindered a deeper reception of his work during the subsequent decades after 1795, the publication of *Origine de tous les Cultes*.

is able to hide that his dry way of writing on even apparently specific subjects presupposes the cosmo-theological framework of the *De coelo* and other cosmological writings. Christian writers followed this path of an imperfect demythologization, while on the metaphysical and religious level the influence of cosmo-theology remained in force.[35]

However, a more substantial wave of demythologizing became possible with the new emphasis on the human subject, the modern principle of the *ego cogito*. With this principle – which had again been known to some ancient authors, such as Augustine – the master role of the heavenly pattern began to decline. Instead, the fundamental role of the human subject as an 'I' came to the fore. By this change, the possibility was given for an overall reassessment of the cosmo-theological pattern. Nevertheless, the *res extensa* of the Cartesian philosophy of nature was still a *natural* entity in its traditional meaning, an entity which could be considered as open to human manipulation. And the notion of the human subject as *res cogitans* did not properly express the character of human personhood except in its relation to the external world as a mathematical-geometrical entity. The way to a gradually emerging new view of reality was opened, however, by the more proper understanding of human subjectivity and personhood, which happened in several steps after Descartes, most importantly in German transcendental philosophies. In the latter tradition, which originated in Kant's famous *Critiques*, the recognition of the genuine nature of human subjectivity smoothed the path to a new, non-cosmo-theological understanding of reality. Reality began to lose its connection to the archaic notion of nature and became more and more emphatically bound up with the human person as its core.

On the other hand, the emphasis on human personhood disclosed the possibility of subjectivism, even solipsism, which degraded human personhood to a worldly entity and blocked the way again to an overall evaluation of the cosmo-theological heritage. In Kant's system a defective notion of human perception, or in Hegel's thought the notion of the universal history of the spirit, lacked important features which did not allow an overall revision of the traditional pattern. Kant remained a sensualist in terms of experience, and Hegel did not

---

[35] Already the New Testament is full with cosmo-theological allusions beginning with the Star of Bethlehem through the heavy Hellenistic astrological symbolism in John's Revelation to Jesus' words referring to the signs in the heavens (Lk. 21.11), or to 'heavens' in the plural *(en tois ouranois)* in the Our Father, a hint to the spherical notion of the universe. A systematic exploration of the cosmo-theological character of the New Testament was offered by Arthur Drews; however, because of the exaggerations of the author's interpretations, his discovery of the cosmo-theological pattern did not have its due recognition.

recognize the Platonic, thus cosmo-theological, roots of an idealizing speculation.[36] Moreover, without a systematic exploration of the fundamental structures of the philosophical tradition, these philosophers and their followers were not able to overcome the defects originating in the centaur-like combination of new insights and traditional structures. The great philosophical rebels of the nineteenth century, such as Kierkegaard or Nietzsche, clearly recognized the insufficiency of transcendentalism as a view open to a subjectivist interpretation of reality and human persons: that is to say, as an approach in which remnants of the old structures of cosmo-theology survived. Kierkegaard emphasized the notion of the godhead as 'absolutely different' from what the human mind can conceive; and Nietzsche, far from being a representative of 'philosophical bestiary',[37] desperately tried to overcome the obscured remnants of a traditional view of morality, politics, culture and metaphysics. Their criticisms did not reach their aim, because these philosophers lacked the recognition of the importance of a systematic and historical demythologization of philosophy.

In the twentieth century, Husserl's experiential idealism or Heidegger's existential ontology were important steps to unmask the cosmo-theological tradition. However, these thinkers did not recognize the necessity of a historical and formal analysis of this heritage.[38] They did offer a 'destruction' of the philosophical tradition. While both Husserl and Heidegger used this expression in slightly different meanings, they lacked the most important tool for a sufficient 'destruction', namely the recognition of the mythical origin and contents of most of the philosophical vocabulary: that is, they did not recognize the cosmo-theological framework. What Husserl wrote on the history of philosophy did not go beyond Kant's schema of a struggle between 'dogmatism' and 'critical philosophy'. What Heidegger offered, most importantly in *Plato's Doctrine of Truth*, was an important criticism of fundamental Platonic notions, mainly

---

[36] Many criticisms of Hegel, such as those of Schelling or Voegelin, emphasized 'positive' philosophy of reality as a whole (Schelling), or reality as an objective history of symbolic forms (Voegelin), in contrast to Hegel's merely conceptual speculation.

[37] MacIntyre, Alasdair: *After Virtue. A Study in Moral Theory* (Notre Dame: University of Notre Dame Press, 1984), p. 22.

[38] In spite of the enormous literature on Plato and other Classical authors, the determining factor of the cosmo-theological view of the universe has not been clearly recognized. The main reason for this is that most of the authors did not see the prevalent nature of the mystical view of the universe. Among the few authors who nevertheless realized the importance of the cosmo-theological view we find the Czech philosopher Jan Patočka. As Patočka explains, Plato first developed the notion of the ideas and then identified the ideas with planets and stars. While this chronology is clearly mistaken, Patočka did recognize the role of cosmo-theology in Plato, while he did not elaborate on this recognition. See Jan Patočka's 'Negative Platonism: Reflections concerning the Rise, the Scope and the Demise of Metaphysics – and Whether Philosophy Can Survive It', in *Jan Patočka: Philosophy and Selected Writings* (ed. and trans. E. Kohák; Chicago and London: University of Chicago Press, 1989), pp. 175–206.

the role of the idea as 'the yoke' of Being. Heidegger, nevertheless, did not see the importance of the cosmo-theological framework in Plato. Neither Husserl, nor Heidegger, realized that not only the history of Western philosophy was 'a footnote to Plato', as Whitehead famously remarked,[39] but the basic conceptions of this philosophical tradition had been determined by the hidden pattern of the cosmo-theological view. Due to this deficiency, the phenomenological and existential-ontological attempts to overcome the cosmo-theological tradition lacked a systematic point of view and remained, in their main structures, attached to transcendentalism.[40]

As a reaction to transcendentalism, several waves of historical criticisms emerged which focused on the history of the forms of human thought, such as those of Dilthey, Jaspers, Cassirer or Voegelin. In fact, the philosophers of symbolic forms added a very important correction to transcendentalism, namely the component of an encompassing historical criticism of the forms of human thinking. In this way, the possibility of an overall criticism of philosophy as it became determined by cosmo-theology was already given. Yet no philosopher so far has endeavoured successfully to map out the range and importance of this criticism in historical as well as transcendental terms. Philosophy had reached the limit of its classical European development by the mid-twentieth century and subsequently it lived on the past results by offering various interpretations, corrections and reconsiderations. In contrast, academic philosophy in the Anglo-American world rarely recognizes the initial character and the natural limits of its heritage. Instead, it concentrates merely on certain perspectives in which the cosmo-theological tradition is not identified and therefore its conceptual schema remains caught up in a philosophical naïveté. As a consequence, in contemporary thought we have a range of philosophies which analyse various aspects of this tradition without recognizing the underlying role of an ancient view of reality, a view determining the self-reflection of mankind for many thousands of years.

---

[39] 'The safest general characterization of the European philosophical tradition is that it consists of a series of footnotes to Plato.' A. N. Whitehead, *Process and Reality. An Essay in Cosmology* (New York: The Free Press, 1979), p. 39.

[40] Heidegger's term of 'onto-theology' expresses a criticism different from my criticism of cosmo-theology. Onto-theology is a Heideggerian term for a metaphysical use of the logical mistake of '*pars pro toto*': Being is seen in terms of beings, the whole is reduced to the level of its parts. The criticism of cosmo-theology, however, is a form of historical criticism. Nevertheless, this criticism points to our insufficient understanding of reality in its entirety and historicity.

The Role of Christian Philosophy

The mere question whether there is 'Christian philosophy' at all may seem to be a kind of academic hypocrisy. For already by raising such a question we logically acknowledge a certain possibility of Christian philosophy inasmuch as the two terms – 'Christianity' and 'philosophy' – are not mutually exclusive and their combination does not entail any apparent contradiction. The counter-argument to the effect that the talk of 'Christian philosophy' is analogous to the talk of 'Christian mathematics' or 'Christian physics' misses the point. The very idea of an eternal and objective philosophy, which Christianity could use for its purposes, is a remnant of the cosmo-theological pattern. In spite of the admonitions of Plato and Aristotle, some philosophers of the subsequent centuries did not see the distinction between special sciences and philosophy as an architectonic kind of knowledge.[41] Philosophy has never been an objective science in the sense of the particular, cosmo-theologically determined sciences, but rather a universal way of experiencing, understanding and contributing to the life of the universe. From the Christian point of view, Christianity was a correction added to pre-Christian thought, and philosophy was fulfilled and perfected in the Christian conception of reality. Philosophy, in this sense, was a corollary to the sciences and pointed to the realm of theology properly so called.[42]

As opposed to various modern philosophies, Christian philosophy has two important advantages: First, traditional Christian philosophy has carefully kept the tradition of the cosmo-theological view. Second, it was Christianity and its philosophical reflections from St Augustine to contemporary attempts which slowly changed the cosmo-theological pattern and secured an appropriate place for an absolutely transcendent God on the one hand and for the importance of human beings as ultimate persons, persons stemming from the free and divine act of creation. These two emphases were going through a long process of articulation, in which the beginnings are massively determined by the externalist cosmo-theological view, but later on, as a result of the efforts of the greatest minds of the Christian centuries, genuine changes occurred: the articulation of God's unique absoluteness and the unique ultimacy of human personhood.[43]

What is often mentioned as the archaism of the tradition of Christian

---

[41] As for instance Aristotle suggests, *Nicomachean Ethics,* 1094 a.
[42] About the famous French debate on the possibility of Christian Philosophy, see especially Gilson's statement in his *The Spirit of Mediaeval Philosophy* (trans. A. H. C. Downes; Notre Dame: University of Notre Dame Press, 1991).
[43] See Mezei, *Reason and Revelation,* pp. 93–177.

philosophy, namely its closeness to Platonism, Aristotelianism and especially the presence of Thomism in many of its branches, is in my view an advantage in our philosophical situation. The great philosophical revolutions of modernity – Cartesianism and transcendentalism, to name only the two main trends – have proved to be important yet failed attempts to overcome the robust tradition of cosmo-theology. Christian philosophy, in contrast, has always emphasized a certain balance between continuity and change, and thus it never attempted to dismantle its foundations. In fact, Christian philosophy has always followed a 'Tychonic' way. As is known, the famous astronomer of the sixteenth century, Tycho Brahe, sought to combine what he saw as the geometrical benefits of the Copernican system with the theological benefits of the Ptolemaic system into his view of the universe. What he proposed was a combination of old and new: the philosophical framework of the cosmo-theological view of Ptolemy enriched by the results and consequences of observations of which Tycho was an important practitioner. Let me consider this well-adjusted combination of old and new a *model*. I claim that Christian philosophy used this model in its renewals and reformations: it aspired to keep the framework of the ancient view and improved it with elements of new philosophical discoveries and perspectives throughout the Middle Ages and modernity up to our day.[44]

The Tychonic nature of Christian philosophy has been pervasive: just think of such different authors as Origen, Augustine, Boethius, Thomas Aquinas, Fénelon, the Neo-Aristotelianism and Neo-Thomism of the nineteenth century and, in our age, the various philosophical proposals by Maritain, Gilson, Rahner, von Balthasar or Jean-Luc Marion, to name only some of the most influential thinkers. The Tychonic model has been applied variously in the works of these authors. It is nevertheless safe to claim without simplification that in all these cases the massive presence of the traditional view has been fundamentally maintained and, at the same time, improved by new thoughts and perspectives. This has taken place, chronologically, in Platonism, Aristotelianism, rationalism, transcendentalism, existentialism, Protestant anti-philosophism (Barth and his followers) and, in our time, in the methodologies of philosophical

---

[44] The tradition of Pseudo-Dionysius has determined Greek Orthodox theology and philosophy in such a measure that philosophy in the Western sense has not developed in Orthodox countries. In the West, nevertheless, the fragmented traditions of Greek philosophy led to the emergence of autonomous attempts to improve the tradition. The condition of possibility of the non-cosmo-theological development in Western philosophy was precisely the fragmented and insufficient knowledge of the tradition and the reaction to this situation by ingenious thinkers, such as Augustine, Bonaventure, Thomas Aquinas, etc. Once this kind of creative philosophizing began, the spell of cosmo-theology became weaker until it was broken – yet not fully unmasked – in the emergence of subjectivist philosophies of modernity.

scientism.⁴⁵ The reason for the dominance of the Tychonic model was the effort to maintain and reinforce the traditional Christian view of reality. And while the latter view has been subjected to several waves of 'demythologization' throughout the centuries, Christian philosophy escorted these changes without offering too much or too little. After the Alexandrian age, Christian philosophy followed an improved version of Platonism; in Augustine's work, it created an existential Platonism; in the first scholasticism it produced Christian Aristotelianism; in the second scholasticism, Christian rationalism; in the nineteenth century, Christian philosophy continued to follow the Aristotelian path with a new emphasis on the importance of common-sense realism and technical knowledge. In the twentieth century, Christian philosophy absorbed some results of transcendentalism, existentialism, hermeneutics and structuralism; and, in our age, some of its important representatives follow the ideal of a scientific philosophy, others the developments of Continental thought with its emphasis on the paradoxical, the negative and the inconceivable.⁴⁶

The advantage of Christian philosophy keeping the traditional cosmo-theological view in its fundamental structures, or the advantage of avoiding an overall demythologization of its traditions, can be expressed as follows. First, it is in Christian philosophy in which we possess a clear example of the cosmo-theological influences. Fundamental notions of Christian philosophy, such as 'nature', 'substance', 'person', 'knowledge', 'metaphysics', 'morals', 'virtue', 'society', 'teleology', 'certainty' and so on maintain their close connection to ancient antecedents and are safely embedded in the cosmo-theological view. The advantage here consists in that a Christian philosopher, being aware of the significance of the cosmo-theological character of the ancient views, can study, explain and reinterpret the cosmo-theological roots of our basic philosophical notions. Second, the Christian philosopher thus becomes able to launch an overall reinterpretation of philosophy, his own philosophical traditions included. Third, on the basis of such a reinterpretation, the Christian philosopher can search for a new understanding of his place in the universe, the significance of his traditions and a new perspective in which he still can be called a philosopher and a Christian at the same time.

At this point we need to answer the following questions: (1) What exactly

---

⁴⁵ Cosmo-theology can be detected even in such authors as Marion, for example, especially when he applies the tradition of negative theology in his thought. A famous representative of scientism in Christian philosophy is Bernard Lonergan.
⁴⁶ See for instance John Haldane's works for a sober and analytical approach to Thomism. And see especially the works of Michel Henry or Jean-Luc Marion for a Continental version of Christian philosophy which absorbed phenomenology and hermeneutics.

does the expression 'renewing' or 'reinterpreting' mean in this context? (2) What is the motive of a Christian philosopher for reinterpreting its philosophical traditions? (3) What kind of assistance can a Christian philosopher receive for his work from the philosophical tradition or from contemporary developments? (4) What are the fundamental structures of a renewed Christian philosophy?

The Vocation of a Christian Philosopher

As briefly explained above, the most important task of Christian philosophy is a clarification of its fundamental philosophical notions. Possible examples abound, but here I focus only on the notion of human personhood. The original notion of personhood is rooted in the optical experience of the external appearance of an individual or a thing.[47] It lasted several centuries until the corresponding Hebrew, Greek and Latin terms assumed a meaning relatively close to our understanding today. Still, even in this notion of a *prosopon* and *persona*, the external appearance remained decisive as the basic background in the semantic circle of the term.[48] The Trinitarian debates of the first Christian centuries and the related dogmatic discussions in the subsequent epochs made it possible to form a notion of personhood equally applicable to every human person and the divine persons; and it was Thomas Aquinas who endeavoured to attribute personhood not only to the persons of the Trinity but also to human individuals.[49] The 'revolution of personhood' in modern philosophy, most importantly in the work of Kant, led to the realization of the unique 'dignity' (intrinsic worth, *Würde*) of human persons, a decisive step on the way leading off the courses of cosmo-theological thinking.[50] However, Western philosophical vocabularies still used versions of the Latin form of *persona* and still kept its rootedness in the ancient worldview in a more or less latent fashion.

---

[47] Mezei, *Reason and Revelation*, p. 129.
[48] In resurrection, as Paul explains in 1 Cor. 15.40ff., human bodies rise just as heavenly bodies rise, and human bodies will possess a spiritual body, just as the Sun, the Moon and other stars possess their own appropriate glorious bodies. In resurrection, moreover, the first living soul of Adam is changed into the life-giving soul of the resurrected. In the background, ancient beliefs of cosmo-theological kind are clearly recognizable, such as that stellar entities are life-creating beings.
[49] Thomas Aquinas, *Summa theologiae*, I, 30, 4.
[50] Immanuel Kant, *Groundwork of the Metaphysics of Morals* (trans. M. Gregor; Cambridge: Cambridge University Press, 1998), p. 42. It is important to see that the Latin *dignitas* and its derivations in contemporary languages do not properly express the notion of an 'inner value' or 'end in itself' as Kant defined them. Dignity comes from the Latin *dignus*, the meaning of which is 'worthy *of* something,' 'deserving *something*'. *Dignus* cannot articulate worth as an end in itself. *Dignitas* basically means 'merit', 'worthiness' (of something), hence 'authority', 'official rank', 'power'.

I believe that this latent connection is responsible for our lack of an obvious distinction between personhood as a *sui generis* entity and personhood as an individual substance in the universe.⁵¹

What a Christian philosopher needs to do in this case is a clarification of the difference between human personhood *sui generis* and personhood as a cosmo-theologically determined individual. For this aim, a Christian philosopher needs to study the documents about the origins of this notion, analyse its historic development and see the philosophical distinction between 'dignity' in a hierarchical universe and *Würde* as inner value, as the basis of personal unity, non-reducibility and irreplaceability.⁵²

In this context, the work of reinterpretation means above all the exploration of the latent remnants of an earlier view of reality in our notions today. Just as Alasdair MacIntyre offered a clarification of the fundamental notions of moral philosophy by referring to their Aristotelian origin,⁵³ we need to clarify the origins of our philosophical notions not only in individual authors of the past but rather in their general view of reality, in the structures of the cosmo-theological thinking, and in the concrete examples of the traces of such structures in the original meaning of these terms. On the other hand, it is not enough to return merely to these ancient authors in order to acquire a proper understanding of our philosophical terms; we need to see the development of the cosmo-theological structures in the philosophical context, the change of the meaning of the fundamental terms of philosophy, the historical process of abstraction in which the cosmo-theological character becomes blurred and, after a certain time, hardly recognizable. This process of abstraction is crucial in *maintaining* the original character of our central notions, because we tend to believe that once a term is used in an abstract sense, its original meaning disappears.⁵⁴ The fact of the matter is different: the more abstract a notion becomes, the more obstinately it maintains its connection, already latent, to its original semantic environment. Philosophical reinterpretation is not only about

---

⁵¹ See Robert Spaemann, *Persons: The Difference between 'Someone' and 'Something'* (Oxford/New York: Oxford University Press, 2006).
⁵² John F. Crosby, *Personalist Papers* (Washington, DC: Catholic University of America Press, 2004), p. 26.
⁵³ MacIntyre, *After Virtue*.
⁵⁴ One of my favourite examples is Thomas's description of contemplation as containing three movements: 'These movements are of three kinds; for there is the "circular" movement, by which a thing moves uniformly round one point as center, another is the "straight" movement, by which a thing goes from one point to another; the third is "oblique," being imposed as it were of both the others.' Thomas Aquinas, *Summa theologiae*, II–II, 180, 6 (trans. Fathers of the English Dominican Providence). The expressions applied here are of astronomical origin and point back, via Pseudo-Dionysius, to Aristotle.

a distinct period of the past, but about the semantic development in which our notions slowly change their meaning and keep their origins in a concealed fashion.[55]

By determining the main lines of the process of a philosophical reinterpretation, we still do not know why a philosopher, especially a Christian philosopher, should embark on such an obviously complicated procedure. If philosophers avoid facing the fundamental character of the tradition of philosophy, they risk the danger of getting caught in a philosophical naïveté and lose the ability to understand their discipline, its vocabulary and methodologies with a sufficient level of clarity. It is a commonplace to say that if we use a certain expression in a philosophical sense, it is important to know its origins, its range of meaning and its historical development. In a general sense the same can be said about the entire spectrum of philosophical terms, or even more of philosophy itself as it evolved from its Greek origins.

Christian philosophers share this motive to understand their philosophical tradition. However, they have additional reasons. It is a common characteristic of Christianity that fundamental historical events compel its representatives to reinvestigate the meaning and role of their identity as Christian thinkers in the new context which emerged in the aftermath of such occurrences. One of the famous examples is Augustine's *City of God* which was composed as a response to the sack of Rome in 410.[56] The fall of Constantinople in 1453, the Lisbon earthquake in 1755 or the Napoleonic wars at the beginning of the nineteenth century offered new contexts in which Christianity, and especially Christian philosophy, had to redefine its meaning and character. It should be the subject of a specific study to explore the reactions to these and similar events in Christian thought. However, it can already be seen that historical events of exceptional

---

[55] As an example, consider the history of the Latin alphabet. We still use letters which originate in Phoenician signs which possessed a concrete meaning, such as 'bull' ('aleph', 'a') or house ('beth', 'b'), etc. Normally, we do not recognize that the system of signs we use to express our concepts in a written form points back to an ancient system of symbols. If we nevertheless realize this connection and study the emergence of modern Western alphabets, we understand more properly the system in which we express our notions and which is so different, for example, from the Chinese approach to conceive and express mental objects in a written form.

[56] Among other sources, see the letters of Jerome, for instance CXXVIII: 'The world sinks into ruin: yes! But shameful to say our sins still live and flourish. The renowned city, the capital of the Roman Empire, is swallowed up in one tremendous fire; and there is no part of the earth where Romans are not in exile. Churches once held sacred are now but heaps of dust and ashes; and yet we have our minds set on the desire of gain. We live as though we are going to die tomorrow; yet we build as though we are going to live always in this world. Our walls shine with gold, our ceilings also and the capitals of our pillars; yet Christ dies before our doors naked and hungry in the persons of His poor.' *The Letters of St Jerome*; available at: http://www.documentacatholicaomnia.eu/03d/0347-0420,_Hieronymus,_Epistolae_%5BSchaff%5D,_EN.pdf (last accessed 28 March 2013).

character did influence or even significantly determined the course of Christian reflection.[57]

The most important occurrence in this series of exceptional events, however, is what we refer to as 'Auschwitz'. In Auschwitz, the Chosen People of the Holy Scriptures were sentenced to annihilation; and this event has a peculiar importance in a tradition the centre of which has been precisely the relationship between 'Jews' and 'Christians'. As I explained it in detail in another work, Auschwitz is the most important motivation for a Christian philosopher to re-examine their philosophical tradition, its origins and developments, and to attempt to transcend the limits of this tradition. Auschwitz is a 'watershed' not only in the context of some centuries but with respect to the entire Christian tradition. For Auschwitz questioned not merely the millennia of Christian thought, but the very foundations of Christianity as well, in which the role of the Chosen People had been considered crucial. Auschwitz invalidates many of our earlier convictions and calls for a thoroughgoing reassessment. One result is what I term here the reinterpretation of philosophy, especially Christian philosophy, not with the purpose of 'destruction' but with the purpose of a sufficient understanding of our tradition and opening a perspective in which this tradition can be explored, understood and properly assessed.[58]

The Christian philosopher is not without assistance in this task. First, we have the tradition of overall reassessments throughout the centuries. Second, in the tradition of Christian philosophy, the Tychonic methodology has an important place. This methodology consists precisely in the attentive perception of 'the signs of the times', that is, the perception of historicity as the most important layer in Christian thought. Thomas Aquinas reacted to the popularity of Aristotle's writings with his universal synthesis. Ficino, Cusanus and other Renaissance philosophers responded to the fundamental changes in their time with broadening their perspectives in a radical way. Malebranche and other rationalistic philosophers used Cartesianism ingeniously and contributed to the modernization of Christian thought. We can witness similar changes in the nineteenth and twentieth centuries with altering accents; the neo-realism and scientific awareness of the nineteenth century cannot be forgotten, just as the existential sensitivity of such thinkers as Gilson or von Balthasar in the

---

[57] Among the authors that are especially important in this respect we find Nicholas of Cusa, Leibniz, Goethe, Burke and Schiller.
[58] See Mezei, *Reason and Revelation*, p. 129; also Johann Baptist Metz, *Memoria passionis. Ein provozierendes Gedächtnis in pluralistischer Gesellschaft* (Freiburg-Basel-Wien: Herder, 2006). Moreover, Steven T. Katz, Shlomo Biderman, Gershon Greenberg (eds): *Wrestling with God. Jewish Theological Responses during and after the Holocaust* (Oxford: Oxford University Press, 2007).

twentieth century. And it is not merely the generally Tychonic characteristic which counts here: in the particular cases we observe, and can explore, sophisticated and well-informed attempts to understand tradition in the light of the new historical developments.

Fides et ratio

One of the most important documents of the application of a Tychonic methodology in philosophy is the encyclical letter *Fides et ratio* by John Paul II. The letter should be seen in a historical context. As the second papal document issued on the problem of philosophy, *Fides et ratio* continues the tradition laid down by the 1879 encyclical letter *Aeterni patris* issued by Pope Leo XIII. At the same time, *Fides et ratio* characteristically differs from some of the main features of its antecedent. *Aeterni patris* aspires to reach the *restoration* of Christian philosophy by turning the readers' attention to the work of Thomas Aquinas. The main merit of the work of Thomas, according to *Aeterni patris*, is not its succinct character, its clarity, its systematic nature, but first of all its openness to the 'physical sciences' which cannot 'suffer detriment, but find very great assistance in the restoration of the ancient philosophy'.[59] *Fides et ratio* still considers the work of Thomas Aquinas crucial, yet it emphasizes a general openness to various philosophical approaches and systems, even Catholic philosophies of the nineteenth century which did not find approval in the time of *Aeterni patris*.[60] *Fides et ratio* offers an encompassing analysis of the philosophical tradition and mentions its positive and negative developments; most importantly, it *encourages* philosophers to return to the original task of philosophy to rise to the horizon of metaphysics and ask 'radical questions about the meaning and ultimate foundation of human, personal and social existence' (§5). This encyclical combines the due respect for the richness of traditional philosophy with a call for 'boldness' and 'courage' to develop new approaches. The text often distinguishes negative and positive philosophy and urges its readers to refute atheism, nihilism, scientism, historicism; it advises us not to remain content 'with partial and provisional truths' (§5), 'with ancient myths' (§36) or 'with more modest tasks such as the simple interpretation of facts or an enquiry into restricted fields of human knowing or its structures' (§55). In other words, the

---

[59] Leo XIII, *Aeterni Patris*, §29.
[60] John Paul II, *Fides et ratio*, §59.

general direction of the encyclical clearly points to a new understanding of philosophy which critically examines its past, continues its valuable insights and understandings, and becomes open to radically new approaches to philosophy. While *Aeterni patris* was about the *restitution* of philosophy on the basis of a tradition, *Fides et ratio* proposes a *renewal* with respect to the future: the renewal of Christian philosophy.

Fundamental Structures of a Renewed Christian Philosophy

I want to emphasize the critical role of philosophy with respect to itself. It is especially Christian philosophy that, as demonstrated splendidly by *Fides et ratio*, is capable of realizing historical self-reflection, clarification and openness to new developments. What I term in this text the reinterpretation or even the renewal of philosophy is indeed a corollary of the main conclusions of *Fides et ratio*.

To say that the task of reinterpreting philosophy would lead to a kind of neglect or destruction of the traditional structures of philosophy is contradictory in more than one sense. It is contradictory because any destructive understanding of demythologization must be based on philosophical insights dependent on earlier philosophical developments and thus indistinctly refuting these developments equals nullifying the philosophical basis on which our reinterpretation would take place. Moreover, the above understanding is contradictory because it does not give us the principles on the basis of which we are justified to reject the philosophical tradition as a whole. In contrast, the task of reinterpreting philosophy is to be understood as a result of the innermost developments of the philosophical tradition and thus it goes hand in hand with a critical yet deep appreciation of these traditions. This task, moreover, is not for its own sake: it serves the understanding of the historical change in which we find ourselves in the context of philosophy, especially Christian philosophy, and in which it becomes possible to build a more appropriate understanding of the human situation, its history and future perspectives. Reinterpreting philosophy is, in this sense, a positive and edifying endeavour which is called to build, not to destroy. The mapping out of the semantic contents and philosophical consequences of the cosmo-theological view is anything other than just a one-sided criticism. Cosmo-theological criticism is actually a radical approach to the tradition of philosophy; it contains a series of radical questions we need to ask with respect to this tradition, its original semantic framework.

I believe that the field is sufficiently prepared for offering a summary of the main features of a renewed Christian philosophy. I wish to consider this philosophy, the Christian philosophy for the twenty-first century, in three clusters: methodology, content and unity.

Methodology. The main method Christian philosophy needs to apply is historical criticism. Most importantly, a critical investigation is needed of the cosmo-theological framework of ancient philosophical concepts, notions and overall views of the universe, human beings and societies. Concretely put, we have to analyse the relevant texts and other monuments, such as for example the *mimema*, the ancient planetarium which is mentioned by many authors, including Plato. The investigation of the significance of findings such as the so-called 'Antikythera Mechanism' is highly relevant here.[61] This historical criticism aims at projecting the outlines and contents of the cosmo-theological view with respect to fundamental philosophical notions. For this endeavour we need to analyse positive evidence, such as astronomical writings, and indirect evidence, such as the role of astronomy in scientific texts. Moreover, the nature of the cosmo-theological view makes it necessary to determine the symbolical and metaphorical presence of cosmo-theology in philosophical texts. For instance, as Eva Brann demonstrated, the philosopher in Plato's understanding shows a close resemblance to the mythical hero Hercules, a hero possessing a cosmo-theological significance not only in his divinization but in the epic deeds he carried out. These deeds, just like the events in the myth of the Golden Fleece, have clear astronomical relevance.[62]

Christian philosophy inherited most of the philosophical vocabulary and with it its cosmo-theological character. It is the task of historical criticism to determine the close connection between pre-Christian and Christian cosmo-theological views. In Christianity, the presence of cosmo-theology is evident in many writings, symbols and cultural phenomena, and the general effect of cosmo-theology can be verified far beyond the beginning of modernity. Christian philosophy uncritically received and applied many such views, and in order to have a clear picture of the effects of this reception we cannot disregard some views of the ancient authors which are embarrassing in the light of modern science and concentrate on an abstract interpretation of these

---

[61] See Gábor Betegh, 'Le problème des représentations visuelles dans la cosmologie présocratique: pour une histoire de la modélisation', in A. Laks and C. Louget (eds), *Qu'est-ce que la Philosophie Présocratique?/What is Presocratic Philosophy?* (Lille: Presses Universitaires du Septentrion, 2002), pp. 381–415.

[62] Eva T. H. Brann, *The Music of the Republic: Essays on Socrates' Conversations and Plato's Writings* (Philadelphia: Paul Dry Books, 2004).

authors. We need to see such views as constitutive in the works of these authors if we really want to understand them, their thinking and the relevance of this thinking in our time. Thereby we become able to grasp the marvelous development Christian philosophy had gone through before the twentieth century: beginning with a quite externalist understanding to the proper conception of crucial philosophical terms and contents, even theological contents.[63]

As mentioned, the most important motive behind the task of historical criticism is history's sudden changes, catastrophes and breakthroughs. It is especially the role of a historical catastrophe which merits particular attention, because it is verified that such catastrophes may lead to fundamental changes in our perception of reality. I repeat here that the catastrophe of 'Auschwitz' offers indeed a new beginning for our reflections. It is by the trauma of Auschwitz that we perceive the need for an overall reassessment of our heritage, its contents and its historical development. Without going into detail in this respect let me point out that Auschwitz in this sense may be seen as a direct consequence of an uncritically received and applied cosmo-theology in which a proper perception of human personhood was not possible. We still live in the aftermath of this occurrence and have not yet assessed appropriately its general significance and concrete consequences for the understanding of our traditions, present situation and future.

The most important presupposition behind historical criticism is that history is a structured whole in which 'change' has a number of well-defined meanings in the context of an overall and meaningful modification of history. The meaningfulness of history cannot be denied because otherwise the possibility of historical criticism is denied as well. And if the meaningfulness of history is explored, then the importance of historical criticism can be defined as an opening of a meaningful perspective in the future of Christian philosophy. Whether we call this thinking 'philosophy', or apply a different name, is not relevant here. We need to see, however, that philosophy as an encompassing, critical and future-oriented thinking, a *sui generis* activity of our human personhood, that remains central to the understanding of history. In this sense, 'Christian philosophy' is openness to the future, to a deeper understanding of our past and to a perspective in which meaningfulness is the most important and overall framework of our personal activity. The traditional distinction between reason and faith remains valid, because human knowledge cannot but

---

[63] Needless to say that, for instance, the so important changes of the notion of personhood are relevant to important theological tenets as well.

presuppose meaningfulness as an absolute given.⁶⁴ *Denying meaningfulness is confirming it.* The human mind cannot produce meaningfulness in its general sense and cannot be detached from it in the same sense; human knowledge is dependent on the fact of a meaningful history of the universe and mankind.

Content. As to the contents of a reinterpreted Christian philosophy, I already mentioned the importance of a revision of fundamental terms. Among innumerable examples let me mention again the importance of the notion of a person, because, in my understanding, personhood should be the centre of a new Christian philosophy. The proper understanding of personhood must be contrasted with earlier views in which personhood was not yet grasped properly in its unity, irreplaceability and non-reducibility. The fundamental problem is not fully conceived if we think that the non-genuine understanding of personhood consists in seeing the person as a substance in the world in line with the material substances of our external experience. Rather, the fundamental problem is that reality itself is seen commonsensically on the level of our external experience of material substances and so we easily fail to perceive the genuine nature of reality which is closer to personal existence than to the rigid material beings given in our external sensation. Personhood is a basic mode of existence and human beings are genuine embodiments of this basic mode. At the same time, personal existence is always existence in a community, and a community has an ultimate source in which the possibility of the community of human existence is organically rooted.⁶⁵

It belongs to the perspective of the reinterpretation of Christian philosophy that a new terminology is to be created. In the past, there have been several similar attempts, beginning with the first Alexandrian theologians through the creative genius of Pseudo-Dionysius in the sixth century or the scholastic innovations in the Middle Ages up to the revolutionary changes in Catholic rationalism and romanticism. In the recent past, the works of Erich Przywara, Hans Urs von Balthasar or Karl Rahner are excellent examples of a philosophical and theological renovation in which the vocabulary changes as well. In philosophy, we see many examples of such a partial or even extensive change of the vocabulary in the works of Kant, Hegel, Nietzsche, Husserl, Heidegger,

---

⁶⁴ See Balázs Mezei, 'Faith and Reason', in Lewis Ayres (ed.), *The Oxford Handbook of Catholic Theology* (Oxford: Oxford University Press, forthcoming).

⁶⁵ This understanding of reality can be interpreted as a philosophical corollary to the Copenhagen interpretation of quantum theory; in the present perspective, it is not centrally important if one follows Heisenberg or Bohr in explaining the contents of this interpretation. On a more general level, see Lanza's paper on biocentrism at: http://www.robertlanzabiocentrism.com/biocentrism-how-life-creates-the-universe/ (last accessed 2 April 2013).

Wittgenstein or Levinas. The reason for such a change is always the perceived inability of earlier terms to express new insights properly. In my perspective of a demythologized Christian philosophy, the need for a significant vocabulary change is perhaps even more urgent than in many other cases. 'After Auschwitz' we do not only need to reassess our traditional ideas and expressions, but we have to attempt to create new expressions for our new understandings as well.

Unity. A reinterpreted Christian philosophy has to reassess the massive tradition of cosmo-theology in general philosophy as well as in Christian thought. Such a Christian thought recognizes history as its overall meaningful framework. History, however, is general and relative openness to the future. Christian philosophy needs to embody a general and relative openness to the future too. It needs to have a general openness because its own history teaches it to attempt fundamental changes at certain points, and it needs to have a relative openness because Christian philosophy remains bound to the tradition precisely as the critical reassessment of this tradition. In this relative openness, we can focus on non-fundamental changes, such as those of Platonism in Augustine's work, or fundamental changes, such as the consequences of Auschwitz. The relative openness of Christian philosophy is rooted in its general openness which can be described as its 'Marian character'. As *Fides et ratio* points out, *philosophari in Maria* implies a fundamental faithfulness to the ultimate meaning of history. *Philosophari in Maria*, on the other hand, means a kind of thinking which points to the future with the clear recognition of the necessity of a general renewal of Christian thought.[66]

Most centrally, however, the general renewal of Christian philosophy may explore the distinction I mentioned at the beginning of my essay between *philosophia* and *philosophos*. Christian philosophy needs to be that of the *philosophos*, the 'lover of the wise one', and build a genuinely personal relationship between the intellectual work and its substantive basis, reality. In the perspective of historical criticism, we cannot consider reality merely in terms of a cosmo-theologically determined objectivity, such as the one we still find in many vistas of our sciences and philosophical reflections today. While earlier notions of objectivity and subjectivity were based on the perception of a closed universe,

---

[66] In Prudence Allen's article, we have a systematic approach to the notion of '*philosophari in Maria*': http://www.secondspring.co.uk/articles/Mary%20and%20Philos%20by%20Prudence%20Allen.pdf (last accessed 29 March 2013). Sister Prudence focuses on the main phases of Mary's life and explains their significance one after the other from the philosophical point of view, always with reference to important theologians and philosophers. There is only one scene that is missing in her list: The Birth of the Savior. In my approach, 'philosophari in Maria' has the central event of preparing and accomplishing the birth of the fully other.

the notion of an open universe has at its core human personhood as *openness*: openness to reality in its entirety and openness to history in its past, present and future dimensions. On the other hand, personal openness entails the openness of the universe, that is, the openness of reality as such. The changing structures of our universe, as we can now already see, correspond to the historical change in which human persons find themselves, and these forms of change are rooted in the fundamental openness of human personhood as the main feature of reality. Thus, in our perception, reality has a personal character in the sense of the personhood we possess today, and thus a personal relationship between the Christian philosopher and its subject matter, reality, needs to be established. The Christian *philosophos* is called to open himself to 'the wise one', the meaningful framework of our existence, which cannot be derived from our efforts.[67]

---

[67] An interesting theory of personal openness in an infinite future can be found in the works of the famous mathematician-priest of the nineteenth century, Bernard Bolzano. See especially his *Athanasia; oder, Gründe für die Unsterblichkeit der Seele* (Frankfurt/Main: Minerva, 1970). Bolzano held that the life of human persons on the Earth is only the beginning of a universal evolution at the end of which we find ourselves in the community of the blessed; human personhood on the Earth is openness to this development. In contemporary science, the 'Goldilocks' or 'anthropic' principle asserts that the universe is tailor-made for us, human beings. Following these investigations, we may overcome the cosmo-theological pattern *not* on the basis of one of its consequences (such as the aspect of rigid objectivity or an objectively conceived subjectivity), but with respect to a new whole. Call this new whole intelligent design or biocentrism, but it still needs to be purged of the remnants of cosmo-theology. It is the notion of *personhood* that helps us to do this job.

Bibliography

Adorno, Theodor W., *The Jargon of Authenticity* (trans. Knut Tarnowski and Frederick Will; Evanston, IL: Northwestern University Press, 1973).
Aquinas, Thomas, *Potency and Act* (trans. Walter Redmond; Washington, DC: ICS Publishing, 2009).
Aristotle, *The Complete Works of Aristotle* (ed. Jonathan Barnes; Princeton, NJ: Princeton University Press, 1991).
Aristotle, *Nicomachean Ethics* (trans. David Ross, Oxford: Oxford University Press, 2009).
Azcuy, Virginia Raquel, *La figura de Thérèse de Lisieux: Ensayo de fenomenología teológica según Hans Urs von Balthasar* (Buenos Aires: Teología, 1997).
Assmann, Jan, *Moses the Egyptian* (Cambridge, MA: Harvard University Press, 1997).
Balthasar, Hans Urs von, *Apokalypse der deutschen Seele: Studien zu einer Lehre von letzten Haltungen*, vol. 3, *Zur Vergöttlichung des Tode* (Einsiedeln: Johannes Verlag Einsiedeln, 1993).
Balthasar, Hans Urs von, *Bernanos: An Ecclesial Existence* (trans. Erasmo Leiva-Merikakis; San Francisco: Ignatius, 1996).
Balthasar, Hans Urs von, *Le chrétien Bernanos* (trans. M. de Gandillac; Paris: Éditions du Seuil, 1956).
Balthasar, Hans Urs von, *Epilogue* (trans. Edward T. Oakes, S.J.; San Francisco: Ignatius Press, 2004).
Balthasar, Hans Urs von, 'Erich Przywara', in Hans Jürgen Schultz (ed.), *Tendenzen zur Theologie im 20. Jahrhundert. Eine Geschichte in Porträts* (Stuttgart: Olten, 1966), 357.
Balthasar, Hans Urs von, *Gelebte Kirche. Bernanos* (Cologne/Olten: Hegner, 1954).
Balthasar, Hans Urs von, *Glaubhaft ist nur Liebe* (Einsiedeln: Johannes Verlag Einsiedeln, 2000).
Balthasar, Hans Urs von, *The Glory of the Lord: A Theological Aesthetics*, vol. 1, *Seeing the Form* (trans. Erasmo Leiva-Merikakis; ed. Joseph Fessio and John Riches; San Francisco: Ignatius Press, 1982).
Balthasar, Hans Urs von, *The Glory of the Lord: A Theological Aesthetics*, vol. 4, *The Realm of Metaphysics in Antiquity* (trans. Brian McNeil C. R. V., Andrew Louth, John Saward, Rowan Williams and Oliver Davies; ed. John Riches; San Francisco: Ignatius Press, 1989).
Balthasar, Hans Urs von, *The Glory of the Lord: A Theological Aesthetics*, vol. 5, *The Realm of Metaphysics in the Modern Age* (trans. Oliver Davies, Andrew Louth, Brian

McNeil C. R. V., John Sayward, Rowan Williams; ed. Brian McNeil C. R. V., John Riches; San Francisco: Ignatius Press, 1991).

Balthasar, Hans Urs von, *The Glory of the Lord: A Theological Aesthetics*, vol. 6, *Theology: The Old Covenant* (trans. Brian McNeil C. R. V. and Erasmo-Leiva-Merikakis; San Francisco: Ignatius Press, 1991).

Balthasar, Hans Urs von, *The Glory of the Lord: A Theological Aesthetics*, vol. 7, *Theology: The New Covenant* (trans. Brian McNeil C. R. V.; ed. John Riches; San Francisco: Ignatius Press, 1989).

Balthasar, Hans Urs von, *In Gottes Einsatz leben* (Einsiedeln: Johannes Verlag Einsiedeln, 1971).

Balthasar, Hans Urs von, 'Introduzione', in Luigi Giussani, *Alla ricerca del volto umano* (Milan: Jaca, 1984), 5–7.

Balthasar, Hans Urs von, *Karl Barth: Darstellung und Deutung seiner Theologie* (Cologne/Olten: Hegner, 1951).

Balthasar, Hans Urs von, 'Die Metaphysik Erich Przywaras', *Schweizerische Rundschau* 33 (1933): 488–9.

Balthasar, Hans Urs von, *My Work: In Retrospect* (trans. Brian McNeill, Kenneth Batinovich, John Saward, and Kelly Hamilton; San Francisco: Ignatius, 1993).

Balthasar, Hans Urs von, 'Le mystérion d'Origène', *Recherches de science religieuse* 26 (1936): 513–62

Balthasar, Hans Urs von, 'Le mystérion d'Origène', *Recherches de science religieuse* 27 (1937): 38–64.

Balthasar, Hans Urs von, *Origen, Geist und Feuer: Ein Aufbau aus seinen Werken* (Salzburg: Otto Muller, 1938; rev. and exp. edn, 1953).

Balthasar, Hans Urs von, *Origen: Spirit and Fire* (trans. Robert J. Daly; Washington, DC: The Catholic University of America Press, 1984).

Balthasar, Hans Urs von, *Our Task: A Report and a Plan* (trans. John Saward; San Francisco: Ignatius Press, 1994).

Balthasar, Hans Urs von, *Parole et mystère chez Origène* (Paris: Cerf, 1957).

Balthasar, Hans Urs von, *Reinhold Schneider: Sein Weg und Sein Werk* (Cologne/Olten: Hegner, 1953).

Balthasar, Hans Urs von, *Romano Guardini: Reform from the Source* (trans. Albert Wimmer and D. C. Schindler; San Francisco: Ignatius Press, 2010).

Balthasar, Hans Urs von, *Theo-Drama*, vol. 2, *Dramatis Personae: Man in God* (trans. Graham Harrison; San Francisco: Ignatius Press, 1990).

Balthasar, Hans Urs von, *Theo-Logic: Theological Logical Theory*, vol. 1, *Truth of the World* (trans. Adrian J. Walker; San Francisco: Ignatius Press, 2000).

Balthasar, Hans Urs von, *Theologik*, vol. 2, *Wahrheit Gottes* (Einsiedeln: Johannes Verlag Einsiedeln, 1985).

Balthasar, Hans Urs von, 'Theology and Sanctity', in idem, *Explorations in Theology*, vol. 1, *The Word made Flesh* (trans. A. V. Littledale with Alexander Dru; San Francisco: Ignatius Press, 1989), 181–209.

Balthasar, Hans Urs von, *The Theology of Karl Barth: Exposition and Interpretation* (trans. Edward T. Oakes; San Francisco: Ignatius Press, 1992).

Balthasar, Hans Urs von, *Tragedy under Grace: Reinhold Schneider on the Experience of the West* (trans. Brian McNeil; San Francisco: Ignatius Press, 1997).

Balthasar, Hans Urs von, *Two Sisters in the Spirit: Thérèse of Lisieux & Elizabeth of the Trinity* (trans. Donald Nichols, Anne Englund Nash, and Dennis Martin; San Francisco: Ignatius Press, 1992).

Barth, Karl, *Church Dogmatics* I/2 (trans. G. T. Thompson and Harold Knight; ed. G. W. Bromiley and T. F. Torrance; Edinburgh: T&T Clark, 1956).

Barth, Karl, *Church Dogmatics* III/2 (trans. Harold Knight; G. W. Bromiley et al; Edinburgh: T&T Clark, 1960).

Barth, Karl, *Church Dogmatics* III/3 (trans. G. W. Bromiley and R. J. Ehrlich; Edinburgh: T&T Clark, 1960).

Barth, Karl, *God Here and Now* (trans. Paul van Buren; New York: Routledge, 2003).

Barth, Karl, *The Humanity of God* (trans. Thomas Wieser and John Newton Thomas; Richmond, Va.: John Knox Press, 1960).

Barth, Karl, *Protestant Theology in the Nineteenth Century: Its Background and History* (trans. Brian Cozens and John Bowden; London: SCM Press, 1972).

Barth, Karl, 'Unsettled Questions for Theology Today', in idem, *Theology and Church: Shorter Writings 1920–1928* (trans. Louise Pettibone Smith; New York: Harper and Row, 1962), 55–73.

Barth, Karl and Eduard Thurneysen, *Karl Barth–Eduard Thurneysen Briefwechsel*, vol. 2, *1921–1930* (Zürich: Theologischer Verlag Zürich, 1974).

Benedict XVI, *"In the Beginning," A Catholic Understanding of the Story of Creation and the Fall* (trans. Boniface Ramsey; Grand Rapids, MI: Eerdmans, 1995).

Bernanos, George, *Essais et écrits de combat* (Paris: Éditions Gallimard, 1995).

Betegh, Gábor, 'Le problème des représentations visuelles dans la cosmologie présocratique: pour une histoire de la modélisation', in A. Laks and C. Louget (eds), *Qu'est-ce que la Philosophie Présocratique?/What is Presocratic Philosophy?* (Lille: Presses Universitaires du Septentrion, 2002), 381–415.

Betz, John R., 'After Barth: A New Introduction to Erich Przywara's Analogia Entis', in Thomas Joseph White (ed.), *The Analogy of Being: Invention of the Antichrist or the Wisdom of God* (Grand Rapids, Mich.: Eerdmans, 2010), 35–87.

Bieler, Martin, '*Analogia Entis* as an Expression of Love according to Ferdinand Ulrich', in Thomas Joseph White (ed.), *The Analogy of Being: Invention of the Antichrist or the Wisdom of God?* (Grand Rapids, MI: Eerdmans, 2010), 314–40.

Bloom, Harold, *The Anxiety of Influence: A Theory of Poetry* (2nd edn; New York: Oxford University Press, 1997).

Bolzano, Bernard, *Athanasia; oder, Gründe für die Unsterblichkeit der Seele* (Frankfurt/Main: Minerva, 1970).

Bonaventure, *Collationes in Hexaemeron*, in St. Bonaventure, *Opera Omnia* (Florence: Ad Aquas Claras [Quaracchi], 1882–1902), 327–454.

Bonsor, J. A., *Rahner, Heidegger, and Truth: Karl Rahner's Notion of Christian Truth, the Influence of Heidegger* (Lanham, MD: University Press of America, 1987).

Borras, Michelle K., 'The Paschal Mystery as Nuptial Mystery in the Theology of Origen of Alexandria', Ph.D. dissertation, John Paul II Institute for Studies of Marriage and Family at The Catholic University of America, 2010.

Brann, Eva T. H., *The Music of the Republic: Essays on Socrates' Conversations and Plato's Writings* (Philadelphia: Paul Dry Books, 2004).

Brassier, Ray, *Nihil Unbound: Enlightenment and Extinction* (London: Palgrave Macmillan, 2007).

Bremond, Henri, *A Literary History of Religious Thought in France*, vol. 3, *The Triumph of Mysticism* (London: SPCK, 1936).

Buber, Martin, 'The Beginnings of Hasidism', in idem, *Mamre: Essays in Religion* (trans. Greta Hort; Westport, CT: Greenwood Press, 1946), 149–82.

van Buren, John, *The Young Heidegger: Rumor of the Hidden King* (Bloomington: Indiana University Press, 1994).

Burrell, David, *Analogy and Philosophical Language* (New Haven: Yale University Press, 1973).

Busch, Eberhard, *Karl Barth: His Life from Letters and Autobiographical Texts* (trans. John Bowden; Philadelphia: Fortress, 1976).

Cadoux, Richard, *Bérulle et la question de l'homme* (Paris: Cerf, 2005).

Calcagno, Antonio, '*Die Fülle oder das Nichts?* Edith Stein and Martin Heidegger on the Question of Being', *American Catholic Philosophical Quarterly* 74:2 (2000): 269–85.

Cantú, Oscar, 'Identity Through Presence and Absence: Robert Sokolowski's Theology of Disclosure and his Contribution to Eucharistic Theology', Ph.D. dissertation, Pontificia Università Gregoriana, 2011.

Caputo, John D., *The Mystical Element of Heidegger's Thought* (New York: Fordham University Press, 1986).

Casarella, Peter, 'Questioning the Primacy of Method: On Sokolowski's Eucharistic Presence', *Communio: International Catholic Review* 22 (Winter 1995): 668–701.

Cicero, *On the Commonwealth. On the Laws* (ed. James E. G. Zetzel; Cambridge: Cambridge University Press, 1999).

Claudianus, Claudius, *Works* (London: W. Heinemann, 1922).

Crosby, John F., *Personalist Papers* (Washington, DC: Catholic University of America Press, 2004).

Crowell, Steven and Jeff Malpas (eds), *Transcendental Heidegger* (Stanford: Stanford University Press, 2007).

Cumont, Franz, *Astrology and Religion among the Greeks and Romans* (New York: Dover Publications, 1960).

D'Acunto, Giuseppe, 'Concretezza e opposizione in Guardini', *Información Filosófica* 8 (2011): 107–20.

Daniélou, Jean, *Origen* (trans. Walter Mitchell; New York: Sheed & Ward, 1955).

Daniélou, Jean, *Origène* (Paris: Table ronde, 1948).

Davidson, Ivor J., 'Reappropriating Patristic Christology: One Doctrine, Two Styles', *Irish Theological Quarterly* 67:3 (2002): 225–39.

Davidson, Ivor J., 'Theologizing the Human Jesus: An Ancient (and Modern) Approach to Christology Reassessed', *International Journal of Systematic Theology* 3:2 (2001): 129–53.

Derrida, Jacques, *Dissemination* (trans. Barbara Johnson; Chicago: University of Chicago Press, 1981).

Derrida, Jacques, 'Force of Law: The "Mystical Foundation of Authority"', in Gil Anidjar (ed.), *Acts of Religion* (New York: Routledge, 2002), 230–98.

Derrida, Jacques, *The Gift of Death* (trans. David Wills; Chicago: University of Chicago Press, 1995).

Derrida, Jacques, *Of the Spirit: Heidegger and the Question* (trans. Geoffrey Bennington and Rachel Bowlby; Chicago: University of Chicago Press, 1991).

Derrida, Jacques, *Sauf le nom* (Paris: Galilée, 1993).

Desmond, William, 'Consecrated Thought: Between the Priest and the Philosopher', *The Journal of Philosophy and Scripture* 2:2 (Spring 2002): 1–10.

Dupuis, Charles-François, *Origin de tous les cultes, ou la religion universelle* (Paris, 1795).

Dupuy, Michel, *Bérulle: une spiritualité de l'adoration* (Paris: Desclée de Brouwer, 1964).

Dupuy, Michel, *Le Christ de Bérulle* (Paris: Desclée de Brouwer, 2001).

Dupuy, Michel (ed.), *Pierre de Bérulle: Oeuvres complètes* (Paris: Éditions du Cerf, 1995–).

Ederer, Martin, 'Propaganda Wars: *Stimmen der Zeit* and the Nazis, 1933–1935', *Catholic Historical Review* 90 (July 2004): 456–72.

Escrivá de Balaguer, St. Josemaría, *Christ is Passing By: Homilies* (Dublin: Veritas 1974).

Fabro, Cornelio, *La nozione metafisica di partecipazione secondo San Tommasio d'Aquino (Opere Complete 3)* (Rome: Editrice verbo incarno, 2005).

Falque, Emmanuel, 'The Phenomenological Act of Perscrutatio in the Proemium of St. Bonaventure's Commentary on the Sentences', *Medieval Philosophy and Theology* 10 (2001): 1–22.

Farias, Victor, *Heidegger and Nazism* (trans. Paul Burrell, Dominic Di Benardi and Gabriel R. Ricci; ed. Joseph Margolis and Tom Rockmore; Philadephia: Temple University Press, 1989).

Feuerbach, Ludwig, *The Essence of Christianity* (trans. Marian Evans; London: Trübner 1881).

Firestone, Chris and Nathan Jacobs, *The Persistence of the Sacred in Modern Thought* (Notre Dame: University of Notre Dame Press, 2012).

Fritz, Peter Joseph, 'Karl Rahner, Friedrich Schelling, and Original Unity', in *Theological Studies* 75:2 (2014): 284–307.

Fritz, Peter Joseph, *Karl Rahner's Theological Aesthetics* (Washington, DC: Catholic University of America Press, 2014).

Frossard, André, *"Be not afraid"*: *Pope John Paul II Speaks Out on his Life, his Beliefs, and his Inspiring Vision for Humanity* (trans. J. R. Foster; New York: St Martin's Press, 1984).

García-Rivera, Alejandro, *St. Martin de Porres: The "Little Stories" and the Semiotics of Culture* (Maryknoll, NY: Orbis, 1995).

Gerl-Falkowitz, H. B., *Romano Guardini* (Kevalaer: Topos, 2010).

Gilson, Étienne, *The Spirit of Mediaeval Philosophy* (trans. A. H. C. Downes; Notre Dame: University of Notre Dame Press, 1991).

Godzieba, Anthony J., *Bernhard Welte's Fundamental Theological Approach to Christology* (New York: Peter Lang, 1994).

Gordon, Richard E., *Heidegger, Cassirer, Davos* (Cambridge, MA: Harvard University Press, 2010).

Grillmeier, Aloys and Heinrich Bacht (eds.) *Das Konzil von Chalkedon. Geschichte und Gegenwart*, vol. 3, *Chalkedon heute* (Würzburg: Echter-Verlag, 1954).

Grossmann, A. and C. Landmesser (eds), *Rudoph Bultmann/Martin Heidegger Briefwechsel, 1925–1975* (Tübingen: Mohr Siebeck, 2009).

Goodstein, Elizabeth S., 'Style as Substance: Georg Simmel's Phenomenology of Culture', *Cultural Critique* 52 (Fall 2002): 209–34.

Guardini, Romano, *Berichte über mein Leben* (ed. Franz Henrich; Düsseldorf: Patmos 1984).

Guardini, Romano, *The Church and the Catholic* (trans. Ada Lane; New York: Sheed & Ward, 1935).

Guardini, Romano, *The Church of the Lord* (Chicago: Henry Regnery, 1966).

Guardini, Romano, *Conscience* (trans. Ada Lane; London: Sheed & Ward, 1932).

Guardini, Romano, 'Das Erwachen der Kirche in der Seele', *Hochland* 19 (1922): 257–67.

Guardini, Romano, *The Essential Guardini* (ed. Heinz R. Kuehn; Chicago: LTP, 1997).

Guardini, Romano, *Freedom, Grace and Destiny* (trans. John Murray; New York: Pantheon Books, 1961).

Guardini, Romano, *Der Gegensatz* (Mainz: Matthias Grünewald, 1925).

Guardini, Romano, *Meditations before Mass* (trans. Elinor Castendyk Briefs; London: Longmans, 1955).

Guardini, Romano, *Preparing Yourself for Mass* (Manchester, NH: Sophia Institute Press, 1997).

Guardini, Romano, *The Rosary of Our Lady* in *The Living God – The Rosary of Our Lady* (trans. H. Von Schwecking; London: Longmans Green: 1957).

Guardini, Romano, *Sacred Signs* (trans. Grace Branham; Dublin: Veritas, 1979).

Guardini, Romano, *The Spirit of the Liturgy* (trans. Ada Lane; London: Sheed & Ward 1937).

Guardini, Romano, *The Spirit of the Liturgy* (trans. John Saward; San Francisco: Ignatius Press 2000).

Guardini, Romano, *The World and the Person* (trans. Stella Lange; Chicago: Henry Regnery, 1965).

Hadot, Pierre, *Qu'est-ce que la philosophie antique?* (Paris: Gallimard, 1996).
Hammond, Wayne G., and Christina Scull (eds), *The J. R. R. Tolkien Companion and Guide* (Boston: Houghton Mifflin, 2006).
Harbert, Bruce, 'The Quest for Melchisedech', *New Blackfriars* 68 (1987): 529-39.
Hawking, Stephen with Leonard Mlodinov, *The Grand Design* (New York: Bantam Books, 2010).
Healy, Emma T., 'The Theory of the Reductio', in St. Bonaventure, *De Reductione Artium ad Theologiam* (St. Bonaventure, NY: The Franciscan Institute, 1955), 119-21.
Hegel, G. W. F., *On Art, Religion, and the History of Philosophy: Introductory Lectures* (ed. J. Glenn Gray; Indianapolis: Hackett, 1997).
Heidegger, Martin, *Being and Time* (trans. John McQuarrie and Edward Robinson; Oxford: Blackwell, 1967).
Heidegger, Martin, *Contributions to Philosophy (from Enowning)* (trans. Parvis Emad and Kenneth Maly; Bloomington: Indiana University Press, 1999).
Heidegger, Martin, *Contributions to Philosophy (of the Event)* (trans. Richard Rojcewicz and Daniela Vallega-Neu; Indianapolis: Indiana University Press, 2012).
Heidegger, Martin, 'The End of Philosophy and the Task of Thinking', in idem, *Basic Writings* (ed. David Farrell Krell; San Francisco: Harper, 1993), 431-49.
Heidegger, Martin, *The Essence of Reasons* (trans. Tom Malick; Evanston: Northwestern University Press, 1969).
Heidegger, Martin, *Gesamtausgabe 15: I. Abt., Veröffentlichte Schriften 1910-1976 Seminare* (ed. Friedrich-Wilhelm von Herrmann; Ingrid Schüßler; Frankfurt: Klostermann, 1986).
Heidegger, Martin, *An Introduction to Metaphysics* (trans. Ralph Mannheim; New Haven: Yale University Press, 1959).
Heidegger, Martin, 'Letter on Humanism', in idem, *Basic Writings* (ed. David Krell; San Francisco: HarperSanFrancisco, 1977), 213-65.
Heidegger, Martin, *The Metaphysical Foundations of Logic* (trans. Michael Heim; Bloomington: Indiana University Press, 1984).
Heidegger, Martin, *On Time and Being* (trans. Joan Stambaugh; New York: Harper and Row, 1972).
Heidegger, Martin, 'The Onto-theo-logical Nature of Metaphysics' ('Die onto-theo-logische Verfassung der Metaphysik' (1956/7)), in idem, *Essays in Metaphysics: Identity and Difference* (trans. Kurt F. Leidecker; New York: Philosophical Library, 1960), 33-67.
Heidegger, Martin, 'The Origin of the Work of Art', in idem, *Poetry, Language, Thought* (trans. Albert Hofstadter; New York: Harper & Row, 1971), 15-87.
Heidegger, Martin, 'Phenomenology and Theology', in idem, *The Piety of Thinking: Essays by Martin Heidegger* (trans. and ed. J. Hart and J. C. Maraldo; Bloomington: Indiana University Press, 1969), 5-21.
Heidegger, Martin, *Sein und Zeit* (Tübingen: Max Niemeyer, 1953).

Hemming, Laurence Paul, *Heidegger's Atheism: The Refusal of a Theological Voice* (Notre Dame: University of Notre Dame Press, 2002).

Henrici, Peter, 'Erster Blick auf Hans Urs von Balthasar', in Karl Lehmann and Walter Kasper (eds), *Hans Urs von Balthasar: Gestalt und Werk* (Cologne: Communio, 1989), 18–61.

Hollingdale, R. J., *Nietzsche: The Man and His Philosophy* (rev. edn; Cambridge University Press, 1999).

Holtmann, Stefan, *Karl Barth als Theologe der Neuzeit: Studien zur kritischen Deutung seiner Theologie* (Göttingen: Vandenhoeck & Ruprecht, 2007).

Howells, Edward, 'Relationality and Difference in the Mysticism of Pierre de Bérulle', *Harvard Theological Review* 102:2 (2009): 225–43.

Illanes, José Luis, 'The Church in the World', in Pedro Rodríguez, Fernando Ocáriz and José Luis Illanes, *Opus Dei in the Church: An Ecclesiological Study of the Life and Apostolate of Opus Dei* (Dublin: Four Courts Press, 1994), 147–90.

Kant, Immanuel, *Critique of Practical Reason* (trans. Mary Gregor; Cambridge: Cambridge University Press, 1997).

Kant, Immanuel, *Critique of Pure Reason* (ed. and trans. Paul Guyer and Allen W. Wood; Cambridge: Cambridge University Press, 1998).

Kant, Immanuel, *Groundwork of the Metaphysics of Morals* (trans. M. Gregor; Cambridge: Cambridge University Press, 1998).

Katz, Steven T., Shlomo Biderman, Gershon Greenberg (eds), *Wrestling with God. Jewish Theological Responses during and after the Holocaust* (Oxford: Oxford University Press, 2007).

Kazimierz, Rafa, 'On Human Being: A Dispute between Edith Stein and Martin Heidegger', *Logos* 10:4 (Fall 2007): 104–17.

Kearney, Richard, *The Wake of Imagination* (London: Routledge, 1998).

Kerr, Fergus, *Twentieth-Century Catholic Theologians* (Oxford: Wiley-Blackwell, 2007).

Kierkegaard, Søren, *Concluding Unscientific Postscript to* Philosophical Fragments (trans. Howard and Edna Hong; Princeton: Princeton University Press, 1992).

Kierkegaard, Søren, 'The Esthetic Validity of Marriage', in idem, *Either / Or, Part II* (trans. Howard and Edna Hong; Princeton: Princeton University Press, 1987), 3–154.

Kierkegaard, Søren, *Fear and Trembling* (trans. Howard and Edna Hong; Princeton: Princeton University Press, 1983).

Kierkegaard, Søren, *Stages on Life's Way* (trans. Howard and Edna Hong; Princeton: Princeton University Press, 1988).

Kisiel, Theodore, *The Genesis of Heidegger's Being and Time* (Berkeley: University of California Press, 1993).

Krieg, Robert, *Romano Guardini: A Precursor of Vatican II* (Notre Dame: University of Notre Dame Press, 1997).

Kuhr, Ilkamarina, *Gabe und Gestalt: Theologische Phänomenologie bei Hans Urs von Balthasar* (Regensburg: Puistet, 2012).

Lacoste, Jean-Yves, *Experience and the Absolute: Disputed Questions on the Humanity of Man* (trans. Mark Raferty-Skehan; New York: Fordham University Press, 2004).

Lacoue-Labarthe, Philippe, *Heidegger, Art, and Politics* (trans. Chris Turner; Oxford: Blackwell, 1990).

Leahy, Brendan, *The Marian Profile in the Ecclesiology of Hans Urs von Balthasar* (Hyde Park, NY: New City Press, 2000).

Lescot, Rémi, *Pierre de Bérulle: Apôtre du Verb incarné* (Paris: Cerf, 2013).

Levinas, Emmanuel, *Otherwise than Being or Beyond Essence* (trans. Alphonso Lingis; The Hague: Nijhof, 1981).

Lind, L. R. (trans. and ed.), *Johann Wolfgang von Goethe's Roman Elegies and Venetian Epigrams* (Lawrence: University Press of Kansas, 1974).

Long, D. Stephen *Saving Karl Barth: Hans Urs von Balthasar's Preoccupation* (Minneapolis: Fortress Press, 2014).

López, Antonio, *Gift and the Unity of Being* (Eugene, OR: Cascade Books, 2014).

López, Antonio, *Spirit's Gift: The Metaphysical Insight of Claude Bruaire* (Washington, DC: The Catholic University of America Press, 2006).

López, José Daniel, 'Aportes sístematicos y metodológicos de una fenomenología de la encarnación para una antropología trinitaria', in Sonia Vargas Andrade (ed.), *Antropología trinitaria para nuestros pueblos* (Bogotá: Publicaciones CELAM, 2014), 75–87.

López Quintás, Antonio, *Cuatro filósofos en busca de Dios* (Madrid: Rialp, 1989).

López Quintás, Antonio, *Romano Guardini y la dialéctica de lo viviente* (Madrid: Cristiandad, 1966).

Löser, Werner *Im Geiste des Origenes: Hans Urs von Balthasar als Interpret der Theologie der Kirchenväter* (Freiburg: Josef Knecht, 1976).

Löser, Werner 'Weg und Werk Hans Urs von Balthasars', in Philosophisch-Theologische Hochschule Sankt Georgen. Frankfurt am Main-Virtueller Leseraum; available online: http://www.sankt-georgen.de/leseraum/loeser12.pdf (last accessed 10 October 2015).

Löwith, Karl, *Martin Heidegger and European Nihilism* (trans. Gary Steiner; ed. Richard Wolin; New York: Columbia University Press, 1995).

Lubac, Henri de, *Catholicisme: Les aspects sociaux du dogme* (Paris: Les Éditions du Cerf, 1938).

Lubac, Henri de, 'La foi chrétienne: Petite introduction au symbole des apôtre (1991)', in idem, *La foi chrétienne: essai sur la structure du symbole des apôtres* (Paris: Cerf, 2008), 517–33.

Lubac, Henri de, *Histoire et esprit: L'intelligence de l'Écriture d'après Origène* (Paris: Aubier-Montaigne, 1950).

Lubac, Henri de, *History and Spirit: The Understanding of Scripture According to Origen* (trans. Anne Englund Nash and Juvenal Merriell; San Francisco: Ignatius Press, 2007).

Lubac, Henri de, 'Le mystère du surnaturel', *Recherches de science religieuse* 36 (1949): 80–121.

Lubac, Henri de, *Le Mystère du surnaturel* (Paris: Aubier, 1965).
Lubac, Henri de, *Pic de la Mirandole: Études et discussions* (Paris: Aubier-Montaigne, 1974).
Lubac, Henri de, *Surnaturel: études historiques* (Paris: Desclée de Brouwer, 1991).
MacIntyre, Alasdair, *After Virtue. A Study in Moral Theory* (Notre Dame: University of Notre Dame Press, 1984).
MacIntyre, Alasdair, *Edith Stein: A Philosophical Prologue 1913–1922* (Lanham, Md.: Rowman & Littlefield, 2006).
MacQuarrie, John, *An Existentialist Theology: A Comparison of Heidegger and Bultmann* (London: SCM Press, 1955).
Marion, Jean-Luc, *Being Given: Toward a Phenomenology of Givenness* (trans. Jeffrey L. Kosky; Stanford: Stanford University Press, 2002).
Marion, Jean-Luc, *Dieu sans l'être. Hors-texte* (Paris: Presses Universitaires de France, 1982).
Marion, Jean-Luc, *God without Being: Hors-Texte* (trans. Thomas A. Carlson; Chicago: University of Chicago Press, 1991).
Marion, Jean-Luc, *Idol and Distance* (trans. and intro. Thomas A. Carlson; New York: Fordham University Press, 2001).
Marion, Jean-Luc, *Reduction and Givenness: Investigations of Husserl, Heidegger, and Phenomenology* (trans. Thomas A. Carlson; Evanston: Northwestern University Press, 1998).
Marion, Jean- Luc, 'Saint Thomas d'Aquin et l'onto-théo-logie', in *Revue Thomiste* 95 (1995): 31–66.
Marion, Jean-Luc, *Sur la theologie blanche de Descartes: Analogie, creation des verites eternelles et fondement* (Paris: Presses universitaires de France, 1981).
Maritain, Jacques, *The Person and the Common Good*, (trans. John J. Fitzgerald; Notre Dame: University of Notre Dame Press, 1966).
Maróth, Miklós, *Die Araber und die antike Wissenschaftstheorie* (Leiden; New York: Brill, 1994).
McCosker, Philip, 'The Christology of Pierre de Bérulle', *Downside Review* 124:435 (2006): 111–34.
McGrath, Sean J., *The Early Heidegger and Medieval Philosophy: Phenomenology for the Godforsaken* (Washington, DC: Catholic University of America Press, 2006).
McInerny, Ralph, *Aquinas and Analogy* (Washington, DC: Catholic University of America Press, 1996).
McInerny, Ralph, *The Logic of Analogy* (The Hague: Martinus Nijhoff, 1961).
McInerny, Ralph, *Studies in Analogy* (The Hague: Martinus Nijhoff, 1968).
McPartlan, Paul, 'Henri de Lubac – Evangelizer', *Priest and People* (August–September 1992): 343–6.
Meillassoux, Quentin, *After Finitude: An Essay on the Necessity of Contingency* (trans. Ray Brassier; London: Continuum, 2008).
Menn, Stephen, *Descartes and Augustine* (Cambridge: Cambridge University Press, 1998).

Merleau-Ponty, Maurice, *Éloge de la philosophie* (Paris: Gallimard, 1953).
Metz, Johann Baptist, *Memoria passionis. Ein provozierendes Gedächtnis in pluralistischer Gesellschaft* (Freiburg-Basel-Wien: Herder, 2006).
Mezei, Balázs, 'Faith and Reason', in Lewis Ayres (ed.), *The Oxford Handbook of Catholic Theology* (Oxford: Oxford University Press, forthcoming).
Mezei, Balázs, *Reason and Revelation after Auschwitz* (New York: Bloomsbury, 2013).
Milbank, John, *Beyond Secular Order: The Representation of Being and the Representation of the People* (London: Wily Blackwell, 2014).
Milbank, John, 'Can a Gift Be Given? Prolegomena to a Future Trinitarian Metaphysic', *Modern Theology* 11:1 (1995): 119–61.
Milbank, John, 'Dignity Rather than Right', *Open Insight* 5:7 (January 2014): 77–124.
Mohr, Daniela, *Existenz im Herzen der Kirche. Zur Theologie der Säkularinstitute im Leben und Werk Hans Urs von Balthasars* (Würzburg: Echter, 2000).
More, Nicholas D., 'Nietzsche's Last Laugh: Ecce Homo as Satire', *Philosophy and Literature* 35:1 (April 2011): 1–15.
More, Nicholas D., *Nietzsche's Last Laugh: Ecce Homo as Satire* (Cambridge: Cambridge University Press, 2014).
Morgan, Stéphane-Marie, *Pierre de Bérulle et les carmélites de France: la querelle du gouvernement, 1583–1629* (Paris: Cerf, 1995).
Moss, David, 'Prayer and the Saints', in Edward T. Oakes, S.J. and David Moss (eds), *The Cambridge Companion to Hans Urs von Balthasar* (Cambridge: Cambridge University Press, 2004), 84–92.
Newman, John Henry, *Parochial and Plain Sermons*, vol. 1 (London: Longmans, Green, and Co., 1907).
Nicolescu, Mihai Vlad, *The Spell of the Logos: Origen's Exegetic Pedagogy in the Contemporary Debate regarding Logocentrism* (Piscataway, NJ: Gorgias Press, 2009).
Nietzsche, Friedrich, *Also Sprach Zarathustra*, Vorrede 4 in Kritische Studienausgabe (ed. G. Coli and M. Montinari; Berlin: De Gruyter, 1988).
Nietzsche, Friedrich, *Ecce Homo: How to Become What You Are* (trans. Duncan Large; Oxford: Oxford University Press, 2007).
Nietzsche, Friedrich, *Ecce Homo and the Antichrist* (trans. Thomas Wayne; New York: Algora Publishing, 2004).
Nietzsche, Friedrich, *Thus Spoke Zarathustra: A Book for All and None* (ed. Adrian del Caro and Robert B. Pippin; trans. Adrian del Caro; Cambridge: Cambridge University Press, 2006).
Nietzsche, Friedrich, *The Will to Power* (ed. Walter Kaufmann; trans. Walter Kaufmann and R. J. Hollingdale; New York: Random House, 1968).
Novak, Michael, 'A Letter to Roberto', *Logos: A Journal of Catholic Thought and Culture* 3 (2000): 70–84.
Nussberger, Danielle, 'Theology Made Flesh: Hans Urs von Balthasar and the Saints', Ph.D. dissertation, University of Notre Dame, 2008.

O'Leary, Joseph S., *Questioning Back: The Overcoming of Metaphysics in the Christian Tradition* (Minneapolis: Winston Press, 1986).

O'Meara, Thomas, *Erich Przywara, S.J.: His Theology and His World* (Notre Dame: University of Notre Dame Press, 2002).

O'Regan, Cyril, *The Anatomy of Misremembering: Von Balthasar's Response to Philosophical Modernity*, vol. 1, *Hegel* (New York: Crossroads, 2013).

O'Regan, Cyril, 'Answering Back: Augustine's Critique of Heidegger', in Fran O'Rourke (ed.), *Human Destinies: Philosophical Essays in Honor of Gerald Hanratty* (Notre Dame: University of Notre Dame Press, 2013), 134–84.

O'Regan, Cyril, *The Heterodox Hegel* (Albany: State University of New York Press, 1994).

O'Regan, Cyril, 'Review of David C. Schindler, *Hans Urs von Balthasar and the Dramatic Structure of Truth: A Philosophical Investigation*', *The International Journal for Systematic Theology* 7:4 (Fall 2005): 585–90.

O'Regan, Cyril, 'Von Balthasar and Eckhart: Theological Principles and Catholicity', *The Thomist* 60:2 (April 1996): 1–37.

Oakes, Kenneth, *Karl Barth on Theology and Philosophy* (Oxford: Oxford University Press, 2012).

Oster, Stefan, 'Thinking Love at the Heart of Things. The Metaphysics of Being as Love in the Work of Ferdinand Ulrich', *Communio: International Catholic Review* 37 (Winter 2010): 660–700.

Patočka, Jan, 'Negative Platonism: Reflections concerning the Rise, the Scope and the Demise of Metaphysics—and Whether Philosophy Can Survive It', in *Jan Patočka: Philosophy and Selected Writings* (ed. and trans. E. Kohák; Chicago and London: University of Chicago Press, 1989), 175–206.

Payne, Steven, *St. Thérèse of Lisieux: Doctor of the Universal Church* (Staten Island: Alba House, 2002).

Pfänder, Alexander, *Die Seele des Menschen. Versuch einer verstehenden Psychologie* (Halle: Max Niemeyer Verlag, 1933).

Pfänder, Alexander, *Zur Psychologie der Gesinnungen* (Halle: Max Niemeyer Verlag, 1913).

Pieper, Josef, *Autobiographische Schriften* (ed. Berthold Wald; Hamburg: Felix Meiner Verlag).

Plato, *Complete Works* (ed. J. M. Cooper; Indianapolis: Hackett, 1997).

Popkin, Richard 'The Religious Background of Seventeenth-Century Philosophy', in Daniel Garber and Michael Ayers (eds), *The Cambridge History of Seventeenth-century Philosophy* (Cambridge: Cambridge University Press, 2003), 393–422.

Prufer, Thomas, 'Husserl, Heidegger, Early and Late, and Aquinas', in idem, *Recapitulations: Essays in Philosophy* (Washington, DC: The Catholic University of America Press, 1993), 72–90.

Przywara, Erich, *Analogia Entis: Metaphysics: Original Structure and Universal Rhythm* (trans. John R. Betz and David Bentley Hart; Grand Rapids, Mich.: Eerdmans, 2014).

Przywara, Erich, *Analogia Entis 1: Metaphysik: Ur-Struktur und All-Rhythmus* (Einsiedeln: Johannes Verlag Einsiedeln, 1962).
Przywara, Erich, *Hölderlin* (Nuremberg: Glock & Lutz, 1949).
Przywara, Erich, *Humanitas: Der Mensch gestern und morgen* (Nürnberg: Glock & Lutz, 1952).
Przywara, Erich, *Katholische Krise* (ed. Bernhard Gertz; Düsseldorf: Patmos, 1967).
Przywara, Erich, *Ringen der Gegenwart, Gesammelte Aufsätze 1922-1927* (Augsburg: Benno Filser-Verlag, 1929), 2 vols.
Przywara, Erich, *Schriften* (ed. Hans Urs von Balthasar; Einsiedeln: Johannes Verlag Einsiedeln, 1962), 3 vols.
Przywara, Erich, *Sein Schrifttum 1912-1962* (ed. Leo Zimny; intro. Hans Urs von Balthasar; Einsiedeln: Johannes Verlag Einsiedeln, 1963).
Przywara, Erich, 'Thomas von Aquin als Problematiker', *Stimmen der Zeit* 109 (June 1925): 188-99.
Przywara, Erich, *Vier Predigten über das Abendland* (Einsiedeln: Johannes Verlag Einsiedeln, 1948).
Radner, Ephraim, *The End of the Church: A Pneumatology of Christian Division in the West* (Grand Rapids, Mich.: Eerdmans, 1998).
Rahner, Karl, 'The Concept of Existential Philosophy in Heidegger', *Philosophy Today* 13:2 (Summer 1969): 126-37.
Rahner, Karl, 'The Concept of Mystery in Catholic Theology', in idem, *Theological Investigations 4: More Recent Writings* (trans. Kevin Smyth; Baltimore: Helicon Press, 1966), 36-73.
Rahner, Karl, *Hearer of the Word: Laying the Foundation for a Philosophy of Religion*, (trans. Joseph Donceel; ed. Andrew Tallon; New York: Continuum, 1994).
Rahner, Karl, *Karl Rahner in Dialogue. Conversations and Interviews 1965-1985* (ed. Paul Imhof and Hubert Biallowons; trans. Harvey D. Egan; New York: Crossroad, 1986).
Rahner, Karl, 'Laudatio auf Erich Przywara', in idem, *Gnade als Freiheit. Kleine theologische Beiträge* (Freiburg: Herder, 1968), 266-73.
Rahner, Karl, *Spirit in the World* (trans. William Dych; New York: Continuum, 1969).
Richardson, William, *Heidegger: Through Phenomenology to Thought* (Dordrecht: Martinus Nijhoff, 1963).
Ricoeur, Paul, 'L'imagination dans le discours et dans l'action', in idem, *Du texte à l'action: Essais d'herméneutique, II* (Paris: Seuil, 1986), 213-36.
Ritter, Cezary, 'Posłowie: Uwagi historyczno-edytorskie w związku z Jana Pawła II katechezami „Mężczyzną i niewiastą stworzył ich", in Karol Wojtyła, *Mężczyzną i niewiastą stworzył ich* (Lublin: Wydawnictwo KUL, 2008).
Rosenthal, Franz (ed. and trans.), *The Classical Heritage in Islam* (Berkeley: University of California Press, 1975).
Rowland, Tracey, *Ratzinger's Faith: The Theology of Pope Benedict XVI* (Oxford: Oxford University Press, 2008).

Rowland, Tracey, 'The World in the Theology of Joseph Ratzinger/Benedict XVI,' *Journal of Moral Theology* 2:2 (2013): 109–32.

Sánchez, José Luis, *San Juan de la Cruz en la revolución copernicana* (Madrid: Editorial de Espiritualidad, 1992).

Sara, Juan M., 'Secular Institutes according to Hans Urs von Balthasar', *Communio: International Catholic Review* 29 (Summer 2002): 309–36.

Scheeben, Matthias, *Die Mysterien des Christentums* (Freiburg i. Br.: Herder, 1958).

Scheler, Max, *Über Scham und Schamgefühl*, in idem, *Schriften aus dem Nachlass*, vol. 1, *Zur Ethik und Erkenntnislehre* (Bern: A. Franke, 1957), 65–154.

Schindler, David C., *The Catholicity of Reason* (Grand Rapids, Mich.: Eerdmans, 2013).

Schindler, David C., *Hans Urs von Balthasar and the Dramatic Structure of Truth: A Philosophical Investigation* (New York: Fordham University Press, 2004).

Schindler, David L., *The Heart of the World, Center of the Church: Communio Ecclesiology, Liberalism, and the Liberation* (Grand Rapids, Mich.: Eerdmans, 1996).

Schindler, David L., 'Introduction', in Henri de Lubac, *The Mystery of the Supernatural* (trans. Rosemary Sheed; New York: Crossroad, 1998), xi–xxxi.

Schindler, David L., 'Norris Clarke on Person, Being and St Thomas', *Communio: International Catholic Review* 20 (Fall 1993): 580–92.

Schleiermacher, Friedrich, *The Christian Faith* (Berkeley, CA: Apocryphile Press, 2011).

Scholem, Gerschom, *Die Vorstellung vom Golem in ihren tellurischen und magischen Beziehungen* (Zürich: Rhein-Verlag, 1954).

Schürmann, Reiner, *Meister Eckhart: Mystic and Philosophy: Translation with Commentary* (Bloomington: Indiana University Press, 1978).

Schürmann, Reiner, *Heidegger: On Being and Acting: From Principles to Anarchy* (trans. Christine Marie Gros; Bloomington: Indiana University Press, 1999).

Shanks, Andrews, *Hegel and Religious Faith: Divided Brain, Atoning Spirit* (London: T&T Clark, 2011).

Sheehan, Thomas, *Karl Rahner: The Philosophical Foundations* (Athens, Ohio: Ohio University Press, 1987).

Siewerth, Gustav, *Das Schicksal der Metaphysik von Thomas von Aquin bis Heidegger* (Einsiedeln: Johannes Verlag Einsiedeln, 1959).

Siewerth, Gustav, *Der Thomismus als Identitätsystem* (Frankfurt: Verlag Schulte-Bulmke, 1939).

Silva, Sergio, 'La teología fundamental de Balthasar', *Teología y Vida* 50 (2009): 225–41.

Simmel, Georg, *The View of Life: Four Metaphysical Essays with Journal Aphorisms* (trans. John A. Y. Andrews and Donald N. Levine; Chicago: University of Chicago Press, 2010).

Sokolowski, Robert, *Eucharistic Presence: A Theology of Disclosure* (Washington, DC: The Catholic University of America Press, 1994).

Spaemann, Robert, *Persons: The Difference between 'Someone' and 'Something'* (Oxford and New York: Oxford University Press, 2006).

Stein, Edith, *Finite and Infinite Being: An Attempt at an Ascent to the Meaning of Being* (trans. Kurt. F. Reinhard; Washington, DC: ICS, 2002).

Stein, Edith, 'Husserl and Aquinas: A Comparison', in idem, *Knowledge and Faith* (Washington, DC: ICS Publications, 2000), 1–63.

Stein, Edith, *On the Problem of Empathy: The Collected Works of Edith Stein (Volume 3)* (trans. Waltraut Stein; rev. 3rd ed.; Washington, DC: ICS Publications, 1989).

Stein, Edith, *Science of the Cross (The Collected Works of Edith Stein (Volume 6)* (trans. Josephine Koeppel; ed. D. L. Gelber, R. Leuven; Washington, DC: ICS Publications, 2003).

Terán-Dutari, Julio, 'Die Geschichte des Terminus "Analogia Entis" und das Werk Erich Przywaras', *Philosophisches Jahrbuch der Görres-Gesellschaft* 77 (1970): 163–79.

Treitler, Wolfgang, 'True Foundations of Authentic Theology', in *Hans Urs von Balthasar: His Life and Work* (ed. David L. Schindler; San Francisco: Ignatius Press, 1991), 169–82.

Thompson, William M. (ed.), *Bérulle and the French School: Selected Writings* (Mawah, NJ: Paulist Press, 1989).

Tolkien, J. R. R., *The Monsters and the Critics and Other Essays* (London: Harper Collins, 2006).

Ulrich, Ferdinand, *Gabe und Vergebung* (Freiburg, i.Br.: Johannes Verlag Einsiedeln, 2006).

Ulrich, Ferdinand, *Homo Abyssus: Das Wagnis der Seinsfrage* (ed. Martin Bieler and Florian Pitschl; Freiburg: Johannes Verlag, 1998).

Ulrich, Ferdinand, *Der Mensch als Anfang. Zur philosophischen Anthropologie der Kindheit* (Einsiedeln: Johannes Verlag Einsiedeln, 1970).

Ulrich, Ferdinand, 'Das Problem einer "Metaphysik in der Wiederholung"', *Salzburger Jahrbuch für Philosophie* 5:6 (1961/62): 263–98.

Varden, Erik, *Redeeming Freedom: The Principle of Servitude in Bérulle* (Rome: Studia Anselmiana, 2011).

Vawter, Bruce, 'Genesis', in Reginald C. Fuller (ed.), *A New Catholic Commentary on Holy Scripture* (Nashville: Thomas Nelson, 1975), 166–205.

Vetö, Miklos, 'La Christo-logique de Bérulle', in Pierre de Bérulle, *Opuscules de piété (1644)* (Grenoble: Jérôme Millon, 1997), 7–136.

Voegelin, Eric, *Modernity without Restraint: The Political Religions, The New Science of Politics, and Science, Politics, and Gnosticism* (ed. Manfred Henningsen; Columbia: University of Missouri Press, 1999).

Wais, Kazimierz, *Ontologja czyli metafizyka ogolna* (Lwów: Towarzystwo „Biblioteka Religijna", 1926).

Waldstein, Michael, 'Introduction', in John Paul II, *Man and Woman He Created Them: A Theology of the Body* (trans. Michael Waldstein; Boston: Pauline Books & Media, 2006), 6–11.

Walsh, David, *The Modern Philosophical Revolution: The Luminosity of Existence* (Cambridge: Cambridge University Press, 2008).

Welte, Bernhard, *Denken in Begegnung mit den Denkern II: Hegel, Nietzsche, Heidegger* (Freiburg: Herder, 2007).

Welte, Bernhard, 'God in Heidegger's Thought', *Philosophy Today* 26 (1982): 85–100.
Welte, Bernhard, *Meister Eckhart: Gedanken zu seinen Gedanken* (Freiburg: Herder, 1978).
Welte, Bernhard, *Zeit und Geheimnis: Philosphische Abhandlungen zur Sache Gottes in der Zeit der Welt* (Freiburg: Herder, 1975).
Whitehead, A. N., *Process and Reality. An Essay in Cosmology* (New York: The Free Press, 1979).
Whitehead, A. N., 'Review of J. H. Randall's Aristotle', *The Objectivist Newsletter* (May 1963): 18.
Wippel, John F., *The Metaphysical Thought of Thomas Aquinas: From Finite Being to Uncreated Being* (Washington: Catholic University of America Press, 2000).
Wippel, John F., *Metaphysical Themes in Thomas Aquinas* (Washington, DC: Catholic University of America Press, 1984).
Wojtyła, Karol (John Paul II), 'The Degrees of Being from the Point of View of the Phenomenology of Action', *Analecta Husserliana* 11 (1981): 125–30.
Wojtyła, Karol, 'The Intentional Act and the Human Act, that is, Act and Experience', *Analecta Husserliana* 5 (1976): 269–80.
Wojtyła, Karol, *Love and Responsibility* (trans. Grzegorz Ignatik; Boston: Pauline, 2013).
Wojtyła, Karol, *Lubliner Vorlesungen* (ed. Anneliese Danka Spranger and Edda Wiener; Stuttgart-Degerloch: Seewald Verlag, 1981).
Wojtyła, Karol, *Man and Woman He Created Them: A Theology of the Body* (trans. Michael Waldstein; Boston: Pauline Books & Media, 2006).
Wojtyła, Karol, *Man in the Field of Responsibility* (trans. Kenneth W. Kemp and Zuzanna Maślanka Kieroń; South Bend: St. Augustine's Press, 2011).
Wojtyła, Karol, 'Natura i doskałność', in idem, *Aby Chrystus się nami posługiwał* (Kraków: Wydawnictwo Znak, 2009).
Wojtyła, Karol, 'Naturaleza y perfección', in idem, *Mi visión del hombre: Hacia una nueva ética* (trans. Pilar Ferrer; ed. Juan Manuel and Alejandro Burgos; Madrid: Biblioteca Palabra, 2010), 44–48.
Wojtyła, Karol, 'On the Metaphysical and Phenomenological Basis of the Moral Norm in the Philosophy of Thomas Aquinas and Max Scheler', in idem, *Person and Community*, 73–94.
Wojtyła, Karol, *Osoba i czyn: oraz inne studia antropologiczne* (Lublin: Towarzystwo Naukowe KUL, 2000).
Wojtyła, Karol, *Person and Community: Selected Essays* (trans. Theresa Sandok; New York: Peter Lang, 1993).
Wojtyła, Karol, *Persona e atto*, in idem, *Metafisica della persona: Tutti le opere filosofiche e saggi integrativi* (trans. Giuseppe Girgenti and Patrycja Mikulska; Milano: Bompiani, 2003).
Wojtyła, Karol, *Rise, Let Us Be On Our Way* (trans. Walter Ziemba; New York: Warner Books, 2004).
Wojtyła, Karol, 'In Search of the Basis of Perfectionism in Ethics', in idem, *Person and Community*, 45–56.

Wojtyła, Karol, *Sources of Renewal: The Implementation of the Second Vatican Council* (trans. P. S. Falla; New York: William Collins & Co.: Glasgow, 1980).

Wojtyła, Karol, 'Subjectivity and the Irreducible in the Human Being', *Analecta Husserliana* 7 (1978): 107–14.

Wojtyła, Karol, 'Thomistic Personalism', in idem, *Person and Community*, 165–75.

Wojtyła, Karol, 'The Transcendence of the Person in Action and Man's Self-Teleology', *Analecta Husserliana* 9 (1979): 203–12.

Wojtyła, Karol, *Valutazione sulla possibilità di costruire l'etica cristiana sulle base del sistema di Max Scheler*, in idem, *Metafisica della persona*, 263–449.

Wojtyła, Karol, *Wykłady Lubelskie* (Lublin: Towarzystwo Naukowe KUL, 2006).

Wolin, Richard, *Heidegger's Children: Hannah Arendt, Karl Löwith, Hans Jonas, Herbert Marcuse* (Princeton, NJ: Princeton University Press, 2003).

Wolin, Richard, *The Heidegger Controversy: A Critical Reader* (Boston: MIT Press, 1991).

Index

Adorno, Theodor W. 57
Aristotle 38, 47, 64, 146, 204–6, 215, 219
Augustine 38, 39, 43, 47, 49, 54, 79, 80, 82, 84–7, 95, 131, 143, 210, 216, 219, 220

Balthasar, Hans Urs von 37, 50–6, 72, 73, 75–7, 87, 111–27, 189, 220, 226, 230
Barth, Karl 73, 74, 75, 78, 86, 97, 88, 93–109, 114, 119, 207, 221
Benedict XVI *see* Ratzinger, Joseph
Bernanos, Georges 119, 180, 201
Blondel, Maurice 41
Bérulle, Pierre de 166–81
Brassier, Ray, 165, 166, 170, 174
Bultmann, Rudolf, 39, 112
Buber, Martin 113

Calvin, John 89, 95
Caputo, John 55
Casel, Odo 63–4
Cassirer, Ernst 42, 47, 75, 90, 218
Cicero, Marcus Tullius 210
Claudel, Paul 126

Deleuze, Gilles 101
Derrida, Jacques 1, 5–8, 56, 102, 165
Descartes, René 2, 3, 47, 98, 175–6, 216
Duns Scotus 38, 89
Durkehim, Émile 116

Fénelon, François 220
Feuerbach, Ludwig 90, 193–5
Fichte, J. G. 100, 109, 198
Foucault, Michel 101
Freud, Sigmund 90

García-Rivera, Alejandro 114
Gilson, Étienne 220, 226
Goethe, J. W. von 101, 102, 104, 115, 118
Guardini, Romano 59–70, 72, 75

Hamann, J. G. 94
Heidegger, Martin 1, 3–6, 37–57, 74, 75, 87, 101, 109, 115, 150, 158, 159, 160, 206, 217, 218, 231
Hegel, G. W. F. 47, 94, 100, 101, 113, 150, 159, 160, 217, 231
Hemming, Laurence Paul 41–2
Herrmann, Wilhelm 94, 96
Hölderlin, Friedrich 48, 53–5
Hume, David 98
Husserl, Edmund 43, 44, 46, 75, 111, 113, 115, 217, 218, 231

Ignatius of Loyola 49, 125
Irigaray, Luce 101

Jaspers, Karl 1, 109, 218
Joachim of Fiore 86
John of the Cross 114, 115, 130, 173
John Paul II *see* Wojtyła, Karol

Kant, Immanuel 1, 3, 9, 10, 12, 14, 38, 42, 54, 68, 69, 89, 94, 99, 100, 101, 165, 174, 175, 193, 217, 222, 231
Kierkegaard, Søren 1–20, 38, 94, 217

Lacoste, Jean-Yves 50, 57
Le Fort, Gertrud von 201
Leibniz, G. W. 47, 109
Levinas, Emmanuel 5–7, 231
Locke, John 98
Lubac, Henri de 102, 112, 178, 179
Luther, Martin 38, 39, 87, 89, 90, 96

MacIntyre, Alasdair 223
Maréchal, Joseph 41
Marion, Jean-Luc 44, 49, 50, 53, 54, 118, 153, 154, 175, 176, 220
Maritain, Jacques 11, 220
Marx, Karl 90
McCabe, Herbert 88
Meister Eckhart 38, 53–6

Möhler, Adam 72, 87
Moss, David 116, 117, 127

Newman, John Henry 75, 84, 86
Nicholas of Cusa 72, 225
Nietzsche, Friedrich 14, 47, 48, 90, 93, 101–8, 196, 217, 231

Origen 112, 121, 126, 220
Otto, Rudolf 38, 62
Overbeck, Franz 94, 101

Péguy, Charles 201
Pico della Mirandola 167–8, 179
Pieper, Josef 72–3
Plato 14, 47, 54, 185, 189, 204, 205, 206, 209, 210, 211, 214, 215, 216, 218, 219, 228
Prufer, Thomas 117
Przywara, Erich 37, 39, 43, 44, 45, 46, 47, 48, 49, 53, 54, 71–92, 118, 230

Rade, Martin 95, 96
Rahner, Karl 37, 39, 40, 41, 42, 43, 44, 45, 52, 72, 75, 76, 126, 220, 230
Ratzinger, Joseph 62, 69, 81
Ritschl, Albrecht 94, 96
Rousseau, Jean-Jacques 98, 196
Rousselot, Pierre 41
Ruysbroeck, John 56

Scheeben, Matthias 72, 113
Scheler, Max 43, 62, 69, 75, 115, 118, 130, 132, 137, 138, 142
Schelling, F. W. J. 100
Schiller, Friedrich 188
Schleiermacher, Friedrich 38, 94, 95, 96, 100
Schürmann, Reiner 55, 56
Siewerth, Gustav 37, 49, 51, 56
Simmel, Georg 116
Sokolowski, Robert 117
Stein, Edith 37, 39, 43–5, 75
Suárez, Francisco 176

Teresa of Avila 115, 166
Thérèse von Lisieux 114–17, 119
Thomas Aquinas 39, 41–5, 47, 49, 51–6, 78, 86, 88, 95, 130, 134, 155, 158, 220, 222, 225, 226
Troeltsch, Ernst 95, 96

Ulrich, Ferdinand 150–63, 200

Voegelin, Eric 218
Voltaire (François-Marie Arouet) 23, 27, 98, 188

Welte, Bernhard 37, 49, 53, 55
Wojtyła, Karol 130–47, 177

CPSIA information can be obtained
at www.ICGtesting.com
Printed in the USA
LVHW02s1740110918
589817LV00007B/71/P